The Diverted Dream

The Diverted Dream

Community Colleges
and the Promise
of Educational Opportunity
in America, 1900–1985

STEVEN BRINT

JEROME KARABEL

New York   Oxford
OXFORD UNIVERSITY PRESS

Oxford University Press

Oxford   New York   Toronto
Delhi   Bombay   Calcutta   Madras   Karachi
Petaling Jaya   Singapore   Hong Kong   Tokyo
Nairobi   Dar es Salaam   Cape Town
Melbourne   Auckland

and associated companies in
Berlin   Ibadan

Copyright © 1989 by Oxford University Press, Inc.

First published in 1989 by Oxford University Press, Inc.,
200 Madison Avenue, New York, New York 10016

First issued as an Oxford University Press paperback, 1991

Oxford is a registered trademark of Oxford University Press

Library of Congress Cataloging-in-Publication Data
Brint, Steven.
The diverted dream : community colleges and the promise of educational
opportunity in America, 1900–1985 / Steven Brint, Jerome Karabel.
p.   cm.   Bibliography: p.   includes index.
ISBN 0-19-504815-6
ISBN 0-19-504816-4 (pbk.)
1. Education, Higher—United States—History—20th century.
2. Community colleges—United States—History—20th century.
3. Education, Humanistic—United States—History—20th century.
4. Vocational education—United States—History—20th century.
I. Karabel, Jerome.   II. Title.
LA226.B74   1989   89-2891
378.73—dc19

9 8 7 6 5 4 3 2 1

Printed in the United States of America

Preface

The invention of the two-year community college is the great innovation of twentieth-century American higher education. Such, in any case, is the claim made recently by Clark Kerr, a key architect of the current system of higher education as well as one of its most perceptive students. Yet when the first public junior college opened its doors in Joliet, Illinois, in 1901, there were grave doubts whether this odd hybrid would survive. Over time, however, it became apparent that this peculiarly American invention was destined to do far more than survive; by mid-century, it had become an integral feature of the American educational landscape.

Today well over 4 million students are enrolled in over 900 public two-year colleges scattered among the fifty states. For more than a decade, the majority of all degree-credit students entering the system of higher education have done so in a two-year institution; in 1983, according to the U.S. Department of Education statistics, almost 54 percent of the nation's first-time college freshmen were enrolled in a two-year college. In recent years, some of the obvious virtues of community colleges—their openness, their flexibility, their inexpensiveness—have attracted considerable attention abroad. The creation of two-year colleges, or something very much like them, now seems to be on the policy agenda in a number of countries, including Yugoslavia, France, and the People's Republic of China.

This book will explore a number of questions about the growth and transformation of the American junior college. What were the forces that brought the two-year college into being? What factors explain the initially regional character of its growth and its later national diffusion? What were the sources of its transformation in recent years from an institution oriented to the provision of college-level transfer courses into one that is predominantly vocational in character? What is its place in the larger system of higher education? And what can its development tell us about the character of the larger society of which it is a part?

In pursuing these questions, we have been guided by the conviction that America's colleges and universities have become central to the contemporary pursuit of the American dream. The United States has always been a land that prided itself on the abundance of its opportunities for individual advancement; in today's increasingly credential-dominated society, the nation's system of higher education has become a crucial gateway to these opportunities. Within this system, the community college has a crucial role to play; it is, after all, the most common point of entry into college for those groups that have traditionally been excluded from higher education. What policies the community colleges pursue—whether, for example, they see themselves primarily as transfer institutions or as providers of terminal vocational training—are thus likely to have important consequences for the life chances of the millions of students who pass through them. As such, these policies are a proper object of both academic and public scrutiny.

A few words may be appropriate here about the values that inform this study. Although our views are not identical, we are both committed to the ideal of an educational system that is dedicated to the cultivation of a democratic citizenry. The purpose of the schools is not, in our view, simply to train skilled workers whose high levels of productivity will facilitate economic growth (though that is a worthy goal); it is also to foster the kind of active and informed citizenry that is the sine qua non of a truly democratic polity. Today, with the growing national preoccupation with America's sagging performance in international economic competition, the mission of schools as what John Dewey called "laboratories of freedom" has been all but forgotten. Instead, we are besieged by a barrage of prestigious commission reports that use the specter of Japanese economic rivalry as legitimation for a program of school reform whose primary agenda is to create a more efficient labor force. This is a far cry from the great democratic tradition in American educational thought and practice, a tradition that recognizes the intimate connections between knowledge and power and sees the democratization of knowledge as indispensable to the project of democratic self-governance. From this perspective, the most urgent task of the schools today is not to produce efficient employees, but rather to encourage the kind of critical literacy that empowers ordinary citizens in their confrontations with powerful public and private institutions.

If the nation's community colleges often fall short of this ideal of democratic empowerment, so, too, we wish to emphasize, does the rest of the educational system. Indeed, one can make a case that there are many features of public two-year colleges—their openness to the entire adult population, their rootedness to the communities in which they are located, and their willingness to deviate from traditional academic patterns—that make them the most democratic component in the system of higher education. Yet community colleges, like other institutions of higher education, are subject to a series of powerful constraints in their relationships to the economy, the polity, and the rest of the system of higher education itself that limit their freedom to maneuver.

The extent of divergence between the democratic ideals of community colleges and some of their actual institutional practices is rooted in the larger political, economic, and organizational context in which community colleges operate. During the course of our research, we were repeatedly impressed by the energy, the intelligence, and the idealism of those who work in the nation's two-year institutions. Because we have often been identified as "critics" of the community college, we wish to be clear on this point. Whatever arguments we may make about negative outcomes that result from some of the institutional practices of community colleges, we believe that these outcomes typically occur despite—and not because of—the intentions of community college administrators, faculty, and staff. In fact, many community college employees do an outstanding job under conditions of powerful external constraints. Identifying these constraints will, we hope, shed light on the dilemmas faced by those who would like the two-year institution to serve, in a phrase that was common in the early years of the junior college movement, as a true *people's college*.

The completion of this project, which was carried out while both of us were involved in a number of other investigations, took far longer than either of us anticipated. Indeed, the book's origins date back to July of 1976, when Karabel submitted a proposal to the National Institute of Education on "Politics and Inequality in American Higher Education." A case study of vocationalization of Massachusetts Community Colleges was a component of this study, and it was funded in July of 1977.

Brint began to work on the community college project in 1978, and we have worked on it together since then—first in Cambridge (at the Huron Institute) and, after 1984, across a distance of 3,000 miles, with Brint having moved to New Haven and Karabel to Berkeley. During these years, we have worked out, over the course of countless conversations and meetings, a common understanding of the place of community colleges in American society. In 1978–1979 and 1982–1983, Brint carried out the fieldwork on which Chapters 5, 6, and 7 are based. The manuscript itself has gone through a number of stages as we clarified our thinking. Brint wrote the first draft of Chapters 1 through 7, and Karabel drafted Chapter 8. Subsequently, the manuscript went through several additional drafts, with each of us revising the work of the other. A wag once said that collaboration is the process whereby two people create something that each thinks is his own, but we would be the first to acknowledge that the volume that has finally emerged is an entirely joint product.

A work of scholarship is part of a larger collective enterprise, and our intellectual debts to colleagues, both living and deceased, are profound. The influence on our work of some familiar figures in the sociology, history, and economics of education will, we hope, be apparent from our references to their work. Less obvious, but equally important, is our debt to a long-standing institutional tradition in the sociology of organizations—one associated with such people as Weber, Michels, Selznick, Mills, Lipset, and Gouldner—that had seemingly fallen out of fashion in recent years. When we began this project more than a decade ago, we conceived of it as (among other things) a case study in the politics of institutional change. It is our hope that this book will find an audience—in addition to those who are interested in American education and its relationship to the larger society—among those students of organizations who are concerned with processes of institutional transformation.

In addition to our debts to the larger intellectual community, we were very fortunate to be part of a group of friends and colleagues who shared our interest in the dynamics of power and inequality in American higher education. During our years in Cambridge, in particular, we benefited enormously from the knowledge of an unusually talented group of colleagues. We are especially indebted to a study group on "Education, Class Structure, and the State" whose meetings at the Huron Institute had a profound impact on our thinking. This group, which existed in various incarnations from 1978 to 1983, included among its members (at one point or another): Stephen Cornell, Charles Derber, Paul DiMaggio, Kevin Dougherty, Anne Hornsby, David Karen, Rebecca Klatch, Katherine McClelland, David Stark, David Swartz, and Michael Useem.

A number of these people—in particular, Dougherty, Hornsby, Karen, McClelland, Swartz, and Useem—worked with us at Huron as members of the larger research project on "Politics and Inequality in American Higher Education." In a group as close as the one at Huron, it is truly impossible to say who was responsible for which idea. Special thanks, however, are due to Kevin Dougherty, whose own work on community colleges exerted a powerful influence on our thinking.

We have benefited also from those colleagues who commented on drafts of this manuscript. Among the many whose criticisms and suggestions proved especially helpful to us were Daniel Asquino, Marzio Barbagli, Michael Burawoy, David Cohen, Paul DiMaggio, Kevin Dougherty, Norton Grubb, Michael Hout, David Karen, Gerald Letendre, Kristin Luker, Ann-Marie McCartan, Katherine McClelland, Michael Olneck, Mark Oromaner, Joel Perlmann, Caroline Persell, Terry Strathman, David Swartz, Gene Tanke, and Michael Useem. Brint would like, in addition, to thank the members of the Complex Organizations Workshop at Yale University for providing a forum to present a draft of the final chapter. Those whose comments proved particularly helpful included Miguel Centano, John Mohr, Mark Suchman, Thomas Schotz, Walter Powell, Charles Perrow, and two colleagues from Huron days, Paul DiMaggio and David Swartz.

A number of undergraduate and graduate students at Harvard University and the University of California at Berkeley helped us collect data for the book. Almost to a person, they did excellent work and were a pleasure to work with. Among these people, Gerald LeTendre, Maureen Scully, Hiroshi Ishida, Julie Brines, Mark Osiel, Juliet Shanks, Terry Strathman, Shantika Emker, Ben Davis, Mike Strong, Sonia Toledo, Bridget Dixon, Lauri Perman, Michael Maloney, and Elizabeth Gessel made particularly noteworthy contributions. We would also like to thank those who assisted us with typing and word processing, especially Cynthia Rose, Karen Georgia, and Sean Senechal. We would like to express our thanks to the Survey Research Center and the Institute of Industrial Relations at UC Berkeley for providing us with important support during the latter stages of the investigation. Finally, we are deeply indebted to our fine editors at Oxford University Press—Susan Rabiner, with whom we began the project, and Valerie Aubry, who helped us bring it to completion.

Throughout the project, our wives, Michele Salzman and Kristin Luker, have been wonderfully supportive. There is no way we can fully express our gratitude to them for what they have brought both to our work and to our lives.

Thanks of a different sort are due to those institutions that provided the generous financial support that made this study possible. In particular, we wish to express our gratitude to the National Institute of Education, which provided funding for the 1977–1981 period (NIE-G-77-0037), and the National Science Foundation, which provided us with resources during 1981–1986 (NSF Grants SES-80-25542 and SES-83-1986). We would also like to thank the Ford Foundation, which provided Karabel with a fellowship during 1981–1983, when cuts by the federal government threatened the survival of the project. Finally, we would like to express our gratitude to Lana Muraskin, formerly of the National Institute of Education, who expressed confidence in our project and helped us obtain support when we most needed it.

The views expressed in this book are, of course, ours alone and should in no way be construed to reflect the perspectives of those who supported the research. In a work of this scope, there will inevitably be some errors, and we apologize for any mistakes we may have made. We are confident, however, that as we have criticized our colleagues where we think they have erred, so too will they criticize us where they are convinced that we have gone astray. As in other domains of scholarly inquiry, this process of critique and reformulation, though untidy, will ultimately result in a deepening of our understanding of the place of community colleges in American society.

Having worked on this volume for so long, it is sheer coincidence that it seems likely to appear at a moment of intense public interest in the state of American education. With the appearance in 1983 of the controversial presidential commission report, *A Nation at Risk,* America entered into one of its periodic debates about the condition of the educational system. Initially, this debate focused on elementary and secondary schools, but in recent years it has come to encompass the nation's colleges and universities as well. Unfortunately, much of this debate has focused on the most elite sectors of the system of higher education (Allan Bloom's best-seller, *The Closing of the American Mind,* is but one example of this preoccupation), leaving the community colleges—which enroll a disproportionately large number of minority, female, and working-class students—largely outside the realm of public dialogue. If this volume does nothing more than contribute in a small way to placing the nation's community colleges on the agenda of the growing policy debate about American higher education, then we will feel that our efforts have been amply rewarded. For the community colleges are, we believe, too important to the American dream of equality of opportunity to remain outside the arena of democratic debate.

Boston   S.B.
New Haven
Berkeley   J.K.
November 1988

Contents

INTRODUCTION

1 Community Colleges and the American Social Order

From the earliest days of the Republic, Americans have possessed an abiding faith that theirs is a land of opportunity. For unlike the class-bound societies of Europe, America was seen as a place of limitless opportunities, a place where hard work and ability would receive their just reward. From Thomas Jefferson's "natural aristocracy of talent" to Ronald Reagan's "opportunity society," the belief that America was—and should remain—a land where individuals of ambition and talent could rise as far as their capacities would take them has been central to the national identity. Abraham Lincoln expressed this deeply rooted national commitment to equality of opportunity succinctly when, in a special message to Congress shortly after the onset of the Civil War, he described as a "leading object of the government for whose existence we contend" to "afford all an unfettered start, and a fair chance in the race of life." [1]

Throughout much of the nineteenth century, the belief that the United States was a nation blessed with unique opportunities for individual advancement was widespread among Americans and Europeans alike. The cornerstone of this belief was a relatively wide distribution of property (generally limited, to be sure, to adult white males) and apparently abundant opportunities in commerce and agriculture to accumulate more. But with the rise of mammoth corporations and the closing of the frontier in the decades after the Civil War, the fate of the "self-made man"—that heroic figure who, though of modest origins, triumphed in the competitive marketplace through sheer skill and determination—came to be questioned. In particular, the fundamental changes then occurring in the American economy—the growth of huge industrial enterprises, the concentration of propertyless workers in the nation's cities, and the emergence of monopolies—made the image of the hardworking stockboy who rose to the top seem more and more like a relic of a vanished era. The unprecedented spate of success books that appeared between 1880 and 1885 (books bearing such titles as *The Law of Success, The Art of Money Getting, The Royal Road to Wealth,* and *The Secret of Success in Life)* provide eloquent, if indirect, testimony to the depth of the ideological crisis then facing the nation.[2]

Clearly, if belief in the American dream of individual advancement was to survive under the dramatically changed economic and social conditions of the late nineteenth century, new pathways to success had to be created. No less a figure than the great steel magnate Andrew Carnegie recognized this. Indeed, in 1885, just one year before the bitter labor struggle that culminated in the famous Haymarket affair, Carnegie conceded in a speech to the students of Curry Commercial College in Pittsburgh that the growth of "immense concerns" had made it "harder and harder . . . for a young man without capital to get a start for himself." A year later, in his widely read book, *Triumphant Democracy,* Carnegie forthrightly acknowledged that opportunities to rise from "rags to riches" had declined with the rise of the giant corporation (Carnegie 1886; Perkinson 1977, pp. 120–121).

Carnegie's solution to the problems posed by the great concentration of wealth was not, however, its redistribution, as was being called for by an increasing number of Americans. On the contrary, in 1889, Carnegie wrote that the "Socialist or Anarchist" who proposes such solutions "is to be regarded as attacking the foundation upon which civilization itself rests." Nevertheless, the man of wealth has a responsibility to administer it in the interest of all so as to promote "the reconciliation of the rich and poor." Perhaps the most effective means of doing so, Carnegie suggested, was to follow the example of such educational benefactors as Peter Cooper and Leland Stanford. The result of such judicious and far-sighted philanthropy would be, he noted, the construction of "ladders upon which the aspiring can rise" (Carnegie 1889, pp. 656, 660, 663).

Yet when Carnegie wrote, the nation's educational institutions were poorly suited to provide such ladders of ascent. In 1890, the average American had not been educated beyond the fifth grade. Moreover, the prevailing assumption—among both businessmen and the population at large—was that an ordinary common school training would provide the skills necessary for economic advancement. The nation's colleges and universities, still largely encrusted by traditional notions of cultural transmission and professional training, stood well to the side of the pathways to business success. As late as 1900, 84 percent of the prominent businessmen listed in *Who's Who in America* had not been educated beyond high school (Wyllie 1954, p. 95). In the late nineteenth century, getting ahead in America thus largely remained a matter of skill in the marketplace, not in the classroom.

If education remained peripheral to the attainment of the American dream, this was in part because, as late as 1890, there was a sense in which no educational system as such had yet been constructed. To be sure, the widely accessible common school had been one of the distinguishing features of American democracy, and one of its tasks was to provide those who attended it with the tools for economic success. But the primary purpose of the common school had been to train citizens for life in a democratic society, not to select workers and employees for their future positions in an increasingly complex and hierarchical division of labor. For this task, a differentiated rather than a common educational system needed to be constructed whose hierarchical divisions would mirror those of the larger society.

The "ladders of ascent" that Carnegie advocated presupposed basic structural changes in the organization of American education. The loose array of high schools, colleges, universities, and professional schools attended in the late nineteenth century by the increasing, though still limited, numbers of students who continued beyond elementary school was not really a system at all. There was not even a clear sequential relationship among the various types of educational institutions. Professional schools did not require the completion of four years of college, and colleges did not require the completion of four years of high school (Collins 1979, pp. 109–130). As a consequence, high schools, colleges, and professional schools sometimes even competed for the same students.[3] For its part, business was largely contemptuous of the diplomas awarded by high schools and especially colleges; in fact, many businessmen contended that college training was positively harmful to young men, in that it made them unfit for the harsh and practical world of commerce and industry (Wyllie 1954, pp. 101–105).

Yet despite the chaotic and relatively undifferentiated organization of American education in 1890, by 1920 the outlines of the orderly and highly stratified educational system that remains with us today were already visible.[4] The emergence of a hierarchically differentiated educational system closely linked to the labor market provided an alternative pathway to success in an era when the traditional image of the self-made man who rose to riches through success in the competitive marketplace was becoming less and less plausible. The creation of "ladders of ascent" through education thus gave new life to the American ideology of equality of opportunity at the very moment when fundamental changes in the economy threatened to destroy it.

In a context of increasing inequality between rich and poor and growing challenges to the established order, the importance of a new pathway to economic advancement is difficult to overestimate. America's large and open educational system now provided an alternative means of getting ahead. Vast inequalities of wealth, status, and power though there might be, the ladders of opportunity created by the new educational system helped the United States retain its national identity as a land of unparalleled opportunities for individual advancement.

Today, the idea that the education system in general, and higher education in particular, should provide ladders of upward mobility is so familiar as to be taken for granted. Yet viewed from a comparative perspective, the emphasis in the United States on individual mobility through education is quite remarkable.[5] To this day, no other society—not Japan, not Canada, not Sweden—sends as many of its young people to colleges and universities as the United States does (Organization for Economic Cooperation and Development 1983). *The vast and expensive system of educational pathways to success that has been constructed in this country is both the institutional embodiment of this commitment to the ideology of equality of opportunity and a constant source of reinforcement of this ideology.* The shape of today's enormous system of colleges and universities—a system in which in recent years almost half the nation's young people have participated—is incomprehensible apart from this commitment.

Central to this distinctive system of higher education is an institution—the two-year junior college (or community college, as it came to be called)—that came into being just when the American educational system was being transformed so as to provide new ladders of ascent. The two-year college, whose pattern of historical development will be the subject of this book, has from its very origins at the turn of the century reflected both the egalitarian promise of the world's first modern democracy and the constraints of its dynamic capitalist economy. Enrolling fewer than ten thousand students in 1920, the American junior college had by 1980 grown to enroll well over four million students (Eells 1931a, p. 70; U.S. Bureau of the Census 1987, p. 138).[6] The most successful institutional innovation in twentieth-century American higher education, the two-year college has in recent years spread beyond the United States and established roots in a growing number of foreign countries, among them Japan, Canada, and Yugoslavia.

Community Colleges and Democratic Ideology

With over one-half of all college freshmen now enrolled in two-year institutions (U.S. Department of Education 1986, p. 111), the community college has come to be an integral feature of America's educational landscape. Yet as recently as 1900, the junior college was no more than a dream in the minds of a few administrators at a handful of America's leading universities. Enrolling under 2 percent of all college freshman in 1920 (U.S. Office of Education 1944, pp. 4, 6), the year in which the American Association of Junior Colleges (AAJC) was founded, the junior college came to play an increasingly pivotal role in the transformation of the nation's system of colleges and universities. Perhaps more than any other segment of postsecondary education, the community college was at the forefront of the postwar demographic expansion that changed the face of American higher education.

The transformation of American higher education was organizational as well as demographic. For the birth of the two-year college marked the arrival of an entirely new organizational form in the complex ecological structure of American postsecondary education. In terms of sheer numbers, no other twentieth-century organizational innovation in higher education even begins to approach the success of the two-year college, which grew from a single college in 1901 to over 1,200 institutions in 1980, representing almost 40 percent of America's 3,231 colleges. In 1984, over 4.5 million students were enrolled in two-year colleges nationwide (U.S. Bureau of the Census 1987, p. 138).

When the junior college first appeared, the outlines of a hierarchical system of colleges and universities were already becoming visible. Nonetheless, the emergence of the junior college fundamentally altered the shape of American higher education, for it introduced a new tier into the existing hierarchy. Thus the two-year institution was not simply another of the many lower-status colleges that dotted America's educational landscape; it was a different type of institution altogether. Unlike even the humblest four-year institution, it failed to offer what had come to be considered the sine qua non of being an "authentic" college—the bachelor's degree.

What was behind the birth of this new institutional form with roots in both secondary and higher education? What explains the extraordinary growth of the two-year college during the twentieth century? And why has the provision of terminal vocational education—a function that, as we shall see, was for decades peripheral to the mission of the junior college—come to occupy an increasingly central place in the community college? The answers to these questions require an understanding of the peculiar political and ideological role that education has come to play in American life.

American Education and the Management of Ambition

All industrial societies face the problem of allocating qualified individuals into a division of labor characterized by structured inequalities of income, status, and power. Since occupying the superordinate positions in such systems provides a variety of material and psychological gratifications not available to those who occupy subordinate positions, the number of individuals who aspire to privileged places in the division of labor not surprisingly tends to surpass, often by a considerable margin, the number of such slots that are available. In advanced industrial societies, all of which have renounced to one or another degree the ideologies that have historically legitimated the hereditary transmission of positions, this problem of a discrepancy between ambition and the capacity of the opportunity structure to satisfy it is endemic. All such societies face, therefore, a problem in what might be called the *management of ambition*.[7]

In the United States, the management of ambition is a particularly serious dilemma, for success—as Robert Merton (1968, pp. 185–214) and others have pointed out—is supposed to be within the grasp of every individual, no matter how humble his (and, more recently, her) background.[8] Moreover, ambition and hard work have been held in more unambiguously high regard in America—a society that was bourgeois in its very origin—than in many European societies, with their aristocratic residues. From Benjamin Franklin to Norman Vincent Peale, the desire to succeed and the willingness to work hard to do so have been seen by Americans as among the highest moral virtues. One consequence of this belief that the "race of life" is both open and well worth winning is that more Americans from subordinate social groups harbor aspirations of making it to the top.

To be sure, not all Americans have joined the race to get ahead. Educational and occupational aspirations are systematically related to social class (Kerckhoff 1974, Spenner and Featherman 1978), and some segments of the population, especially in the racial ghettos of the nation's inner cities, have withdrawn from the competition all together (Ogbu 1978, 1983).[9] Even among those individuals who do harbor hopes of upward mobility, the depth of their commitment is highly variable and shifts in aspirations are common. Upward mobility has real social and psychological costs, and not everyone is willing—or able—to pay them. For many Americans, hopes of a "better life" crumble in the face of obstacles; consigned to low-status jobs, they nonetheless find fulfillment in the private sphere of family and friends. Moreover, aspirations to move ahead are often accompanied by a belief in the legitimacy of inequalities that are based on genuine differences in ability and effort [10]—*and* by doubts about whether one measures up.

The problem of managing ambition is particularly difficult in the United States. In 1980, for example, over half of high school seniors "planned" (not "aspired to") careers in professional/technical jobs. But in that same year, only 13 percent of the labor force was employed in such jobs (Wagenaar 1984). Even if one assumes that there will be a considerable increase in the number of such jobs in the future and that there is significant uncertainty in many of these "plans," it seems clear nonetheless that American society generates far more ambition than its structure of opportunity can satisfy.

As early as the 1830s, there was a powerful popular demand for free schooling, although it should be noted that the early workingmen's organization of New York, Boston, and Philadelphia looked on the provision of free, public education not as a way of getting ahead but as indispensable to the exercise of their rights as democratic citizens (Welter 1962, pp. 46–47).[11] By the middle of the nineteenth century, free elementary education in America's "common schools" had become a reality in many states. Much as the early granting of "universal" suffrage (limited in fact to white males) promoted the incorporation of American working people into the existing political order, so too did the early provision of free public schools (Katznelson and Weir 1985).

As schools became more relevant to economic success and correspondingly more attractive to ambitious young men and women during the early twentieth century, popular demand for the expansion of education intensified. Between 1920 and 1940, over 20 percent of the age-eligible (fourteen to seventeen) population in the United States was enrolled in secondary schools; in eleven European countries, including Great Britain, France, Germany, and Sweden, the proportions nowhere surpassed 8 percent (Rubinson 1986, p. 522). The same pattern could also be seen in rates of attendance in higher education. An examination of statistics regarding college enrollments in twenty-two countries, including Japan and Russia as well as the major nations of Western and Central Europe, reveals that no country enrolled even half as many students as did the United States during the period 1913 and 1948 (Ben-David 1966, p. 464). From a sheer demographic perspective, then, the educational system has nowhere been as central to the life experiences of the population as it has been in the United States.

In light of the extraordinary emphasis in the United States on individual economic success and on the role of education as a pathway to it, it is hardly surprising that there has been such a powerful demand from below to expand the educational system. What is perhaps more difficult to understand is the readiness of the state to provide the additional years of schooling demanded by the populace. After all, one can well imagine the state trying to control public expenditures by limiting the amount of education. Yet for the most part, governing elites have joined in a broad national consensus that favored the construction of an educational system of unparalleled dimensions.

There have been many sources of elite support for the expansion of education, among them adherence to the classic Jeffersonian view that a democratic citizenry must be an educated one, and a related commitment to the task of nation building (Meyer et al. 1979). But also critical, we wish to suggest, has been the implicit recognition that a society that promises its subordinate classes unique opportunities for individual advancement needs to offer well-developed channels of upward mobility.

No one could deny the inequalities of wealth and power in the United States. But what made these inequalities tolerable, perhaps, was that everyone—or so the national ideology claimed—had a chance to advance as far as his ability and ambition would take him. And once education became established as the principal vehicle of this advancement, it became politically difficult for any group to oppose its expansion.

The result of this interplay of popular demand and elite response was the creation of a huge but highly differentiated educational system, with unequaled numbers of students enrolled in it. America's commitment to the idea of equal opportunity guaranteed that there would be a tremendous amount of ambition for upward mobility among the masses; somehow the educational system would have to find a way to manage the aspirations that its own relative openness had helped arouse. The junior college was to play a critical role in this process, and it is to the complex pressures it has faced both to extend and to limit opportunity that we now turn.

The Contradictory Pressures Facing the Junior College

From its very beginnings, the junior college has been subjected to contradictory pressures rooted in its strategic location in the educational system in a society that is both democratic and highly stratified. Its growth in substantial part a product of the responsiveness of a democratic state to demand from below for the extension of educational opportunity, the junior college's trajectory has also been shaped by the need to select and sort students destined to occupy different positions in the job structure of a capitalist economy. In the popular mind—and in the eyes of the many dedicated and idealistic men and women who have worked in the nation's two-year institutions—the fundamental task of the junior college has been to "democratize" American higher education, by offering to those formerly excluded an opportunity to attend college. But the junior college has also faced enormous pressure to limit this opportunity, for the number of students wishing to obtain a bachelor's degree—and the type of professional or managerial job to which it has customarily led—has generally been far greater than the capacity of the economy to absorb them. Poised between a burgeoning system of secondary education and a highly stratified structure of economic opportunity, the junior college was located at the very point where the aspirations generated by American democracy clashed head on with the realities of its class structure.

Like the American high school, the community college over the course of its history has attempted to perform a number of conflicting tasks: to extend opportunity and to serve as an agent of educational and social selection, to promote social equality and to increase economic efficiency, to provide students with a common cultural heritage and to sort them into a specialized curriculum, to respond to the demands of subordinate groups for equal education and to answer the pressures of employers and state planners for differentiated education, and to provide a general education for citizens in a democratic society and technical training for workers in an advanced industrial economy.[12]

Burton Clark, in a seminal article on "The 'Cooling-Out' Function in Higher Education," put the dilemma facing the junior college well: "a major problem of democratic society is inconsistency between encouragement to achieve and the realities of limited opportunity" (Clark 1961, p. 513). By virtue of its position in the structure of educational and social stratification, the junior college has confronted the necessity of diverting the aspirations of students who wish to join the professional and managerial upper middle class, but who are typically destined by the structure of opportunity to occupy more modest positions. In such a situation, Clark notes bluntly, "for large numbers failure is inevitable and *structured*" (Clark 1961, p. 515, emphasis his).

The junior college has thus been founded on a paradox: the immense popular support that it has enjoyed has been based on its link to four-year colleges and universities, but one of its primary tasks from the outset has been to restrict the number of its students who transfer to such institutions. Indeed, the administrators of elite universities who developed the idea of the junior college (and who later gave the fledgling organizational form crucial sponsorship) did so, as we shall show in Chapter 2, with the hope that it would enable them to divert from their own doors the growing number of students clamoring for access to higher education. These university administrators recognized that the democratic character of American culture and politics demanded that access to higher education be broad; in the absence of alternative institutions, masses of ill-prepared students would, they feared, be clamoring at their gates.[13]

The junior college thus focused in its early years on offering transfer courses. The reason was simple: Students who attended two-year institutions did so on the basis of their claim to be "real" colleges, and the only way to make this claim convincing was for them to offer liberal arts courses that would in fact receive academic credit in four-year institutions. For the first three decades of their existence, the junior colleges thus concentrated on constructing preparatory programs that, as the catalogues of the two-year institutions were fond of characterizing them, were of "strictly collegiate grade."

There was almost a missionary zeal among the predominantly small-town Protestant men who presided over the early junior college movement; their task as they saw it was to bring the blessings of expanded educational opportunity to the people. Proudly referring to their institutions as "democracy's colleges," they viewed the two-year institution as giving thousands of worthy students who would otherwise have been excluded a chance to attend higher education. Yet they were also aware that the educational and occupational aspirations of their students outran their objective possibilities by a substantial margin; while some of their students had great academic promise, well under half of them, they knew, would ever enter a four-year college or university. Something other than college preparatory courses, therefore, would have to be provided for them if they were to receive an education appropriate for their future place in the division of labor.

The solution that the leaders of the junior college movement devised bore a striking resemblance to the one developed earlier by the administrators of secondary education at the point when the high school was transformed from an elite to a mass institution: the creation of a separate vocational education track. The underlying logic of the vocational solution is perhaps best captured in a speech given in 1908 by Dean James Russell of Teachers College, Columbia University, to a meeting of the National Education Association. Entitling his presentation "Democracy and Education: Equal Opportunity for All," Russell asked:

> How can a nation endure that deliberately seeks to raise ambitions and aspirations in the oncoming generations which in the nature of events cannot possibly be fulfilled? If the chief object of government be to promote civil order and social stability, how can we justify our practice in schooling the masses in precisely the same manner as we do those who are to be our leaders? (quoted in Nasaw 1979, p. 131)

Russell's answer was unequivocal: The ideal of equal education would have to be forsaken, for only *differentiated education*—education that fit students for their different vocational futures—was truly democratic. Paradoxically, then, if mass education were to realize the promise of democracy, separate vocational tracks had to be created.

In a society that generated far more ambition for upward mobility than its structure of opportunity could possibly satisfy, the logic of vocationalism, whether at the level of secondary or higher education, was compelling. The United States was, after all, a class-stratified society, and there was something potentially threatening to the established order about organizing the educational system so as to arouse high hopes, only to shatter them later. At the same time, however, the political costs of turning back the popular demand for expanded schooling were prohibitive in a nation placing so much stress on equality of opportunity. What vocationalism promised to do was to resolve this dilemma by, on the one hand, accepting the democratic pressure from below to provide access to new levels of education while, on the other hand, differentiating the curriculum to accommodate the realities of the economic division of labor. The aspirations of the masses for upward mobility through education would not, advocates of vocationalization claimed, thereby be dashed; instead, they would be rechanneled in more "realistic" directions.[14]

The leaders of the junior college movement enthusiastically embraced the logic of vocationalism and, by the 1930s, had come to define the decided lack of student enthusiasm for anything other than college-transfer programs as the principal problem facing the two-year institution. Their arguments in favor of expanding terminal vocational education in the junior college were essentially identical to those used by advocates of vocational education in the high school: Not everyone could be a member of the elite; vocational programs would reduce the high dropout rate; and occupational training would guarantee that students would leave the educational system with marketable skills.

At times, junior college leaders were remarkably forthright about the fate that awaited these students in the labor market. For example, Walter Crosby Eells, founder of the *Junior College Journal* and executive secretary of the American Association of Junior Colleges from 1938 to 1945, noted that while universities tend to train leaders, democratic societies also needed "educated followership" and so proposed junior college terminal education as a particularly effective vehicle for training such followers (Eells 1941b, p. 29). Under Eells's leadership, by 1940 a consensus had been reached among key junior college leaders that between two-thirds and three-fourths of junior college students should be enrolled in terminal vocational education programs.

Yet the junior college leaders who advocated vocationalization faced a formidable obstacle: the widespread and persistent lack of interest among their own students. Despite encouragement from local administrators and counselors, no more than 25 to 30 percent of junior college students had ever enrolled in vocational programs. Their chances of getting ahead in a nation increasingly obsessed with educational credentials depended, they believed, on transferring to a four-year institution. The students realized that junior college occupied the bottom rung of higher education's structure. But as long as they were enrolled in college-parallel transfer programs, the possibility that they could obtain a professional or upper managerial job survived. Faced with the energetic efforts of junior college administrators to expand occupational education, the students—many of whom were of modest social origins—sensed that the attempt to vocationalize their institutions threatened to divert them from their educational and occupational aspirations.

This pattern of student opposition to vocational programs continued after World War II. The enrollment target of vocational education advocates remained two-thirds to three-quarters of junior college students, but at no time from the mid-1940s to the late-1960s did the proportion of two-year college students in the vocational track surpass one-third of the entire enrollment. Remarkably, this pattern of resistance to vocational education continued despite a dramatic increase in the number of students enrolled in community colleges, from just over 200,000 students in 1948 to almost 1.3 million in 1968 (U.S. Bureau of the Census, 1975, p. 383). Throughout this period, approximately two-thirds of community college students continued to be enrolled in college preparatory programs; of these, fewer than half ever transferred to a four-year institution (Medsker 1960, Medsker and Tillery 1971).

After decades of student resistance, enrollments in community college vocational programs finally surged after 1970, following a decline in the market for college graduates. By the mid-1970s, the percentage of students in programs specifically designed to provide occupational training had risen to at least 50 percent, and by 1980, the proportion had grown to approximately 70 percent.[15] Simultaneously, transfer rates fell drastically (Baron 1982, Cohen and Brawer 1982, Friedlander 1980, Lombardi 1979).

Although it would be misleading to hearken back to a mythical "golden age" when the junior college catapulted the majority of its students onto the pathway of educational and occupational success, the community college has historically provided a ladder of upward mobility to at least some of its students.[16] Especially in an institution that claimed as its *raison d'être* the democratization of American higher education, the sharp rise in vocational enrollments and the corresponding decline in the rate of transfer warrant careful examination. Increasingly, it seems, the community college has become a vocational-training institution, more and more divorced from the rest of academia, with potentially serious consequences for the life chances of its students.[17]

Curricular Change in the Community College

Observers of the transformation of the community college from an institution oriented to college-preparatory transfer programs to one emphasizing terminal vocational training have tended to focus on one of two forces as the principal cause: either the changing preference of student "consumers" of community college education or, alternatively, the decisive influence of business elites. In the first, which might be called the *consumer-choice model,* institutions of higher education are regarded as responding exclusively to students' curricular preferences: what the consumers of higher education demand, they receive. In the second, which we shall refer to as the *business-domination model,* the curricular offerings of the community colleges are seen as reflecting the imprint of powerful business interests, which prefer programs that provide them with technically trained workers. Drawing, respectively, on classical liberal and Marxist approaches to the problem of institutional change, each of these models provides a theoretically plausible explanation for the trajectory of community college development, and, accordingly, commands our attention.

The Consumer-Choice and Business-Domination Models

The consumer-choice model is an application of the more general "rational-choice" model of human behavior popular among economists (see, for example, Becker 1983) and an increasing number of social scientists in neighboring disciplines. This model sees students' preferences as based on perceptions of the labor market "returns" that are yielded by different programs (Freeman 1971, 1976). According to this perspective, the enormous growth in community college vocational programs reflects the shift in the preference of hundreds of thousands of educational consumers. The aggregate consequence of all these individual shifts is the increasing predominance of occupational training in the two-year colleges.

The consumer-choice model views students as highly rational economic maximizers.[18] They wish to obtain the highest possible rates of return for the lowest cost in time, effort, and expense. Consequently, as the rate of return to liberal arts education begins to decline and opportunities for relatively high returns to low-cost vocational education increase, students make the rational choice: they begin to invest more heavily in vocational education, and colleges in turn expand their vocational course offerings to meet the increased demand. Especially in light of the widely publicized decline in the early 1970s in the economic returns for a college degree, the consumer-choice model offers a parsimonious explanation of the community college's vocationalization.

The unit of analysis in the consumer-choice model is not the group or the institution but, rather, the individual. As with the other approaches embodying "methodological individualism," the underlying assumption of this model is that social processes can be reduced to individuals' preferences and activities (Lukes 1968).

The other explanation of the community colleges' vocationalization, the business-domination model, emphasizes the power of large corporations to shape the educational system to serve their own interests. This perspective is in many ways an application to education of a broader Marxist "instrumentalist" theory of the role of the state in advanced capitalist societies.[19] Advocates of this view see the rise of vocationalism as primarily caused by the active intervention of business in shaping the community college's curricular offerings. Seeing in vocational education an opportunity to train at public expense a labor force of narrowly educated but technically competent middle-level specialists, big business has moved— through private donations, control of boards of trustees, and influence on trend-setting private foundations—to tailor the community college to its particular needs. In the business-domination model, the primary unit of analysis is social class, viewed in the Marxist framework as embedded in a capitalist mode of production.

Given the historical enthusiasm of the business community for vocational training (Lazerson and Grubb 1974) and its often-expressed concern in recent years about the tendency of four-year colleges and universities to produce masses of "overeducated" workers, the role attributed by the business-domination model to large corporations in the process of vocationalization seems plausible. According to this perspective, community colleges are seen as eager "to do the errands of business interests," having "no broader conception of education . . . than one that narrowly serves these interests" (Pincus and Houston 1978, p. 14). Bowles and Gintis, authors of *Schooling in Capitalist America,* believe that the increasingly vocationalized community college is well designed to produce that particular combination of technical competence and social acquiescence that is required to occupy skilled but powerless positions in the corporate economy: "The social relationships of the community college classroom increasingly resemble the formal hierarchical impersonality of the office or the uniform processing of the production line" (Bowles and Gintis 1976, p. 212).[20]

Both the consumer-choice and the business-domination perspectives capture something important, we believe, about the forces shaping community college development. Market forces have influenced student preferences, and the downturn in the labor market for college graduates in the early 1970s was indeed a major factor in the rapid community college vocationalization of the following years. And especially since the mid-1970s, business has influenced (occasionally directly, but more often indirectly) the shape and content of the curricula from which community college students select their programs.

Today student "consumers" eagerly enroll in community college occupational programs that they hope will lead them into relatively high-paying, secure jobs with opportunities for advancement. These choices, though based, we shall argue, on imperfect labor market information, are in part logical responses to the overcrowded market for college-trained persons and the difficulties of competing in such a market. The programs in which these occupational students enroll, in turn, are determined in part by industry's needs for particular types of "middle-level" manpower.

We believe that the indirect influence of business on community college curricula has always been great. The colleges have for some time sought to keep pace with manpower developments in the private economy. Indeed, the more enterprising two-year college administrators have studied regional and national labor projections almost as if they were sacred texts. Arthur Cohen, now director of the ERIC Clearinghouse for Junior Colleges at the University of California at Los Angeles, was hardly exaggerating when he wrote that "when corporate managers . . . announce a need for skilled workers . . . college administrators trip over each other in their haste to organize a new curriculum" (Cohen 1971, p. 6).

Yet despite the consumer-choice and business-domination models' contributions to our understanding of recent developments in the community college, neither is an adequate guide to the past. Rather, they are most useful for the period since 1970, the year of the first signs of decline in the labor market for college graduates—and of little help for the period before that year. Since some of the most influential community college officials have been attempting, as we shall show in Chapters 2 and 3, to vocationalize their institutions since at least 1930, that leaves forty years of history almost entirely unaccounted for by either model. Moreover, we shall argue, neither model captures some of the key dynamics of the process of vocationalization since 1970.

Before 1970, our study reveals, neither students nor businessmen were very interested in vocational programs. Most students (and their families) desired the prestige of a baccalaureate degree and resisted terminal vocational training. But despite the students' overwhelming preference for liberal arts programs, the leaders of the American Association of Junior Colleges and their allies pursued a policy of vocationalization for over four decades before there was any notable shift in the students' preferences. This policy decision cannot be explained by the consumer-choice model.

Similarly, most members of the business elite were indifferent to community colleges before the late 1960s. Indeed, for almost another decade after that, business interest in the community colleges remained modest and picked up only in the late 1970s, after the colleges had already become predominantly vocational institutions. The indifference of business people to programs ostensibly developed in their interests cannot be readily explained by the business-domination model. An adequate explanation of the community college's transformation thus requires a fundamental theoretical reformulation.

Toward an Institutional Approach

The framework that we propose to account for the transformation of American community colleges may be called, albeit with some oversimplification, an *institutional model*. Inspired in part by the classical sociological tradition in the study of organizations,[21] this approach can, we believe, illuminate processes of social change beyond the specific case of education. Perhaps the model's most fundamental feature is that it takes as its starting point organizations themselves, which are seen as pursuing their own distinct interests. Within this framework, special attention is focused upon "organizational fields" (e.g., education, medicine, journalism), which may be defined as being composed of "those organizations that, in the aggregate, constitute a recognized area of institutional life: key suppliers, resource and product consumers, regulatory agencies, and other organizations that produce similar services or products" (DiMaggio and Powell 1983, p. 148).[22] Relations among organizations within the same field are often—but not always—competitive; accordingly, understanding the historical trajectory of a particular organization generally requires an analysis of its relationship to other organizations offering similar services. The dynamics of specific institutions, in turn, are rooted in their relationships to other major institutions. For example, the educational system must be analyzed in relation to the state and the economy. If the focus of the consumer-choice and the business-domination models is on the individual and the class respectively, the focus of this approach will be, accordingly, on the institution.

According to this perspective, neither the consumer-choice nor the business-domination model pays sufficient attention to the beliefs and activities of the administrators and professionals who typically have the power to define what is in the "interest" of the organizations over which they preside. Much of our analysis will focus, therefore, on explaining why these administrators chose to vocationalize despite what we shall document was the opposition of the student consumers (an opposition that casts doubt on the consumer-choice model) and the indifference of potential sponsors in the business corporations (which in turn undermines the business-domination model). Our analysis assesses the beliefs and organizational interests of those who pursued the vocationalization policy and the techniques they used to implement this policy over time. It also examines the forces, both external and internal to the community college movement, that facilitated or hindered implementation of the policy at different historical moments.

In skeletal form, our basic argument is that the *community colleges chose to vocationalize themselves, but they did so under conditions of powerful structural constraints.* Foremost among these constraints was the subordinate position of the community college in the larger structure of educational and social stratification. Put more concretely, junior colleges were hampered by their subordinate position in relation to that of the older and more prestigious four-year colleges and universities and, correspondingly, a subordinate position in the associated competition to place their graduates into desirable positions in the labor market.

Perhaps the best way to capture this dual structural subordination is to think of the structure of stratification faced by community colleges in terms of two parallel but distinct components—one a structure of labor market stratification and the other a structure of institutional stratification in higher education. From this perspective, educational institutions may be viewed as competing for training markets—the right to be the preferred pathway from which employers hire prospective employees. Access to the most desirable training markets—those leading to high-level professional and managerial jobs—is, and has been for decades, dominated by four-year colleges and, at the highest levels, by elite graduate and professional schools. Community colleges, by their very location in the structure of higher education, were badly situated to compete with better-established institutions for these training markets. Indeed, it is not an exaggeration to say that by the time that two-year colleges established a major presence in higher education, the best training markets were effectively monopolized by rival institutions.

Training markets are critical to the well-being of higher-education institutions. In general, those that have captured the best markets—for example, the top law, medical, and management schools—are the institutions with the most resources, the greatest prestige, and the most intense competition for entry. Viewed historically, community colleges had lost the most strategic sectors of this market before they could enter the competition. The best that the community colleges could hope to do, therefore, was to try to situate themselves favorably for the next available market niche. Therein resided the powerful organizational appeal of the two-year college's long-standing vocationalization project, a project that, as we shall show, had become widely accepted among community college administrators long before there was any decline in the demand for graduates of four-year colleges or any demand for vocational programs from the community college students themselves.

Because of their precarious position in the competition for training markets, community colleges tried desperately to fit themselves to the needs of business despite the absence of direct business interest in the colleges. Indeed, far from imposing on the community colleges a desire for a cheap docile labor force trained at public expense, as the business-domination model would have it, big business remained indifferent to the community colleges for the first sixty years of their existence. Yet because of the structural location of business in the larger political economy—and, in particular, its control of jobs—community colleges had little choice but to take into account the interests of their students' future employers. Thus business exerted a profound influence over the direction of community college affairs and pushed them in the direction of vocationalization without any direct action whatsoever. This capacity to exert influence in the absence of direct intervention reflects the *structural power* of business.[23]

Reduced to its essentials, then, our argument is that the community colleges found themselves in a situation of structured subordination with respect to both other higher-education institutions and business. Within the constraints of this dual subordination, the vocationalization project was a means of striking the best available bargain. We refer in the text to this deference to the perceived needs of more powerful institutions—even when such institutions made no conscious efforts to control their affairs—as *anticipatory subordination.*

This anticipatory subordination was rooted in the recognition by the community colleges that if they tried to compete with the existing better-endowed, higher-status institutions on their own terrain, they would face certain defeat. A far better strategy, it was determined after much internal debate with the junior college movement, was to try to capture an unexploited—albeit less glamorous—market in which they would not compete directly with institutions with superior resources. In return for accepting a subordination that was, in any case, inherent in their structural location, the community colleges would use vocationalization to bring a stable flow of resources linked to a distinctive function, a unique institutional identity, and above all, a secure—indeed, expanding—market niche. Only the students' resistance stood in the way of this project's realization.

The Outline of This Volume

Our study of the American junior college is divided into two sections. Part I, which includes Chapters 2 through 4, is a historical analysis of the origins of the two-year institution, its growth and development, and its transformation into a predominantly vocational institution. The focus of Part I is on developments at the national level, and it attempts to trace the spread of junior colleges during this century from a few states in the Midwest and West to every corner of the United States. We shall pay particular attention in Part One to the trajectory of junior college development in the state that for decades was the uncontested leader of the national movement: California. For California was not only the first state to develop a coherent "master plan" for higher education; as late as 1968, it enrolled over one-third of all the junior college students nationwide (Carnegie Commission 1970, p. 59).[24]

Part II, which covers Chapter 5 through 7, is a detailed case study of the development of community colleges in Massachusetts. The history of junior colleges in this state encapsulates, in telescoped fashion, developments at the national level. Founded initially as institutions primarily devoted to the provision of liberal arts–transfer programs, Massachusetts's community colleges were transformed during the 1970s into overwhelmingly vocational institutions. Broadly representative of national trends over the past two decades, the case of Massachusetts's community colleges will illuminate the dynamics which have led to the triumph of vocationalism in so many other states.[25]

We have included both national-level and state-level studies because of our conviction that each is critical to understanding junior college development. The study of national-level events is crucial for tracing the rise to prominence of the two-year college. By 1920, with the founding of the AAJC, the junior college movement had become nationwide, and developments in national institutions often had major consequences for two-year colleges at state and local levels. In particular, the national level was where the campaign for vocationalization originated and gained momentum; indeed, it is hard to imagine that the "comprehensive model" of the community college, with its strong emphasis on vocational programs, would have been embraced by state systems from Florida to Washington without the help of such national organizations as the American Association of Junior Colleges and the Carnegie Foundation.

Yet an analysis of national-level forces and developments can tell us only part of the story of the two-year colleges' transformation. Although it can illuminate the historical evolution of program preferences, it cannot give us a detailed account of the reactions to these preferences at the state and local levels, the independent sources of change at these levels, or the means through which policy preferences were implemented on specific community college campuses. Such issues require both archival data and field work for the purposes of examining processes of change in state coordinating bodies and on individual community college campuses. A case study was thus necessary, we believed, to complement and give texture to our broader analysis of national trends, and it is for this reason that we examined the rise and transformation of Massachusetts community colleges.

Finally, in the last chapter, we attempt to bring together the findings of our national-level study and our case study of Massachusetts and to identify the theoretical implications of our investigation. The development of junior colleges reveals much about not only the educational system but also the character of American society: the two-year college has been a distinctively American creation, and nowhere else has it attained such prominence. How and why this peculiar institution developed—and through what processes it was fundamentally transformed—will be the subject of the remainder of the book.

PART I Community Colleges in the United States: From Liberal Arts to Vocational Training

2 Organizing a National Education Movement: 1900–1945

Of all the changes in American higher education in the twentieth century, none has had a greater impact than the rise of the two-year, junior college. Yet this institution, which we now take for granted, was once a radical organizational innovation. Stepping into an educational landscape already populated by hundreds of four-year colleges, the junior college was able to establish itself as a new type of institution—a nonbachelor's degree–granting college that typically offered both college preparatory and terminal vocational programs. The junior college moved rapidly from a position of marginality to one of prominence; in the twenty years between 1919 and 1939, enrollment at junior colleges rose from 8,102 students to 149,854 (U.S. Office of Education 1944, p. 6). Thus, on the eve of World War II, an institution whose very survival had been in question just three decades earlier had become a key component of America's system of higher education.

The institutionalization and growth of what was a novel organizational form could not have taken place without the support and encouragement of powerful sponsors. Prominent among them were some of the nation's greatest universities— among them, Chicago, Stanford, Michigan, and Berkeley—which, far from opposing the rise of the junior college as a potential competitor for students and resources, enthusiastically supported its growth. Because this support had a profound effect on the subsequent development of the junior college, we shall examine its philosophical and institutional foundations.

University Sponsorship and the Rise of the Junior College

In the late nineteenth century, an elite reform movement swept through the leading American universities. Beginning with Henry Tappan at the University of Michigan in the early 1850s and extending after the 1870s to Nicholas Murray Butler at Columbia, David Starr Jordan at Stanford, and William Rainey Harper at Chicago, one leading university president after another began to view the first two years of college as an unnecessary part of university-level instruction. This idea was enunciated in 1896 by the president of the University of Missouri:

> The first two years in college are really secondary in character. I always think of the high school and academy as covering the lower secondary period, and the freshman and sophomore years at college as covering the upper secondary period. In the secondary period, and at least the freshman and sophomore years of the college, not only are the students identical, but the character of the teaching is the same. (Jesse, quoted in Monroe 1972, p. 8)

Two years later, Harper commented along the same lines in a speech to the National Education Association:

> The work of the freshman and sophomore years is only a confirmation of the academy or high school work. It is a confirmation not only of the subject matter but of the methods employed. It is not until the end of the sophomore year that university methods of instruction may be employed to advantage. (Harper, quoted in Monroe 1972, p. 8)

These sentiments were part of a general desire to reconstitute the universities as research and training centers for an intellectual elite, and they led to efforts by some university presidents to purge the freshman and sophomore years from their institutions. This movement to create "pure" universities—universities uncontaminated by any responsibility for a general education—was greatly influenced by world economic competition. Many university presidents believed that Germany's head start in the development of highly specialized universities had led directly to major German achievements in science and technology, which in turn had helped Germany become a leading industrial power. The importation of the German model of the university into the United States would therefore be a crucial step in improving America's economic position in the international system (Veysey 1965).

But narrower organizational interests were also at work in the desire of many American universities to divest themselves of their freshman and sophomore classes. By "purifying" their institutions through the removal of the intellectually less capable students, the presidents hoped to achieve for their institutions something approaching the status enjoyed by the German universities. Alexis Lange, dean of the School of Education at the University of California, was one of the many leaders who acknowledged an elitist ideal as the core of the movement to reform the universities:

> The work of the first two years [of university education], as a matter of history and fact, is all of a piece with secondary education and should, therefore, be relegated as soon and as far as practicable to secondary school. . . . The upward extension of the high school [would be] in the educational interests of the great mass of high school graduates who cannot, will not, should not, become university students. (Lange 1915, p. 119)

Almost to a man (and they all were men), the leading university presidents of the late nineteenth century—many of whom had either studied in Germany or visited its universities—agreed with Lange's analysis. The first two years of college work, they felt, could be more appropriately handled in a reconstituted high school organized along the lines of the German *gymnasium* (Bledstein 1976, Zwerling 1976). Only the most academically adept graduates of the new six-year high school would proceed to the university. "The junior college," wrote Lange, "cannot make preparation for the university its excuse for being. Its course of instruction and training are to be culminal rather than basal" (Lange, quoted in Aldridge 1967, p. 73).

For the university sponsors of what later came to be known as the "people's colleges," the growth of the two-year institution had little to do with the democratization of higher education. On the contrary, the diffusion of the junior college was primarily a means of diverting students away from the university into an upward extension of the high school. Thus protected from those clamoring for access, the university would be free to pursue its higher tasks of research and advanced professional training.

William Rainey Harper of the University of Chicago was the first to find organizational forms appropriate to this elitist model. Harper pursued the plan to purify the universities in two ways. He introduced innovations into his own university that were aimed at reducing movement into the junior year, and he lobbied Chicago area high schools to extend their offerings to include college-level courses.

In 1892 Harper separated instruction at the University of Chicago into two divisions—one for the first two years of instruction and one for the last two—and by 1896 these two divisions were known as the Junior College and the Senior College. In 1900 he convinced the faculty and trustees to grant an "associate's degree" to students who completed work at the Junior College. His hope was that many students would voluntarily terminate their education at this point, so that only the most gifted would go on to the upper division and graduate work. In the 1902 president's annual report, Harper made explicit that an important purpose of the associate's degree was to encourage students to "give up college work at the end of the sophomore year" (quoted in Zwerling 1976, p. 47). He believed that this degree would someday allow the universities to cease offering lower-division courses altogether, leaving them to the extended high schools and to colleges that offered only the associate's degree (Harper 1900). Many of Harper's innovations at the University of Chicago—including the name he gave to the lower division and the degree he granted to sophomores—later reemerged in the two-year colleges.

The origin of the public junior college as a distinct organizational form, however, can be traced more directly to Harper's efforts to persuade Chicago area high schools to introduce college-level courses. After many years of fruitless lobbying by Harper among these high schools, J. Stanley Brown, the principal of Joliet High School, began to work on a plan to expand his school's curriculum to include college-level courses. Brown's move was apparently influenced not only by his personal association with Harper but also by Harper's offer to grant Joliet students advanced standing at the University of Chicago. In 1901 Joliet Junior College opened its doors, with much fanfare, as the country's self-proclaimed first independent public junior college (Eells 1931a, p. 54).

Table 2-1. Growth of Junior Colleges 1918–1928

	All Junior Colleges		Publicly Controlled		Privately Controlled	
	Number	Enrollment	Number	Enrollment	Number	Enrollment
1917–1918	46	4,504	14	1,367	32	3,137
1919–1920	52	8,102	10	2,940	42	5,162
1921–1922	80	12,124	17	4,771	63	7,353
1923–1924	132	20,559	39	9,240	93	11,319
1925–1926	153	27,095	47	13,859	106	13,236
1927–1928	248	44,855	114	28,437	134	16,418

Source: U.S. Office of Education 1944, p. 6.

The junior college idea hardly swept the nation immediately. By 1910, only three public two-year colleges had been founded (Eells 1931, p. 74). But by 1918, there were fourteen public and thirty-two private junior colleges enrolling over 4,000 students (see Table 2-1). Nonetheless, junior colleges remained on the periphery of American higher education, for in that same year (1918), four-year colleges enrolled well over 400,000 students (U.S. Bureau of the Census 1975, p. 383).[1]

Sponsorship in California, Illinois, Michigan, and Missouri

During this first period of junior college development, California took over the lead from Harper and his associates in Illinois. As in Illinois, the key actors in California were top university administrators. Two, in particular, played a leading role: Alexis F. Lange,[2] dean of the School of Education at the University of California at Berkeley, and David Starr Jordan, president of Stanford University. Like Harper, Lange and Jordan were motivated not only by nationalist economic concerns but also by a desire to improve the status of their own institutions.[3] Both believed that the junior colleges would eventually assume all routine teaching functions, thereby enabling them to drop freshmen and sophomore instruction. This in turn would enable the university to concentrate on its proper functions: research and scholarship.

With these goals in mind, Lange and Jordan had already begun to lobby the state legislature in the 1890s to permit California's high schools to teach college-level courses. Although Lange was the more continuously active promoter, Jordan made some important contributions. In particular, according to Lange, "while Berkeley had been in the habit of speaking of six-year high schools, Dr. Jordan gave general currency to the name junior college, and this proved much more potent in suggestible communities" (Lange 1915, p. 91). This apparently minor linguistic shift—which directed attention away from the new institution's ties to secondary education and toward its linkages with four-year colleges and universities—was crucial in helping to gain popular legitimacy for the two-year college.

The lobbying efforts by Stanford and Berkeley eventually were successful. In

1907 the California legislature passed a law permitting high school boards of education to provide the first two years of college work, and in 1910 the first public junior college in California opened in Fresno as a department of the local high school. The Fresno Board of Education soon received congratulatory notes from both Jordan and Lange. Jordan wrote that he was looking forward "to the time when the large high schools of the state . . . will relieve the two great universities from the expense and from the necessity of giving instruction of the first two university years." Lange added, "The State university has stood for the junior college plan for more than fifteen years, and its policy is to further the establishment of junior colleges in every way possible" (quoted in Zwerling 1976, p. 50).

State laws passed during the next twelve years continued to encourage the establishment of junior colleges in California. Until 1921 most of them were funded as departments of high schools that served local school districts. When the first independent junior colleges began to appear, after 1921, they continued to be organized on a district basis, so that several local communities would be served by a single district junior college. By 1930 California had thirty-five junior colleges enrolling 13,392 students, which was slightly over one-third the total of public two-year college enrollment in the nation at the time and about half the total public higher education enrollment in California (Eells 1931a, p. 24).

Following in the footsteps of Harper and the California pioneers, state university presidents in several industrial states sponsored the development of junior colleges as a means of diverting the flow of students away from their own institutions. President Edmund James of the University of Illinois had urged as far back as 1905 that secondary schools and junior colleges take up much of the university's lower-division work, leaving it free to concentrate on specialized professional and scientific programs (Eells 1931a, p. 46). Although Illinois's junior colleges grew more slowly than Harper and James had hoped, by 1930 the two universities' efforts to stimulate interest in local communities had created the third largest public system in the country, with a total of 4,767 students (Eells 1931a, p. 24).

President Little of the University of Michigan helped establish seven junior colleges in his state in the 1920s, and wrote in 1925 that the "university . . . rejoices that the [junior college] movement is growing so rapidly here" (Little, quoted in Eells 1931a, p. 138). The efforts of the University of Missouri's president, S. D. Brooks, were even more successful: by 1928 seven public colleges and eleven private colleges closely associated with the university were operating. Beginning in 1911, Brooks and his assistants persuaded several four-year colleges in the state "that their own interest and honesty in education required them to devote all of their resources to two years instead of four years of work." This reduction suited the University of Missouri and also proved satisfactory to the colleges themselves. As Brooks recalled, "Parents who could not be persuaded to send their children to a small college for four years could be induced to send them to a junior college near at home for two years, provided transfer to the university without loss of credit could then be made" (Brooks, quoted in Eells 1931a, pp. 64–65).

Table 2-2. Number of and Enrollment in Junior Colleges by Types of Control, 1929–1930 (states with nine or more colleges)

State	Total		Public		Private	
	Number	Enrollment	Number	Enrollment	Number	Enrollment
Arkansas	11	1,956	7	1,363	4	593
California	49	13,922	35	13,392	14	530
Georgia	13	1,435	4	640	9	795
Illinois	18	6,514	6	4,767	12	1,747
Iowa	28	1,858	21	1,177	7	681
Kansas	19	2,232	10	1,178	9	454
Kentucky	17	1,664	1	107	16	1,557
Michigan	9	2,046	7	1,949	2	97
Mississippi	18	1,396	11	563	7	833
Missouri	23	5,554	7	2,517	16	3,037
Nebraska	9	805	2	159	7	646
New York	11	1,087	0	—	11	1,087
North Carolina	18	2,439	3	306	15	2,133
Oklahoma	14	1,744	11	1,591	3	153
Pennsylvania	9	1,000	0	—	9	1,000
Tennessee	13	1,680	1	151	12	1,529
Texas	47	8,886	19	4,755	28	4,131
Virginia	12	1,586	0	—	12	1,586

Source: Eells 1931a, p. 24.

Junior College Growth in Other States

In the first years of the junior college movement, university sponsorship contributed heavily to the building of respectably sized institutions. The states in which such sponsorship was most vigorous—California, Illinois, Michigan, and Missouri—enrolled nearly three-fifths of all public junior college students by 1929–1930 (calculated from Eells 1931a, p. 24). But for sheer institution-building energy, other sources of development were more important elsewhere. In parts of the South and Midwest, the lingering Populist impulse, usually combined with local boosterism, encouraged the founding of public two-year colleges as an avenue of cultural and social mobility for the children of farmers, shopkeepers, artisans, and workers. In 1929–1930, only six states had ten or more public junior colleges: California, Iowa, Texas, Oklahoma, Mississippi, and Kansas (see Table 2-2).[4] Except for California, all these were states in which the Populist political legacy apparently combined with municipal pride to support efforts to build institutions dedicated to cultural enlightenment and social opportunity.

Only in Mississippi and in the three Texas colleges linked to Texas A&M did the zeal for higher education become directly linked to the state's economic interests.[5] In other areas, the emphasis was on bringing the fruits of a traditional liberal arts education directly to the people. Communities in Iowa, Louisiana, and several other states competed to fund new two-year colleges. Often two-year colleges were founded too close to one another, leaving them inadequately supported (see Eells 1931a, pp. 132–133, 136).

In much of the South and in parts of the Midwest, religious enthusiasm was a major source of private junior college development. Methodists, Baptists, and Catholics were particularly active in founding denominational colleges, which became prevalent in the "Bible Belt," the band of states arching from Virginia through the border South into the agrarian Midwest. Between 1900 and 1916, more than half of all junior colleges in the nation were denominational (McDowell 1919); by 1930, after the first wave of public development, this proportion had fallen to just under half (Eells 1931a, pp. 47). Although they remained the single most numerous type, the religious colleges were generally small, with typically under one hundred students. Some of them had always been two-year institutions but many had begun as four-year schools and then found themselves forced by financial pressures to cut back to two years. In Texas, for example, three of the weaker four-year Baptist colleges were cut back to two-year colleges feeding into Baylor College, the best-established Baptist college in the state (Eells 1931a, pp. 63–64). A similar pattern was common in several other states.

In the Northeast, the first junior colleges were exclusively private. Although sometimes denominational, they were often built by independent proprietors on the model of the prestigious private liberal arts colleges in that region. Many of the colleges for men were explicitly preparatory and attracted academically marginal sons and daughters of the upper and middle classes. They aimed at preparing their students for successful completion of four-year programs and claimed to offer the advantages of small classes and individualized instruction (Winslow 1933). The colleges for women typically sought to provide cultural finishing for the daughters of the well-to-do. Such students might read "Livy, Tacitus, and Horace. . . . They study logic and ethics, as well as 'moral philosophy.' " (Keep, quoted in Winslow 1933, p. 346). These private colleges were generally quite small, and at first a majority of them aspired to become full-fledged four-year liberal arts colleges (McDowell 1919).

In addition to these regional variants, the movement also included a few profit-making schools aimed at teaching specific job-related skills; some experiments in the two-year teacher training programs; and some unclassifiable institutions, such as the five YMCA colleges that taught general morality along with academic and vocational subjects (Eells 1931a, pp. 125–159).

Business played a secondary role in the founding of the first community colleges; university sponsorship, Populist and "community pride" impulses, and religious motives were far more important. Nonetheless, individual businessmen were often enthusiastic supporters of the colleges. In California, the junior colleges were strongly supported by many local chambers of commerce, primarily because of the increased business that the schools brought into their communities (Boren 1928). And some businessmen liked the "sound business principles" on which junior colleges were founded (Allison 1928, p. 10). But there is no evidence that, as the business-domination model might suggest, businessmen regarded the first colleges as potential suppliers of trained manpower. Instead, their support seems to have been entirely based on their pride in new community institutions, their hopes for increasing commercial volume, and their appreciation of

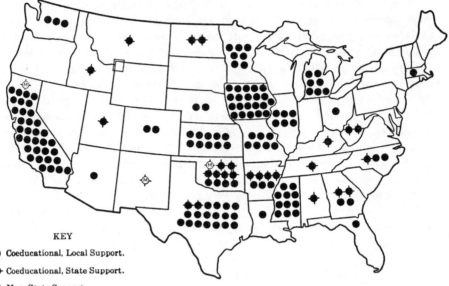

KEY

● Coeducational, Local Support.

◆ Coeducational, State Support.

◈ Men, State Support.

Figure 2-1. Number of public junior colleges of various types in the United States, 1930. *Source:* Eells 1931a, p. 30.

the lower cost and greater "efficiency" of operating junior, as compared with senior, colleges (see Eells 1931a, pp. 194–197).

An examination of the geographical distribution of public and private junior colleges in 1930 reveals much about the organizational ecology of American higher education and the factors that both facilitated and impeded the development of the two-year college. A brief glance at Figure 2-1 shows that public junior colleges were heavily concentrated in the Midwest (especially the Plains states), the Southwest (including Texas), and the Far West (predominantly California)—regions with strong traditions of public education and relatively few private institutions. In the densely populated Mid-Atlantic and New England regions, however, there was only one public junior college.[6] Public junior college development in these regions was blocked not merely by the public sector's traditional weakness in higher education but also by the presence of a dense network of private four-year colleges and universities—institutions that as we shall later show, often viewed junior colleges as potential competitors. Nonetheless, it was precisely in these regions (along with the Old South) that the private junior colleges made their greatest inroads.

The Common Focus on Transfer

During the first quarter of the twentieth century, two-year colleges were both extraordinarily diverse and relatively isolated from one another. They catered to different publics, were controlled by different types of authorities, and responded to different social and economic agendas. Not even their basic institutional affiliations were similar. Many hoped to "grow into" four-year colleges, and others sought to become closely linked to secondary schools. As late as 1928, a junior college administrator observed: "The junior college is, as yet, in that interesting stage where there is nothing standardized about it—not even its name. . . . The term 'junior college' has become generic, like church or education, covering a multitude of experiments on the borderline between . . . secondary and higher education" (Coats, quoted in Eells 1931, p. 160).

Within this highly diverse set of institutions, however, a definite central tendency could be discerned. Two out of three of the colleges were secular, and the vast majority (both public and private) were liberal arts institutions that emphasized curricula that could be transferred with credit to senior colleges.

Vocational programs were found from the beginning in some junior colleges, but they were seldom important features of the institutions. For example, when junior college presidents were surveyed by the U.S. Bureau of Education in 1917–1918, fewer than one-quarter of non-California presidents said that providing occupational programs had been an important commitment of their colleges at the time of their founding. Moreover, only 4 percent of private junior college courses and only 17 percent of public junior college courses were categorized by the bureau as vocational (McDowell 1919). The college preparatory programs were dominant even in states like California and Texas, where many officials favored "practical" training and the public two-year colleges were considered to be part of secondary education.

Administrators found that to legitimate their institutions, they had to emulate the first two years of a traditional college education. In the institutions that offered them, vocational courses were stigmatized as "dumb-bell courses" (see Eells 1931a, p. 310). Indeed, one reason for the irregular growth of California's junior colleges in the 1920s was the stigma attached to the institutions itself. As one researcher noted in the mid-1920s, "High school graduates were not inclined to regard them as 'real colleges' and many preferred to wait in the hope of attending a larger institution rather than become identified with the unappreciated junior college which seemed to them a mere appendage of the high school, and even lacking the . . . high school life and attractiveness" (quoted in Eells 1931, p. 99). The junior colleges tried first to overcome the students' misgivings, and as one writer noted, any institution that "was not giving courses of real college grade could not expect long to survive" (Eells 1931, p. 249).[7]

Many parents felt that the junior colleges would offer their children brighter futures than they themselves had, by enabling them to enter and do well in the higher-level institutions. Among the junior college presidents surveyed by the U.S. Bureau of Education in 1917–1918, 90 percent said that public demand for greater educational opportunity was an important reason for the founding of their colleges, and 50 percent said that it was the most important reason (McDowell 1919). According to the president of a Detroit junior college: "I think that it is a great mistake to limit the scope of the junior college. . . . If democracy is to be preserved by education, it will be by bringing education down to the masses. There are many intelligent people in large communities who are capable of profiting by college work. . . . The junior college ought to offer a large number of courses that will appeal to such persons'' (MacKenzie, quoted in Eells 1931a, p. 236).

Sometimes this sentiment was given larger civic significance:

> It was believed by many citizens of Chicago that junior colleges should be encouraged in the city for the purpose of developing home talent that might be utilized in solving some of our city problems. . . . After graduating, our city boys, familiar with city conditions, framed in our city colleges, would be better than outsiders to solve our problems. (Bogan, quoted in McDowell 1919, p. 25)

At other times it was put in less grandiose terms. For example, educational opportunities in local communities were often thought to be desirable by parents who felt their children were "still too immature to be safe in the freedom-loving atmosphere of a large institution." But for whatever reason, virtually everyone felt that opportunities for higher education should be "brought within the reach of all" (McDowell 1919, p. 24).

The Founding of a National Association: The American Association of Junior Colleges

Despite their diversity, the two-year colleges faced some common problems stemming from their marginal position and their efforts to tailor their course offerings to university requirements. In particular, most junior colleges faced the continuing problem of designing procedures and policies that would maximize the transferability of course credits and yet fulfill the special needs of two-year college students. Standards for admission and requirements for degrees were also affected by having to contend with the changing policies and moods of the four-year institutions.

Perhaps the greatest problem facing the two-year college movement, however, was coping with the low esteem in which their institutions were often held. This issue was almost never addressed publicly, but it was acutely felt. In later reminiscences, early junior college presidents frequently mentioned how angry they felt to hear their institutions dismissed as "glorified high schools" or "bargain basement colleges" (Bishop 1950, Campbell 1936, "Impressions of the Berkeley Convention" 1931).

Given the differences among the junior colleges, the rapid changes in their fortunes, and the pressures of day-to-day affairs, the junior colleges had been unable to act in concert and lacked even a forum for discussing common problems. When representatives from the colleges finally met together for the first time in 1920, they did so at the invitation of two prominent educators of the period: George F. Zook, a higher education specialist for the U.S. Bureau of Education, and James M. Wood, a well-known Missouri junior college president and a disciple of William Rainey Harper. Both men had been impressed by the steady, if haphazard, growth of the junior colleges since 1901, and both were disturbed by their lack of a common identity. This combination of optimism and concern led

Zook and Wood to convene a conference in St. Louis in 1920 to discuss, as they put it, the "mutual interest and problems" of junior college officials. Sponsored by the U.S. Bureau of Education, the conference brought together thirty-four educators from twenty-two junior colleges in thirteen states (Brick 1964, p. 32). The officials who gathered in St. Louis shared little except a common anxiety about the status and prospects of their hybrid institutions.

It is significant that the conferees talked mainly about their colleges' proper mission, as there could hardly have been less agreement on this score. Relieving the universities of "routine" functions, teaching useful skills, and extending educational opportunities all received some measure of support, but each participant seemed to have his or her own position on the issue. If the sometimes acerbic comments directed toward the universities are indicative, there was considerably greater unanimity in a feeling of shared victimization. "I wonder," said one participant, "whether we are going to assert our right to 'a place in the sun' . . . or whether we are just going to be a tail for the universities to wag" (Loomis, quoted in Zook 1922, p. 20).

After two days of intermittently contentious but apparently satisfying meetings, the participants in St. Louis conference decided to establish a permanent organization to provide leadership for the junior college movement (Brick 1964, pp. 30–34). It is clear that this organization, the American Association of Junior Colleges (AAJC), was formed as much from a need for mutual support as from a sense of shared interests. In the words of Doak S. Campbell, one of the Association's early leaders: "At first I think we should characterize [the association's activities] . . . as defensive. We came together, a small group seemingly for the purpose of defending this child which appeared to be greatly in need of defense just at that time" (Campbell, quoted in Eells 1931a, p. 78).

The sanctuary, however, soon became an important vehicle for shaping institutional interest and identity. Indeed, the founding of the association was a critical event in the history of the two-year college movement. The AAJC's organizational presence provided for the first time the possibility of overcoming the centrifugal force of decentralization and forging a common identity among the member institutions. It offered both a forum for debate about the proper role and organization of junior colleges and an instrument for the realization of ascendent views. Again, according to Campbell: "A little later, this program turned from the defense to forward movement, a promotional program" (Campbell, quoted in Eells 1931a, p. 78). Most importantly, it provided an organizational center whose goal was to shape the emerging institution of community colleges and, in turn, to shape the destinies of those who would attend them.

The Junior College Vanguard and the Universities

In the Association's early years, junior college administrators, particularly those from the southern and eastern states, spent much of their time in Association meetings discussing problems related to the transfer of junior college graduates to four-year institutions (Bishop 1950, Brick 1964). Several of the other early meetings of the AAJC were spent in long debates about academic standards. Most of the participants argued for maintaining standards at or above the levels required by higher education accrediting agencies, but a minority argued that these standards imposed severe burdens on junior colleges that had grown out of secondary education. Other prominent issues concerned the recruitment of students and the training and qualifications of faculty members (Brick 1964). The early meetings of the AAJC were thus dominated by the activities of junior college officials who were preoccupied with acceptance in established higher education circles.

But this preoccupation was less visible among a new group of leaders that began to emerge during the first years of the AAJC. These men emphasized the importance of occupational training as the primary function of junior colleges in all parts of the country, no matter what had been the conditions of their founding. They also emphasized the need to maintain transfer tracks while using counseling and guidance procedures to ensure that their students would enroll in the curriculum most appropriate to their abilities and likely occupation. Given their later influence and power, it would not be inaccurate to refer to these men as the "vanguard" of the junior college movement.

The universities' preferences were influential in the formation of this vanguard, for the early vocationalizers were academic men attuned to the interests of the universities and skeptical of the free play of student choice. The principal leaders of the vocationalizing movement in the AAJC were Leonard V. Koos, Walter Crosby Eells, and Doak S. Campbell.[8] Both Koos and Eells were professors of education—Koos at Minnesota (later at Chicago) and Eells at Stanford—and both were in close contact with the most advanced trends in thought regarding junior colleges. Campbell's convictions seem to have been forged mainly by his early experiences as a junior college president, but he, too, had been a professor of education, at George Peabody College in Tennessee (Goodwin 1971, pp. 95–116).

The early leaders of the junior college movement were typically men of small-town Protestant backgrounds, and they were often of modest social origins. Some, like Campbell, came from families that were far from affluent (Campbell was born in a log cabin in Arkansas); others, like Koos, were from more prosperous backgrounds (Koos's father was a successful German-born tailor who had settled in Aurora, Illinois). Despite their origins, all of them had completed college. But few had attended undergraduate schools attached to leading universities; Campbell, Eells, and Koos, for example, were, respectively, alumni of Quachita (a small college in Arkansas), Whitman (in Walla Walla, Washington), and Oberlin (in Ohio).[9]

Much of the language used by the early leaders of the junior college movement displayed an almost missionary zeal, and it seems likely that they, like many Progressives of the era, were channeling fundamental moral and ethical concerns into a secular outlet. Koos, for example, had been persuaded to attend Oberlin by a Congregational minister, and Campbell received his undergraduate education at a Baptist institution before going on to spend a year as the state secretary of Baptist sunday schools in Arkansas[10] (Goodwin 1971, pp. 97, 111). While no systematic data on the religious origins of the early junior college leaders are available, it seems that many of them were raised in religious Protestant families and carried their commitment to moral uplift into their professional careers. Indeed, in many ways, they resembled the "managers of virtue" described by David Tyack and Elizabeth Hansot (1982): those men of small-town pietist origin who presided over American elementary and secondary education during this same period.

George Zook once described the junior college movement as an army of "struggling frontiersmen" put together by "General Koos" and "Colonels Eells and Campbell," who then led them into all parts of the country, "even storm(ing) the New England citadel" (Zook 1940, p. 618). The analogy is apt in many ways. These intellectual commanders did undertake a massive job of organization. They did lead their recruits to fight many battles before their institutions were accepted, and many more before their vision of the junior colleges became widely adopted. Zook's metaphor is misleading only insofar as it suggests that the battles were mainly fought against university educators and other skeptics outside the movement. In fact, the first battles were fought within the junior college movement to gain consensus on the need for vocationalization, and some of the struggling junior college frontiersmen's most important allies were in fact those cosmopolitan gentlemen who ran the nation's leading universities.

The strong preference of the universities for terminal two-year colleges had changed little since William Rainey Harper's time, but the principal rationale had shifted somewhat. During World War I, as college enrollments declined, many university presidents had come to appreciate the extent to which their institutions depended on freshmen and sophomore tuitions. By the end of the war, appreciation of this economic constraint had greatly lessened the appeal of earlier plans to "amputate" the first two years of university instruction (Zwerling 1976, pp. 45–46).

Within a few years, another reason to support the development of junior colleges as terminal institutions had emerged. After the war, college enrollments began to grow so rapidly that many university presidents feared their institutions would be overwhelmed (D. Levine 1986). Junior colleges thus were welcomed, in the words of president Raymond Wilbur of Stanford, as "shock absorbers" (Eells 1931a, p. 49).

University officials in California continued to lead the way in conceiving of the junior colleges as institutions that would divert those clamoring for higher education away from the nation's four-year colleges and universities. Until his death in 1924, Alexis Lange, the dean of the University of California's School of Education, continued to argue that "junior college, in order to promote the general welfare . . . cannot make preparation for the university its excuse for being" (quoted in Monroe 1972, p. 11). Increasingly, university administrators in other sections of the country came to favor this new definition of the role of junior colleges.

As A. Lawrence Lowell, president of Harvard, explained, "One of the merits of these new institutions will be the keeping out of college, rather than leading into it, young people who have no taste for higher education" (Lowell 1928, p. 284). Robert G. Sproul, president of the University of California from 1930 to 1958, emphasized that the state's educational system should allocate students in accord with the natural distribution of talent in the society. Insisting that "the university is primarily designed for one type of mind and the junior college for another," he argued that what was needed was "not more colleges and universities of the traditional type . . . but altogether different institutions which will suitably train [less able] students and get them to their life work sooner" (Sproul 1931, pp. 279, 276–277).

Koos, Eells, and Campbell all were clearly influenced by the views of university men on the proper role of the junior college, particularly as emphasized in the earlier writings of Alexis Lange. In Lange's mind, the success of the junior colleges in diverting students away from the university was connected to their providing an alternative to university-type training. He argued that most junior college students were "intended" for life work "just as noble as, but quite different from, that for which a university prepared one" (Lange 1911, p. 8). For these students, "probably the greatest and certainly the most original contribution to be made by the junior colleges is the means of training for the vocations occupying the middle ground between those of the artisan type and the professions" (Lange 1918, p. 213). Lange later traveled throughout California imploring junior college administrators to prevent the "wrong students" from attempting to transfer to the universities. He believed that university training would be harmful for students whose intellectual capacities were not up to the level required, and he encouraged administrators to direct those students toward vocational subjects (Brick 1964, p. 22).

Koos, a popular lecturer at AAJC meetings, argued that the junior colleges could "democratically" guide less capable students toward their place in society without subjecting them to the "ruthless" but socially necessary elimination awaiting them at the university (Koos 1930). Eells wrote that it would be "unwise and unfortunate" if all junior college students "tried to enter a university and prepare for professions which in most cases are already overcrowded and for which their talents and abilities in many cases do not fit them." It was his belief that "the junior college must offer something more than a simple university preparatory course, if it is to live up to its true destiny. The development of the terminal function is an essential corollary of the success of the popularization function" (Eells 1931a, p. 289). Campbell, though he often spoke of the need for strong transfer programs, also accepted the idea that the junior colleges had an obligation to "provide training suitable to the needs of those it serves" (Campbell 1930, p. 150).

None of these leaders of the junior college vanguard favored an exclusively vocational curriculum. Rather, they believed that general education courses should be a part even of the vocational tracks and that preparatory (or transfer) curricula should be an option in all colleges. The reforms they urged were designed to bring about a change in emphasis, not a complete reconstitution. But this change in emphasis was to be far-reaching: all three believed that between two-thirds and three-quarters of junior college students should properly be enrolled in terminal occupational training programs.

The AAJC was sufficiently fragmented in the early years, and sufficiently sensitive to the universities' interests, to ensure the early vocational leaders a forum. Indeed, the early leaders of the vocationalizing movement moved quickly into positions of prominence in the AAJC. Campbell was elected executive secretary in 1922 and held that position for the next sixteen years. Eells became the first editor of the *Junior College Journal* in 1930 and then appointed Campbell his deputy. When Campbell retired in 1938, Eells assumed the position of executive secretary, which he held through World War II. Koos, though he devoted most of his time to consulting and teaching at the University of Minnesota and later at the University of Chicago, was a tireless writer and lecturer on junior college subjects. He conducted research for the association and was a favorite speaker at its meetings. In addition, several of the early presidents of the AAJC (elected annually) were sympathetic to the vocationalizing wing (Brick 1964, Goodwin 1971).

Koos, Eells, Campbell, and their followers were articulate, well connected to the universities, and not afraid to argue their position. But more than these facts are necessary to explain their quick success in gaining positions of prominence. The academic colleges were still most numerous in the AAJC, but they seemed content to go their own way, using the annual conventions less as forums for arguing policy than as retreats for rest and relaxation.

It seems likely that the cause of the academic colleges' passivity resided in the status problems they faced. It is clear that the early junior colleges were not highly respected by many higher-tier institutions, however much the universities may have applauded their "shock-absorbing" functions. As one early junior college leader recalled: "When the Association came into being, the few junior colleges that existed were regarded by institutions of higher learning—if indeed, they were regarded at all—with something [like] disdain. Senior colleges and universities viewed the junior colleges with attitudes varying from skepticism to virtual contempt" (Bishop 1950, p. 501). This lack of respect was a problem for all the junior colleges, but it must have been felt particularly keenly by the academic colleges. The more vocationally oriented colleges, after all, were not in the business of producing classically educated men and women. Pushed by parents and students, the more academic colleges may have had sufficient incentive to keep their own programs transfer based, but apparently they did not have sufficient courage, in the face of university skepticism and organized internal opposition, to promote their preferences in any vigorous fashion among their fellow institutions.

The Development of an Ideology of Vocationalism

University administrators may have seen the junior college as an institution designed to divert students, rather than as a place of preparing students to transfer, but they were not in a position to make their vision a reality. The task of developing the organizational innovations needed to reform the junior colleges thus fell to those directly involved with them and, in particular, to the vanguard of the junior college movement.

More than any other junior college leaders, Leonard Koos and Walter Crosby Eells developed the ideas and techniques that were later used in the campaign to "sell" terminal vocational education to academically oriented junior college administrators, faculty, and students. These ideas and techniques included a conception of the potential training markets open to the community colleges, the formulation of a "counterideology" to combat the prevailing academic ideology, and the promotion of intelligence testing and guidance counseling in the junior colleges as means of channeling students into occupational programs.

Koos's concept of "semiprofessional training" provided a focus for the leaders of the vocationalizing movement in describing the types of training that most junior college students should receive. Koos consistently argued that the community colleges should allow the universities to be the main providers of training for higher-status professional and managerial occupations and that they should try to carve out a distinct market niche for themselves as centers of training for the next highest levels in the occupational hierarchy (1924, pp. 144–166; 1925, pp. 121–145). He defined the "semiprofessions" as occupations that are "to be distinguished, on the one hand, from *trades,* the training for which is concluded during the secondary school period, and, on the other, from *professions,* adequate preparation for which requires four or more years of training beyond the high school" (Koos 1924, p. 144, emphasis his). The length of training required to enter a semiprofession—"a course of training approximately two years in length, with a high school education or its equivalent as a prerequisite" (Koos 1924, p. 153)—corresponded to that offered by terminal programs in the junior college. In looking to the semiprofessions as occupations for which the junior college should strive to provide training, Koos's intent was clear: to capture for the junior college the best training markets available, given that the universities and four-year colleges already virtually monopolized the pathways to the higher professions and top management.

The kinds of jobs that people trained in the semiprofessions would obtain included work as assistants to professionals in engineering, health, and agriculture, such as "insurance agents," "shipping department heads," "forest rangers," and "foremen on truck farms" (Koos 1925, pp. 136–138). In addition, Koos suggested that such occupations as "managers of commercial, institutional, and industrial cafeterias," "professional shoppers," "designers," "lithographic and photo engravers," and "masseurs" might be logical lines of development for semiprofessional training (Koos 1925, pp. 140–141). Since this manifestly heterogenous set of occupations had no common relationship to the established professions, one might well ask in what sense, if any, they constituted genuine semiprofessions. But to dwell on this is to miss the hidden unity of Koos' list, for what all of these occupations had in common was their location in the middle levels of the stratification system.

Koos's method of identifying potential training markets for the two-year college reveals much about the constraints facing the early leaders of the movement. In searching for a stable market nice in America's highly competitive system of higher education, Koos's first step was to examine the changing American occupational structure, consulting data gathered by the U.S. Bureau of Labor Statistics, the U.S. Army, and various employer surveys (Koos 1924, p. 153). Having done his best to ascertain the structure of the labor market for middle-level jobs, he then proceeded to survey university administrators and to pore over university catalogues to determine the highest status "semiprofessional" occupations not already provided for by the four-year institutions. The final step of the process was to recommend that the junior college move expeditiously to develop curricula and programs in the still unoccupied market niches (Koos 1924, 1927; Goodwin 1971).

Koos's efforts to channel curricular development into semiprofessional training illustrate the willingness of junior college leaders to acknowledge the primacy of the universities in relation to the highest rungs of the occupational structure. Koos thus made no attempts to compete directly with the universities; indeed, he accepted that the best the junior college could do was to provide training for the most prestigious fields that the university had not yet claimed. Vocationalization may thus be viewed as a strategy devised in substantial part in response to the constraints on junior college development posed by the university's links to the existing structure of educational and social stratification. More compelling testimony of the enormous structural power of the university—its capacity to influence profoundly the direction of junior college development even in the absence of direct intervention—is hard to imagine.

In addition to his pioneering role in advocating semiprofessional education in the junior college, Koos was among the first to champion the standardized aptitude tests developed by such psychologists as Edward L. Thorndike and Lewis M. Terman as the most acceptable means for tracking students into vocational programs, a suggestion that would have enduring appeal. He cited the statistical distributions of Army Alpha Tests from World War I as proving that many students who were not capable of mastering a four-year college course could still profit from an education beyond high school (Koos 1924, pp. 87–122; 1925, pp. 102–121). Koos also strongly supported the further development of intelligence testing and argued that it could provide an even better means for scientifically distributing students among tracks.

Standardized tests enjoyed widespread prestige during this period (see Gould 1981), and members of the junior college movement were quick to follow Koos's lead. At the AAJC's national convention of 1928, for example, L. W. Smith, the president of Joliet Township High School and Junior College proposed a definition of semiprofessional education that would continue to carry weight in junior college circles: such education was distinctly below the level of university-level specialization because of its less demanding cognitive content, but it differed from training for the skilled crafts because it required students to prepare for life "on the level of intellectual routine rather than manipulative routine." Nonetheless, those who graduated from junior college vocational programs for the semiprofessions would be entering vocations "that have a great deal of routine work in them" (Smith, quoted in Goodwin, 1971, p. 157).

Koos was also a pioneer in foreseeing the potential importance of guidance counseling as a means of softening the conflict between the high aspirations held by junior college students and the limited occupational opportunities available to them. Koos argued that intelligence testing should form the basis for guiding students into jobs and that counselors should make it easier for students to accept their scientifically prescribed life trajectories by pointing out the correspondence between their individual abilities and the cognitive demands of special occupations. Although Koos's vigorous advocacy of expanded guidance counseling rested on a naive faith in the precision of recently developed standardized tests, his underlying impulse was, it should be emphasized, a humanitarian one. The alternative, in his view, to increased reliance on standardized tests and counseling was to follow the brutally competitive model of American universities, in which the "large-scale elimination" of students was accompanied by "ruthless disruptions of life plans" (quoted in Goodwin 1971, p. 103).

Though also favoring expanded testing and counseling, Walter Crosby Eells was perhaps the first of the vocationalizing leaders to recognize that students might object to the outcomes of "scientific selection" and to contend that the most effective guidance would be to influence preferences rather than to prescribe courses. The students' resistance to vocational programs and their preference for an academic curriculum, Eells noted, was a natural expression of their interest in social mobility:

> It is very difficult to enroll students in a curriculum upon the gates of which are inscribed the motto, "abandon all hope, ye who enter here." Many students who . . . will profit by a junior college education . . . probably should never enter the university for professional work, but . . . they will refuse to submit to any doctrine of academic predeterminism which forever forbids possible entrance to educational paradise. (Eells, quoted in Goodwin 1971, pp. 163–164)

Eells dismissed this interest in mobility and the corresponding resistance to tracking as inconsistent with the natural distribution of talents and abilities and, therefore, as unrealizable (Eells 1931a, p. 289). Although students could not be forced to take terminal courses, he said, they could be "led, enticed, and attracted" into taking them, largely through the efforts of guidance counselors who were motivated to "popularize" them (Eells 1931a, p. 310). Left to the vicissitudes of "consumer choice," however, the junior college was destined to remain overwhelmingly college preparatory in orientation.

Like other leaders of the vocationalizing wing, Eells had deep faith in the results of standardized tests and tended to assume a suspiciously precise correspondence between the structure of available jobs and the distribution of individual abilities and talents. At times the hierarchical division of labor even seemed to take its shape not from the demands of the economic structure but from the innate characteristics of individuals. The very possibility that there might be more people capable of performing professional and managerial jobs than there were slots available for them in the labor market seems not to have been entertained by any of the early leaders.

The underlying logic of the junior college vanguard's vocationalization project was rooted in its members' forthright recognition of the hierarchical character of the division of labor in industrial societies and their conviction that the educational system should be consciously designed so as to produce trained workers to fill the slots in this hierarchy. Writing in 1931, Eells noted that "census figures indicate that less than ten per cent of the population of the country is required for the professions" (1931a, p. 289). A central task of the junior college, Eells believed, was to prevent the popular clamor for educational and economic mobility from leading the system of higher education to produce more highly trained graduates than the economy could absorb. But this structurally based diversion of students away from the universities (and from the ranks of the professions and higher management) was simultaneously legitimated in terms of the individual deficiencies of those who attended the junior college.

As part of their efforts on behalf of vocationalization, Koos, Eells, and Campbell also led the way in developing a coherent counterideology that could blunt the continuing appeal of the explicitly academic ideology still favored by many junior college educators. This vocational counterideology celebrated "practicality" and "realism." Eells, for example, maintained that if the junior colleges wanted to popularize higher education, they would have to provide curricula that would be of practical advantage to the increasing number of students they hoped to attract. He also contended that most junior college students were terminal students—in fact if not in desire—because they lacked the money, the motivation, or the qualifications to gain admission to the four-year colleges and universities. Given this situation, he argued, the only reasonable approach was to offer courses suited to the actual life prospects of most junior college students.

Koos and Campbell, for their part, pioneered the popular use of the term *democratic* to describe the vocational track in the junior college. For Campbell, who had become executive secretary of the AAJC in 1922, terminal vocational education was "democratic" because, unlike "elitist" academic course work, it provided knowledge "suitable to the needs of those it serves" (Campbell 1931, p. 150). Like Eells, Koos saw higher education as social engineering, a system for channeling individuals of differing abilities to appropriate occupational levels. In his view, the more sensitive, personally negotiated forms of guidance found in the junior colleges deserved to be called democratic, whereas the more impersonal forms of selection associated with universities, were relatively undemocratic (Goodwin 1971, pp. 103–104, 161–163).

Koos, Eells, and Campbell were frank in characterizing the vocational programs that were central to their vision of the role of junior colleges. They usually spoke of them as the "terminal curricula" or the "terminal functions." These phrases sound harsh to modern ears, accustomed to hearing comparable curricula described as "career programs." But the older terms did convey an important truth about these programs: students taking them would in fact terminate their education with two-year degrees and little hope of realizing higher educational or occupational aspirations. This reality was intuitively grasped by junior college students, and it became an important source of their resistance to vocationalization for years to come.

Converting the Unconverted

Once in positions of prominence, the leaders of the AAJC's vocationalizing movement pressed their case in a variety of ways. Their first task was to gain some degree of consensus for expanding what was then called the terminal function. According to Brick (1964, p. 120), "hardly a meeting of the Association throughout the 1920s and 1930s failed to discuss terminal education." At least one of the leaders of the vocationalizing wing spoke at every annual meeting, and Koos spoke at virtually all of them.

The founding in 1930 of the Association's *Junior College Journal* under Eells's editorship provided a crucial forum for promoting vocational curricula. During the first year of his editorship, Eells made it clear that he appreciated the opportunities for "consciousness building" that the *Journal* provided. "This journal," he wrote, "should be a powerful factor in giving greater unity and consciousness to the junior college movement" (Eells 1931b, p. 80). Eells and his deputy editor Doak Campbell tried to offer something for practically everyone in the Association, but they did not cease arguing that colleges and universities were improper reference points to guide further junior college development. As an editorial signed by Campbell in 1932 put the case: junior college "curricular practices have reflected faithfully the practices of four-year institutions. . . . There seems to be small hope that the junior college will make its distinctive contribution until it shall adopt curricular procedures based upon other premises" (Campbell 1932, p. 63).

Another selection by Eells, developing a theme that would become increasingly important in the future, championed "looking outward upon the community" rather than "upward to the university" (Eells 1932, p. 2). The *Journal* never turned all of its attention to the terminal programs—to do so would have been to risk a loss of credibility—but it went to considerable lengths to advertise successes in this area. Curricular shifts toward vocational subjects were highlighted, and among the seven "representative junior colleges" featured in the first several numbers of the 1932 *Journal* were at least four that could be considered highly vocationalized for the period.

While the *Junior College Journal* and the annual national meetings were important avenues of persuasion, the forces favoring vocationalization had other vehicles at their disposal as well. Between 1924 and 1931, Koos, Eells, and Campbell had published four treatises on junior college education. All four books (Campbell 1930; Eells 1931a; Koos 1924, 1925) charged that junior colleges were concentrating far too much on the "preparatory function" and neglecting the more important "terminal function."

Probably the decisive contribution here was Koos's *The Junior College Movement* (1925), a widely read popularization of his two-volume scholarly monograph on the junior college published a year earlier. Koos's work had a profound impact on future generations of junior college leaders, including such key figures as Jesse Bogue, executive secretary of the AAJC from 1946 to 1958, and Leland Medsker, perhaps the leading junior college scholar in the years after World War II (Goodwin 1971, p. 104). Eells's own 1931 text, *The Junior College,* was greatly influenced by Koos's work, as was Campbell's more specialized 1930 monograph, *A Critical Study of the Stated Purposes of the Junior College.* Together, these works— commonly used as required reading in education courses for junior college administrators—set the terms of the debate about the proper mission of the junior college. Indeed, already by the mid-1930s, it had come to be taken for granted by policymakers that terminal vocational programs were—despite the lack of much popular demand for them—at the very center of what the junior college was about.

The Vocationalization Project and Student Choice

Despite their tireless efforts in the 1920s and early 1930s, the national leadership failed to dampen the enthusiasm of junior college students for academic courses that paralleled those of the four-year colleges. The most extensive development of vocational courses and enrollments was found in the California junior colleges, which had the enthusiastic support of the University of California and Stanford, but even there the results were modest. As late as 1929–1930, fewer than one-sixth of California's junior college students were enrolled in vocational programs (Eells 1931a, p. 309). Outside California, vocational programs in the late 1920s remained poorly developed. There are no precise data on vocational enrollments nationwide, but they probably did not exceed the California average of 16 percent in 1929–1930, and most likely were a good deal lower (Eells 1931a, p. 308).

Just how completely students identified junior college education with traditional academic course work can be seen from several surveys carried out in the 1920s. In the largest study, students from twenty-nine California junior colleges were asked to state their reasons for deciding to attend a junior college. The reasons most frequently mentioned were "to save money" (60 percent) and "to prepare for the university" (58 percent). Fewer than 30 percent of the students mentioned vocational preparation, and under 10 percent said it was their most important reason (Eells 1931a, pp. 217–218). In this same study, more than 2,900 students responded to a question asking them to name the outstanding advantages of junior colleges. Small classes, low costs, personalized instruction, and the opportunity to live at home were the advantages most frequently mentioned. About 15 percent of the respondents mentioned improved chances of getting into a four-year college. By contrast, only 31—barely more than 1 percent—mentioned advantages related to occupational training[11] (Eells 1931a, p. 222).

A 1924 study of more than nine thousand California junior college students revealed that 80 percent of them intended to go on to four-year colleges and universities (Eells 1931a, p. 250). Though no direct data on their occupational aspirations are available, it seems likely that their desire to obtain a bachelor's degree was linked to their ambition to enter the kinds of professional and managerial jobs traditionally held by college graduates. For Eells, the results of this study suggested that although "the junior college is succeeding in the first step of its preparatory function, namely, in giving its students an ambition to go on to further work in the university . . . there are many reasons to suppose that it is succeeding too well" (Eells 1931a, pp. 250–251).

The parents of junior college students were even less interested in vocational programs than their children were. When Koos (1924, pp. 123–125) asked 199 such parents from Minnesota, Michigan, Texas, and California why they had sent their children to junior college, not one of them mentioned occupational training opportunities as a reason. Not surprisingly, parents most often mentioned "low cost" (72 percent) as a reason that their child was attending a local two-year college rather than a college or university elsewhere (Koos 1924, pp. 123–125).[12]

Although junior college students (and their parents) were not lacking in ambition, they often lacked the social status and financial resources of four-year

Table 2-3. Percentage Distribution by Occupational Groups of Fathers of Students in Public High Schools, Public Junior Colleges, Private Junior Colleges, and Other Higher Education Institutions

Parental Occupation	Public High Schools	Public Junior Colleges	Public Junior Colleges, Sophomores Only	Private Junior Colleges	Sophomores in Colleges and State Universities	Freshmen in Large Eastern University
1. Proprietors	19.8	19.1	17.8	29.5	25.1	35.7
2. Professional service	9.4	14.0	15.3	15.3	20.8	30.3
3. Managerial service	16.5	16.3	17.8	9.4	7.8	5.4
4. Commercial service	9.5	9.3	9.6	6.9	8.7	8.6
5. Clerical service	5.8	3.8	2.8	1.1	3.5	2.4
6. Agricultural service	2.4	14.2	11.7	26.9	22.5	1.4
7. Artisan-proprietors	4.2	2.8	3.2	1.7	2.6	0.3
8. Manual labor	29.1	15.6	18.3	6.7	7.1	6.5
9. Unknown	3.3	4.9	3.6	2.4	2.0	9.4
Total	100.0	100.0	100.1	99.9	100.1	100.0

Source: Koos 1924, p. 138.

college students. In his 1924 study of 2,744 college students, Koos combined his own data with evidence presented in Counts's classic *The Selective Character of American Secondary Education* (1922) and found that only one-third of public junior college students had fathers who were either professionals or proprietors, compared with over 45 percent of sophomores at "colleges and state universities" and almost two-thirds of the freshmen in a "large eastern university" (see Table 2-3). The results of a later study of fifty-five colleges and universities (also modeled on that of Counts) by Reynolds (1927) generally confirmed these findings and established that there was, by this time, a clear-cut social hierarchy of institutions, with state teachers' colleges near the bottom, public universities in the middle, and private women's and men's colleges at the top. The public junior college was at the very bottom of this hierarchy, even though it was more middle than working class in composition and considerably more exclusive socially than the American public high school (an institution that, as Counts had documented, itself significantly underrepresented the children of manual workers).

Ironically, at a time when more and more junior college and university leaders were criticizing the wastefulness of providing college preparation for those whom they felt should not or could not continue their training on a higher level, junior college transfer students were busy demonstrating the flaws of that assumption. Comparisons of the academic performance of junior college transfers and "native" students at nine universities in the late 1920s showed only one case (the

University of Texas) in which junior college students performed significantly less well than native students. Transfer students performed at roughly the same level as native students at the University of Minnesota and the University of Chicago. At the other schools—Stanford University, the University of California at Berkeley, UCLA, the University of Southern California, the University of Colorado, the University of Iowa, and the University of Michigan's engineering school—the grades of transfer students were on average higher than those of native students. (For details of these studies, see Eells 1931a, pp. 254–274.)[13]

Leaders of the junior college vanguard were curiously unmoved by this evidence that junior college students could succeed in the "ruthless competition" of university life. After reporting the "good average performance" of junior college transfers, Eells praised not the students but the junior colleges, for their success in acting as "a protective sieve, a bumper, tending to select only the superior student for university work" (1931a, p. 277). For Eells and other leaders, the notable success of junior college transfers did not lead to a reconsideration of assumptions—only to renewed efforts to close the gates to protect the universities.

When 294 junior college presidents were asked in 1928–1929 to discuss the special purposes of their institutions, 43 percent of private college presidents and 24 percent of public college presidents mentioned opportunities for occupational training. Another 35 percent of private college presidents and 23 percent of public college presidents mentioned "completion of training for those not going on" (Whitney 1928, pp. 31–46). At a time when students (and their parents) continued to see the junior colleges as a means of demonstrating the ability to transfer and to pursue a higher degree, administrators were apparently beginning to warm to the calls of Koos, Eells, and other junior college leaders to de-emphasize college-transfer programs and to expand alternatives to the academic model.

Nevertheless, programs that prepared students for further academic study remained a dominant concern. From a systematic content analysis of 343 junior college catalogues, Campbell concluded that "those responsible for junior college programs attach more import to the preparatory function and purpose than to all other functions and purposes combined" (Campbell 1930, p. 80). The vocationalizing leaders could not help but regard figures like these with dismay. "The outstanding achievement of the past decade" Eells wrote, "has been the development and success of the preparatory function; the outstanding achievement of the next decade should be similar [achievement] and success of the terminal function. It, too, must be popularized, standardized, and recognized" (Eells 1931a, p. 311).

But the leaders of the movement to vocationalize the junior college recognized that their plans faced serious obstacles. For the truth was that, as Eells wrote, there was a stigma attached to vocational programs in many institutions, a stigma based in part on the widespread belief that those students capable of taking preparatory courses did so while the rest were "ignominiously shunted into the 'dumb-bell' courses." Given such formidable obstacles, Eells believed that it would "require missionary work to make the terminal courses successful" (Eells 1931a, p. 310).

Efforts to encourage this missionary effort were hindered by limited resources.

As late as 1930, the association had annual receipts of only $2,323, and it employed no salaried staff (Brick 1964, p. 55). Furthermore, the leadership was apparently unable to capture the imagination of outside sponsors who might have contributed to the cause. In 1926, when AAJC President L. W. Smith initiated efforts to gain foundation support to study effective terminal education programs, he found no willing sources of funding (Goodwin 1971, p. 183). Nor were state legislators necessarily supportive of terminal education. Even in California, the center of junior college strength and vocationalizing sentiment, the state legislature in 1930 briefly considered transforming the two-year colleges into four-year liberal arts institutions (Goodwin 1971, p. 147). The federal government had already expressed indifference to the junior colleges as training centers, by excluding them from eligibility for federal vocational education funds under the Smith–Hughes Act of 1917, and this attitude remained unchanged through the 1920s and 1930s (Venn 1964).

The California Example

In 1930 the AAJC held its annual meeting in Berkeley (the first time the Association had met in a western state), and this enabled the leadership to showcase the burgeoning junior college movement in California. The responses of past presidents of the Association indicate that many left Berkeley inspired by the California model ("Impressions of the Berkeley Convention" 1931): "The manner in which California is pouring its money into education, especially into its more than thirty public junior colleges is marvelous to one from the conservative East" (H. Gnuffsinger of Virginia). "The program from beginning to end was a great source of inspiration and information" (J. Thomas Davis of Texas). "It was a California convention . . . with a California program, presided over by a California chairman, manned with California spellbinders. . . . This was exactly as it should be, for is not California the golden embodiment of American education, the father of the best brands of junior institutions?" (Thomas F. Marshall of Arkansas).

The extraordinary growth of junior colleges in California had occurred in an unusually supportive economic and institutional environment. By 1900 the state was both populous and wealthy. Rapid industrial and agricultural expansion after the Civil War had built a strong revenue base, which was further strengthened by royalties from the lease of rich mineral lands. High school enrollments, a precondition for higher educational development, were significantly higher in California than elsewhere in the nation. These enrollments reflected the new demands of a booming economy, the influx of upwardly mobile migrants from other states who were eager to compete for the riches promised by vigorous growth, and the increasingly widespread popular belief in education as a vehicle of upward mobility (Eells 1931a, pp. 117–121; Starr 1986).

In addition, junior college development was favored by the unusual organizational ecology of higher education in California. Both the University of California and Stanford University had adopted restrictive admissions policies in the late nineteenth century, and compared with other large states California had relatively few small private colleges to absorb the increasing numbers of high school graduates not admitted to the state university system or to Stanford (Eells 1931a, pp. 117–121). Junior colleges developed rapidly to fill this gap, and by 1930, over one-third of all public junior college students nationwide were enrolled in a California institution.

As editor of the *Junior College Journal,* Eells printed several articles in which California educators announced the state's contributions to the movement, described some of the experimental forms developed in the state, and discussed some of the difficulties they had encountered in trying to combine transfer and terminal programs. In one of these articles, the director of Los Angeles Junior College argued that the junior college "should never allow itself to become an academic hospital where intellectual convalescents are encouraged to try for the university." This policy, he said, would undermine morale and "stultify the most essential mission of the junior college" (Snyder 1931, p. 78). In another, a University of Southern California professor urged junior college administrators to see their institutions as "a sort of university of the common people, serving the needs of all types of students—industrial, commercial, and semi-professional, as well as pre-collegiate and pre-professional" (Weersing 1931, p. 364).[14]

California's prominence in the movement was only partly due to the national leadership's ability to throw a spotlight on developments there. The success of the California colleges—their rapid growth and stable finances—naturally attracted the attention of junior college administrators in other states. In Texas, for example, the general law of 1929 setting requirements for the establishment of a junior college was modeled explicitly on the California district law of 1921 (Eells 1931a, p. 149). Both the ability of leaders to organize a vision of standard practice and the natural propensity of administrative elites to emulate stable, successful forms combined to place the California colleges in a widely recognized position at the forefront of the junior college movement.

The Carnegie Report on Public Higher Education in California

Junior college development was given added impetus in 1932 by a report on public higher education in California by the Carnegie Foundation for the Advancement of Teaching. The report had been commissioned by the governor after the state legislature had become stalled in a debate over the desirability of transforming two-year junior colleges and state teachers' colleges into four-year liberal arts colleges (Goodwin 1971, p. 147). In its inquiry, the Carnegie panel (called the Commission of Seven) touched on virtually every higher education controversy in the state, but its focus was on creating a formal division of labor among what was still a relatively fluid group of institutions with overlapping tasks and responsibilities. Its report, *State Higher Education in California,* published in June 1932, was a landmark in the rationalization of public higher education in the United States and had profound implications for junior colleges not only in California but across the nation.

The views of those who favored junior college vocationalization and retricted entry into university work were well represented on both the Commission of Seven itself and the various committees that advised it. Robert G. Sproul, president of the University of California, and Walter Eells were among those who participated in the commission's meetings. Three important advocates of vocationalization—William Snyder, the director of Los Angeles Junior College, Nicholas Ricciardi of the California State Department of Education, and F. W. Thomas of Fresno Junior College—were appointed to subcommittees concerned with junior college education (Carnegie Foundation, 1932, pp. 7–12). In addition, Leonard Koos was a friend and colleague of Henry Suzzallo, the president of the Carnegie Foundation, and was on friendly terms with at least two members of the Commission of Seven. Koos submitted considerable information to the commission, including a survey of California educational needs that the commission used in formulating its recommendations (Goodwin 1971, p. 147).

The Commission of Seven itself was selected by Suzzallo and included a number of prominent university administrators—among them, Lotus D. Coffman (president of the University of Minnesota), Charles H. Judd (dean of the School of Education at the University of Chicago), and James E. Russell (dean emeritus of Teachers College, Columbia University)—but no one directly connected to a junior college. The Commission did, however, have among its members one individual with long-standing and close ties to the junior college movement—George F. Zook (at that time president of the University of Akron), the co-organizer of the founding conference of the American Association of Junior Colleges and a strong advocate of vocationalization. The Commission's chairman was Samuel P. Capen, chancellor of the University of Buffalo.[15]

The Commission of Seven was not a completely disinterested group. It was dominated by university administrators, and its members were part of a loosely organized but relatively cohesive national and state educational policymaking elite.[16] Their views were far more homogeneous than those of educators at large and were organized around a vision of rationalization, institutionally based stratification, "scientific" educational selection, and "efficient" labor allocation, a vision that had been shaped by the characteristic Progressive impulses of the period.

The Commission's report vigorously endorsed the view that the primary function of the junior college was not the preparation of students for transfer to four-year institutions but, rather, the provision of terminal education for the vast majority of its students. Indeed, the junior college was, according to the Commission (Carnegie Foundation 1932, p. 34), not really part of the system of higher education but, instead, the "last stage of the upper or secondary period of common schooling." The very term *junior college*, the report suggested, is "unfortunate." For the two-year college is "not junior . . . to the university in its primary or main functions" but is in fact "senior to all common schooling below it—the capstone of socializing or civilizing education"[17] (Carnegie Foundation 1932, p. 43).

Detouring the junior college from its proper course, in the Commission's view, was "a false pride on the part of the town, the school authority, and the students which . . . has abetted the early tendency of junior college faculties to make junior colleges mere university preparatory schools." What the report was responding to here was the public's widespread support for the two-year college's role as a steppingstone to the university—a support that was based in part on the perception that policies that reduced opportunities for transfer would also reduce opportunities for upward mobility. As an alternative to the junior college's traditional emphasis on providing college-transfer courses, the Commission proposed a view of the junior college as "the highest part of community education for a general civilized life." In a statement foreshadowing the junior college's later linguistic transformation into the community college, the report suggested that the two-year institution "ought" to be looking outward upon the community and its life to discover how all its unselected and different kinds of students may be educated to intelligent cooperation and useful membership in society' (Carnegie Foundation 1932, p. 43).

The Commission of Seven was clear and forceful in its proposals to change the junior college's basic purpose. Advocating an "extensive reorganization" of the curriculum, the Commission suggested that the two-year colleges' "principal energies . . . be directed towards the large majority who (regardless of misleading statistics of intention) will not enter the university courses, rather than the small minority who will. This is the reverse of the present emphasis" (Carnegie Foundation 1932, pp. 39–40). Approximately 85 percent of all junior college students should, the report estimated, be enrolled in terminal education. Because 79 percent of junior college freshman in California reportedly intended to transfer to a four-year institution (Eells 1931a, p. 250), the Commission's plan obviously called for a vast lowering of student aspirations.

To accomplish this reorientation, the Commission argued, the junior colleges would have to reverse their emphasis on academic course work in two ways: by introducing a "new curriculum for social intelligence" that would attract a majority of junior college students and by improving the existing vocational offerings for most other students. The curriculum for social intelligence would "organize knowledge and intelligence for effective social behavior rather than for the intense and detailed mastery required for professional or avocational scholarship." [18] It would emphasize "literature" rather than "languages," "social values" rather than "scientific facts" (Carnegie Foundation 1932, p. 36). The report was thus proposing a diluted curriculum targeted at students who were destined to occupy not professional or upper-managerial positions but the growing ranks of semi-professional and other white-collar workers.

The Commission's advocacy of a curriculum for social intelligence was an apparently innovative solution to a thorny problem. Where both academic and vocational tracks were offered, the academic tracks were preferred by a vast majority. The Commission reasoned that most junior college students preferred liberal studies to vocational programs but suggested that many could be diverted into liberal studies of less than a collegiate grade. The proposed curriculum for "social intelligence" or "social citizenship" was based on the work of Progressive educators who had popularized "life adjustment" curricula in the high schools during the previous decade (see Cremin 1961, pp. 274–327; Ravitch 1983, pp. 43–80). It also responded to the Depression-era concern about strengthening shared values in face of widespread social unrest. [19]

In its quest to reduce the proportion of junior college students enrolled in college preparatory programs, the Commission of Seven also emphasized the importance of building enrollments in vocational programs. Aware of the pervasive student unwillingness to enroll in vocational programs, the Carnegie panel recommended three strategies for increasing enrollments: (1) careful study of the types of occupations that could appropriately fit under the rubric of semiprofessional training; (2) increased training and hiring of guidance counselors; and (3) improvement of student placement, particularly by making surveys of local employment needs and by creating college employment offices to enlist the cooperation of employers. Without these efforts, the Commission warned, junior colleges were "doomed to ineffectiveness in the vocational field" (Carnegie Foundation 1932, p. 38).

Yet the Carnegie panel also recognized the difficulty of attracting students to vocational programs, for only 17 percent of subject enrollment in California junior colleges in 1931–1932 was, by its own figures, in vocational or semiprofessional courses. While noting that "students can not be forced to elect this work when, and if, they do not wish it," the Commission elsewhere insisted that junior college students "ought" to take these courses but do not do so "because of their inferior status in a school community." Then in a rhetorical twist used time and again by advocates of vocationalization, the Commission thundered: "This undemocratic trend must be reversed" (Carnegie Foundation 1932, pp. 49, 43). From this perspective, it was the critics of vocational tracking rather than its advocates who were "undemocratic," for they failed to recognize that "social and educational justice is far more nearly realized by treating students differently than by treating them identically" (Carnegie Foundation 1932, p. 19). That the creation of formalized vocational tracks might restrict opportunities for immigrants and workers[20]— a charge made by several labor and independent radical organizations with respect to vocational education at the high school level (see Hogan 1985, Shapiro 1978)[21]— was a possibility that had no place in the Carnegie panel's orderly and meritocratic vision of a reformed and rationalized system of higher education.

The Commission of Seven's report sharpened the curricular differences between the University of California and the two-year colleges and made more pronounced the division within the junior colleges between terminal and transfer programs. In light of these recommendations arose the issue of which students would be eligible for which institutions and programs. The Commission's approach to this sensitive issue was straightforwardly technocratic: recent advances in psychological testing had revealed an "astounding range of individual differences," and so the educational system should be differentiated so as to reflect these differences (Carnegie Foundation 1932, p. 19). The "accumulation of psychological evidence of great importance" had made possible a new level of rationality in educational and occupational selection:

> In the past, educational careers have been too largely determined by personal whim. Now that experience and psychological investigation indicate that a specific educational or vocational interest is not a good index to the possession of ability in a specific field, we are compelled to take into account both ability and interest, the first for social efficiency, the second for personal happiness. (Carnegie Foundation 1932, p. 41)

If part of the Carnegie panel's justification for increased tracking in higher education derived from the growing conviction that scientific research had established the enormity of "individual differences," another, less visible component was rooted in a sober assessment of the realities of the division of labor. "Under our economic system of the subdivision of work or services," the Commission noted, "every person has . . . a particular obligation which he meets, usually by the services he renders through his special renumerative occupation" (Carnegie Foundation 1932, p. 17). A key function of the educational system is, therefore, to provide young people with appropriate occupational training. Problems arise, however, when the number of people who wish to perform a particular type of work exceeds the number of positions available.

Citing university admissions as an arena in which societal interests must be taken into account, the Carnegie panel stated that the right to refuse to admit students into particular professional courses "rests in some measure upon grounds other than that of personal fitness' (Carnegie Foundation 1932, p. 21). Policymakers must be mindful "of the necessity of giving some attention to the relation of supply to probable demand in the several professions . . . [as] overproduction in these particular fields might become a social and professional evil" (Carnegie Foundation 1932, p. 21). Phrased differently, the Commission was acknowledging that educational institutions might have to restrict certain curricular opportunities not because the aspiring individuals were intellectually "unfit" to handle them but because the number of qualified students surpassed the economy's capacity to absorb them.

The massive diversion of junior college students from college-transfer programs advocated by the members of the Commission of Seven—though justified by them primarily in terms of an ideology of "individual differences"—may thus also be viewed as an attempt to avoid the overproduction of professionals and managers. Writing in the midst of the Great Depression, the Carnegie panel could hardly have failed to notice the growing gap between individual aspirations for mobility and available job opportunities. Increasing the proportion of junior college students in terminal curricula—even if it relegated some unfortunate individuals into programs that did not tap their highest intellectual abilities—was central to their program for addressing this dilemma.

Sponsored by a powerful national foundation and written by a prestigious group of educators, *State Higher Education in California* had a profound effect on the way in which policymakers conceived of the role of the junior college. At a time of considerable flux and fluidity in American higher education, with state colleges becoming universities, normal schools becoming state colleges, and many junior colleges still aspiring to become four-year institutions, the Carnegie panel came down firmly on the side of those who emphasized the differences in the functions of different types of institutions. In what came to be known as the "California model," the state university had an effective monopoly on research and training for the higher professions; the state colleges concentrated on preparation for such middle-level professions as teaching and social work; and the junior colleges focused on training for the semiprofessions, general education for the masses, and vocational education. The Commission of Seven thus provided a philosophical rationale for the tracking structure that was then emerging in higher education and also a set of concrete proposals designed to sharpen the lines of demarcation between the tracks.[22]

Perhaps the greatest effect of the Commission of Seven's report was to legitimate the junior college's further growth in a time of fiscal crisis. Presenting the junior college as a relatively inexpensive way of increasing educational opportunities, the Carnegie panel's message reinforced the idea long held by leaders of the junior college movement that the two-year institution was the logical locus of the expansion of higher education. In California alone, the number of public junior colleges grew from thirty-five to forty-eight during the 1930s, with the number of students increasing from 13,392 to 82,666 (Eells 1931a, p. 24; 1941a, p. 3).

At the same time, however, the Commission of Seven (Carnegie Foundation 1932, p. 39) emphasized that the junior college was not to be primarily a college preparatory institution; indeed, the fact that the majority of students enrolled were taking "university preparatory courses of either academic or professional type" was described as "the largest single functional failure of the junior-college system in California." As proposed by the Carnegie panel, the California model did, to be sure, promise to make college more financially and geographically accessible than ever before. But its adoption in other states also meant that more and more students would be entering institutions that were designed to divert the vast majority of them from the bachelor's degree.

The Depression Boom

The Great Depression brought an unexpected boost to the junior college movement. Whereas the junior colleges, both public and private, enrolled under 56,000 students in 1929, by 1939 the figure had risen to almost 150,000 (see Table 2-4).

The largest increase came in the public sector between 1933 and 1939 after state legislatures had had time to respond to the twin pressures of increased demand and fiscal stress, by authorizing the establishment of new or expanded two-year colleges. In these six years, sixty-five public junior colleges were founded, and enrollments surged from 55,869 to well over 100,000. Whereas in 1930, barely 5 percent of all students in higher education attended a junior college, by 1940 one student in ten was enrolled in a two-year institution (calculated from U.S. Office of Education 1944, pp. 4, 6).

Much of the growth in the 1930s came in states that had already become established centers of junior college activity in the 1920s: Illinois, Minnesota, Iowa, Kansas, Oklahoma, Texas, and California all added five or more public colleges in the 1930s (Eells 1931a, p. 24; 1941a, p. 3). California, in particular, grew stronger still. Just three states, the three largest in the 1920s—Texas, Illinois, and California—enrolled almost two-thirds (66 percent) of all public junior college students by the end of the decade (calculated from Eells 1941a, p. 3). But several new public systems were also introduced, including relatively large ones in Wisconsin, Georgia, and Utah. Other new public systems opened in New Jer-

Table 2-4. Junior Colleges and Their Enrollments, 1929–1930 to 1939–1940

	All Junior Colleges		Publicly Controlled		Privately Controlled	
	Number	Enrollment	Number	Enrollment	Number	Enrollment
1929–1930	277	55,616	129	36,501	148	19,115
1931–1932	342	85,063	159	58,887	183	26,176
1933–1934	322	78,480	152	55,869	170	22,611
1935–1936	415	102,453	187	70,557	228	31,896
1937–1938	453	121,510	209	82,041	244	39,469
1939–1940	456	149,854	217	107,553	239	42,301

Source: U.S. Office of Education 1944, p. 6.

sey, Pennsylvania, Indiana, and Virginia (Eells 1931a, p. 24; 1941a, p. 3). The junior college movement continued, however, to be divided along regional lines in 1940, with public development strongest in California, the agricultural and industrial Midwest, and the South, and private development most pronounced in New England, the Middle Atlantic states, and the South. Public junior colleges, in particular, continued to be something of a regional phenomenon; under 2 percent of enrollments nationwide were in the eleven states of the Northeast, and not a single public institution had yet opened in New England or New York (Eells 1941a, pp. 3–7).

Pressures for Expansion

The junior colleges flourished, it seems, primarily because they were relatively inexpensive to attend and to operate at a time when demand pressures continued to encourage the expansion of higher education. High school enrollments had doubled every ten years since 1880, so that by 1930 some 4.7 million students were enrolled in secondary schools, nearly eight times as many as thirty years before (Eells 1941b, p. 44). This growth was due in part to compulsory schooling legislation and the passing of child labor laws, but it also reflected the increasing status and economic value of a high school degree. In addition, more students were graduating. Whereas only 40 percent graduated from high school in the early 1920s, by the 1930s over half were graduating. There were nearly 650,000 high school graduates in 1930, up from fewer than 100,000 in 1900 (Eells 1941b, p. 46).

If the desire of students to attend college had simply remained constant, the larger pool of college-eligible students would have led to much greater pressures on the colleges and universities. But other forces operating during the Depression actually increased students' interest in attending college. The most important factor was the difficulty that college-age students had in finding employment. With jobs scarce, employers preferred to hire older workers, and this preference was strongly encouraged by labor unions. Whereas only 5 percent of eighteen- and nineteen-year-olds had been unemployed in 1920, nearly 15 percent were unemployed in 1930 and nearly 25 percent in 1937 (Eells 1941b, p. 22).

If young people had fewer alternatives to pursuing higher education, they also had somewhat stronger inducements, as college education had already been firmly established in the 1920s as the principal avenue to social and economic mobility during an era of rapid corporate growth and declining opportunities for entrepreneurship. As David Levine observed: "The myth of 'the self-made man' was supplanted in the 1920s by the ideal of 'the man who worked his way through college' " a man who had all the "traditional virtues—determination, honesty, and the like—[and] was clothed in a football uniform rather than frontier garb" (D. Levine 1981, pp. 55–59, 72–73).

But the four-year colleges and universities would have had difficulty accommodating all of the new students even if they had wanted to—and by and large, they did not. Indeed, increasing doubts arose from the universities about the educability of the mass of high school graduates. Many states felt an obligation to respond to the new demand pressures, if only because high unemployment among young people increased the welfare rolls and raised concerns about the potential for crime and social disruption. The junior colleges thus emerged more or less naturally as a solution. They were less expensive to operate than four-year schools, and they served a useful custodial function in that they kept late adolescents off the unemployment rolls and police ledgers. As Eells (1941a, p. 33), in an argument common during the Depression, put the matter: "Certainly investment in junior college education even entirely at public expense is much more economical as well as socially far preferable than investment in care of young men in state and Federal penitentiaries."[23]

For many, junior colleges provided the only possible way to attend college. Tuition charges were low or nonexistent at a time when most families could not afford to send their children away, even to the relatively inexpensive public universities. In 1935–1936, when one-third of the families in the United States had an annual income of less than $750, total student costs at the more prestigious private colleges ran in excess of $1,000 per year (Eells 1941b, p. 37). As a result, the majority of students continued to attend junior colleges more in order to save money than for any other purpose (Eells 1941b, p. 36). By attending a local junior college, students could live at home and save room, board, and tuition costs.

Organizational Forms and the Debate over Function

During the 1930s, a consensus began to emerge in the AAJC on the proper functions of junior colleges. The idea of a curriculum with two tracks—one for students who would continue their education and another for those who would not—gradually gained general approval. By the late 1930s, at least one terminal program was offered at 70 percent of junior colleges. In some states, this was mandated by law. The laws establishing junior colleges in Colorado, Connecticut, Nebraska, and Pennsylvania all specified that both academic and vocational tracks should be provided, and similar provisions had been made earlier in California, Texas, and Mississippi (Eells 1941a, p. 32). But the consensus on basic functions seems to have been shaped more by other factors: the unwillingness of the universities to accept increasing numbers of junior college students, the promotional efforts of the vanguard leaders, the increasing integration of member colleges into the national association, and the shifting center of gravity within the movement toward state-supported junior colleges with less of a stake in traditional academic identities.

The national integration of junior colleges into the AAJC is of particular importance. Before national integration, junior college administrators necessarily concerned themselves with local matters as they worked to survive in an environment of limited resources and threatening competitors. Their activities followed the interests of their particular clientele; the peculiarities of their regional, state, and local cultures; and the expectations of local college and high school officials. Indeed, in the 1930s, national identification seems to have been a major source of the junior college administrators' optimism. Though often operating small, underfunded institutions with ambiguous identities and insecure status, they repeatedly expressed their sense of being involved in the most important educational innovation in American history (see Eells 1941b, pp. 88–115). As this integration grew, national objectives and standards began to exercise an influence in many ways more profound than that of strictly local factors. In this way the AAJC leadership, as a force of standardization and collective organization, overcame the heterogeneity inherent in local control.

Integration was encouraged by both expansion and the standardization of organizational forms and ambitions. During the 1930s, a declining number of two-year colleges aspired to "grow into" four-year institutions (Kelly 1940, p. 222). The four-year institutions, in turn, made it clear that they would keep their lower divisions, ending the hope of some administrators that two-year colleges would eventually absorb all undergraduate teaching for the first two years after high school.

Nor were other possible forms of organization successful. Several school systems in California and the Midwest experimented with four-year junior colleges that combined the last two years of high school with the first two years of college, but this form also gradually lost out to institutional rigidities. Most high schools were reluctant to give up half of their traditional responsibilities. As the report of the Carnegie panel, *State Higher Education in California,* observed, "only a few places" proved able to overcome "the existing inflexibilities of school support and school accounting and the traditional notion that the junior college is a two-year unit of the old college type" (see also Snyder 1941). Organizational interests also seem to have impeded the growth of branch junior colleges connected to four-year schools (Eells 1931a, pp. 13–15). Only a few institutions in the country were able to sustain a commitment to enrolling all graduates of their junior college branches. In addition, the tendency to starve these branch campuses proved difficult to overcome during periods of tight finances.

Clearly, many organizational forms were considered in the period before the independent two-year college emerged as a standard, and it may be illuminating to identify these historical roads not taken. All the discarded organizational forms— the "amputated" four-year college discussed above, the expanded high school, and the branch college for lower-division work—had some pedagogical or administrative merits. Indeed, the independent two-year college idea could be seen as comparatively illogical by contrast—an awkward insert into an existing organizational ecology. But it was that organizational ecology that proved most important: the process of selecting a standard form was based more on the interests of existing organizations than on the logic of purely educational considerations.

Throughout the 1930s, the junior college movement continued to be divided over the issue of proper program emphasis. Most presidents had come to believe that the colleges should be predominantly terminal, but there were pockets of dissent in both public and private colleges: indeed, almost 30 percent of junior college presidents continued to regard the transfer function as the most important (see Eells 1941b, p. 78). The dominant sensibility among junior college administrators who favored terminal programs combined meritocratic assumptions with social engineering goals. Most junior college students, these administrators argued, were not suitable candidates for professional training in the universities and should therefore be trained for the best jobs available to them. This required not only teaching occupational skills but also offering instruction in attitudes and values that encouraged "good citizenship," efficiency, and adjustment to industrial and commercial life. As a junior college administrator in Pennsylvania put it, because

> only a very low percentage of high school graduates go on with the traditional type of higher education, and since even this percentage is probably too high, the influence is clear that a great mass of needy and desirable students are being overlooked. This is the group of young people who in the best interests of the social structure, should be given the opportunity of adequate terminal training to provide them with the necessary equipment to earn a decent living and become intelligent [contributors to society]. (quoted in Eells 1941b, 112)

A few vocationally oriented administrators cited "increasing technological complexity" as a reason for the insufficiencies of high school vocational education, and others noted the increasing demand for persons to work in semiprofessional occupations. Some administrators endorsed terminal programs mainly because they would benefit youths who would otherwise remain unemployed in the Depression era. Finally, a handful of administrators saw no special virtue in the programs but regarded them as inevitable (see Eells 1941b, pp. 88–115).

Most of those who continued to favor the transfer programs argued along populist and democratic lines. The junior colleges brought opportunity to "underprivileged groups of young people," according to one Mississippi junior college president (quoted in Eells 1941b, p. 98). A few also considered a liberal arts education superior to vocational training as a preparation for democratic and independent living. As one college president in Kansas, emphasizing the role of higher education in training democratic citizens, contended: "Democracy needs liberal arts colleges to develop independent thinkers. Junior colleges with mere emphasis in vocational training may become tools of totalitarianism" (quoted in Eells 1941b, p. 127). But by the late 1930s, such notes were increasingly rare, for the growing dominance of the ideology of vocationalism emphasized the development of a skilled labor force far more than it did an enlightened citizenry.

Indeed, most junior college leaders were not interested in developing independent, much less critical, thinkers of the sort essential to the classical democratic ideal. Convinced that junior college students were destined for middle-level rather than professional or managerial positions in the occupational structure, they were concerned with developing an "educated followership." As Eells wrote:

> Increasingly is there need for young people to be prepared better for civic responsibility, social understanding, home duties and responsibilities, law observance, and devotion to democracy. At a time when the democratic way of life is on trial as never before, it is essential to have a well-educated and intelligent citizenry. Educated leadership is not sufficient. Educated followership is also essential. . . . On the whole the university tends to select and educate the young people of superior native ability and intelligence. In a democracy, however, the vote of the citizen of moderate or inferior ability counts quite as much in the ballot box as the vote of the genius. (Eells 1941b, 29)

Other association leaders stated such elitist views with equal bluntness. According to John Harbeson, the principal of Pasadena Junior College, "Independence consists in choosing when to follow rather than in following one's own devices." In the place of initiative, Harbeson advised junior college students to develop "a wholesome respect for authority" (Harbeson 1926, p. 260).

During the 1930s, the issue of whether junior colleges should be considered part of secondary or higher education was often debated in meetings of the AAJC (Brick 1964). At first, the lines of cleavage predictably divided the western from the eastern colleges and the public from the private schools, with sentiment for identification with secondary education strongest in the West and in public institutions. Over time, however, the advocates of an identification with higher education gradually won out.

The emergence of the junior college's identification with higher education did not come easily. Influential national policymakers (including the 1932 Carnegie panel and important university presidents) favored defining the junior college as a part of secondary, rather than higher, education. As late as the 1930s, well over three of four junior colleges were in fact still housed in high schools (Levine 1986, p. 175). Indeed, the junior college movement's most influential figure, Leonard V. Koos, was strongly committed to the so-called 6-4-4 plan of public education, with a redefined high school covering not only the traditional junior and senior years of secondary education but also the freshmen and sophomore (or lower-division) years of college.[24]

Almost alone among the major early leaders of the junior college movement, Walter Crosby Eells favored a 6-3-3-2 plan in which the junior college would be considered part of higher education. When Eells originally suggested this at the 1930 AAJC convention, it ignited the first of many heated debates. A year later, when he formally proposed it in his text on the two-year college movement, it provoked one of the few major disagreements among the junior college vanguard. Koos, who agreed on most issues with Eells, attacked the 6-3-3-2 proposal in a book review in *School Review,* suggesting that Eells was more attuned to higher than to secondary education (Goodwin 1971, pp. 175–176). Yet it was Eells's plan that ultimately triumphed despite its relative unpopularity inside the junior college movement, for it spoke to the desire of a population thirsty for upward mobility to attend a genuine "college."

Eells described the issue forcefully in *The Junior College* (1931a, pp. 726–727):

> Going to college has been the great American ambition, and it is rapidly becoming the Great American habit. America may not know exactly what the college stands for, . . . but it is very sure that college means something distinctive and worthwhile . . . In the popular mind college means an institution in advance of high school graduation, not merely a glorified and amplified high school. It is difficult enough to get the notion into the public consciousness that the two-year junior college is a real college; it will be far more difficult for it to feel that "college" is a centaur-like hybrid, half high school and half college.

As this quote makes clear, Eells' reasons for favoring the incorporation of the junior college into higher education were quintessentially practical: the American people wanted the opportunity to attend 'college' and, as he put it, this was "a powerful factor that must be considered" (1931a, p. 728).

Eells's program did, to be sure, offend those who saw the junior college as the capstone of secondary education. But it enjoyed broad popular support, especially in vote-conscious state legislatures. Unlike the 6-4-4 plan favored by Koos, Eells's proposal did not require the radical restructuring of the existing institutional realities of secondary and higher education. Its ultimate triumph was thus rooted in the sober recognition that if the junior college was to flourish in the American political and cultural context, it had no alternative but to be organizationally and symbolically linked to 'higher' education.

Like the ill-fated 6-4-4 plan, the popularity of the terminal "social intelligence" curriculum gradually faded in the face of powerful organizational, political, and cultural countertendencies. Critics argued that it risked throwing terminal students onto the labor market with no marketable skills, and this, they suggested, could eventually threaten the colleges' legitimacy. Another more diffuse factor also seems to have diminished popularity of the terminal "social intelligence" curriculum; as the immediate shock of the Depression faded, so too did the search for common values to sustain civic commitment in the face of extraordinary stress.[25]

Increasingly, the general cultural courses became less important as a distinctive curriculum than as one component of the program in the occupational curricula. In Eells's view, junior college vocational education could be promoted as superior to similar programs in trade schools because it combined cultural and technical training rather than focusing on narrowly occupational skills. "Each is important," he wrote, "and each is incomplete without the other" (Eells 1941b, p. 8). AAJC leaders argued that social attitudes, such as dependability, cooperativeness, thoroughness, and loyalty, were just as important to employers as were occupational skills, and indeed in many cases more important. In the mid-1930s these arguments were supported by a survey of California businessmen. The results, reported to members attending the AAJC's 1937 national convention, indicated that the businessmen recommended attitude training as the best way to ensure "good and efficient" employees (Goodwin 1971, p. 149). Junior college leaders contended that these "proper attitudes" could be instilled through courses aimed at developing "social intelligence."

The side of general education that aimed for responsiveness to authority was sometimes promoted with an ardor that is jarring to modern sensibilities. For example, Byron S. Hollinshead, an AAJC activist and president of a Pennsylvania junior college, wrote the following assessment of psychology and economics courses taught at Rochester Atheneum, a vocationally oriented two-year college in New York:

> The [student] leader gives examples, called "thought denominators" from the texts provided by [the instructor], and the group discusses the illustration. The effect is that of a controlled "bull session." There is much discussion of attitudes and work habits in these courses and the tabulated results achieved by the men in them would seem to indicate that the inculcation of proper attitudes has been quite effective. . . . Probably the best indication of the value of the courses is that employers frequently pay the cost of the course for employees who do creditable work. (Hollinshead 1941, p. 164)

For some, support for general education as a component of the vocational curricula sometimes had a more idealist cast. For example, Jesse P. Bogue, then president of Green Mountain Junior College in Vermont and later executive director of the AAJC, was asked: "Why should not a cabinet maker or a die cutter, or an expert draftsman, or a doctor's assistant, or a registered nurse, or a private secretary be entitled to those insights and social understandings which come from the study of sociology, economics, political science, and psychology?" (quoted in Eells 1941b, p. 303). But few administrators had such idealistic reasons for wanting to integrate general education requirements into vocational programs. For them, the fundamental feature of vocational education was that it was terminal. A smattering of general education would help legitimate such programs as not merely technical and would, it was hoped, elevate the students' general cultural level. Whether or not terminal vocational education succeeded in this task of cultural elevation, it would at least preserve the junior college's function as a vigilant gatekeeper, not only for the nation's universities, but also for its professional and managerial classes.

Administrative Pioneers in Vocational Education

Many of the techniques that helped transform the junior college into an institution oriented to vocational education—elaborate guidance procedures, surveys of employer demand, placement services, follow-up studies, citizen advisory boards, and the development of a "community service" identity—were developed and perfected during the 1930s by administrators in a handful of California and Chicago area junior colleges.

Pasadena Junior College, under its principal John W. Harbeson, was a pioneer in vocationalization and a leader in the guidance field. At a time when guidance counselors were weakly organized in most junior colleges and counseling was handled as an extra chore by overworked faculty members, Pasadena employed two deans of guidance, six full-time counselors, and eight part-time counselors (Eells 1941b, p. 67). The Pasadena policy emphasized the first interview with incoming freshman, which parents were also asked to attend.

According to Pasadena Junior College guidance counselor H. I. Weitzel, the guidance service made a point of granting no appointments for interviews unless it had received a transcript of the student's previous record.

> [With] a student, parent, counselor, and record sheet . . . assembled at a given place and ample time provided to discuss the student's vocational choice, . . . one merely has to point out the 'amounts' and 'kinds' of intelligence necessary for success in the semiprofessions as opposed to the strictly professional fields, the recommended high school patterns of subjects involved, the quality of high school work and later college work demanded . . . "opportunity to work one's way through school," etc. . . . and then leave the decision to the common sense of the student and parents.

Weitzel was "gratified . . . to observe that at least two times out of three the student and parent jointly will choose . . . a terminal curriculum as most nearly meeting the several needs of the case" (Weitzel, quoted in Eells 1941b, p. 67).

With such pressures on consumer choice a matter of institutional policy, vocational enrollments rose dramatically. Whereas in 1926 "semiprofessional" enrollments at Pasadena were a mere 4 percent, by 1938 they had risen to 67 percent. As Eells acknowledged in his 1941 volume on vocational education, "Results such as Dr. Weitzel describes do not just happen. *They are caused*" (quoted in Eells 1941b, pp. 64–67, emphasis ours).

Pasadena also pioneered techniques for building cooperation with local employers. Businessmen were invited to the campus to give talks on such subjects as "Opportunities in Department Stores," "What the Insurance Field Offers Youth," and "What May Young People Find in the Field of Accounting." Harbeson also set up advisory committees of local businessmen to provide feedback in the development of specific vocational courses. Members of the advisory councils and other local businessmen were also recruited to offer practical work experience to junior college vocational students (Eells 1941a, p. 153).

Los Angeles Junior College, under the leadership of William Snyder and later Roscoe Ingalls, ranked with Pasadena as the most highly vocationalized California college in the 1930s. Its contribution to the movement came in the area of employer surveys and in the creation of business advisory committees. From the beginning, Snyder insisted on offering vocational programs only in areas in which employment opportunities were considered good. Snyder described his first survey of employers as a "rapid but somewhat comprehensive" effort (Snyder 1941, p. 262). When a field looked promising, Snyder and his staff made a preliminary study of the technical requirements of jobs in the field and developed a tentative course of study. Employers were then invited to the campus to discuss the proposed curriculum with interested faculty. These discussions, according to Snyder, "were very enlightening and aided greatly in developing not only the technical courses but also the subject matter of the supplementary liberal arts courses" (Snyder 1941, pp. 262–263). Riverside Junior College, another California campus, initiated the first junior college cooperative work–study plan, a course option that allowed vocational students to gain study credit for supervised work experience. The program was soon adopted by numerous California junior colleges and by many two-year institutions in other parts of the country as well (Eells 1941a, pp. 141–142).

The Chicago area colleges, under the leadership of Leland Medsker, added innovations in the area of occupational placement and follow-up. Before graduation, students were asked to register with state and federal employment offices and to leave copies of their registration with the colleges' Bureau of Occupational Research. The Bureau then coordinated efforts by the Chicago area schools to place graduates in jobs (Hollinshead 1941, p. 170). Under Medsker, the Chicago junior colleges also conducted elaborate surveys on employer demand in a wide range of semiprofessional, technical, clerical, and craft fields, and these were used to organize the development of vocational curricula.

One of the most striking departures from traditional academic practices occurred at San Francisco Junior College under A. J. Cloud, who set about to serve the instructional interests of many community groups, not just college-age students. During most of the 1930s the college had no regular campus and instead offered an extraordinarily wide range of courses at over twenty centers scattered throughout the city. Cloud may have been the first to use the term *community college*. In response to a 1940 survey questionnaire, he wrote: "The junior college is properly a community college. It seeks to make a continuous study of community needs, and to respond in developing types of instruction or training that will meet such needs" (quoted in Eells 1941b, p. 92). Cloud's ideas had little immediate impact on the movement, but they were revived and became an important influence in the 1960s.

Within a year or two after the original innovation, many Texas and California colleges became active in the guidance field, and extensive testing programs for guidance purposes were set up at colleges in all parts of the country. Indeed, junior colleges in Colorado and Vermont were among the most avid users of the full range of tests for ability, vocational interest, and personality (Eells 1941a, pp. 129–130; Hollinshead 1941, pp. 166–167). At the Opportunity School in Denver, for example, counselors used forty separate tests to identify vocationally relevant aptitudes, interests, and personality attributes (Hollinshead 1941, pp. 166–167).

By the late 1930s most junior colleges used some test information in guidance (Eells 1941a, pp. 126). At least one-quarter of them offered occupational exploratory programs or courses; one-fifth or more collected at least some basic information on employment opportunities; and at least thirty colleges were conducting relatively comprehensive surveys of local employers (Eells 1941a, pp. 134–143). Thus although the various administrative techniques used in pursuit of vocationalization were still not fully developed in the 1930s, many of the most important were already being diffused throughout the country.

The Terminal Education Project

Despite the growing consensus among administrators on the importance of terminal vocational curricula, the forces favoring vocationalization faced a fundamental problem: their programs were unpopular with students. Junior college students "insist on preparing for the university," Eells (1941b, p. 65) noted, even though most of them "will never enter any higher educational institution."

Eells was correct about the low status of vocational programs. In 1938–1939, barely one-third of junior college students were enrolled in terminal programs (Eells 1914a, p. 24). Clearly this was a far cry from the 75 percent favored by most AAJC leaders.

Dismayed by the slow progress of vocational programs in 1937, the AAJC leadership established a policy committee to investigate terminal education. This committee, later renamed the Commission on Terminal Education, recommended studies of successful vocational education programs that might serve as models for member institutions. Following solicitation by commission chairman Doak Campbell, the Rockefeller-funded General Education Board (GEB) made a grant of over $100,000 to the AAJC to conduct these studies and pursue other activities designed to promote terminal education (Brick 1964). In announcing the grant, the GEB emphasized that semiprofessional courses would provide an "increasing number of young people" with "greater economic competence and civic responsibility" (quoted in Eells 1940b, p. 244). This grant, which ran from 1939 to 1943, was the first significant outside funding received by the AAJC. Such funding had been sought by the AAJC since at least 1926 (Goodwin 1971, p. 183).

All aspects of the terminal education project were designed to be both informational and "inspirational." According to Eells, the "most important contribution" of the study would be to stimulate "hundreds of junior college administrators and faculty members" to devise "terminal curricula suited to the needs of their own constituencies" (Eells 1941b, p. xi).

The 1939 grant money financed surveys of existing terminal programs, which were coordinated by the boundlessly energetic Eells and published as three monographs in 1941. The first monograph was an annotated bibliography of articles and books on terminal education in junior colleges. The second summarized data on enrollments and curricula, highlighting programs and techniques that Eells and Hollinshead considered exemplary. The third monograph presented Eells's own case for terminal education and the views of some 1,900 "leaders" (1,225 educators and 675 laypersons) on the value of junior colleges and their terminal programs.

Elite Opinions Regarding the Junior College

The third monograph, entitled *Why Junior College Terminal Education?* and based on a survey conducted by Eells, is a unique resource for understanding the position of the junior college movement in 1940. Eells sent questionnaires to over 3,700 people defined as leaders: presidents of public and private junior colleges, presidents of public and private universities, city superintendents of schools, editors of educational journals, and miscellaneous leaders in labor unions, the professions, and business. More than half of those contacted returned the questionnaires, and only labor leaders responded at a rate of less than 48 percent (Eells 1941b, pp. 70–72). The results indicated a broad acceptance of junior colleges and strong support for their further growth; indeed, almost two-thirds of the respondents favored the establishment of more junior colleges in their own state. The results also showed a very strong preference for "terminal education" as the "most important" junior college programs, though Eells lamented that only three out of four junior college presidents took this position (Eells 1941b, pp. 79–82).

The final question of the survey asked respondents for their "general judgment of the significance of the junior college movement, particularly with reference to its terminal aspects." The responses to this question indicate that institutional elites were nearly as supportive of the terminal programs as was Eells himself. Only a few, in unsolicited comments, argued that liberal arts constituted the core of any authentic higher education. "The junior college is fundamentally a college," said Robert S. Reed, president of St. Petersburg Junior College, and "if this means anything, it means that its primary emphasis must be intellectual, the training of the head, not of the hand" (quoted in Eells 1941b, p. 104). But the majority said they wanted students to get an "appropriate" education, with appropriateness apparently measured by the tightness of the fit between their schooling and their subsequent position in the hierarchical division of labor. Several were at pains to note that not everyone can be of the "white-collar" type. Some praised the terminal programs as "antidotes to idleness," but most emphasized the junior colleges' responsibility to meet industry's increasing needs for middle-level skills and to provide graduates with "marketable skills" that they could use in a "new scientific and cultural world." Judging from Eells's survey, the idea of tailoring education to the needs of industry was nearly as popular among community elites in 1940 as it is today (see Eells 1941b, pp. 190–244).

Educators were generally enthusiastic about the terminal programs. They applauded the junior colleges for their efforts to provide useful training, and relatively few of them expressed concern that opportunities for students might thereby be narrowed. Nor did many object to the junior colleges' de-emphasis of traditional liberal arts training. Instead, the statements stressed industrial training. For example, one educator approvingly called the junior college "an industrial finishing school" (Eells 1941b, p. 262). One Michigan junior college dean wrote: "The terminal curricula can provide a broader and more economical training than it is possible for business and industry to supply. . . . However, if the movement is to continue to grow, students must be kept intelligent enough to insure that graduates will be both competent and industrious" (quoted in Eells 1941b, p. 96). Another junior college dean observed: "As the rest of our democratic civilization continues to rise and our industrial life becomes more highly complicated and technological, high school graduation cannot give the great mass of young people, who do not go on to the university, adequate training for their proper place in society" (quoted in Eells 1941b, p. 94).[26]

Only among private college presidents was there any strong dissent. Part of this dissent represented a clash between upper-class and utilitarian-status cultures, but most of it reflected antagonism among organizational competitors. The private four-year college administrators, especially those located in weaker market positions, sometimes had harsh words for the junior college. The president of Baldwin Wallace College in Ohio wrote: "I do not think the junior college has arrived. It copies the liberal arts college in a cheap way and promises more than it delivers. The president of Jamestown College in North Dakota was even more negative in his assessment: "I think the so-called junior college is a misnomer. It ends nowhere and upsets the whole scheme and purpose of an adequately educated citizenship" (quoted in Eells 1941b, pp. 131–132).

Not all administrators at private four-year colleges were as hostile as those quoted, but among the groups that Eells polled, they were by far the most negative in their views of the junior college. Whereas 65 percent of all respondents favored an increase in the number of junior colleges, only 38 percent of the presidents of private colleges and universities supported their expansion. When asked whether the junior college was primarily an institution in competition or cooperation with other institutions of higher education," only 17 percent of all respondents saw the two-year college in competition, but almost half (48 percent) of the heads of private four-year institutions did so. Insofar as there was opposition to the further growth of the junior college, it came precisely from that sector of higher education—the private four-year colleges and universities—whose "market share" was most threatened by the rise of cheap and accessible two-year public institutions. In regions where such institutions were both numerous and politically powerful, as in the New England and Mid-Atlantic states, public junior college development lagged.

In Eells's own view, the "democratization" of higher education required the expansion not only of the two-year college, but of terminal programs within it. Terminal education was justified mainly because most junior college students were in fact terminal, regardless of whether they were enrolled in terminal programs; few actually went on to four-year colleges, and fewer still completed bachelor's degrees. This being the case, junior college students should receive a suitable education, one that fitted them for work at the level of the class structure to which they were destined. This was the only sensible thing to do and also the most beneficial policy for students who faced limited futures. "It should be axiomatic," Eells observed, "that these continuing thousands of young people should not be educated primarily for something they will not do if they can be educated better for the things they will do" (Eells 1941b, p. 65).

Subsequent General Education Board (GEB) grants through 1943 allowed the AAJC to conduct twenty-four regional conferences to explain the theory and practice of terminal education. The AAJC also used the GEB money for vocational development at eight junior colleges. These eight included virtually all of the pioneering vocational institutions of the 1930s, and they used the GEB money to perfect techniques that had already been substantially developed either on their own campuses or elsewhere. The AAJC hoped that their experiments could serve as models for vocational development throughout the country.

The Impact of the Terminal Education Project

By the end of the project, AAJC leaders certainly had a sharper sense of who supported and who opposed their policies. They had publicized the successes of certain model institutions and called attention to the techniques these schools had found useful in promoting vocationalization. The project also enabled them to disseminate a coherent justification for the further development of vocational programs. The centerpiece of their argument was Eells's conception of what later came to be called *latent terminal students:* students enrolled in the transfer curriculum who would nevertheless end their education in the junior colleges (see Eells 1941b, pp. 58–65). Other features of the AAJC's philosophy—its emphasis on semiprofessional labor markets, intelligence-based selection, guidance counselors, and cooperation with employers—reached a wider audience thanks to the GEB grants.

Perhaps the project's most important impact was on the organizational capacity of the AAJC itself. By 1943 the Association's income from dues and the sale of publications had risen to $21,000, which was almost ten times higher than its income in 1930 (Brick 1964, p. 55). Larger budgets in the late 1930s and early 1940s permitted the hiring of salaried staff for the first time and the extension of organizational influence. Successful completion of the project had required efficient planning and coordination, and the leadership had proved capable of supplying it. This fostered a new activist spirit in the Association. For the first time, in the late 1930s, the AAJC lobbied Congress for legislation that would allow federal vocational education funding for programs "of less than senior college level" (Brick 1964, Goodwin 1971). This effort failed, but it set a precedent for more successful efforts in later years.[27]

This period was also marked by a new interest in other external constituencies. Beginning in 1938, three association activists—Leland Medsker of Wright Junior College in Chicago, James Reynolds of Fort Smith Junior College in Arkansas, and James Harbeson of Pasadena Junior College—began systematically questioning employers about how best to design curricula for the maximum practical benefits to industry. This was the first organized campaign to interest business and industry in junior college semiprofessional programs, and it was among the earliest manifestations of the structural power of business—its capacity, derived from its control over jobs, to influence curricular and other policies at the junior college in the absence of direct intervention.

Nonetheless the project provided few concrete suggestions about how to surmount the obstacles to vocationalization that Eells's surveys had revealed.

Only in regard to the largest obstacle to vocationalization, the students' longstanding resistance, did it attempt to provide practical guidance. But even this amounted to little more than a restatement of the standard formula—testing, then the offer of guidance, placement, and linkage with employers—that the leadership had been promoting for years with only modest success. Indeed, few in the movement sufficiently appreciated the strength of the American dream of upward mobility and the depth of students' unwillingness to be diverted into terminal vocational programs that they viewed as a detour from the realization of their educational and occupational aspirations.

But despite lagging vocational enrollments, the leadership of the junior college movement was in a much stronger position by the early 1940s than it had been only a few years before. It was better organized, more confident, and it had strong support in elite opinion. Academic opposition among administrators and faculty, never that strong in the first place, had begun to melt away. Moreover, outside sponsors were beginning to take an interest in the junior colleges as potential developers of middle-level manpower. The coming of World War II interrupted this progress, as national attention turned to producing good soldiers and patriots.[28] But partisans of vocationalization were confident enough in the days immediately before the war to predict that henceforth the preparatory function would "apply only to the minority of students enrolled" in junior colleges (Eells 1941b, p. viii).

Toward Vocationalization: Sponsorship and Opposition

By the time that the United States entered World War II, the junior college had become established as the major organizational innovation in twentieth-century American higher education. Spurred on by both sponsorship from above and popular demand from below, the junior college grew at a truly extraordinary rate. Enrolling only 4,504 students in 46 institutions in 1918, by 1940 two-year colleges enrolled 149,854 students in 456 institutions (U.S. Office of Education 1944, p. 6). Between the end of World War I and the beginning of World War II, the proportion of American undergraduates enrolled in junior colleges grew from less than 1 student in 100 to about 1 in 10 (calculated from U.S. Bureau of the Census 1975, p. 383).

Yet despite the efforts of the junior college vanguard and its allies and the infusion from the outside of what were, for the time, large sums of money, student resistance to terminal programs remained strong, and vocational enrollments continued to lag. The main reason was that the vocationalization project favored by most junior college administrators was not rooted in student preferences; indeed, it had arisen in direct opposition to these preferences. For their part, the students—many of them of modest social origins—came to the junior college in search of upward mobility. The best route for this mobility seemed obvious to them: a college-parallel transfer program that would gain them access to a senior college and to the occupations for which such colleges had traditionally prepared their students. But their aspirations clashed directly with the preferences of both university and community college administrators, who wished to divert students away from four-year colleges and universities. How this conflict was played out in the decades after World War II will be the subject of the next two chapters.

3 The Takeoff Period: 1946–1970

At the end of World War II, a sense of expectancy pervaded America's colleges and universities. Enrollments had dropped during the war years, and many institutions looked forward to the return of millions of veterans. These veterans were themselves eager to get ahead in civilian life after the hardships of war, and the nation was eager to reward them for the sacrifices that they had made.

Already in 1944, as the war was coming to a close, the prestigious Education Policies Commission of the National Education Association and the American Association for School Administrators came out with a report entitled *Education for All American Youth*. Though focused more on secondary than higher education, the report sounded some themes that were to shape thinking about education for veterans as well. Perhaps the most powerful of these themes was the belief that the war had called on all of the American people to make sacrifices and that efforts must be made to see that no segment of the population would be excluded from the rewards of American society. For higher education, in particular, this meant that new measures would be required to realize the traditional American dream of equality of opportunity.

Alongside the idealistic impulse to extend to veterans unprecedented educational opportunities, there was also the fear that the nation's economy would be unable to provide work for the millions of returning soldiers. The massive unemployment of the Great Depression had, after all, been relieved only by the boost that war production had given the economy. The end of the war therefore threatened—or so it was widely believed at the time—to send the economy back into a terrible slump. With so many soldiers returning home, the possibility of such a downturn frightened policy elites and the public alike, for it was almost certain to revive the bitter social and political conflicts of the 1930s.

Together with more idealistic factors, this concern with the effects of the returning veterans on domestic stability led to one of the major higher education acts in American history: the G.I. Bill of 1944. Designed in part to thank American veterans for their service during the war, the bill also had the goal of using the nation's colleges and universities to keep masses of veterans out of a labor market that might not be able to absorb them. As Keith W. Olson wrote in *The G.I. Bill, the Veterans, and the Colleges:*

> The origins and motives for enactment of the G.I. Bill revealed a widespread awareness of the past and an attempt to ward off a recurrence of undesirable conditions and events. . . . Almost everyone realized that war spending had ended the depression that had lasted throughout the 1930s and that during the war the nation had enjoyed the rarity of full employment. Politicians and other leaders had little faith that the economy could sustain this full employment as it moved from war to peace, yet they were convinced that the United States could not safely allow veteran unemployment. If the man in uniform would go from the battle line to the breadline, the common theme ran, he probably would demand radical economic and political changes. The fear of unemployed veterans, not the fear of maladjusted veterans, motivated the persons who enacted the G.I. Bill. (Olson 1974, pp. 23–24)

The influx of huge numbers of new students, following the passage of the G.I. Bill, raised fundamental issues regarding the future organization of higher education. What policies would be most helpful to the expansion of educational opportunities? How could higher education best be organized so as to serve the interests of the returning veterans? And of particular interest to the junior college, what institutional forms would be most appropriate for handling the unprecedented numbers of students seeking higher education?

In July 1946, with these and other such questions in mind, Harry S Truman established the President's Commission on Higher Education. A year and a half later, in December 1947, the Commission released a landmark six-volume report, *Higher Education for American Democracy*.

The Truman Commission Report and the Junior College

Fortunately for the junior college movement, the chairman of the twenty-eight member President's Commission on Higher Education (commonly known as the Truman Commission) was an old friend of the two-year college and, indeed, the co-organizer of the founding conference of the AAJC: George F. Zook. Zook, born in Fort Scott, Kansas, in 1885, had come a long way since heading the Division of Higher Education at the U.S. Bureau of Education from 1920 to 1925. After a stint as president of the University of Akron (until 1933), Zook served as U.S. Commissioner of Education under Franklin Roosevelt and then as president of the most influential organization of institutions of higher education, the American Council on Education (ACE). It was from his position as head of the ACE that President Truman recruited him.

Zook had written widely on the junior college (see, for example, Zook 1932, 1940, 1946), and his views were well known. Consistently looking at the junior college from the perspective of four-year colleges and universities, Zook had in

1929, in an article entitled "Is the Junior College a Menace or a Boon?" insisted that the two-year institution, far from being "a fundamental attack on the liberal-arts college" was, rather, "a supplement, which by drawing off pre-professional and semi-professional students from the present colleges . . . will enable us to more nearly approach the standard of our ideals in college education" (Zook 1929, p. 425). Zook thus had a clear vision of the proper role of the junior college. It was to "draw off" substantial numbers of students who might be headed for existing colleges, to serve as a sieve for the minority that was capable of transferring to a four-year institution, and to provide terminal vocational training for the remainder. This vision bore a striking resemblance to that of the junior college vanguard, and it greatly influenced the work of the Truman Commission.

Despite Zook's rather restrictive views on the mission of the junior college, the final report of the Truman Commission, *Higher Education in American Democracy,* was in many ways a remarkably liberal document.[1] Taking a populist stance on the fundamental issue of who should go to college, the report declared:

> The Commission does not subscribe to the belief that higher education should be confined to an intellectual elite, much less a small elite drawn largely from families in the higher income brackets. Nor does it believe that a broadening of opportunity means a dilution of standards either of admission or scholarly attainment in college works. (U.S. President's Commission 1948, vol. 3, p. 6)

In addition, the Truman Commission called for full equality of educational opportunity:

> If the ladder of educational opportunity rises high at the doors of some youth and scarcely rises at all at the doors of others, while at the same time formal education is made a prerequisite to occupational and social advance, then education may become the means, not of eliminating race and class distinctions, but of deepening and solidifying them. *It is obvious, then, that free and universal access to education, in terms of the interest, ability, and need of the student, must be a major goal in American education.* (1948, vol. 1, p. 36, emphasis theirs)

The Commission's call for equality of opportunity was followed by a proposal for the massive expansion of higher education. Basing its recommendations on an analysis of the test scores of college freshmen in relation to the "mental ability" of the population, the Truman Commission concluded that at least 49 percent of the population had the capacity to complete fourteen years of schooling and that at least 32 percent were able to complete "an advanced liberal or professional education" (1948, vol. 1, p. 41). These figures represented a tripling of the college-attending population of 1940, when only 16 percent of American youth even entered the system of higher education (calculated from U.S. Bureau of the Census 1975, p. 379).[2]

The junior college was central to the Commission's plans for expanding educational opportunity. Recommending that the number of community colleges be increased, the report declared that the "time has come to make education through the fourteenth grade available in the same way high school education is now available. To achieve this, it will be necessary to develop much more extensively than at present such opportunities as are now provided in local communities by the 2-year junior college" (1948, vol. 1, p. 37).

The Truman Commission also recommended that the two-year institution emphasize programs of terminal education (1948, vol. 1, p. 68). Its rationale was virtually identical to that offered by Leonard Koos (1924, 1925) almost a quarter of a century before: the economy required an ever-increasing number of semi-professional workers for such jobs as medical secretary, electrical technician, and dental hygienist, and the junior college was the appropriate institution to provide training for such middle-level positions. For such "semiprofessional occupations," the Commission noted, "a full 4 years of college training is not necessary." Indeed, it "is estimated that in many fields of work there are *five* jobs requiring 2 years of college preparation for every *one* that requires 4 years" (1948, vol. 1, p. 69).

But even in its advocacy of expanded terminal vocational education in the junior college, the Commission's generally liberal and democratic orientation was apparent. In order for the "semiprofessional curriculum . . . to accomplish its purpose . . . it must not be crowded with vocational and technical courses to the exclusion of general education, but must instead aim at developing a combination of social understanding and technical competence" (1948, vol. 1, p. 69). Sounding a theme that placed them squarely with the democratic tradition of American educational thought, the Commission emphasized that the "vocational aspect of one's education must not . . . tend to segregate 'workers' from 'citizens' " (1948, vol. 3, p. 7). One of the most interesting aspects of the Truman Commission's report was its proposal to abandon the term *junior college* in favor of the term *community college*. The Commission's logic here was tied to its endorsement of the vocationalization project of the junior-college vanguard: because one of the principal tasks of the two-year institution was to provide "terminal curricula" to the majority of students who will never transfer to a four-year institution, "a change of name is suggested because 'junior' no longer covers one of the functions being performed" (1948, vol. 3, pp. 7–8). Since such an institution "must fit into the community life as the high school has done," the Commission suggested "the name 'community college' to be applied to the institution designed to serve chiefly local community education needs" (1948, vol. 3, p. 5). What the Commission had in mind here was a vision of the community college as a "people's college" (see Koos 1947): an institution designed, at least in principle, to serve the needs of the entire local population.

The Truman Commission's proposal to change the name of the two-year institution from the 'junior college' to the 'community college' did, to be sure, provoke some controversy in the movement (see for example, Unruh 1949), but most administrators seemed eager to abandon the old term, with its connotations of inferiority and subordination. According to Jesse Bogue, executive secretary of the AAJC from 1946 to 1958, both "practical experience and wide contacts with the movement" suggested that *"community college* more nearly approximates trends of thinking as well as observable usage of the name itself" (Bogue 1950, p. xviii). As a reflection of both the democratic aspirations of the two-year institution and its desire to declare itself independent of its higher-status partners in "senior" institutions, the new name of "community college" had wide appeal. Though the idea of renaming the junior college dated back at least to the 1930s, the Truman Commission's endorsement of the 'community college' label played a key role in setting in motion the process that led to its official adoption by the AAJC more than two decades later.

But the greatest impact of the Commission's report on the two-year college movement was not the symbolic one of changing a name, but the more substantive one of legitimating an enormous increase in the prominence of the community college within the larger system of higher education. Between 1947 and 1960, the Commission proposed, the number of young people in higher education should increase from fewer than 2,100,000 to a "minimum of 4,600,000," of whom "2,500,000 should be in the thirteenth and fourteenth grades" (1948, vol. 1, p. 39; vol. 3, p. 21). Although not all of these students were to be channeled into two-year institutions, the Commission repeatedly made clear that its central goal of extending educational opportunities could not be achieved without a drastic expansion of the community college.

The junior college leadership was understandably delighted by the attention showered on it by the President's Commission. Placing the community college at the center of future developments in higher education, the recommendations of the Truman Commission could hardly have been better had they been written by Leonard Koos himself. For a movement wracked by feelings of insecurity and marginality from its beginning, the public recognition that it had sought so long had finally arrived.

Junior College Growth in the Postwar Years

In the years immediately following the war, junior college enrollments passed the 200,000 mark, rising to about 10 percent of all higher education enrollments nationwide (U.S. Bureau of the Census 1975, p. 383), and they climbed much higher in the succeeding years. The growth included both a massive expansion of facilities—the average college campus more than quadrupled in size (Hillway 1958, p. 19)—and the opening of many new campuses. According to AAJC figures, between 1938 and 1953, the number of public junior and community colleges increased from 258 to 388 (Fields 1962, p. 42).[3]

The largest new building projects took place in Florida, North Carolina, Maryland, New York, Wisconsin, and Washington. With the creation of new public systems in the South and Middle Atlantic states, the development of state-supported two-year colleges became less and less a western phenomenon. In New York State, junior college expansion was particularly impressive. After a hiatus in the development of public higher education, owing to the strength of private colleges (Medsker 1960, p. 255), New York emerged as a leader in 1948 with its plan for the State University of New York, a decentralized set of campuses that included teachers' colleges, universities, and professional schools. The community colleges in the system began to open in 1950, and by the mid-fifties, new campuses had opened throughout the state (Medsker 1960, pp. 248–256). New York's master plan, drawn up by the university and approved by the governor in

1950, described the goals of the community colleges and presented a plan of development that identified special areas of the state that needed community colleges (State of New York 1950). The community colleges were divided into two types: technical institutes (some of which had already been founded before World War I) and comprehensive community colleges. The thirteen technical institutes were designed almost exclusively for vocational students. The four comprehensive community colleges mainly enrolled students in academic preparatory programs, though they were intended to offer a significant number of technical programs (Medsker 1960, p. 251). Including six small agricultural and technical institutes established before 1946, public two-year college enrollments in New York numbered over 24,000 by 1955, which placed the state system fourth behind California, Texas, and Illinois, the long-standing leaders in public junior-college enrollment (Hillway 1958, pp. 15–16). For the first time in the history of the two-year college movement, a northeastern state was at the forefront of junior college development.

The systems that became enrollment leaders in the early 1950s—New York, Washington, Pennsylvania, and Georgia—were developed more as a result of state planning than local initiative. These state plans were simultaneously efforts to respond to demand, to expand access, and to coordinate public higher education along the lines of a hierarchically segmented system, with the California system as a model. From the beginning, these state plans accepted the AAJC's definition of junior colleges as institutions that offered terminal vocational as well as college preparatory programs.

In several states, the junior colleges were designed as buffers between the high schools and the four-year colleges. Planners envisioned them as diverting students away from the university and directing them toward jobs in emerging nonprofessional occupations. Such a perspective informed the planning documents shaping the development of junior colleges in Georgia, Florida, and Washington. New legislation in Mississippi, Texas, and Minnesota also authorized a coordinated system for matching student demand to labor market openings (Medsker 1960, pp. 207–295.)

Of the new and expanded systems of the early postwar period, only those in Indiana, Wisconsin, and Pennsylvania, which were organized as extensions of the state universities, were relatively immune to the appeal of schemes based on the California model.[4] The case of Indiana, a relative laggard in public junior college development, is especially interesting, for there the major public four-year institutions—Indiana University and Purdue University—apparently blocked the growth of junior colleges. Instead, the only public two-year institutions that were allowed to develop were extension centers operated by Indiana and Purdue (Medsker 1960, pp. 227–231). The principal reason for this opposition was that the major state universities feared that the community colleges would become competitors for both students and resources (Dougherty 1988b).

Opposition by existing state colleges and universities to the development of junior colleges was perhaps even more intense in Ohio where, through the 1950s, there were no public junior colleges at all. In Ohio, five public universities maintained branches in twenty-two communities (Medsker 1960, pp. 259–264). Ohio

State University, the flagship institution, had long followed a policy of open admissions for all high school graduates from the state and maintained the position that no public junior colleges were needed. The case of Ohio, perhaps even more than those of Indiana, Pennsylvania, and Wisconsin, suggests that there was nothing inevitable about the channeling of much of the expansion of the postwar decades into two-year rather than four-year institutions. Yet by 1968, as we shall show later in this chapter, public junior colleges had opened in every state of the union except Nevada.

By 1958, junior colleges enrolled almost one out of four new freshmen, and in the fast-growing public sector, junior colleges enrolled nearly one out of three freshmen (Medsker 1960, p. 13). Low (or free) tuition and convenience to home continued to be the primary attractions of the community college; opportunities for career preparation were much less important (Hillway 1958, p. 19).

The Political and Economic Context of Expansion

Yet the attempts by community college leaders to expand the vocational track during the 1940s and 1950s were largely frustrated. Indeed, in the late 1940s and early 1950s, the proportion of junior college students transferring to four-year schools increased from about one-quarter to about one-third, and the proportion enrolling in transfer programs remained stable at about 75 percent (Medsker 1960, p. 24). Junior college expansion during this period was not, however, accompanied by increased differentiation—despite the tendency, observed by both classical and modern functionalists, for such differentiation to occur during periods of rapid growth (Clark 1962; Durkheim 1938, 1956; Trow, 1970). To understand why the vocational tracks remained relatively undeveloped, we shall next discuss the larger political and economic context in which the expansion occurred.

Curriculum and Market Conditions

Both market conditions and student performance shaped what might otherwise have been a fertile opportunity to develop the occupational tracks. The optimism and prosperity generated by a vastly expanded United States role in the postwar era seems to have favored a tolerance for the mobility aspirations of working-class students. After World War II, the economy's annual growth averaged 4 percent, and the gross national product doubled between 1946 and 1969 (Freeman 1976). The dream of upward mobility seemed within reach of everyone.

As the economy expanded, so did openings for people with college-level training. From 1950 to the mid-1960s, the expansion of opportunities outpaced the increase in college graduates (Carnegie Commission 1973; Freeman 1976, pp. 51–73). The economist Richard Freeman and others have called this period the "golden age" for college graduates, for their salaries rose more rapidly than did the salaries of any other group. Opportunities appeared to exist for everyone, and thus choosing a particular course of study was less consequential than it might otherwise have been. Many of the new students may have lacked some of the manners,

Table 3-1. Comparison of Four Colleges[a] by Occupation of Student's Father
(in percentages)

College	Upper White-Collar	Lower White-Collar	Upper Blue-Collar	Lower Blue-Collar	Total
Stanford University	87	7	6	0	100 (N = 55)[b]
University of California	69	14	11	6	100 (N = 52)
San Jose State College	38	17	29	16	100 (147)
San Jose Junior College	23	15	45	17	100 (N = 95)
City of San Jose[c]	26	17	38	19	100 (N = 23,699)

[a]Based on freshmen from the city of San Jose.

[b]N = number of cases.

[c]Employed males, fourteen years and over, occupation reported, San Jose as "urban place," 1950 census.

Source: Clark 1960, p. 54.

linguistic stye, and cultural interests—in short, the markers of "status-group" membership (Collins 1979)—of traditional college students, but they faced a labor market for professional and managerial work that was expanding rapidly. College students in general were in a enviable position; it was a seller's market and good jobs sought graduates.[5]

Moreover, student performance helped reinforce this laissez-faire attitude. Studies from the late 1940s and the 1950s repeatedly show that junior college transfers performed as well or better than "native" students in four-year college programs in a variety of disciplines (DeRidder 1951; Medsker 1960, pp. 119–140).[6]

These findings are particularly interesting in view of the marked change in the colleges' social composition before the war. The junior colleges then had been predominantly middle-class institutions, but after the war they became predominantly lower middle–class and working-class institutions. Though estimates vary, it appears that students from lower middle– and working-class backgrounds made up a majority, perhaps as much as two-thirds, of the new entrants to the public junior colleges in the first ten years after the war (Clark, 1960, Darley 1959, Havinghurst and Neugarten 1957). Data from the mid-1950s for the San Jose–San Francisco area, though not nationally representative, point up the increasingly working-class character of community colleges—and the social distance between their student bodies and those of four-year colleges and universities, especially the prestigious ones (see Table 3-1).

When a similar influx of working-class students had reached the high schools in the late nineteenth and early twentieth centuries, curricula were rapidly differentiated through the creation of vocational tracks for large numbers of working-class students (Nasaw 1979). None of the documentary evidence from the 1950s suggests, however, that the same kind of intense reaction to nontraditional populations occurred at this time in the case of the community colleges. Indeed, sentiment for vocational programs as the main curriculum seems to have been higher in the prewar years, when the colleges still enrolled mainly middle-class students.

Some junior college faculty wanted the colleges to put greater emphasis on vocational training, but even among teachers of vocational courses, fewer than 30 percent felt that the main aim should be vocational-technical training. Fewer than 10 percent of academic faculty members wanted to stress vocational education (Medsker 1960, p. 181). Administrators, too, were less likely than they had been in 1940 to endorse the vocational programs as the primary curriculum. Instead, they tended to consider preparatory and vocational curricula as equally important (Medsker 1960, p. 197).

In the new climate of opportunity, even some of the staunchest advocates of terminal programs softened their labeling of junior college students. Instead of being just "average" and "not suited for higher education," as they were in the 1930s, junior college students were reported to show some signs of "superior abilities," and indeed "a very large segment of students . . . are able to carry on college work as rigorous as that offered in other higher institutions[7] (Medsker 1960, p. 38).

Administrators who favored a vocational emphasis realized that they faced an uphill struggle. Medsker reported that "administrators, counselors and teachers in most of the two-year colleges visited [in 1957–1958] agreed that no matter how hard an institution endeavors to effect a terminal occupational program, it is difficult to interest students in the program" (Medsker 1960, p. 131). In Texas, administrators even went along with state aid programs that benefited transfer students because, they admitted, junior college students were "not as a group interested in terminal courses" (Medsker 1960, p. 283).

Indeed, the strong labor market for college graduates led to a decline in the proportion of vocational students, from about one-third in the immediate prewar years to less than one-fourth by the early 1960s (Venn 1964, p. 88). In California, about one-third of the students in two-year schools remained enrolled in occupational training programs, but community colleges in most of the other state systems experienced dropoffs in their vocational enrollments, sometimes to "token" levels (Medsker and Tillery 1971, p. 61).

Curriculum and the Cold War

The outbreak in the late 1940s of the Cold War between the United States and the Soviet Union also played a role in temporarily sidelining efforts to vocationalize the two-year college. Amid much talk of crisis and national defense, many junior college officials began to oppose narrow skills training as inimical to democratic principles. This reaction was part of a larger effort to protect American institutions from policies that might, it was thought, eventually lead to their collapse. In place of technical training, a liberal arts–general education curriculum was promoted as the best means of promoting national unity and thereby combating Soviet ambitions.

The Truman Commission endorsed the views of those who saw general education as a vehicle for combating social and political fragmentation.

> The failure to provide any core of unity in the essential diversity of higher education is a cause for grave concern. A society whose members lack a body of common experience and common language is a society without a fundamental culture; it tends to disintegrate into a mere aggregation of individuals since community of values, ideas, and attitudes is essential as a cohesive force in this age of minute division of labor and intense conflict of special interests. (U.S. President's Commission 1948, vol. 1, pp. 48–49)

Even so strong an advocate of vocational training as Leland Medsker, who had served as secretary of the AAJC's Commission on Terminal Education, was convinced for a time that general education had to be promoted in order to defend the country against external aggression (Medsker 1952). Those who favored academic education on other grounds could take advantage of this concern and align themselves with the general education movement. Sentiment for this trend reached a higher water mark at the AAJC's 1950 national convention when three different reports submitted definitions of "general education," each emphasizing the need to "minister to the common needs of human beings in contemporary democratic society" (Bigelow 1951).

But the proponents of vocationalization quelled this last major thrust of curricular dissent in relatively short order by absorbing it into the vocationalizing program. Jesse Bogue, a former Methodist minister and junior college president who succeeded Eells as executive secretary of the AAJC in 1946, took the lead in defending the principles of vocationalization. Bogue himself felt that general education should "be at the heart" of the junior college curriculum, but he favored integrating this education with practical training attuned to emerging industrial requirements for skilled personnel at the semiprofessional level. He insisted that there was no conflict between occupational training and general education. For the community college to do its job, both were necessary and neither alone would suffice (Bogue 1950). He also disputed contentions that terminal vocational programs were less "democratic" than other curricula:

> People are becoming increasingly convinced that the spirit and processes of democracy apply with equal force and value to business, industrial, and professional development as they do to any other aspect of life. . . . There was a time when an employee perhaps of less than professional standing was regarded as a hired hand. Today, however, in a democratic society this concept is giving way to that of the dignity and worth of *man* . . . [which] views him as a person endowed with all the rights, emotions, desires of all men, regardless of their so-called station in life. (Bogue 1950, p. 183, emphasis his)

Some sharper critiques were also advanced by those who equated the new proponents of general education with the older type of university emulators. One article in the *Junior College Journal,* for example, predicted that "[a] lot of hot air and hot ink will be shed before we hear the end of . . . the twin bogeymen, respectability and prestige" (Wood 1950, p. 519)).

With the decline of early Cold War anxieties, Jesse Bogue and the postwar leaders steered the AAJC closer to the ideals put forth by Koos, Eells, and Campbell. Some of the proponents of general education as the primary curriculum were converted (or reconverted) to the view that general education and semiprofessional training were complementary goals. Once the general education partisans were divided, their program quickly lost momentum. The more committed general education enthusiasts never gained a foothold in the national offices, and by the mid-1950s they had lost whatever footholds they had gained in the Association in the immediate postwar period (Brick 1964).

Bogue made particularly good use of the annual AAJC conventions to gain support for his concept of comprehensive community colleges. Like many of his predecessors in the junior college vanguard, Bogue was a man of strong religious convictions, and he stated his political understanding in the rhetoric of moral uplift: "The breath of life for educators is a better idea, an advancing ideal, inspiration and encouragement caught from contacts with like-minded associates who seem to be gifted with a little clearer thinking and ideals, more profitable experiences and practices" (Bogue 1953, p. 292). This clearer thinking and these more profitable practices meant the creation of programs that would give equal emphasis to preparatory and vocational training. By the mid-1950s the focus of the national meetings had shifted from advocating general education and "democratic ideals" to increasing the "diversity" of community and junior college programs.

The attitudes of campus officials soon reflected the renewed consensus on the importance of vocational programs as part of a comprehensive community college identity. In 1957–1958, a survey by Leland Medsker—a junior college administrator turned scholar, who by the late 1950s had replaced Koos as the movement's's leading researcher—showed that nearly three-fourths of the academic faculty in public junior colleges and four-fifths of the vocational faculty regarded vocational programs as "very important" parts of the two-year college curriculum. Administrators, too, showed very high levels of support for vocational programs. Moreover, some 86 percent of junior colleges offered at least one vocational program, up from 70 percent in 1940 (Medsker 1960, pp. 169–205).

New Techniques for Social Engineering

Although administrators had trouble convincing students of the desirability of the occupational offerings, many continued to experiment with the techniques of curricular tracking. In his classic study of guidance practices at San Jose Junior College in the late 1950s, Burton Clark (1961) described the postwar guidance system as a "cooling out process." According to Clark, this process consisted of several gently but cumulatively convincing steps designed to convince "marginal students" to substitute vocational for academic training. The first step was preenrollment testing, whose result led to the construction of "objective records of ability" and sometimes also the assignment of low-scoring students to remedial work. The second step consisted of holding counseling interviews before the beginning of each semester.

Clark found that the students' desires carried considerable weight in these counseling sessions: counselors "limited themselves to giving advice and stating the probability of success" in higher-status careers, and they began to suggest alternatives to the transfer program only when the accumulating record indicated that a student was having a difficult time. The idea, according to one counselor, was to "edge [students] toward a terminal program by gradually laying out the facts of life." A third step was a required freshman-level orientation course, which paralleled Pasadena's general orientation course of the 1920s and 1930s. Here students were given tests for vocational aptitude, and teacher-counselors helped students "in evaluating their abilities, interests, and aptitudes." In these presentations, counselors emphasized the opportunities offered by vocational training programs (Clark 1961, p. 517).

Through these and other methods, including required follow-up counseling for below-average performance, many students found their futures slowly being redefined. Only after a long process were they led to relinquish their original intentions and, in some cases, induced to accept a lower-status substitute. When most effective, Clark concluded, these procedures "let down hopes gently and unexplosively" and brought the student "to realize, finally, that it is best to ease himself out of the competition to transfer." At every step, counselors encouraged "latent transfer" students to give up their unrealistic goals and stood "ready to console [them] in accepting a terminal curriculum" (Clark 1961, p. 519). In fact, the process worked much better in sidetracking students from four-year colleges than in channeling them into semi-professional curricula. Many of those who were "cooled out" left school before receiving an associate of arts degree, and many others continued to pursue liberal studies while reassessing their desire for two more years of college.

There were also some important public image advances during this period that facilitated vocationalization. A new terminology, promoted by Jesse Bogue in particular, helped give a more attractive image to the vocational track in two-year colleges. Bogue rarely referred to vocational programs as *terminal*. Instead, he substituted the terms *technical* and *semiprofessional*. "Students rebel against the thought that they are entering blind alleys," he commented in rejecting the terminal label (Bogue 1950, p. 33).

Following the Truman Commission, Bogue also championed the new term *community college* as more descriptive of the type of two-year institutions that would dominate in the future. Such colleges did not simply lead into the senior colleges; they also provided two-year occupational programs that would lead directly into the labor market, and they offered community service and adult education activities as well. They were more comprehensive institutions, having the "total community" rather than the higher levels of academe as their points of reference. As Bogue put the matter in the preface to *The Community College:* "Semantically, *junior* connotes a restricted formation for these institutions that more aptly describes a role they were supposed to play in former days. Present trends and future needs that must be met at the community level cannot well admit that *junior* is an accurate and inclusive term for the institutions" (Bogue 1950, p. xvii).

Bogue's advocacy of the new term community college revealed some of the status anguish that had so long haunted the two-year college movement. Bogue used a developmental metaphor to ridicule the junior college label and to assert the status value of two-year college programs. One does not have to be a psychoanalyst to detect some anger in his apparently whimsical metaphor of "junior growing up:"

> There are signs on every hand that *junior* has cast off his swaddling clothes. He is certainly out of the cradle and stoutly refuses the confinement in which well-meaning but traditional-minded . . . persons would keep him. He is speaking for himself, writing his declaration of independence, constitution and bill of rights. He is ready, willing, and able to cooperate with others in the task of education on terms of equality. He is no longer junior to anything or anybody. His personality and worth entitle him to a seat at council tables rather than the little chair in the corner of the conference room. (Bogue 1950, p. xviii)

This "declaration of independence" reinforces our sense that old status injuries, the result of long subordination to four-year colleges and universities, contributed to the push of national junior college leaders for a predominantly nonacademic identity, even though most students continued to prefer college-transfer programs.

Meritocracy, the Cold War, and the Junior College

The tendency of junior college administrators to withdraw from the academic hierarchy of higher education institutions and to occupy the apex of an alternative nonacademic hierarchy was boosted by the emergence of powerful external allies and sponsors during the 1950s and early 1960s. This new sponsorship was associated with changes in Cold War thinking on higher education. Throughout the period, the most influential writers on educational policy, including James B. Conant (1948, 1953, 1956, 1959, 1961, 1964), Dael Wolfle (1954), and, somewhat later, Hyman Rickover (1959) and John Gardner (1961), linked the future prosperity of the United States and the security of the Western democracies to the widest possible search for academic talent. Echoing themes from the Truman Commission report, they exhorted policymakers to encourage equal educational opportunity so that America's "human resources" would not be wasted. They argued that the widest possible pool of educable youth should be assigned to appropriate levels of higher education on the basis of criteria designed to maximize the selection of those with the highest ability and motivation. These themes were substantially embraced by President Eisenhower's Committee on Education Beyond the High School (1957) and by the National Education Association's *Higher Education in a Decade of Decision* (1957), a report of its prestigious Education Policies Commission.

The new ideology represented a subtle but important shift from earlier Cold War preoccupations with national unity. The earlier concerns had encouraged efforts in the two-year colleges to develop a common curriculum. But the new ideology, with its emphasis on selection by ability, advocated differentiated curricula based on a link between occupations and "required" intelligence levels. Such efforts were, of course, consistent with traditions in community college administration dating back to the 1920s.

Conant's Blueprint

The key figure in developing a coherent vision of the role of the junior college in the nation's emerging postwar "meritocracy" (see Young 1958) was James Bryant Conant. Conant, the president of Harvard from 1933 to 1953 and the nation's leading spokesman on educational policy in the decade after his retirement from Harvard, was a self-conscious carrier of the Jeffersonian tradition of universal schooling and the paramount importance of equality of opportunity.

Conant's concern with the threat that inequalities of educational opportunity posed to the social order was already visible before World War II. In "Education for a Classless Society," written during the Great Depression and published in the *Atlantic Monthly* in May 1940, he lamented that the "ruthless and greedy exploitation of both natural and human resources" accompanying the arrival of modern industrialism and the passing of the frontier "has hardened the social strata and threatens to provide explosive material beneath" (p. 597). What must be avoided if America is to remain "classless" is not inequality among groups in the resources they possess, but the inheritance of these differences. For Conant, as for many American liberals and progressives, a classless society is, quite simply, a fluid one: "a high degree of social mobility is the essence of . . . a classless society" (1940, p. 598).

Higher education played a pivotal role in Conant's vision of a classless society. Quoting from Jefferson, Conant believed it a key task of the educational system "to call from every condition of our people the natural aristocracy of talent and virtue" (1938, p. 563). The creation of this natural aristocracy of talent would call for a major redistribution of educational opportunity. Conant suggested that "the country at large would benefit by an elimination of at least a quarter, or perhaps one-half of those now enrolled in advanced university work, and the substitution of others of more talent in their place." This "untapped reservoir" of "promising material" should, he believed, come from those of "high ability" among the 89 percent of the population between eighteen and twenty-one not attending college in the 1930s (1938, pp. 564–566).

Conant's vision of a reformed system of higher education was at once meritocratic and technocratic: the most academically talented students, regardless of social background, would be channeled into a hierarchically differentiated system of colleges and universities closely coordinated with the manpower needs of the economy. The existing system of higher education not only included many of the wrong students; it also simply enrolled too many. Like many policymakers both inside and outside higher education, Conant was worried that the nation's colleges and universities were producing more graduates than the economy could absorb: "I doubt if society can make a graver mistake than to provide *advanced* higher education of a specialized nature for men and women who are unable subsequently to use this training" (1938, pp. 565–566). His concern about overproduction was, Conant made clear, social and political as well as economic: "The existence of any large number of highly educated individuals whose ambitions have been frustrated is unhealthy for any nation" (1938, p. 566). Lest there be any confusion, he cited the case of Germany in the decade of the 1920s as a warning "against the perils lying in wait for a nation which trains a greater number of professional men than society can employ'' (1938, p. 565).

Conant's solution to the overproduction of the highly educated was the ''differentiation of higher education'' (1938, p. 564). For the academic elite (perhaps 10 percent of the population), attendance at a research university or a first-class liberal arts college was desirable—subsidized, if necessary, by large scholarships. For the large majority of high school graduates who ''do not contemplate entering a learned profession,'' however, a university education is ''not essential'' (1938, p. 569). Because some of these high school graduates wish to proceed to education beyond secondary school, Conant recommended that additional opportunities to attend college be created. His preference was that most of these opportunities be offered by the two-year junior college—an institution in which a ''general education can be given at greatly reduced cost locally, since students live at home.'' Then, in a suggestion that echoed the most expansionist voices in the junior college movement, Conant proposed that ''a two-year course in a junior college . . . might conceivably be desirable for every boy and girl'' (1938, pp. 569–570).

In the years after the Second World War, Conant was to develop these ideas on the role of the junior college in several influential books on educational policy (Conant 1948, 1953, 1956, 1961, 1964). First as president of Harvard University and then as a kind of elder statesman of educated policy, he hammered home the Cold War theme that the United States, if it was to be able to compete with the Soviet Union, could no longer afford to squander valuable ''human resources'' by failing to give students of ''high ability'' the most rigorous possible education. Junior colleges played a key role in Conant's ideal system of higher education; indeed, in his widely read 1948 work, *Education in a Divided World,* he looked to community colleges as offering the ''best hope of meeting the postwar surge for the vast expansion of education beyond the high school'' (Conant 1948, p. 200).

But like such founders of the junior college movement as William Rainey Harper of Chicago and David Starr Jordan of Stanford, Conant's main preoccupation was not with the junior college; it was with the type of institution over which he presided, the elite research university. Like the earliest advocates of the junior college, Conant wished to expand the two-year institution so that the university could concentrate on its principal tasks of research and graduate and professional training. ''No one can be more eloquent as to the necessity for providing advanced education locally (through community colleges),'' he shrewdly observed, ''than those who are responsible for the state universities'' (1948, p. 204). For many such administrators, as for Conant himself, the influx of new students threatened to undermine the university's true function of training the intellectual elite of the next generation. Far better, they reasoned, to divert such students into a rapidly expanding network of local two-year institutions.

Though Conant's discussion of junior colleges in *Education in a Divided World* was framed in the context of his very genuine desire to expand educational opportunities, his specific vision of the community colleges emphasized that they ''should be defined as *terminal* two-year colleges'' (1948, p. 200, emphasis ours). While subscribing to the official AAJC ideology that the junior college should be a "comprehensive" institution offering college preparatory, general, and vocational programs, his clear preference was for the terminal functions. "An occasional transfer of a student from a two-year college to a university should not be barred," Conant wrote (1948, p. 200). But such cases were, his writings made clear, to be very exceptional indeed.

Conant's master plan for American higher education was thus one in which a higher percentage of young people would attend college at the same time that a smaller proportion would be enrolled in four-year institutions. In *Education and Liberty,* his first major work on education published after his retirement from Harvard, he suggested a policy in which a rapid expansion of junior colleges, a tremendous increase in the number of young people, and a deliberate decision not to expand four-year institutions would combine to reduce the "percentage of the total number of 18 to 22 year olds enrolled in four-year liberal arts colleges and four-year university programs . . . by at least a half" (1956, p. 58). The underlying logic of his plan bore a striking resemblance to that of the vocationalization project of the junior college vanguard; in *The Citadel of Learning,* published in 1953, he declared that only 5 percent of young men and women were destined to be professionals (an estimate, it is worth noting, that is even lower than those offered by Koos and Eells). The junior college, Conant suggested, was ideally suited to handle the "flood of college students" that threatened to inundate the universities (1953, p. 71). And in protecting the university, Conant implied, the junior college would protect the larger society as well. For by reducing the likelihood that the system of higher education would produce more highly trained individuals than the economy could employ, the junior college would also, as he had argued in *Education in a Divided World,* reduce the number of "frustrated individuals with long education and considerable intelligence" who become "the leaders of anti-democratic movements whether they originate from the right or left" (Conant 1948, p. 199).

The increasing appreciation of junior colleges by educational opinion leaders such as Conant was complemented by the favorable treatment of the two-year colleges in the nation's business press and elsewhere. An article published in 1956 in *Nation's Business,* for example, predicted that community colleges would grow more and more important because they were "good institutions" for students "not qualified" for four-year institutions and also because they provided job-related training with "no stigma attached" (Lindsey 1956). In that same year the President's Committee on Education Beyond the High School (1956, p. 641) remarked that the "expansion of the two-year colleges has been one of the most notable developments in twentieth century America."

The Sputnik *Scare*

The successful Soviet launching of the satellite *Sputnik* in 1957 led to further aid for two-year colleges. Politicians, military men, journalists, and educators all were alarmed. So, too, was the public. Indeed, according to Michael Brick, author of a scholarly study of the first four decades of the AAJC, "Sputnik, not speeches, made the concept of [technical] training acceptable" (Brick 1964, p. 130).

Although Brick's assessment is perhaps exaggerated, *Sputnik* was undoubtedly important as a symbol, for it crystalized the growing concerns about U.S. strength in geopolitical competition with the Soviet Union, the perception of new technical needs in industry, and the increasing acceptance of Cold War meritocratic ideas (see, for example, Rickover 1959). All of these factors encouraged national elites to take a greater interest in community college vocational programs. *Sputnik* condensed all of these concerns into a single symbol and made action seem imperative.

In the middle and late 1950s the AAJC tried to take advantage of the new climate of opinion. In 1957, under the direction of former AAJC president Edmund J. Gleazer, Jr., it raised $20,000 from member institutions for a "public information campaign." In his prospectus, Gleazer noted that the environment was "decidedly getting warmer" for junior colleges, and he advocated taking advantage of this fact through persistent and determined selling efforts (Gleazer 1957, p. 515). "I am not advocating that we fight in an unpleasant way," he wrote, "but that we become more aggressive in a polite, persistent and competent way."

Potential sponsors, Executive Secretary Jesse Bogue wrote, must be convinced that junior college education "is interlocked with business and industrial progress, social advancement, [and] better citizenship" (Bogue 1957, p. 227). At least four other articles appeared in the *Junior College Journal* in 1956 and 1957 describing effective public relations techniques (Compton 1956, Priest 1956, Rowe 1957, Taylor 1957). They stressed the need for a businesslike approach and conveyed a simple message: community colleges should be sold as inexpensive, convenient, multifaceted institutions that are attractive to parents and good for local business.

In 1958, on the eve of a new era of respectability and growth, the AAJC's institutional membership numbered nearly five hundred, up from the thirty-four members originally enrolled in 1920 (Brick 1964). The AAJC leadership, under Bogue's guidance, had triumphed over the partisans of a more strictly academic definition of purpose. It had thereby gained a working internal consensus on the desirability of diversity in curricular offerings and had also refined various techniques for encouraging this diversity.

The junior college had gained an important degree of visibility from the Truman Commission report, and it had benefited enormously from the favorable publicity it had received in the writings of such educational leaders as James Bryant Conant. By 1958, the movement seemed better situated than ever before to realize the goals set by Koos, Eells, and Campbell more than three decades before. And to direct its efforts in this regard, the AAJC had an energetic new leader, Edmund J. Gleazer, Jr.,[8] who had risen, like Campbell and Bogue before him, from the presidency of a two-year religious college to become executive secretary of the Association.

The Great Enrollment Surge

With the arrival of the postwar baby-boom generation on the nation's campuses, higher education enrollments swelled, and the community colleges grew at an unprecedented rate. Indeed, during the 1960s, community colleges grew more

Table 3-2. Enrollment in Two-Year Institutions, 1950–1970

Year	Total Enrollment (in thousands)
1950	217
1952	238
1954	282
1956	347
1958	386
1960	451
1962	590
1964	711
1966	945
1968	1,289
1970	1,630

Source: U.S. Bureau of the Census 1975, p. 383.

rapidly than any other segment of American higher education had ever grown: during the last four years of the decade, new campuses opened at a rate of more than one a week (U.S. Bureau of the Census 1975, p. 382). By the late 1960s, the junior colleges' share of total higher education enrollments had risen to nearly three in ten, up from one in six in 1955 (Medsker and Tillery 1971, pp. 16, 27). According to government figures, degree-credit enrollments at the two-year colleges more than tripled between 1960 and 1970, from 451,000 to 1,630,000 (see Table 3-2).

This rapid growth took place almost entirely in the public sector, for by 1970, public institutions enrolled more than 95 percent of all junior college students (National Center for Education Statistics 1981, p. 105). By 1968, forty-nine of the fifty states had at least one public two-year college (Nevada was the lone exception). However, more than two-thirds of all community college students were still enrolled in only seven states—California, New York, Illinois, Michigan, Florida, Texas, and Washington (Medsker and Tillery 1971, p. 22). Two of these seven, Washington and Florida, were new among the leaders of the movement, and sizable systems were built virtually from scratch in various regions: Massachusetts, Delaware, Rhode Island, and New Jersey in the Northeast; South Carolina and Alabama in the South; and Idaho, Oregon, Arizona, and Wyoming in the West.

A useful indicator of the relative magnitude of state community college systems is the ratio of community college enrollments to total higher education enrollments (see Table 3-3). By this criterion, the states in the West and the South were clearly the leaders. In all of the states in the Deep South, with the exception of Louisiana, 20 percent or more of higher education enrollments were in community colleges. In the West, where the California model was especially influential, five states (California, Washington, Oregon, Arizona, and Wyoming) had enrolled 30 percent or more of their undergraduates in community colleges by 1968, and another two (Hawaii and Idaho) had enrolled 20 percent or more in them. Among the remaining populous and highly industrialized states outside the Sunbelt, only Illinois, Michigan, and New York had enrolled over 30 percent of their undergraduates in community colleges by 1968.

Table 3-3. Enrollment in Two-Year Institutions of Higher Education As a Percentage of Total Undergraduate Enrollment, by State, 1968

State	Percent
Very high (30 percent or more)	
California	61.2
Florida	52.0
Washington	48.6
Arizona	41.3
Wyoming	39.4
Illinois	35.0
Mississippi	34.7
Michigan	34.2
New York	30.5
Oregon	30.4
High (20 to 30 percent)	
Hawaii	29.2
Texas	28.7
North Carolina	28.1
Delaware	27.8
Maryland	25.5
Idaho	25.2
South Carolina	25.1
Connecticut	23.9
Alabama	22.8
Iowa	20.7
Georgia	20.6
Virginia	20.4
Missouri	20.2
Moderate (10 to 20 percent)	
North Dakota	19.9
Massachusetts	18.4
Pennsylvania	17.8
Wisconsin	17.7
New Jersey	17.2
Kansas	17.1
Rhode Island	17.7
Colorado	15.0
Ohio	14.6
Kentucky	14.3
Minnesota	12.2
Oklahoma	11.7
Vermont	11.2
Low (less than 10 percent)	
Alaska	9.7
District of Columbia	9.0
New Mexico	9.0
Tennessee	8.3
Arkansas	7.9
Utah	7.9
West Virginia	7.8
Nebraska	6.7
Louisiana	6.6
Indiana	5.1
Montana	5.0
New Hampshire	4.9
Maine	1.6
South Dakota	1.3
Nevada	0.0

Source: Medsker and Tillery 1971, pp. 24–25.

The 1960s were also years of rapid growth for the nation's four-year colleges and universities, whose enrollment doubled from 3,130,000 in 1960 to 6,290,000 in 1970 (U.S. Bureau of the Census 1975, p. 383). Yet the growth rate of community college enrollments during the same period far surpassed that of four-year institutions: 361 percent compared with 201 percent. During the 1970s the growth of four-year colleges slowed dramatically, whereas that of community colleges continued to burgeon.

The California Master Plan

The impending arrival on the nation's campuses of the postwar baby-boom generation put enormous pressure on state governments, and in response, many of them attempted to rationalize as well as to expand their system of public education. During the 1960s, almost all the states set up new coordinating or governing boards (Berdahl 1970), and nineteen of them adopted master plans for community colleges. Although none of these state plans required a particular level of vocational offerings, most called for "comprehensive community colleges," the AAJC term for multipurpose institutions with strong vocational curricula (Hurlburt 1969).

The model for many states was the California system and, in particular, the famous 1960 California Master Plan for Higher Education. As had been the case before World War II, California remained the national leader in junior college development; in 1958, well over 40 percent of all junior college students nationwide were enrolled in California institutions (Gleazer 1960, p. 30). Ever since the report of the Carnegie panel of 1932, *State Higher Education in California* had been published, California's system had been considered a model for other states. And with the rise to international prominence in the postwar years of its flagship institution—the University of California at Berkeley[9]—the California plan was widely viewed as a model in providing for both broad popular access and the maintenance of academic excellence.

Designed with the consultation of University of California President Clark Kerr, the California Master Plan of 1960 recommended a hierarchically segmented system based on the allocation of students by high school grade point averages.[10] It also proposed diverting large numbers of matriculating high school students away from the state colleges and universities. Kerr foresaw that the tremendous increase in the national birthrate after the war would soon result in vastly increased enrollments in California colleges. If the state colleges and universities were to maintain their current percentages of lower-division enrollments (approximately 51 percent in both cases), they would soon reach an "unmanageable size" (Liaison Committee 1960, p. 58). This, in turn, would weaken the capacity of these institutions to perform their proper "differentiated functions": lower-division and technical education for the junior colleges, and upper-division, graduate and professional education, and research for the state colleges and universities.

The master plan recommended reducing the number of lower-division students in the state colleges and universities to 41 percent by 1975 and proportionately increasing the numbers of students enrolled in the junior colleges. In order to reach this goal, the committee proposed the "diversion . . . of approximately 50,000 lower-division students from the State College system and the University of California to junior colleges." Recognizing that this task might prove difficult, the master plan suggested that "persuasive counseling might help 'sell' the merits of the junior colleges" (Liaison Committee 1960, p. 79).

The committee also recommended new admissions requirements. Instead of admitting any student with a B average over the last three years of high school, the University of California would restrict admission to the top 12.5 percent of high school graduates in the state. Similarly, the state colleges, which had also based admission on minimum grades achieved, would limit admission to the top one-third of high school graduates. The junior colleges, meanwhile, would remain open to all high school graduates. These more stringent admissions criteria, the master plan argued, would by 1975 substantially reduce the number of students admitted to lower-division work in the top two segments and ensure that "the best students get into the right institutions" (Liaison Committee 1960, p. 66).

By limiting access to the top tiers, the master plan strengthened the long-standing role of the junior college as a "shock absorber." It set a minimum requirement of a 2.4 grade point average for the admission of junior college transfers to the university and a 2.0 average for admission to the state colleges. These minimum requirements appear to be relatively generous, as a 2.0 grade point is equivalent to a C average. Nevertheless, the committee was well aware only a relatively small proportion of their community college students would ever transfer.

From the University of California's perspective, a principal function of the community college had always been, as Alexis Lange put it in 1920, "to prevent annual cloudbursts of freshmen and sophomores from drowning the university proper" (Lange 1920, p. 483). Clark Kerr, who succeeded Robert Sproul as president of the University of California in 1958 and remained in that position until 1967, stated the university's viewpoint:

> When I was guiding the development of the Master Plan for Higher Education in California in 1959 and 1960, *I considered the vast expansion of the community colleges to be the first line of defense for the University of California as an institution of international academic renown.* . . . Otherwise the University was either going to be overwhelmed by a large number of students with lower academic attainments or attacked as trying to hold on to a monopoly over entry into higher status. (Kerr 1978, p. 267, emphasis ours).

"Mass and universal access higher education," he noted, "can make it possible for the elite sector to become more elite" while at the same time helping to "identify new talent for the elite sector." An important consequence of "mass and universal access higher education" was its capacity to "help to soften class distinctions and antagonisms" (Kerr 1978, pp. 266–267).[11]

Yet despite the democratic rhetoric, the master plan in fact tightened and further institutionalized the three-tiered tracking structure already long in place in California's public higher education. Against those who wished to channel the masses of baby-boom students into four-year colleges and universities, it argued

Table 3-4. Distribution of High School Graduates by Eligibility for Public Higher Education in California, by Type of Education and Family Income, 1966

	Percentage Distribution of High School Graduates by Eligibility for	
	University of California	University of California and State Colleges[a]
Family Income		
$ 0–3,999	10.7	28.0
4,000–5,999	11.5	26.3
6,000–7,999	11.9	30.5
8,000–9,999	16.2	33.2
10,000–12,499	19.4	37.1
12,500–14,999	22.5	39.8
15,000–17,499	27.9	45.4
17,500–19,999	29.5	45.1
20,000–24,999	33.3	46.1
25,000 and over	40.1	54.3
Not Reported	13.3	28.0
All	19.6	36.3

[a]The figures in this column refer to students who are academically eligible to attend both the California state colleges and the University of California.

Source: Hansen and Weisbrod 1969, p. 72.

for diverting the majority of them into junior colleges. This was not a response to popular demand; on the contrary, the public remained eager to send its children to four-year institutions. The decision to expand the bottom track of the system far more rapidly than its upper two tiers was by no means inevitable. Instead, it was a policy choice based in part on a desire to insulate the University of California from those demanding access and in part on the substantially lower cost of educating freshman and sophomores in junior colleges.

The effect of the institutionalization of the three-tiered structure, though not its intent, was to create a system of tracking in public higher education closely linked to students' social origins. In California, in particular, black and Hispanic students were least likely to enroll in the University. Although comprising 7.0 and 11.6 percent, respectively, of California high school students, blacks and Hispanics made up only 0.8 and 0.7 percent, respectively, of the student body at the University of California (excluding the Berkeley campus) in 1967. Whites, in contrast, though comprising up to 78.6 percent of high school students, accounted for 93.7 percent of students at the University (Joint Committee on Higher Education 1969, p. 66).

Although all residents of the state over eighteen years of age were eligible to attend the community colleges, eligibility to attend the state colleges and the state universities was clearly related to family income (see Table 3-4). In regard to actual attendance, data from 1964 reveal that the social composition of the universities was more exclusive than that of the state colleges, with the state colleges,

Table 3-5. Percentage Distribution of Families by Income Level and Type of College or University, California, 1964

Income Class	All Families	Families with Children in California Public Higher Education		
		JC	SC	UC
$ 0–3,999	16.1	8.1	4.1	5.0
4,000–5,999	14.8	15.9	10.2	7.5
6,000–7,999	18.9	19.6	17.0	11.1
8,000–9,999	18.1	16.9	17.2	13.1
10,000–11,999	12.4	14.4	19.9	13.3
12,000–13,999	7.4	17.2	10.8	11.3
14,000–19,999	7.9	11.1	13.0	20.3
20,000–24,999	1.8	2.6	3.3	6.6
25,000 and over	2.6	4.2	4.5	11.8
Median Income	$8,000	$8,800	$10,000	$12,000

Source: Hansen and Weisbrod 1969, p. 69.

in turn, enrolling more affluent students than those in the junior colleges (see Table 3-5). The proportions of students from families with 1964 incomes of over $14,000 at the junior colleges, state colleges, and universities were, respectively, 17.9, 20.8, and 38.7 percent (calculated from Table 3-5).[12]

The Impact of the California Master Plan

Nationwide, state plans modeled on the California system were widely adopted during the 1950s and 1960s, and the results in terms of the emergence of a class-linked structure of tracking were similar.[13] A 1959 study of sixteen communities in the Midwest and Pennsylvania as well as California revealed that more than twice as many children of professionals and managers attended public universities than public junior colleges (Medsker and Trent 1965). Studies of the systems of higher education in Illinois, Massachusetts, and North Carolina in the mid-1960s revealed some state-by-state variations, but a remarkably similar overall pattern (Cross 1971, Medsker and Tillery 1971, Tillery 1973). And nationally representative data for 1966 gathered by the American Council on Education demonstrated that the student's track position in American higher education was closely associated with the father's education (see Table 3-6).

Perhaps the greatest impact of the California model nationwide was the subtle one that it had on the admissions policies of public colleges and universities in other states. T. R. McConnell, chief consultant to *A Restudy of the Needs of California in Higher Education* (1955) and chairman of the Center for the Study of Higher Education at Berkeley, described the impact of the creation of a large public junior college system on the University of California, but he could well have been speaking for a number of public institutions elsewhere when he wrote:

Table 3-6. Father's Education by Type of College Entered in 1966 (percentages)

Type of College	Grammar School or Less	Some High School	High School Graduate	Some College	College Graduate	Post-graduate Degree	Total
Public Two-Year	12.7	21.3	31.7	19.1	11.5	3.8	100
Public Four-Year	12.1	19.4	34.7	17.9	11.1	4.8	100
Public University	8.0	13.9	29.0	20.3	19.0	9.8	100
Private University	4.6	9.6	21.9	18.9	24.4	20.5	100
Elite[a]	1.2	3.5	10.6	13.1	31.3	40.5	100

[a]Elite colleges are defined as institutions with average freshman SAT scores of over 650. For more data on elite colleges, see Karabel and Astin (1975).

Source: American Council on Education 1967, p. 22.

> The University of California could not have become so selective without the system of state colleges, which admit students with a wider range of ability, and junior colleges, which are essentially unselective. . . . The existence of sixty-nine junior colleges makes it possible for the public four-year institutions to reject a student without denying him an opportunity for higher education. This is a cardinal factor in maintaining a selective state college and university system in the face of widespread public demand for access to higher education. (McConnell 1962, p. 11)

The expansion of the junior college in the 1950s and 1960s thus made it politically possible for state colleges and universities, many of which had traditionally been open-admission institutions, to become more exclusive. In many states, it became more difficult during these years for high school graduates to be admitted to a four-year institution. In the Midwest, for example, where two-thirds of public four-year institutions had been open to all high school graduates in 1958, only one-fourth were in 1968. For the nation as a whole, eighty-eight public institutions that had operated under open admissions in 1958 had by 1968 restricted their admissions procedures (Ferrin 1971, pp. 58–63). The irony in this tightening of admissions requirements was considerable, for its precondition had been the radical expansion of the very institution whose most compelling public mission had, from its earliest days, been the thoroughgoing democratization of American higher education.

Democratization or Diversion?

The state plans to expand community colleges in the 1960s were often undertaken in the belief that the junior college was, in fact, a powerful force for the democratization of higher education. This followed a long-standing tradition in the junior college movement and was consistent with the existing research literature. From Eells's 1931 volume to a study by Koos in 1944 to Medsker's Carnegie-funded 1960 monograph, *The Junior College: Progress and Prospects,* the empirical evidence confirmed what seemed intuitively obvious: the presence of a local two-year institution substantially increased the proportion of young people attending college (Eells 1931a, Koos 1944, Medsker 1960). Moreover, the most extensive study ever conducted on the effects of the availability of a junior college on patterns of college attendance—a longitudinal examination of almost ten thousand members of the high school class of 1959 in sixteen selected communities—not only corroborated the previous findings but also established that the junior college attracted some "high-ability" students, especially men, who would otherwise have forgone higher education altogether (Medsker and Trent 1965).

Yet these early findings tended to neglect an important dimension of the effect of the community college on patterns of college attendance: although the presence of a local junior college unquestionably brought some students into higher education who would otherwise never have attended (what might be called the *democratization effect*), it also drew some students away from four-year institutions who would have gone to college in any event (what might be called the *diversion effect*). This latter effect was, as our analysis of the junior college reveals, partly an intended one, for part of the junior college's *raison d'être* was to channel students away from more selective and expensive four-year colleges and universities (see also Dougherty 1983, 1988b). Yet studies of the community college largely ignored this diversion effect.

The first investigation to examine this issue of democratization versus diversion was a University of Chicago doctoral dissertation by Vincent Tinto (1971); additional results were reported in a volume sponsored by Carnegie and coauthored by Tinto (Anderson et al. 1972) and in a pair of journal articles (Tinto 1973, 1975). Through the use of longitudinal data on high school graduates in Wisconsin, which had relatively few junior colleges, and Illinois and North Carolina, which had many junior colleges, Tinto was able to establish that the independent effect of the junior college on rates of college attendance—after controlling for academic ability and socioeconomic status—was quite small. Yet if the widespread availability of junior colleges did not greatly affect the proportion of young people attending college, it did affect where they went. In communities where a public junior college was easily accessible, students tended to substitute attendance at a four-year state college or the state university for attendance at the junior college. Tinto referred to this tendency as the junior college's *substitution effect* (Tinto 1975).

A disproportionate number of students who attended a junior college instead of a four-year institution, Tinto's findings suggested, were of relatively low socioeconomic status (Tinto 1971, p. 309). Affluent students were apparently more likely to attend a four-year institution out of town even if there were a junior college in their home community (see also Tinto 1975). The enormous expansion of the junior college in the 1960s thus had a dual effect: it brought some students into the system of higher education who would not otherwise have attended col-

Table 3-7. Proportion of Students Receiving Bachelor's Degrees Among Senior and Junior College Entrants with Similar Academic Aptitudes, by Sex

Academic Aptitude and SES by Type of College	Percentage Graduating from College, Men	Percentage Graduating from College, Women
Academic Aptitude		
High		
Senior College	70	74
Junior College	31	40
High-Medium		
Senior College	55	60
Junior College	19	20
Socioeconomic Status		
High		
Senior College	67	70
Junior College	21	26
High-Medium		
Senior College	57	63
Junior College	23	21

Source: Folger et al. 1970, p. 176.

lege, but it also channeled other students, many of them of modest origins, away from four-year institutions that they would have attended in the absence of a local junior college.

In light of some findings appearing at that time that suggested that individuals who entered community colleges were considerably less likely to obtain a B.A. than were students of comparable academic ability and socioeconomic background who had attended a four-year institution, the documentation of a diversion effect was sobering indeed.[14] In a massive longitudinal study of 1960 high school seniors, the Commission on Human Resources and Advanced Education found sizable differences between two-year and four-year college students in the likelihood that they would obtain a bachelor's degree five years after entering college (see Table 3-7). Reviewing its findings, the commission concluded that although "the community colleges appear to have increased college opportunity for low-status youth," they also seem "to have increased socio-economic differentials in college completion" (Folger et al. 1970, p. 319). The more-than tripling of community college enrollments during the 1960s thus had expanded educational opportunities for some, but whether democratization had been its principal effect was now an open question.

External Support and the New Push for Vocationalization

The growing prominence of the community colleges helped the national leadership attract aid for its vocationalization project. In the almost four decades between

1920 and 1958, only two foundations (the Carnegie Foundation in the early 1930s and the General Education Board in the late 1930s and early 1940s) had financially supported the junior college movement. But between 1958 and 1962 eight foundations offered support to the Association or its member institutions.

AAJC leaders continued to play the role of entrepreneurs in selling the vocational project to potential sponsors. Edmund Gleazer's skillful promotional efforts as part of the AAJC's "public information" campaign were particularly important in encouraging initial foundation support for the Association.[15] The postwar growth of the community colleges gave Gleazer a strong arguing point. According to one historian of the movement, at least some of the foundations first supported community colleges because they believed that they were already a significant part of the system of higher education and "were destined to become more significant in the future" (Brick 1964, p. 59).

Early Foundation Support

The first foundation awards contributed both to building the organizational capacity of the AAJC and to communicating the perspective of its leaders to relevant publics. The U.S. Steel Foundation granted $10,000 annually for research and planning sessions organized by the Association's national office. Shortly thereafter, the Carnegie Corporation of New York provided funds to AAJC scholar Leland Medsker for research on the national movement. The Sears Roebuck Foundation sponsored the distribution of a brochure about junior colleges to the nation's secondary schools, and the Fund for the Advancement of Education sponsored a conference on the "central problems" facing junior colleges. The red, white, and blue Sears-funded brochure was especially important, for it presented a positive image of community college education for "middle-ability" students to every high school principal in the country.

Though important, these funds in no way compared with the contributions made by the W. K. Kellogg Foundation beginning in 1959, when Kellogg's education division announced a five-year, $240,000 grant to the AAJC for the purpose of "strengthening and expanding professional services to junior colleges, and to communities planning the establishment of [junior colleges]" (Gleazer 1959). Under the direction of Maurice Seay, who had once studied under Leonard Koos at the University of Chicago, Kellogg's education division had begun to study development in the community colleges as early as 1956. By the time the Association approached Seay and other Kellogg representatives with a development proposal in 1958, the Kellogg staff had already decided that the junior college movement merited broadly based institutional support (Brick 1964).

In 1961, Kellogg announced an additional six-year grant of $340,000. Combined with smaller grants from the Lilly Endowment, the U.S. Steel Foundation, and the General Electric Foundation, the Kellogg money allowed the AAJC to vastly increase its services to member institutions. Some of these funds were used to help colleges improve their administrative and financial organization and to educate staff in the philosophy and practices in guidance and curriculum development favored by the national leadership. In 1962, the Association inaugurated a program of "professional advisory services" which made advisors available to individual campuses in such areas as finance and development, student personnel and guidance counseling, curriculum construction, and community relations. Another program was designed to "upgrade" administrators through "leadership seminars" that would present, among other topics, the latest ideas on building comprehensive community colleges and techniques for promoting vocational curricula.

The funds also helped the AAJC expand its publishing activities on behalf of the vocationalization project. J. W. McDaniel's foundation-sponsored guide to administrators on "essential student personnel practices" communicated to a national audience the guidance techniques prescribed by the California junior colleges and other leaders in the field. Norman Harris's *Technical Education in the Junior College* (1964), sponsored by the Sloan Foundation, described methods of surveying local areas to determine emerging labor needs and also the most up-to-date techniques for "building status for middle-level occupations" (Harris 1964, p. 81). Harris also proposed a battery of status-conferring techniques: identifying vocational programs "with prestige companies and with new and popular industries such as space research, operations research, medical research, aviation, communications, electronics and pharmaceuticals"; making color slide presentations of vocational programs to community groups; building strong ties with high school counselors and teachers through campus symposia and workshops on vocational programs; offering "career days" on campus for high school seniors; and using bulk-rate mail to promote occupational programs. Harris predicted that vocational programs, when properly packaged and promoted, would attract half or more of all new students from the outset and that most "borderline" transfer students would "move willingly" into vocational programs after one or two semesters if they did not achieve immediate success in academic courses.

The Slow Emergence of Federal and Business Support

National commissions continued to look favorably on the community colleges during this period. In 1960, the Rockefeller-sponsored Commission on National Goals predicted that two-year colleges would soon enroll more than 50 percent of the students entering college for the first time. In 1964, the Education Policies Commission of the National Education Association called the community colleges the primary vehicle for achieving the national goal of equal educational opportunity. The federal government and private corporations, however, were slower than the foundations and the national commissions to acknowledge the unique capacity of community colleges to attract large numbers of students and provide training for middle-level occupations.

Congress remained tied to a traditional notion of educational organization, identifying vocational education with secondary education and specialized professional training with higher education. For example, in the 1958 National Defense Education Act, Congress judged that training for technicians and other "skilled workers in occupations requiring scientific or technical knowledge" could be provided more effectively by secondary schools than by junior community colleges.

And over the next four years Congress turned down three separate AAJC appeals for funds to build new facilities (Dougherty 1980).

The distance between the federal government and the community colleges began to close in 1963. The colleges were allowed to share up to 22 percent of the grant money from the Higher Education Facilities act with other postsecondary vocational training institutions. More important, the 1963 Vocational Education Act provided vocational education funds to postsecondary institutions. But in the end, these two bills brought very little material gain to the community colleges, as program administrators tended to direct the authorized funds to noncollegiate postsecondary institutions, such as technical institutions, rather than to the community colleges (Dougherty 1980). Apparently, state officials still felt more comfortable distributing vocational education money to institutions specifically designed for job training. Nevertheless, the 1963 bills signified the first departure from traditional thinking in Congress about the appropriate educational level for vocational training.

New Resources for Occupational Training Programs

In 1965 the Kellogg Foundation announced a new five-year grant of $750,000—later raised to $1.5 million—for projects to assist the AAJC in "the development of semiprofessional and technical programs." This grant was a crucial event in the AAJC's long-standing vocationalization campaign. It enabled the Association to hire four full-time specialists in occupational education to travel throughout the country offering advice on program development and implementation. It also enabled the Association to hold five regional conferences (attended by one thousand teachers and administrators) to "acquaint college personnel with new developments" in occupational education (AAJC 1969). The grant also helped finance new publications. A monthly newsletter, the *Occupational Education Bulletin,* was distributed to every junior and community college in the country, and other publications provided "guidelines and concepts for the establishment of new programs and expansion of existing training courses" (AAJC 1969). In 1965, the Sloan Foundation joined the project by providing a grant to help the AAJC identify "pockets of excellence" in the areas of medical engineering and business-related semiprofessional programs.

The mid-1960s also saw breakthroughs for the community colleges with respect to federal legislation. In the Higher Education Act of 1965, they became eligible to receive 22 percent of the authorized "developing institutions" funds, which they used to introduce new curricula, to train faculty, and to develop cooperative arrangements with business and public employers. The Adult Basic Education Program of 1966 and the Allied Health Professions Act of 1966 also directed federal funds specifically to the community colleges. Overall, between 1964 and 1966, federal funding increased from $7.4 million to $31.4 million, and the federal share of total community college budgets increased from under 2 percent to 4.5 percent (O'Neill 1973).

During the lobbying for these "Great Society" bills, community college officials were able for the first time to convey to Congress a persuasive view of their institutions' role in higher education and American society. In these presentations, the themes of manpower development, fiscal responsibility, and democratization all were used to good effect. Influenced by the arguments of AAJC officials, congressional supporters of the movement argued that community colleges were effective means of meeting the liberal goal of expanding access to higher education while at the same time satisfying both taxpayers' demands for fiscal responsibility and industrial needs for manpower development in technical and semi-professional fields (Dougherty 1980).

Emerging Organizational Interests Within the AAJC

Support from foundations and state and federal governments in the early and mid-1960s affected also the AAJC leadership's support for the policy of vocationalization. The national leaders had begun to push for vocationalization largely in response to the domination of the best training markets by the already-existing four-year colleges and universities and the junior colleges' corresponding need to establish their own stable market niche. This response had been reinforced by the leaders' concern with providing useful preparation for the majority of junior college students who would not finish four years of college. In the mid-1960s, when the Association gained its first significant outside sponsorship, its further growth and prominence became increasingly dependent on the success of the vocationalization project. As a consequence, we believe, the national leaders during this period developed an even stronger direct organizational interest in the project's success. The status consequences of the new rewards were also great. As funds grew to encourage AAJC efforts to link curricula to manpower projections, community college leaders began to shrug off the low status forced on them by those situated higher in the academic hierarchy, and they began to assume a rewarding new status atop the hierarchy of educational institutions that were guided by "practical concerns."

These emerging organizational and status interests can be seen in the changing tone of advocacy adopted by Association leaders. Although they had vigorously promoted the vocational programs in the past, their advocacy of them had always been encumbered by a sort of poor man's utilitarianism. The education and occupational worlds were depicted as grim and uninviting places for junior college students, and the junior colleges were urged to do the best they could for their students under these harsh conditions. Though seldom said, it was often implied that the junior colleges might not be able to do much for their students, most of whom were destined for very modest occupational attainments. In an unguarded moment, Walter Eells had used the phrase "eternal damnation" to describe students' perceptions of the occupational trajectory associated with vocational training (Eells, quoted in Goodwin 1971, p. 164).

By the mid-1960s this gloomy tone had entirely disappeared. In its place, Association leaders spoke of the great opportunities and grand national purposes represented by the further development of vocational tracks. For example, Harris's guide to technical education stated:

By 1970 one-fourth of the nation's labor force will be employed in semiprofessional and technical jobs which did not even exist in 1930. . . . Our society can no longer operate efficiently with the four-year education gap which exists between the high school graduate and the college graduate. The two-year college is the logical answer to the problem of closing this gap; and among the two-year colleges, it is the community junior college which can make the greatest contribution to the nation's . . . need. (Harris 1964, pp. 19, 28)

One year later, Executive Director Edmund Gleazer of the AAJC championed the vocational curricula in equally enthusiastic terms. They were, he wrote, "the right kind of education" to meet "the most critical problems in American society" (Gleazer 1965b, p. 4).

The Campaign for an Alliance with Business

Perhaps surprisingly, the AAJC's increasing visibility and effectiveness did not immediately lead to significant changes in business's long-standing lack of interest in the movement. Business took a far more active role in founding local community colleges than it did in supporting them at the national level or in their ongoing activities. Case studies in the 1960s suggest that local business and industry officials often played a crucial promotional role in building community support and that they sometimes also played an important financial role in capitalizing the institutions (see Fields 1962, Lustberg 1979, Singleton 1967, Thornton, 1972). According to one observer of these studies, businessmen, tended to support the founding of community colleges "in the hope of attracting other commerce to the area; or developing a trained manpower pool; or increasing the purchasing power of the whole community; or introducing concepts of industrial efficiency" (Lustberg 1979, p. 91).

At the national level, however, business support for the community colleges lagged well behind foundation and federal support. Private gifts and grants accounted for only 0.5 percent of total community college funds. In 1967, they rose to 0.7 percent, but by the end of the decade they were back down to 0.5 percent again (National Center for Educational Statistics, Financial Statistics of Higher Education 1969, O'Neill 1973). Foundations alone gave ten times as much money to the community colleges as the corporations provided (Bremer and Elkins 1965). This indifference of national business elites and their organizational representatives reflected two historical legacies: an ideology of anti–New Deal fiscal conservatism that sometimes led to reflex opposition to public spending, even when it was clearly meant to benefit business, and the long-standing relationship between corporate wealth and private colleges (Dougherty 1980, Jencks and Riesman 1968).[16]

Echoing the public relations efforts of the 1950s, community college writers in the early 1960s stressed the potential support of business and industry and the responsibility of junior colleges officials to seek it more actively. According to one of these writers, "In general, local business and industry may well be willing to lend financial support to the public community college. It is the task of the administration . . . to solicit this source of revenue more diligently than presently. The colleges must have the ability to 'sell' their program to business and industry'' (Thomas 1961, p. 368).

In subsequent presentations to business officials, community college spokespersons stressed the colleges' ability to socialize the costs of training for occupations that were increasingly critical to industry. Other benefits often mentioned were the provision of retraining facilities for older workers, the appeal of a nearby higher education facility to persons considering employment in local companies, and the likelihood that the college itself could become a large consumer of local goods and services (Blocker et al. 1965).

By the late 1960s, these arguments had been accepted by a growing list of business organizations that supported the movement. In 1967 *Nation's Business,* the magazine of the U.S. Chamber of Commerce, predicted the increasing vocationalization of community colleges and commended this as a trend that would be responsive to "the industrial or commercial needs of the locality" ("A Look Ahead in Education" 1967). But such support by business had been slow in coming and followed decades of general corporate indifference. Indeed, business, far from imposing its own vocationalization project on the junior college, was generally uninterested in its affairs. Only in the late 1950s and early 1960s—after the junior college had become simply too large to ignore—did business pay any attention to it. And even then, it would be far more accurate to see the community college as trying to court business than to see business, as one version of Marxist theory would have it, as trying to dominate the junior college and use it as its own instrument.

The Junior College Movement Looks to the 1970s

By the end of the decade, AAJC leaders enjoyed considerable support. Some eighteen different foundations had helped sponsor the Association during the decade, contributing millions of dollars directly to the vocationalization project and additional millions to general institutional support (AAJC 1967, 1968, 1969). In addition, the 1968 amendments to the Vocational Education Act substantially increased the federal contribution to community colleges. The leadership's efforts had also been enhanced by the trend toward state-level coordination and control of community colleges, which replaced some local idiosyncrasies with rationalized systems that were sympathetic to AAJC goals. Partly through sponsored research, the leadership had been able to use labor market surveys, sophisticated promotion efforts, pre-entrance testing, and firm but gentle guidance to raise curricular tracking to the level of a highly sophisticated technique.

In short, by the late 1960s Association leaders were better situated to realize their goals than ever before. The old problems of low institutional status and confused identity were nearing a definitive solution. More and more community colleges were assuming a new identity as low-cost institutions that emphasized occupational training. This new identity brought material rewards; by persuading outside elites that vocationalization could address critical national problems, the AAJC leaders had vastly increased the Association's budget. The new identity was also rewarding in status terms, for community colleges were now increasingly insulated from invidious comparisons with more strictly academic institutions. Their new positions as schools at the top of the occupational training hierarchy had its own status in the eyes of the outside world, if not within academe. In a 1969 editorial for the *Junior College Journal,* Edmund Gleazer well expressed this recently acquired self-confidence:

> Community and junior colleges, especially those which are willing to depart from tradition if necessary to carry out their mission, have their own kind of prestige. If we are honest about it, we would not trade that kind of status for the . . . repute and renown of the Harvards and Stanfords. (Gleazer 1969b, p. 5).

After the Kellogg grants and the dissemination of techniques to encourage vocational enrollments, there were some signs of slow change in the proportion of transfer and vocational students in community colleges. Between 1960 and 1968 the proportion of students enrolled in occupational programs increased nationally from less than one-quarter to nearly one-third (Medsker and Tillery 1971, p. 62; Venn 1964, p. 88).[17] Washington state, in particular, had shown that rapid growth and increased vocationalization were compatible; by 1968, nearly two out of five students in its community colleges were preparing for work rather than transfer to academic institutions (Medsker and Tillery 1971, p. 62).

Changes in the labor market do little to explain this trend, for between 1960 and 1968 the labor market for college graduates remained inviting (Freeman 1976, pp. 51–73). For full-time workers over the age of twenty-five who were surveyed by the U.S. Census Bureau in 1968, each additional year of college education was associated with a 12 percent increase in annual earnings (Jencks et al. 1972). Furthermore a college degree was more and more becoming a prerequisite for access to the better jobs; among young males with professional and managerial jobs in the late 1960s, more than four in five had graduated college (Jaffe and Adams 1972, p. 249).

To some degree, the arrival in the community college of new, lower-scoring students may have played a role in the gradual increase in vocational enrollments (Cross 1971, Medsker and Tillery 1971). But the policies of most junior college officials to channel enrollments away from the academic transfer track may have been equally important. Cross, for example, reported the results of a 1967 four-state survey (1971) which indicated that one-fifth of community college students felt that counseling had made them less certain of their career plans or encouraged them to change them. In 1966, nearly two-thirds of community college students said they hoped to enter managerial or professional occupations (Cross 1968), and throughout the 1960s, over 70 percent of entering two-year college students said they aspired to a baccalaureate or higher degree (American Council on Education 1966–1970, Medsker and Tillery 1971).

The desire for mobility continued to push junior college and community college students toward the higher levels of the educational system. Indeed, many AAJC leaders throughout the period attributed the slow growth of the vocational programs to their low status in the eyes of students. In the mid-1960s, for example, Norman Harris wrote: "Pressures from parents, fellow students and from high school teachers and counselors motivate thousands of high school youngsters to elect the academic program when their interests and abilities actually lie in more practical fields. . . . Nationwide, the average junior college student, *even after testing and counseling procedures,* shows a predilection [for the transfer programs] (Harris 1964, p. 81, emphasis in the original). And four years later Edmund Gleazer, still worrying about lagging vocational enrollments, wrote: [The] problem begins with an enthusiasm in our society for the 'upper' occupations, emphasizing the professional and managerial categories, and consequently, giving lower status to other occupational categories. . . . [This is] a notion which encourages aspiration and puts its faith in economic and social mobility'' (Gleazer 1968, p. 71).

The continued resistance of many community college students to explicit vocational training—a policy favored as the 1960s came to a close not only by higher-education administrators within and without the junior college movement, but also by foundation executives, federal officials, and a growing number of business leaders—was the last obstacle to its realization. For the most part, this resistance was individual and basically passive; indeed, even during the peak periods of activity during the student movement of the late 1960s and early 1970s, there was relatively little collective protest against the push from above for an expanded junior college vocational track. Instead, the majority of resisting students simply voted with their feet against efforts to "cool them out" of college-parallel transfer courses and into terminal vocational programs, with many of them dropping out of community colleges altogether.

Insofar as there was an exception to this pattern of disorganized and individualized resistance to vocationalization, it came from the black community which, unlike the white working and lower-middle classes, was extremely sensitive to the threat that an expanded vocational track in the community college might pose to equality of educational opportunity. Thus in May 1970, a group of seven prominent black junior college leaders from around the country issued a statement expressing concern about the higher education policy of the federal government, stating that its emphasis "on vocational training at the expense of greater Black participation in higher education strongly indicates that the [Nixon] administration views the community college as a ceiling for Black educational achievement" (AAJC 1970, p. 2). Black opposition to channeling minority students into terminal vocational programs—where they were in fact disproportionately concentrated (Cross 1970, p. 191)—was also visible at Seattle Community College in 1968–1969 (A. Cohen et al. 1971, p. 142). Moreover, the bitter struggle at the City College of New York over open admissions raised fundamental questions about the tracking of minority students, not only into community college vocational programs, but into the community college itself (Karabel 1983, Lavin et al. 1981). But such cases of organized resistance to vocationalization were relatively rare, even in institutions with large black populations.

The primary barrier in 1970 to the vocationalization project so long favored by junior college leaders remained the same one it had been immediately after World War II: the desire of students, many of them of working and lower middle–class origins, to use the community college as a steppingstone to four-year colleges and universities and to the professional and managerial jobs that graduates of such institutions had traditionally obtained. Yet if the quest of junior college students for upward mobility via higher education in 1970 remained remarkably similar to what it had been nearly twenty-five years before, the numbers involved had grown enormously. Whereas in 1946, just 17 percent of all students who entered higher education started in a junior college, by 1970 the proportion had grown to more than 40 percent (U.S. Department of Education, Center for Statistics 1986, p. 111).

One part of the original vision of the founders of the junior college movement had thus become a reality in the two and one-half decades after World War II: the two-year college had spread to virtually every state in the union and, in so doing, had become an integral part of the system of higher education. Proponents of vocationalization remained frustrated, however, at the failure of vocational enrollments to rise above one-third of all community college students. Yet that, too, was finally to change in the 1970s, as the strong postwar market for college graduates faltered seriously for the first time since the Great Depression.

4 The Great Transformation: 1970–1985

During the 1970s, the community colleges were finally able to realize the vocationalization project that visionaries in the junior college movement from Koos to Gleazer had favored for almost half a century. Since the 1920s, as we saw in Chapters 2 and 3, the advocates of junior college vocationalization pursued their project in the face of persistent student indifference and occasional overt opposition. But in the early 1970s, a complex concatenation of forces—among them, a changed economic context and an unprecedented degree of support for vocational education from key institutions—including private foundations, the federal government, and business—tilted the balance in favor of the vocationalizers.

A key factor behind the sharp increase in vocational enrollments at the community college, we shall argue, was the declining labor market for graduates of four-year institutions. But the objective change in the structure of economic opportunities for college graduates was not, as the consumer-choice model would have it, the sole factor responsible for the shift in junior college enrollments; indeed, the impact of such objective changes is, of necessity, mediated through subjective perceptions—perceptions that, we shall attempt to demonstrate below, tended to exaggerate the economic plight of college graduates. Moreover, the community college itself, driven by a powerful organizational interest in expanded enrollments and in carving out a secure niche for itself in the highly competitive higher education industry, actively shaped its economic environment by pursuing those segments of its potential market—in particular, adults and part-time students—most likely to enroll in occupational programs.

By almost any standard, the rise in vocational enrollments during the 1970s was remarkable. Between 1970–1971 and 1979–1980, for example, the proportion of A.A. degrees awarded in occupational fields rose from 42.6 percent to 62.5 percent (Cohen and Brawer 1982, p. 203). With respect to total enrollments (full-time and part-time) the picture was similar: between 1970 and 1977, the proportion of students enrolled in occupational programs rose from less than one-third to well over half (Blackstone 1978). In the midst of a long-term decline in the liberal arts, Cohen and Brawer (1982, p. 23) observed, "occupational education stands like a colossus on its own."

In just a decade, then, the community college was transformed from an institution primarily devoted to its traditional function of providing transfer programs to one whose identity and curricular offerings increasingly revolved around occupational training. As late as 1971, Medsker and Tillery had bemoaned the "academic syndrome" and "negative attitudes towards vocational education" that depressed occupational enrollments; by 1979, however, community college leaders were expressing alarm at the drastic decline of transfer education (Lombardi 1979, Medsker and Tillery 1971, p. 140). In this chapter, we will attempt not only to explain why this transformation occurred, but also to examine its implications for the life chances of community-college students.[1] By 1980, over 40 percent of all undergraduates were enrolled in a community college, and more than half of all students entering higher education for the first time did so in a two-year rather than a four-year institution (American Council on Education 1982, U.S. Bureau of the Census 1987). More than ever before, the American dream of upward mobility through education depended on the fate of the millions of students in the nation's community colleges.

External Support for Vocationalization

The Carnegie Commission on Higher Education

When the 1970s began, the debate in policymaking circles about the future of the nation's system of higher education was already being shaped by the Carnegie Commission on Higher Education. Founded in January 1967 under the auspices of the Carnegie Foundation for the Advancement of Teaching (CFAT), the Carnegie Commission had been created to provide a coherent plan for national higher education policy at a time of great social and political upheaval on the nation's campuses and in society at large. The original idea of creating a commission to review the structure and financing of higher education was that of Alan Pifer, a graduate of Groton, Harvard, and Emmanuel College, Cambridge, who in 1965 had succeeded John Gardner as president of the CFAT.[2] A firm believer that foundations should sponsor "objective appraisals in the best possible manner by the best possible people," Pifer was strongly committed to maintaining a strong "philanthropic presence" in higher education. When the time came to pick someone to direct the Carnegie Commission, the choice was obvious: University of California President Clark Kerr, who was not only one of "the best possible people," but also a key force behind California's three-tiered system of higher education which Pifer deeply admired (Lagemann 1983, pp. 129–132, Stuart 1980, pp. 274–276).[3]

The historic moment at which the Carnegie Commission came into being was, as the author of the major study of the CFAT has noted, one in which "established patterns of social deference and social authority were being seriously challenged" (Lagemann 1983, p. 128). Liberal elites, in particular, believed that threats to the stability of American education threatened the stability of American society, and the Carnegie Commission was formed to provide the kinds of rational and pragmatic proposals that would constitute an alternative to the escalating 1960s dynamic of politicization and turmoil.[4] By offering the kind of objective analysis and expertise that befitted a prestigious institution dedicated to its own powerful vision of the public interest, the Carnegie Commission would, like its CFAT-sponsored predecessor in California more than three decades before, prove to be a force for the legitimation and rationalization of a hierarchical system of American higher education.

As a body composed of prominent individuals, the Carnegie Commission was, like most foundation entities of the time, dominated by men who occupied positions of leadership in key corporate and educational institutions.[5] The sheer stature of the Commission's members gave it legitimacy and its recommendations special weight. Over the seven years of its existence (1967–1973), the Commission— aided by a highly able professional and technical staff—issued over twenty official reports. Spending roughly $6 million on its activities, the Commission also sponsored over sixty separate research reports, many of them of interest to policymakers and scholars alike (Carnegie Council 1980, Lagemann 1983, Stuart 1980). All in all, historians John S. Brubacher and Willis Rudy (1976, p. 216) were certainly not exaggerating when they described the work of the Carnegie Commission as "by far the most thorough and comprehensive study of higher education ever undertaken in this country."

The Commission's vision of higher education was of an orderly and rational hierarchical system dedicated to providing broad access to college at the same time that the highly selective character of the elite institutions was to be protected—a system, in short, much like the three-tiered California model over which Clark Kerr had himself presided. In a formulation strikingly similar to that expressed in former Carnegie President John Gardner's influential 1961 volume, *Excellence,* the Commission described itself as committed to the pursuit of both "quality" and "equality" in higher education. And when the Carnegie group issued its first report in December 1968, its chosen title was *Quality and Equality: New Levels of Federal Responsibility for Higher Education* (Lagemann 1983, p. 138).

What the Commission had in mind when it spoke of "quality" and "inequality" became more clear when its report, *The Open-Door Colleges: Policies for Community Colleges,* was published in June 1970. The report embodied the two-pronged strategy for community college development that had been popular in elite polcymaking circles for over four decades: to increase the proportion of college students in two-year, as opposed to four-year, institutions and to decrease the proportion of community college students enrolled in transfer programs. In this way, the community colleges would relieve growing popular pressures for expanded access to four-year colleges and universities at the same time that they would channel an increasing proportion of two-year college students into terminal occupational programs.

In a sense, the Carnegie Commission was calling for an acceleration of the already existing trend toward what might be termed the "Californiaization" of American higher education. The California Master Plan of 1960, the Commission noted, had been "a landmark in the evolution of the community colleges" which was "extensively studied throughout the country." During the 1960s, *The Open-Door Colleges* observed approvingly, "a number of states adopted plans with similar objectives" (Carnegie Commission 1970, pp. 10–11).

The influence of the California model was visible in the specific recommendations of the Carnegie Commission concerning community colleges. By 1980, the two-year colleges were to expand to the point that 95 percent of all Americans would be within commuting distance, and in order to accomplish this, 230 to 280 new two-year institutions would need to be built (Carnegie Commission 1970, pp. 33–39). As in California, the community college should be an "open-door" institution, charging no or low tuition and admitting "all applicants who are high school graduates or are persons over 18 years of age who are capable of benefiting from continuing education." At the same time, "access to four-year institutions should generally be more selective" (1970, p. 15). Over time, the proportion of all undergraduate students (including juniors and seniors) enrolled in community colleges should increase from an estimated 29 percent in 1968 to 40 to 45 percent by the year 2000 (1970, pp. 33–34, 52).

The Carnegie Commission favored the "comprehensive" model of the community college, long advocated by the AAJC, over more specialized versions (e.g., those exclusively devoted to liberal arts–transfer programs or vocational training), but its main thrust was clearly to expand the occupational programs and to solidify the community college's position at the bottom of higher education's tracking structure. To those two-year colleges that still aspired to become four-year institutions, *The Open-Door Colleges* therefore specifically stated that such conversions "should be actively discouraged by state planning and financing policies"; such upgraded institutions, the Commission worried, "might place less emphasis on occupational programs" (1970, p. 16). For those forces within the community college favoring vocationalization, however, the Commission proved a reliable ally: in particular, *The Open-Door Colleges* recommended "coordinated efforts at the federal, state, and local levels to stimulate the expansion of occupational education in community colleges" (1970, p. 21). The Commission also proposed strengthening occupational guidance in the community college, for a proper guidance program would lead students to recognize that "the ultimate objective" of all junior college programs is "preparation for an occupation." Such a realization would, the Commission hoped, overcome the unfortunate tendency of community college students to "regard occupational curricula as 'dead-end' or inferior" (1970, p. 21).

Underlying the Carnegie Commission's recommendations regarding the community college was a coherent vision of an orderly and integrated system of higher education flexibly feeding manpower into an advanced, technology-based economy. In a sense, this hierarchical and rationally structured system of higher education was but the mirror image of the orderly, stratified, and increasingly meritocratic occupational structure into which its "products" would be channeled.[6] From this technocratic perspective, any force that seriously interfered with a harmonious balance between the "supply" of education labor and the "demand" for it in the economy would threaten the stability of the system of higher education.

Such a force appeared in the form of the sudden downturn in demand for college graduates in 1970–1971, and the Carnegie Commission noted this new disequilibrium with alarm. In words reminiscent of the concerns expressed by Eells, Conant, and other educators during the Great Depression, the Commission, in its April 1973 report *College Graduates and Jobs,* worried that the declining market situation foreshadowed more social tension as "some college-educated persons fail to find jobs for which they are academically qualified" (Carnegie Commission 1973, p. 17). Without "adequate adjustments," the United States could end up with a chronic excess of college graduates. The Commission feared that such overproduction could lead to "a political crisis because of the substantial number of disenchanted and underemployed or even unemployed college graduates—as in Ceylon or in India or in Egypt." Were such a condition to materialize, "higher education will then have become counterproductive" (1973, pp. 4–5).

Although the Carnegie Commission rejected the kind of blunt-edged manpower planning characteristic of state socialist societies,[7] it favored a less visible but nonetheless far-ranging type of planning. Indeed, the Commission's basic program for higher education—the extension of universal access, but with an increasing proportion of students channeled into community colleges and the terminal occupational programs within them—constituted a long-term plan to create a flexible and hierarchical set of institutional structures that would avoid the type of disjuncture between the university and the economy that had frequently "plagued many societies not only in the Third World, but in Western Europe as well."[8] The Commission's detailed blueprint for American higher education was, in essence, one of diversion—from the nation's selective universities and from the professional and upper managerial occupations to which they gave entrée.

The expansion of community colleges—and of their terminal occupational programs—was central to its plan of diversion, and the Commission vigorously promulgated it. Each of its reports was sent "as promptly and directly as possible" to "officials in the national and state governments, to presidents of all colleges and universities in the United States, to the principal officers of certain educational and civic organizations, to executives of major foundations, and to certain other individuals designated by the Chairman or the Commission" (Carnegie Council 1980, p. 472). Although it is impossible to quantify the precise influence of a group such as the Carnegie Commission, it seems likely that at the very least, it strengthened those forces wishing to diffuse further the California model of higher education at a particularly crucial moment in its history. Moreover, for those who wished to vocationalize the community college, these lucid and widely read reports provided a valuable resource. The community vocationalizers now had the support of an enormously respected, independent body of educational policymakers, and the legitimacy that this brought to their long-standing cause would be put to good use in the years ahead.

Additional Sources of Foundation and Corporate Support

Although the Carnegie Commission provided moral and political support to the community colleges, other groups continued to contribute in more material ways. Between 1970 and 1975 for example, sixteen foundations provided a total of $1 million annually to the AAJC, roughly twice the average annual amount of the previous five years. Approximately half of these funds went directly or indirectly to projects that promoted occupational training.

The Kellogg Foundation continued as the leading foundation sponsor, helping strengthen the AAJC's organizational capacity. In 1970, Kellogg provided $250,000 for an institutional self-study entitled "Project Focus." Two years later, it granted over $100,000 for strengthening the council system organized by the Association. In another growth-oriented project, Kellogg contributed several hundred thousand dollars to a "community-service program" designed to link the colleges in regular exchanges with the local community institutions. Overall, during the period between 1958 and 1978, the Kellogg Foundation contributed over $29 million to the two-year college movement. More than $3.8 million of this sum went directly to the AAJC (Gleazer 1978, p. 2).

Whereas Kellogg concentrated on organization building, other foundation sponsors took the lead in funding curricular development projects. In the early 1970s major grants for vocational projects were provided by the Commonwealth Fund ($63,000 for developing allied health curricula), the Robert Wood Johnson Foundation ($183,000 also for studies of allied health education), the Alfred Sloan Foundation ($20,000 for a study of technical education in the community colleges), and the Aerospace Foundation ($18,000 for developing aerospace technology curricula). The National Science Foundation also contributed $20,000 for developing marine technology curricula.[9]

After decades of unsuccessful attempts to court business, the Association also finally began in the early 1970s to win the support it had so long desired from corporate leaders. Between 1969 and 1973, some thirty-seven major corporations joined an advertising campaign to "upgrade the image" of the community colleges' technical programs. Sponsored by the Conference Board and the Manpower Institute, two consortia of major corporate executives, the campaign's aims were "to urge increasing numbers of people to pursue a postsecondary technical education" and "to promote the attitude that a baccalaureate is not the only passport to an attractive and satisfying vocation" (Rhine 1972, p. 5). As part of the campaign, a free booklet entitled "25 Technical Careers You Can Learn in 2 Years or Less" was offered via television and in magazines and newspapers.

During the same period, another important corporate group, the Council for Financial Aid to Education (CFAE), hailed the community colleges as "the most important innovation in American education during the twentieth century" and called their vocationalization project one of "the strongest movements in higher education today" (CFAE 1973, p. 1). "There is a direct relation between business and industry and the two-year colleges," the CFAE noted, "which provide a trained workforce in literally hundreds of fields" (CFAE 1973, p. 7).

During the early 1970s, perhaps in response to the writings of such groups as the Carnegie Commission and the Conference Board, individual corporations began to give donations to the community college movement. Between 1970 and 1973, seven corporations contributed nearly $100,000 to the AAJC for general institutional support. Although the sum was not large, especially in comparison with the much bigger sums given to prestigious private universities, the list of donors—Ford, General Motors, IBM, AT&T, Gulf Oil, City Services, and Olin-Mathiesen—clearly indicated that the community colleges had finally gained the attention of some of the most powerful segments of the American business community.

Federal Higher Education Policy

Despite increasing foundation and business support, the most important source of outside material support for the community colleges in the early 1970s came from a newly responsive federal government. Between 1969 and 1973, the federal government under the Nixon administration moved from providing just over 6 percent of the community colleges' revenues to 8.4 percent—in dollar terms, from $91 million to $256 million (Mertins and Brandt 1979).

Like members of the Carnegie Commission, Nixon administration officials were clearly impressed by the growing popularity of the two-year institutions. Some, like Chester Finn, a participant in the administration's education policy group, explicitly noted the administration's desire to channel this popularity into pathways consistent with an expansion of vocational programs. According to Finn:

> The community colleges constituted much the fastest growing sector within the world of nonprofit post-secondary education and already enrolled nearly one out of every five students. An obvious role for the federal government was to provide financial incentives to channel this growth in the direction of 'career education' rather than liberal arts. (Finn 1976, p. 64)

Finn's remarks support our sense that the relationship between the community colleges and powerful outside sponsors was one that might be described as a process of "contingent adoption." For several decades, the community colleges made their way more or less on their own, and only when they had proved that they were a popular and successful organizational form did outside sponsors respond to their persistent courting. Far from being vocationalized by powerful external institutions such as major corporations or the federal government, the community colleges could not, for the most part, even gain their attention until they had become a major presence in higher education. Nonetheless, the enormous structural power of these institutions subtly shaped the direction of the movement, for its leaders believed (not incorrectly, as it turned out) that an emphasis on practical, job-oriented education would ultimately be rewarded.

The administration's first major endorsement of the colleges came in President Richard Nixon's "Special Message to Congress on Higher Education" in March 1970. Echoing a common refrain of junior college leaders from Koos to Gleazer, he contended in this speech that "too many people have fallen prey to the myth that a four-year liberal arts diploma is essential to a full and rewarding life, whereas in fact other forms of postsecondary education—such as a two-year community college or technical training—are far better suited to the interests of many young people" (Nixon 1970, p. 37A). Nixon added that the programs were not only appropriate for many students but also important to the nation as a means of filling manpower needs in government and industry.

> Critical manpower shortages exist in the United States in many skilled occupational fields such as police and fire science, environmental technology and medical paraprofessionals. Community colleges and similar institutions have the potential to provide programs to train persons for these manpower deficient fields. (Nixon 1970, p. 39A).

Nixon also praised the community colleges for their relative tranquillity at a time when students in many four-year schools were actively engaged in militant political protests. The community colleges, Nixon argued, avoided the characteristics of four-year institutions that contributed to "the isolation, alienation and lack of reality that many young people find in universities or campuses far from their own communities" (Nixon 1970, p. 37A). And one year later, Health, Education and Welfare Secretary Elliot Richardson testified before Congress that the number of students that go through a four-year program "is probably higher than it needs to be . . . not enough prestige and recognition is attached to the pursuit of career education offered in two-year colleges" (U.S. House of Representatives 1971a, p. 92).

The Nixon administration's policy on higher education, formed in 1969 under the intellectual guidance of Democrat Daniel Moynihan, a former Harvard government professor and at the time a counselor to the president, had both a reformist and an elitist cast. One of Moynihan's consuming interests was "the threat to scholarly excellence in the prestigious research universities that were running out of money, besieged by their own students, and seemingly less esteemed by the society. . . . These ideas converged in his mind blending liberalism with elitism and federal restraint with governmental activism (Finn 1976, pp. 50–51).

Science adviser Lee A. DuBridge joined Moynihan in playing an active role. A former president of the California Institute of Technology, DuBridge shared Moynihan's concern with the fate of the elite research university. His interests were in advanced research, particularly in the hard sciences, which "demanded outstanding scholars, ample funds, and an atmosphere free from distraction." Yet he also saw a broader role for the federal government: "Curriculum reform also interested him, as did the need to build community colleges and strengthen society's capacity to provide technical and vocational training to those for whom a classical liberal arts education was unsuited" (Finn 1976, pp. 50–51).

Not all Nixon administration officials wanted to broaden the definition of higher education to include training for job-relevant skills, but many wanted to give an added boost to the community colleges, whose institutional goals were so similar to the administration's own objectives of broadened access tied to utilitarian training (Finn 1976, p. 64). The administration's enthusiasm for the community colleges was attached to specific policy proposals that favored further development. In his "Special Message on Higher Education" in 1970, President Nixon called for a "career education" program designed to assist the colleges in meeting the costs of starting vocational programs in "critical skills areas," and he suggested funding of $100 million for the first year. When the Education Amendment Act of 1972 was finally passed two years later, the proposal had been modified to provide an even larger grant to the community colleges. Although the actual appropriations were smaller than the authorized levels, they were still substantial: $707 million in 1972 (to be distributed over three years) and another $981 million in 1974 (again to be distributed over three years). These funds were augmented by additional monies for occupational programs for the disadvantaged and the handicapped. Overall, federal appropriations for postsecondary vocational education were more than fifteen times as large in 1972 than they had been a mere four years before (Cohen and Brawer 1982, p. 192).

The federal funds, channeled through state allocation boards into many community colleges throughout the country, were used mainly to develop new occupational programs that would train people for the kinds of middle-level jobs emphasized by advocates of community college vocationalization. The language of the Higher Education Act of 1972 made clear that the funds were not to be used to train professionals or to subsidize four-year colleges and universities:

> The term "postsecondary occupational education" means education, training, or retraining . . . conducted by an institution . . . which is designed to prepare individuals for gainful employment as semi-skilled or skilled workers or technicians or sub-professionals in recognized occupations (including new and emerging occupations) . . . but excluding any program to prepare individuals for employment in occupations . . . to be generally considered professional or which require a baccalaureate or advanced degree. (Higher Education Act of 1972, p. 87).

The channeling of students away from four-year institutions and into community college terminal occupational programs—a policy favored by the Carnegie Commission as well as many leaders of the junior college movement—was for the first time being reinforced by major federal financial incentives.

In addition to the material resources provided by favorable legislation, Nixon administration officials also contributed symbolic support for the community colleges' vocationalization efforts through their vigorous promotion of the "career education" concept. Sidney P. Marland, U.S. Commissioner of Education from 1970 to 1972, was most responsible for the idea. In Marland's view, all education was directed toward a job, and thus all education was career education, whether it was directed toward blue-collar, lower white-collar, or upper white-collar jobs (Marland 1972a, 1972b).

Marland's formulation blurred the distinction between terminal and transfer education—a point not missed by the critics of career education (see, for example, Grubb and Lazerson 1975). But this blurring was precisely what was appealing about the concept, for it conferred status on occupational programs by suggesting that everyone (and not just privileged professionals and managers) could have not just a job, but a *career*. What used to be called, grimly if rather accurately, terminal vocational education was now referred to by a sunnier term that, in characteristic American fashion, suggested abundant possibilities for upward advancement. If the term vocational education carried with it connotations of dead-end jobs, then career education suggested orderly, upward movement. The public relations value of this linguistic shift was obvious, and the AAJC adopted the new terminology almost immediately.

The early 1970s also witnessed a second major shift in the terminology of the two-year college movement: the change from *junior* to *community* college that had been suggested by the Truman Commission almost a quarter of a century earlier. This change had important implications for the public's perception of the two-year institutions. For unlike the term *junior college,* which drew attention to the subordinate position of the two-year institution within the system of higher education, the term *community college* focused on the institution's ties to the local community, a shift that had the effect of differentiating it horizontally rather than vertically from the more prestigious four-year colleges and universities. Whereas a junior college quite naturally emphasized transfer to a senior college, a community college might rightfully concentrate on terminal occupational training for employment in the local community.[10]

After years of intense promotional effort, the AAJC suddenly found itself at the center of a well-supported and highly visible national movement. The attendance of a large number of national political figures at its 1971 annual convention—Health, Education, and Welfare Secretary Elliot Richardson; Senators Harrison Williams of New Jersey, Robert Taft of Ohio, and Alan Cranston of California; and Representatives Roman Pucinski of Illinois, Parren J. Mitchell of Maryland, and Albert H. Quie of Minnesota—provided a tangible symbol to many that the community colleges had "arrived" (Shannon 1971b). Following the convention, AAJC president Edmund Gleazer proclaimed that the hard years of promotion were ending: "Ten to fifteen years ago, community colleges were faced with the need to promote themselves—to establish recognition as educational institutions of worth. One senses that this is no longer a need of paramount importance" (Gleazer 1971a, p. 7).

Market Forces in Context: Perception and Reality

Yet as some of the new sponsors were beginning to recognize, the early 1970s witnessed the development of a marked downturn in the market for college-educated labor. Slow occupational growth and in some cases actual decreases in the kinds of jobs that educated workers traditionally filled, combined with continued expansion of higher education enrollments, had gradually begun to create an oversupply of college graduates for college-level jobs (Carnegie Commission 1973, Freeman 1976, Rumberger 1981). These labor market shifts thus changed the environment in which community colleges had been pursuing their organizational interests, and they were destined to play a pivotal role in overcoming students' preference for liberal arts–transfer programs.

The Changing Market

The first indications of difficulty in the market for college graduates emerged in the late 1960s, but it was not until 1970–1971 that clear signs of decline could be seen nationwide. New market conditions were created from the interaction between the unprecedented growth in the supply of new graduates and a relative slowing down of the rate of growth in industries that made intensive use of college-educated labor. These new forces reversed the trends of the previous twenty-five years, when the supply of new graduates had grown much more slowly than demand, creating the "golden age" of the 1950s and 1960s for college-educated labor (Carnegie Commission 1973; Freeman 1975, 1976; Gordon 1974; Rumberger 1981, 1984).

Supply forces were especially important in shaping the new market situation. Contrary to what is often believed, in the 1960s there had been a relatively low supply of college-educated labor.[11] Although there were sizable increases in the number of new college graduates, the enormous growth of graduate programs delayed the entrance of many new graduates into the labor market. In the late 1960s, however, these temporarily diverted new graduate and professional degree-holders began to enter the labor market along with an ever-increasing number of B.A. holders. At the same time, because of the baby-boom, colleges continued to increase in size (Freeman 1976, pp. 51–73).

Unfortunately for the new graduates, the peak era of job expansion in industries and occupations that traditionally employed college labor had passed. Millions of new high-level jobs were created each year, and millions more became vacant through retirement, but this was still not enough to absorb the unprecedented increases in the supply of new college graduates. By the late 1960s, at least three important sectors that made intensive use of college-educated labor—education, government, and research and development—were entering periods of slow growth or decline relative to the overall state of the economy. With the gradual decrease in the birthrate after 1957, employment growth ended first in the elementary schools and later in the secondary schools.[12] The 1969–1971 recession slowed growth in government spending, and research firms were hurt by both the recession and the winding down of the war in Vietnam (see Freeman 1976, pp. 62–73).

As graduate education became less attractive because of the weakening of these traditional high-demand sectors, the supply problem was further exacerbated. Between 1969 and 1972, the net number of new college graduates seeking work (that is, the number of new graduates minus the number of first-time enrollees in graduate and professional schools) relative to the total male work force increased threefold (Freeman 1976, p. 67). The relative supply of new college-educated workers in the labor market dwarfed the supply of the 1960s: whereas the number of new college-graduate workers had increased by 1.2 percent each year from 1959 to 1967, it increased by 7.6 percent each year in the late 1960s and early 1970s (Freeman 1976, pp. 67–68).

As a result of these new market factors, many new college graduates were forced into positions other than professional or managerial jobs. Among students receiving bachelor's and master's degrees in 1972, for example, slightly over 30 percent of the men and 25 percent of the women took nonprofessional and non-managerial jobs. By contrast, just over 5 percent of 1958 bachelor's and master's recipients were employed in such jobs at a roughly comparable point in their lives (Freeman 1976, p. 20). These high levels of underemployment persisted through the 1970s; in February 1978, for example, 21.6 percent of 1976–1977 bachelor's degree recipients were described by government studies as "underemployed,"[13] with humanities and social science graduates faring even worse[14] (National Center for Education Statistics, *The Condition of Education 1979*, p. 242).

The income effects of the new surplus of graduates were also pronounced. Between 1969 and 1975, the earnings of bachelor's degree graduates in the humanities and social sciences dropped from $608 per month (in constant 1967 dollars) to just $470 per month (Freeman 1976, p. 12). Not surprisingly, the depressed market for educated labor led to a decline in the relative earnings advantage of college graduates over high school graduates (see Figure 4-1). Among young men aged twenty-five to thirty-four, the decline was particularly sharp, dropping from 1.39 in 1969 to 1.16 in 1974 (Freeman 1976, pp. 13–15).

Yet as marked as the decline was, it is important to note that *college graduates still maintained relative advantages in the labor market over the less educated.* College graduates continued to hold the great majority of the higher-paying, higher-status jobs, and they continued to be by far the least likely to be unemployed (Brown 1979, O'Neill and Sepielli 1985). Indeed, as applications for desirable jobs piled up and employers could afford to be more selective, a queuing like process combined with "educational upgrading" to reinforce the quasi-monopoly that graduates held on these jobs (Rodriguez 1978, Thurow 1975).

Rates of return on an investment in a college education (after-tax income minus the costs of college) constitute another revealing measure of the continuing advantages of graduates. Some economists suggest that although rates of return for graduates of the 1970s probably dropped by 2.5 to 3.5 percent from the average of 11 to 12 percent in the 1960s, college graduates maintained at least a 7.5 percent rate of return, still an impressive yield on investment (Freeman 1976, pp. 24–29). Moreover, college graduates continued to hold a substantial lifetime earnings advantage over those with "some college"[15] (O'Neill and Sepielli 1985). Whether measured by income, occupational status, or rates of unemployment, the college graduate in the 1970s still enjoyed a substantial advantage over both the high school graduate and the college dropout.

Media Coverage of the Changing Market

In spite of the continuing advantages of four-year college graduates over nongraduates during the 1970s, the mass media focused its attention sharply on the distress of the minority of graduates who experienced exceptional difficulties. Indeed, a regular viewer of the media might well have concluded that the shortest route to a low-status job (or no job at all) was by way of a college campus.[16] A CBS television special entitled "Higher Education: Who Needs It?" broadcast in the spring of 1972 is representative of the early expressions of this view. The

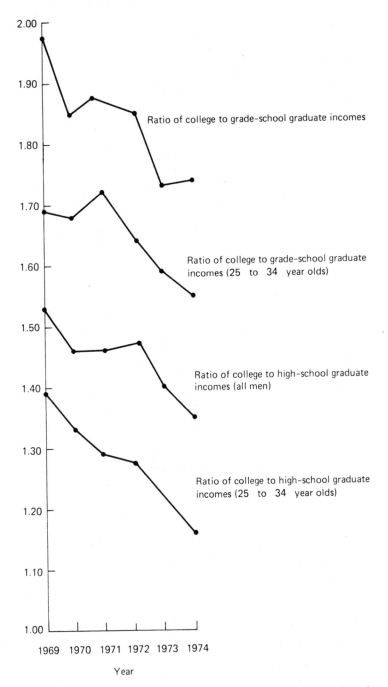

2.00

1.90

1.80

Ratio of college to grade-school graduate incomes

1.70

Ratio of college to grade-school graduate
incomes (25 to 34 year olds)

1.60

1.50

Ratio of college to high-school graduate
incomes (all men)

1.40

1.30

Ratio of college to high-school graduate
incomes (25 to 34 year olds)

1.20

1.10

1.00

1969 1970 1971 1972 1973 1974

Year

Figure 4-1. The falling relative income of year-round, full-time, employed, male college graduates, 1969–1974. (Incomes refer to the mean incomes of year-round, full-time workers.) *Source:* Freeman 1976, p. 14. From U.S. Bureau of the Census "Consumer Income," *Current Population Reports,* Series P-60, Nos. 66, 75, 80, 92, 97, 101.

show opened with a scene of a college commencement. Several recent graduates were then interviewed, and not one of them had been able to obtain a job; the consensus was that with a bachelor's degree it was almost impossible to find work. Later in the show some more fortunate graduates were introduced. These young people had found jobs, but they were working as cab drivers, painters, parking-lot attendants, and newspaper delivery men. Not once during the hour did the program suggest that nongraduates faced even more difficult circumstances, or that a relatively high proportion of graduates continued to obtain higher-level employment. Near the conclusion of the program, it was noted that of 1,200 students registered at the placement office of a state college in New York, only sixteen had firm job offers at graduation.

Media messages of this sort were common for the next several years. The *Wall Street Journal* described the plight of a National Merit Scholar who had accumulated awards and graduated with high honors but still could not find a job ("Sally Gerhardt" 1975). *Time* reported that graduates of one respected college had obtained jobs ranging from janitor to dog warden ("America's New Jobless" 1975). The image of college graduates driving taxis was presented so often that *Newsweek* ran a tongue-in-cheek article recommending the formation of the "The Intellectual Taxicab Company" (Carson 1974). In April of 1976, young men in graduation robes appeared on the cover of *Newsweek* drilling with jackhammers under the headline "Who Needs College?" Other headlines of the period read: "Grads and Jobs: A Grave New World," "The Agony of the Overskilled Man," and "The Welder with the Ph.D." *Time* magazine's feature-length story, "Slim Pickings for the Class of 1976," was accompanied with one photo of an honors student holding a packet of rejection letters and other pictures of graduates hard at work in blue-collar and routine white-collar jobs. The story included a cartoon of robed graduates standing in a line to collect their unemployment benefits. Another cartoon in the April 21, 1975 *Time* magazine showed a diploma at the bottom of a bird cage next to a graduate thumbing through the want ads.

Not all the stories were as sensational as these, and some of them mentioned in passing that college graduates would still earn more than nongraduates in the long run. None of the reports, however, emphasized the continuing advantages of college graduates. Instead, the press suggested that technical training at community colleges and similar institutions was an increasingly sound investment in the face of worthless liberal arts degrees.[17] According to a *Fortune* article in 1970, "The colleges and universities are now turning out too many school teachers and Ph.Ds . . . and too few graduates with vocational certificates for technical level jobs" (Faltemeyer 1970, p. 100). In the same vein, the CBS special noted above quoted college president Robert Ewigleben's expert view that "in this very community there isn't a licensed plumber, and yet we could tomorrow hire twenty Ph.Ds in physics." Later in the broadcast, CBS predicted that enrollments would increase in the "already popular" community colleges as high school students realized that bachelor's degrees no longer assured employment.

CBS noted that among the great attractions of the two-year colleges were their "excellent career training facilities." The magazines also touted vocational training as the major solution to the ills of "overeducation." *Time* magazine wrote glowingly of a Midwestern college that offered associate's degrees in automobile repair and body mechanics ("College, Who Needs It?" 1972). *Newsweek* noted that "of all the alternatives to the traditional college degree, it is the community college that has attracted the most attention," because it offered courses that could "lead to paraprofessional jobs in health and law, and [could] train people as nurses, computer and lab technicians, and even flight controllers" ("Who Needs College?" 1976).

The Surge in Vocational Enrollments

Just as the media had predicted and as many policymakers had hoped, students began to look with increasing favor on vocational training programs. Between 1970 and 1977 the proportion of full-time students enrolled in occupational programs rose from no more than one-third to well over 50 percent—the largest and most rapid shift in the history of the junior college (Blackstone 1978; Bushnell 1973; Cohen and Brawer 1982, pp. 200–203; Medsker and Tillery 1971; Parker 1974, 1975).

Technical difficulties with national enrollment data make precise estimates of the shift impossible.[18] But within states where the criteria for classifying students have been standardized for some period of time, the results all point toward sizable increases in the percentage of vocational enrollments (Lombardi 1978). Moreover, the shift carried through to graduation. By 1975–1976 over 55 percent of all associate's degrees were being awarded in occupational programs, an increase of 110,000 per year from the first years of the decade when most degrees were awarded in arts and sciences or general programs (see Table 4-1).[19] And in the second half of the decade, even the absolute number of nonoccupational associate's degrees fell, with the number of such degrees awarded dropping by over 24,000 between 1976 and 1980.

The Students and the New Market Situation

How did students understand the new market pressures, and why did they respond to them in the way they did?

In Chapters 2 and 3 we stressed the high educational and occupational aspirations of community college students and their strong opposition to programs that might compromise these aspirations. Indeed, even after the shift in the labor market in the early 1970s, between 70 and 80 percent of full-time community college freshman surveyed by the American Council on Education said they planned to obtain at least a baccalaureate degree (American Council on Education 1973–1979).[20] Yet despite these high aspirations, research conducted on community college students in the late 1960s and early 1970s—in particular, the ethnographic study of a working-class community college by London (1978) and the survey analyses by Cross (1971)—suggest that other characteristics must be taken into account to understand the students' responses to the new market pressures. These studies indicate that although community college students wished to be upwardly

Table 4-1. Associate Degrees Conferred by Institutions of Higher Education by Type of Curriculum, 1970–1971 to 1979–1980

Year	All Curricula	Arts and Sciences or General Programs	Percentage of Total	Occupational Curricula	Percentage of Total
1970–1971	253,635	145,473	57.4	108,162	42.6
1971–1972	294,005	158,496	53.9	135,509	46.1
1972–1973	318,234	161,291	50.7	156,943	49.3
1973–1974	347,173	165,520	47.7	181,653	52.3
1974–1975	362,969	167,634	46.2	195,335	53.9
1975–1976	395,393	176,612	44.7	218,781	55.3
1976–1977	409,942	172,631	42.1	237,311	57.9
1977–1978	416,947	168,052	40.3	248,895	58.7
1978–1979	407,471	158,738	39.0	248,733	61.0
1979–1980	405,378	152,169	37.5	253,209	62.5

Source: Cohen and Brawer 1982, p. 203.

mobile, many of them also were fearful about their abilities to do so and were vulnerable to anti-academic pressure from family and peer groups. Such fears and vulnerabilities interacted with the changed labor market environment of the early 1970s—and, in particular, sensationalized media portrayals of the changed labor market—to push many students toward vocational programs.

Both Cross and London found a strong fear of academic work among many community college students. The "hidden curriculum" of primary and secondary education had taught them that their position was highly precarious, their abilities in doubt, and their performance potentially embarrassing. Students often reported feeling nervous and tense in class, and they indicated an aversion to intellectualizing in classroom situations. These feelings and experiences encouraged them to adopt or reaffirm nonintellectual hobbies and interests (Cross 1971, pp. 22, 38, 56–61).

In contrast, many of them felt safe performing the mechanical tasks typical of some vocational programs, and experienced the conceptual demands of academic courses as serious threats to self-esteem (London 1978, pp. 61–114). Moreover, the students who enrolled in transfer programs were more regularly confronted with the possibility of failure than their counterparts in vocational programs. According to London, "to enroll in these curricula and then do poorly was publicly and privately mortifying" (1978, p. 95). This made academic education a gamble, even under favorable market conditions.

Less obviously, success in the academic programs, so central to being able to transfer, also had costs in terms of social dislocation. For many community college students, success in academic courses meant turning away from the values, lifestyles, and self-images of their predominantly working-class and lower-middle-class friends and families. Valuing intellectual activity often meant adopting unfamiliar attitudes, and sometimes constructing an entirely new self-image. Students who attempted to construct such a new identity were especially susceptible to subtle social-class pressures.

In observing community college classrooms, London found that less mobile students often acted as enforcers of the claims of the community by ridiculing students whom they perceived as too strongly committed to success in school. In the college he studied, these taunts took the form of unflattering imitations of intellectual demeanors, barbs about "uppity" attitudes or "educated" vocabulary, and swipes at "pushy" or "brown-nosing" activities in class. London noted that serious transfer students were resented: "In effect they were willing to leave others behind. If they were seen as doing too well without seeing anything wrong with that, then they were deserters; they had shown how weak their allegiances were." For many community college students, these reactions from peers—and sometimes also from family—were especially difficult to handle. "Ostracism," London concluded, "is difficult no matter what the principle involved, but it is especially so for a student not fully confident of sustaining intellectual performances needed to alter his very identity. In such cases, a student is doubly vulnerable—he risks ostracism yet has no guarantee that his efforts will pay off" (London 1978, pp. 100–104).

With social and psychological pressures such as these, it is no wonder that many students began to reevaluate their career plans. When they found that college degrees had become more difficult to convert into high-status jobs, the potential disappointment and ostracism associated with academic preparation took on a new salience—and a new cost—and the security of vocational programs gained a new appeal.

The objective decline in the job prospects of college graduates did, of course, influence these perceptions. But it is also likely that the sensational images of worthless degrees and widespread unemployment that were disseminated by the media had considerable impact. Few students had full and accurate information on labor market trends, but most had access to the images conveyed by the networks and the press. Indeed, surveys suggest that community-college students and their families were relatively likely to rely on the mass media for their information. One study found that low- and lower-middle-income families were three to four times as likely as middle- and upper-middle income families to regard the mass media as "a very important source" of information about colleges. Families headed by persons who had never attended college were also far more likely to regard the media as a very important source of information about college (Group Attitudes Corporation 1982). Because in the early and mid-1970s roughly three-quarters of community college students came from low- and lower-middle-income families, and approximately two-thirds came from families headed by persons who had not attended college (American Council on Education 1971–1976), the mass media probably played a major role in shaping these students' beliefs about the costs and benefits of college.[21]

The massive shift to vocational programs in the early and mid-1970s was more, therefore, than a rational adjustment to changed objective conditions; it was also a response of vulnerable students based on subjective perceptions of these conditions. Stimulated by fear and misinformation as well as by a genuine decline in the market position of the highly educated, the surge in occupational enrollments at community colleges reflected a decisive weakening of the traditional pattern of resistance to programs that were structured to divert students from transfer to a four-year institution. Still hoping to use higher education as a vehicle of upward mobility, many community college students had finally ceased to believe that a bachelor's degree was the pathway to a better life. In this dramatically changed context, the junior college vocationalization project that began more than four decades before was finally being realized.

Changes in Student Composition

Many analysts see the transformation of the community colleges as based in part on the increased numbers of older, part-time, disadvantaged, and low-ability students who entered the community colleges in the 1970s (Cohen and Brawer 1982, Friedlander 1980, Lombardi 1978). From this perspective, the colleges' new emphasis on vocational programs reflects the interests of the new kinds of students attending; as more students from groups traditionally favoring vocational programs are enrolled by the colleges, the curricula will naturally change to mirror their preferences. In its purest form, this argument is a variation of the consumer-choice model, but one that is grounded in the proclivities of particular social categories rather than the preferences of individuals. As Lombardi observed:

> The growth in part-time, women, disadvantaged, handicapped, and older students has contributed to the rise in vocational enrollments. Bushnell points out in his study that while 40 percent of all full and part-time students enrolled in career-training programs, only 25 percent of full-time students did so. The proportion of women who chose career programs was 35 percent, while among men it was only 17 percent. . . . State and local college reports indicate that adults desire occupationally related courses. The large occupational enrollments in California, Florida, Iowa, North Carolina, and Oregon consist largely of older, part-time students. (Lombardi 1978, p. 17)

Simply stated, the argument is that a change in the proportion of students traditionally receptive to vocational programs leads to a change in the proportion enrolled in those programs.

Although it is true that there have been important demographic changes in the kinds of students attending community colleges, there are problems in arguing that these changes caused the transformation of community colleges away from transfer and toward a focus on two-year terminal vocational education. According to Lombardi (1978) and Blackstone (1978), vocational enrollments had already begun to climb in the late 1960s. Yet in many instances, the growth of groups supposedly receptive to vocational education came only after 1970. With respect to age, for example, in the late 1950s roughly 43 percent of community college students were under twenty years of age, and one-sixth were thirty years or older (Medsker 1960, p. 43). The age distribution of community college students in 1970 was not very different from the distribution of the late 1950s; in fact, in 1970 the proportion of students under twenty years of age was higher, according to Cohen and Brawer (1982, p. 32). The decline of the traditional college-age group as a percentage of community college students did not begin in earnest until the mid-1970s, that is, until after the major shift in enrollments.

Similarly, with respect to part- and full-time status, the proportion of part-time to full-time enrollments in the community colleges did not really take off until well into the 1970s. According to AACJC data, the proportion of part-time students remained stable between 1967 and 1971 at 47 to 48 percent, having earlier reached a level of 53 percent in 1963. The 50 percent mark was not again attained until 1972, and it was not until 1978 that 60 percent of community college students were enrolled on a part-time basis (Cohen and Brawer 1982, p. 33).

Even where real changes in composition can be demonstrated between the early 1960s and the mid-1970s, we are skeptical of arguments claiming that these changes had a large independent impact. We have already shown, for example, that the increase in the proportion of working-class students enrolled in the community colleges in the 1950s did not, as a simple compositional argument would predict, lead to increased vocationalization; instead, labor market conditions helped keep the transfer enrollments high. Any consideration of compositional effects that does not take into account institutional goals and labor market conditions is bound to be incomplete and misleading.

Though we are skeptical of most compositional explanations for the early period of decisive change in the community colleges, we do think compositional changes eventually did play a role, especially during the later 1970s and early 1980s. The enrollment of greater numbers of part-time, working-class, and older students furthered a process already in motion by encouraging the colleges to adopt an even more complete vocational orientation. Certainly, the enrollment of such students would not favor a high transfer rate, other things being equal. But we would suggest that even in the late 1970s, institutional goals and labor market conditions strongly mediated the effects of changes in student composition.

Indeed, it may be misleading to talk of student composition as an independent causal force. Increasingly in the 1970s, community college officials recruited older and part-time students whom they felt would be especially receptive to the vocational programs they were constructing. But the new students did not create the programs. Instead, the colleges created the programs and then recruited the students they thought would be most willing to attend, given the changed institutional atmosphere. To an extent, therefore, the colleges created their own compositional change.

Vocational Programs and the Labor Market

By the late 1970s, community colleges had become predominantly vocational institutions, with estimates of the proportion of students enrolled in occupational programs ranging as high as seven in ten (Grubb 1984, p. 431). At the same time, enrollment in college-parallel transfer programs fell, and the overall rate of transfer to four-year colleges and universities plummeted to an all-time low. According to sources within the community college movement itself, the proportion of two-year college students transferring to four-year institutions had dropped everywhere, and in some states fell below 10 percent (Baron 1984; Cohen and Brawer 1982; Friedlander 1980; Lombardi 1979, p. 24).

Table 4-2. Average Weekly Earnings of Community College Vocational Graduates with Jobs Related to Their Training (1973)

Position	Weekly Earnings
Electronics technician	$175.25
Programmer	158.00
Accountant	154.15
Secretary	120.25
Dental assistant	100.75
Cosmetologist	82.25

Source: Wilms 1974, pp. 78, 104, 121, 133, 150, 154.

With the community colleges enrolling, by some estimates, over 2 million students in vocational programs (Blackstone 1978), the issue of their impact on students' lives took on particular importance. The popular assumption—shared by community college administrators, the mass media, and students alike—was that these programs provided a secure route to well-paid, if sometimes unglamorous, jobs. Yet there was little solid evidence on which to base this assumption and some reason to doubt that such programs would, in the aggregate, expand economic and social opportunities, especially in light of the historical failure of vocational education at the elementary and secondary level to expand economic and social opportunities (Kantor and Tyack 1982, Lazerson and Grubb 1974).

In one of the earliest studies of community college vocational education, Wilms (1974) surveyed graduates and dropouts from occupational programs in four metropolitan areas. All of those surveyed attended programs designed to train students for one of six occupations: accounting, computer programming, electronics technology, secretarial work, dental assisting, or cosmetology. Wilms found that few students, whether graduates or dropouts, obtained professional, managerial, technical, or sales jobs. Only a minority of the graduates of the higher-status programs (accounting, computer programming, and electronics technology) obtained jobs in the fields for which they were trained. Moreover, those who dropped out of these programs did just as well on average as did those who graduated; the majority of both groups obtained clerical or lower-level jobs.

Earnings and raises, Wilms found, were more closely related to socioeconomic background than to program completion. Students from higher-status backgrounds did better, independent of whether or not they completed the program. Only in the three lower-status fields studied (secretarial training, dental assistance, and cosmetology)—all of which are dominated by women—did program completion make a difference. In these programs, most graduates obtained jobs in the occupations for which they were trained, whereas many nongraduates did not. However, the average earnings of graduates in these female-dominated programs were considerably lower than the earnings of graduates in the predominantly male fields of electronics technology and programming (see Table 4–2). Interestingly, accounting—the one field with substantial numbers of both male and female graduates—occupied an intermediate position in the labor market.[22]

Table 4-3. Average Values of Outcomes in 1976, by Educational Status in 1972

Measure of Outcome, October 1976	Vocational Program in Community College	Academic Program in Community College	Four-Year College or University
Percentage holding bachelor's degree	3.0	16.0	44.2
Years of postsecondary education completed	1.6	2.3	3.1
Occupational status[a]	426	429	486
Weekly earnings[b]	167	153	142

[a]For those employed. The scale runs from 1 to 999, with higher numbers representing greater socioeconomic status.

[b]For those employed.

Source: Breneman and Nelson 1981, p. 81.

The few available studies that compare community college vocational students with four-year college students tend to underline the continuing advantages of a bachelor's degree. In a major national study, Breneman and Nelson (1981) found that the occupational status of vocational entrants was significantly lower than that of four-year college entrants four years after high school graduation (see Table 4-3). Multivariate analyses indicated, moreover, that the advantage in occupational status held by four-year college students continued to hold true even when controls were introduced for individual differences in social background, aspirations, and ability.

The early earnings of those who had enrolled in community college vocational programs were higher than those of their counterparts who had enrolled in four-year colleges. But as Breneman and Nelson noted, because "occupational status is found to be highly correlated with earnings, the positive impact of attending a four-year institution on occupational status bodes ill for future earnings for those who choose a community college instead of a university right after high school" (Breneman and Nelson 1981, p. 86).

A study by Monk-Turner (1983) compared the returns between two- and four-year colleges over a considerably longer time frame than that used by Breneman and Nelson. Using data from the National Longitudinal Surveys of young men and women who were followed up almost ten years after high school graduation, Monk-Turner found that community college students were at a disadvantage in the labor market compared with otherwise similar students who entered four-year colleges. Controlling for social background, ability, race, gender, and other individual characteristics, she found that attending a community college rather than a four-year college negatively affected occupational status, as did acquiring only an A.A. degree. A decade after high school graduation, there were significant differences in occupational status between community college entrants and students who attended four-year colleges, with almost twice as many of the latter in the ranks

Table 4-4. Occupation by First College Entered and Highest Degree Achieved

Occupation	First College Entered		Highest Degree Achieved	
	Community	Four-Year	A.A.	B.A.
Blue collar	21.4	10.4	20.2	5.8
White collar	55.3	46.8	58.6	38.7
Professional and managerial	23.3	42.9	21.2	55.4
Total	100.0	100.1	100.0	99.9
	(318)	(870)	(104)	(720)

All X^2 for each column and row in this table are significant beyond the 0.05 level.

Source: Monk-Turner 1983, p. 398.

of professionals and managers (see Table 4-4). Moreover, Monk-Turner found that community college students with associate's degrees in vocational fields of study, as opposed to liberal arts, were more likely to be employed in low-status occupations, with twice as many (23.7 versus 11.8 percent) working in blue-collar jobs. Her overall conclusion was that "entering a community college instead of a four-year college, obtaining an A.A. vs. a B.A. degree, and concentrating in a vocational, rather than liberal arts, field in acquiring an A.A. degree, all entail a significant penalty in terms of occupational status" (Monk-Turner 1983, p. 397).[23]

In a 1985 article, Monk-Turner suggested that the occupational-status penalty associated with attendance at a two-year, as opposed to a four-year, institution may have especially serious implications for women. Since 1977, women have constituted an absolute majority of all two-year college students (55 percent in 1980). Indeed, 48 percent of all female undergraduates were enrolled in two-year institutions in 1980, compared with only 41 percent of male undergraduates (calculated from Monk-Turner 1985, p. 91). If attending a community college has, as Monk-Turner's findings show, a negative effect on occupational status, then these negative effects will fall disproportionately on women.[24]

A series of state-level studies comparing community college vocational and four-year graduates are generally consistent with the national studies already considered. In a review of those studies, Pincus (1980) found usable comparative data on income for vocational and four-year college graduates from reports in four states. In two of these states, mean earnings for two-year vocational graduates were less than for four-year college graduates, and in the other two states they were roughly equivalent. Pincus also located data suggesting that unemployment may be somewhat higher among two-year college vocational graduates than among college graduates nationwide. Finally, addressing the issue of gender inequality, Pincus noted that among vocational graduates, women make less than men because they tend to enroll in lower-paying, sex-stereotyped jobs (Pincus 1980, pp. 347–354).

Although the fragmentary nature of the available evidence requires caution, and considerably more research on what happens to graduates of community college vocational programs in the labor market is needed, existing studies are more than sufficient to raise serious questions about the returns to occupational training.[25] In particular, existing data suggest that the alumni of vocational programs frequently are unable to find work in the occupations for which they were trained and, overall, may be more likely to suffer from unemployment than those who hold bachelor's degrees. Moreover, contrary to some of the more exaggerated claims for vocational education appearing in the mass media, graduates of occupational educational programs in two-year colleges tend to occupy lower-status jobs than their counterparts who have graduated from four-year colleges. Furthermore, this status differential, though reduced, does not disappear when controls are introduced for prior differences between two-year and four-year college students in social backgrounds, aspirations, and academic ability. The short-term earnings of alumni of community college vocational programs seem to be roughly comparable to those of the alumni of four-year institutions, but there is reason to believe that over the course of the life cycle a substantial advantage will accrue to those who attend four-year colleges and universities as they translate their higher occupational status into earnings. The outcomes of vocational education are, to be sure, positive for some community college students in some occupational programs (certain technical and health-related fields would seem to be especially likely candidates). But overall, there is little in existing research to suggest that, as the consumer-choice model would have it, the extraordinary expansion of community college occupational educational programs can be explained solely in terms of the rational choices of economically maximizing students who recognized the capacity of vocational education to "deliver the goods" in the labor market.[26]

The AAJC and the Growth of Marketing

The shifting emphasis in the community colleges away from transfer and toward vocationalization did not go uncriticized. Although most community college administrators and faculty members at least tacitly endorsed the trend toward vocational education, a few asked whether high occupational enrollments might not result in second-rate curricula for the least advantaged students. Of the challenging groups, black educators and students were particularly persistent. In 1970, as noted in Chapter 3, a group of black college presidents suggested in an open letter to President Nixon that the administration's emphasis on the community colleges could put "a ceiling on black educational achievement" ("Open the Doors," 1970).[27]

Yet as the period of protest receded, new troubles for community colleges appeared from an unexpected quarter. In an article entitled "After the Boom: What Now for the Community Colleges?" written early in 1974, Gleazer noted that community colleges were no longer alone in their efforts to supply vocational curricula for postsecondary students. He observed that many four-year institutions, faced with declining enrollments, had begun to introduce vocational curricula that were often very similar to those found in the community colleges. For the community colleges, this was a disturbing trend, for it threatened their hold on a stable and growing market niche (Gleazer 1974a).

Gleazer's analysis proved prescient. By 1976, vocational programs were being offered at well over two hundred four-year institutions (Harris and Grede 1977, p. 89). In their quest for job-oriented students, underutilized four-year institutions seldom attempted to coordinate their offerings with those of nearby community colleges. Consequently, the programs often overlapped, and sometimes duplicated, existing programs in the two-year colleges. By 1977, higher education appeared to some observers to be headed toward competitive anarchy, with the weaker four-year institutions battling the two-year colleges for scarce students (Harris and Grede 1977).

Defending Curricular Turf

With their characteristic attentiveness to emerging occupational fields, the community colleges were usually the first institutions to offer training opportunities in emerging subprofessional fields. In the early and mid-1970s, the colleges developed new occupational programs in such areas as hotel and motel management, agribusiness, instrument repair, medical laboratory technologies, energy technologies, and a variety of social welfare support services (Harris and Grede 1977). In most of the states, the colleges continued to emphasize technician and semi-professional training, but some colleges diversified by providing training for skilled blue-collar service and clerical jobs, as well as the traditional middle-level occupations.

As the two-year colleges pushed to beat competitors to new markets, they also fought to keep them out of old ones. Community college officials testifying in Congress accused the four-year schools of being poorly prepared for vocational training and being interested in the programs for mercenary rather than educational reasons (Berkenkemp 1977, U.S. House of Representatives 1975a). Some criticized four-year programs for operating with "inadequate facilities" and with "faculty reassigned from teacher training programs" (Harris and Grede 1977, p. 95). Others argued to state policymaking boards in favor of discontinuing four-year programs that directly competed with those offered in nearby two-year institutions (Berkenkemp 1977, Harris and Grede 1977).

Toward a Marketing Philosophy

The AACJC's response to the new competition included a long-range plan designed to secure expanding markets for the community colleges. Gleazer unveiled the proposal in the same 1974 article that first raised the specter of increasing competition with four-year institutions. Drawing on the work of marketing analyst Theodore Levitt (1960), Gleazer argued that the community colleges should adopt a marketing strategy designed to uncover the full range of services that the largest potential pool of consumers might wish to purchase. More specifically, he suggested that the colleges could provide new goods and services in four areas: "career development" for adult workers; "individual development" for recreational users of higher education; "family development" courses primarily for women; and educational and research services for local government, business, and cultural institutions. He also urged the colleges to expand their concept of the potential market for their services. Services should be provided for all, he wrote, including the large number of demographic groups not traditionally found in postsecondary education, such as "adults unemployed or in jobs that are obsolete, the hard-core unemployed, women in the community including young mothers with children at home, [and] senior citizens" (Gleazer 1974a, p. 11).

Procedures should also be transformed, according to Gleazer. Serving new consumers would mean that "unjustified rigidities of calendar, campus, and courses would have to go"; procedures should "meet the convenience and the needs of . . . clients." No longer would the colleges assume that the colleges and citizens have "only one short period of association." Instead, the colleges would be used any time citizens had a "need or interest" in their services (Gleazer 1974a, p. 9).

Gleazer's proposal included several ideas for diversifying the vocational programs. He recommended expanding training programs to reach beyond the college-age group to adults interested in upgrading the skills used in their current jobs and in retraining for new jobs. He suggested offering psychological testing services to any adult workers who were interested in identifying their "own interests, aptitudes, and potential" (Gleazer 1974a, p. 8). Gleazer also urged selling the new vocational services to employers through the development of subcontracting relationships to provide specialized training and "job orientation" courses. He further recommended that the colleges explore opportunities for consulting in the development of corporate on-the-job training programs. Overall, the aim of Gleazer's proposals for expanding vocational training was to deepen the community colleges' ties with—and dependence on—major private corporations.

Gleazer's marketing strategy carried the entrepreneurial instinct of the movement a qualitative step beyond its previous boundaries. The community college, he contended, should no longer feel constrained by any traditional notions of who should receive postsecondary instruction, what they should receive, or how they should receive it. Gleazer did not hesitate to spell out the new opportunities he had in mind: "For better or worse, most of those who seek a share of [the postsecondary] market are prevented by their traditions from playing a thoroughly opportunistic role." The community colleges had been no exception to this rule, but the times now required that the AACJC "bring together the practices which place more emphasis on 'community' than 'college' " (Gleazer 1974a, p. 8). The Association's "mission statement" for 1974–1975 adopted the essence of Gleazer's program and many of his specific objectives. The statement called for efforts to provide leadership in "community-based, performance-oriented postsecondary education" (AACJC 1976), a phrase that was Gleazer's thumbnail description of the proposed market philosophy.

The Enrollment Surge Continues

Not all community colleges attempted as vigorously as Gleazer had proposed to "market" their wares. For example, reaching new student markets through the use of traditional curricula proved far more popular than diversifying programs. In part this was because new programs required new funding at a time when additional resources were particularly hard to find. The recession of 1974–1976 and the state fiscal crises that followed took a serious toll on the colleges' balance sheets. Equally important, many administrators were reluctant to sever all ties with the traditional academic model of education. Both inertia and continued concerns about legitimacy kept administrators from even attempting to transform their schools into the educational supermarkets that Gleazer envisioned.[28]

In contrast, the idea of reaching out to nontraditional students had great appeal. The costs of recruitment were relatively low and the benefits self-evident. With the proportion of eighteen- to twenty-four-year-olds beginning to decline and nontraditional enrollments already high, the incentives were strong to recruit still more part-time, older, and disadvantaged students. The new competition for markets added to the momentum.

During the 1970s, the community colleges continued to grow rapidly, almost tripling from over 1.6 million students in 1970 to more than 4.5 million in 1980. When the decade began, community colleges enrolled less than 24 percent of undergraduate students; by 1980, they enrolled over 41 percent (calculated from U.S. Bureau of the Census 1987, p. 138). In 1968, slightly more than four in ten college freshman nationwide were enrolled at two-year colleges; a decade later in 1978, the figure had reached 52 percent (U.S. Department of Education 1986, p. 111).[29]

A portion of the new increases in enrollment, especially after the early 1970s, was due to the expansion of nontraditional enrollments: adult women, middle-aged part-time attenders, senior citizens, and minorities. The colleges made deliberate efforts to attract part-time students, especially by making it easy for them to attend. They created senior-citizen institutes and weekend colleges and offered courses at off-campus centers, in workplaces, and in rented and donated housing. In California, for example, some 60 percent of the community colleges used special publicity campaigns and ties to other community agencies to recruit older students (Cohen and Brawer 1982, pp. 31–33).

The two-year colleges also tried to recruit more economically disadvantaged and minority students. The increasing availability of student financial aid greatly facilitated these efforts. Student assistance programs were found in fewer than half the states in 1970, but in nearly every state ten years later. Federal student loans and work–study grants rose from less than $120 million in 1974 to nearly $450 million in 1978 (Breneman and Nelson 1981, p. 138).

These funds, combined with the growing number of open-door institutions located in or within easy access to minority populations, greatly increased the number of minority students in the nation's community colleges. The two-year institutions thus became the major point of entry into the system of higher education for recent immigrants: for Cubans in Florida, Asians in California, Puerto Ricans in the Mid-Atlantic states, and Mexican-Americans in the Southwest (Astin 1982, Olivas 1979).

By the late 1970s, the major subordinate racial minorities, including blacks, were disproportionately concentrated in two-year institutions (see Table 4-5). The

Table 4-5. Percentage of College Students Enrolled in Different Types of
Institutions, Fall 1978, by Racial or Ethnic Group

| Group | Public Institutions | | |
	Universities	Other Four-Year Institutions	Two-Year Colleges
Whites	19.7	24.8	33.2
Blacks	9.7	30.6	39.3
Hispanics	8.6	25.0	53.3
Native Americans	12.5	22.4	53.0
All students	18.4	25.2	34.5

| Group | Private Institutions | | |
	Universities	Other Four-Year Institutions	Two-Year Colleges
Whites	6.5	14.6	1.3
Blacks	4.3	13.5	2.7
Hispanics	4.1	7.9	1.1
Native Americans[a]	2.9	7.1	2.1
All students	6.4	14.1	1.4

[a] Includes Alaskan Natives.

Source: Astin 1982, p. 130, adapted from Dearman and Plisko 1980, p. 110.

structure of tracking in American higher education had thus come to mirror the
larger society's structure of racial stratification. For the nation's minority communities, the key question was what effect this pattern of disproportionate concentration in the nation's community colleges would have on the life chances of the
hundreds of thousands of students enrolled in them.

Institutional Climates, Transfer Patterns, and Students' Life Chances

The massive influx during the 1970s of nontraditional students, many of them
white as well as minority, changed the climate of the community college in two
important ways. First, an increasing number of part-time "personal development"
students took a course or two at a time, dropped in and out at their own convenience, and chose courses they were interested in rather than programs that would
prepare them for more schooling. As Cohen and Lombardi observed, "students
are taking the 'transfer' course in photography to gain access to the darkroom, the
'transfer' course in arts to have their paintings criticized, the 'transfer' course in
a language so that they can travel abroad" (Cohen and Lombardi 1979, p. 26).

Traditional liberal arts courses often lost enrollments to what Cohen and Brawer
(1982, pp. 290–291) called "specialized, current interest courses" on such subjects as folklore, magic and mythology, "Tidepools of California," and "Urban
Life." By the end of the decade, Cohen and Lombardi (1979, p. 25) found that

"except for U.S. history, Western civilization, American and state government, introductory literature and Spanish, little in the humanities remains."

Concomitantly, there was a second trend, which reflected the declining academic achievement levels of recent high school graduates and the growing numbers of disadvantaged students in the system, namely, the expansion of remedial courses. In 1977–1978 nearly one in three mathematics classes taught arithmetic at a level lower than college algebra, and 37 percent of English courses were offered at levels below general college grade (Center for the Study of Community Colleges 1978). John Lombardi noted "the most nettlesome paradox" surrounding the community college: "It is called a college, but elementary grade subjects—arithmetic, reading, and writing—rank high in terms of courses offered and students enrolled" (Lombardi 1982, p. xii). In many two-year colleges, more students were enrolled in courses in basic reading and writing than in traditional college-level liberal arts courses (Cohen and Lombardi 1979).

These two trends—casual attendance and remedial courses—together had significant negative effects on transfer rates. Although the absolute number of students transferring declined relatively little (owing to the vast expansion of the community college system as a whole), the rates of transfer plummeted from approximately 25 percent at the beginning of the 1970s to perhaps 15 percent by the end of the decade (Anderson 1981, Cohen and Brawer 1982, Cohen and Lombardi 1979, Lombardi 1979, Peng 1977).[30] Moreover, among the minority of students who did transfer to a four-year institution, those of higher socioeconomic status were overrepresented (Velez 1985).

When total enrollments are used as a base for computing transfer rates, figures from state-level studies suggest that transfer programs have become peripheral to the actual functioning of community colleges. According to studies conducted in New York, Washington, and Illinois, less than 6 percent of all students enrolled in community colleges transferred to a four-year institution in a given year (Baron 1982).[31] Even if one doubled the estimated rates of transfer in these studies (a procedure that seems reasonable given that two years are needed to complete an associate's degree), the chances of a given community college student's ever enrolling in a four-year college or university had by the late 1970s become shockingly low for institutions whose primary source of public support still is, according to public opinion polls conducted for the AACJC in 1981 and 1984, their transfer programs (AACJC 1981, 1984).

For evidence on patterns of transfer, data from California—which in 1980 enrolled about one-fourth of community college students nationwide—are especially revealing, for they shed light on the rates of transfer to the different tiers of the tracking structure. Overall, the figures from California suggest both a relative and an absolute decline in the number of transfers, especially to the top tier (see Table 4-6). Transfers to the University of California (UC) peaked in 1973 at 8,193 but dropped to 5,649 in 1979. During the same years, the number of transfers to the intermediate tier, the California State Universities and Colleges (CSUC), declined only slightly, from 33,089 to 30,428. Thus, whereas in 1973 there were slightly more than four transfers to CSUC for every transfer to UC, the ratio had risen to well over five to one by 1979.[32]

Table 4-6. First-Time, Fall-enrolled Transfer Students from California Community Colleges to UC and CSUC, As a Percentage of Full-Time Community College Students Two Years Prior

Year	Number to UC	Percentage to UC	Number to CSUC	Percentage to CSUC
1971–1973	8,193	2.7%	33,089	11.1%
1973–1975	8,002	2.6	35,537	11.9
1975–1977	6,392	1.6	34,001	9.1
1977–1979	5,649	1.8	30,428	9.5

Source: California Postsecondary Education Commission 1984, p. B-4.

It is important to keep in mind, however, that the low transfer rates of the late 1970s, in California and elsewhere, merely accentuated a long-standing pattern in which most community college students never transferred to a four-year institution. The vocationalized community college was a particularly inhospitable institutional environment for transfer, yet the fact of the matter is that the junior college was, as we showed in Chapter 2, designed to divert students from senior institutions as well as to bring a selected few into them. In a society in which over half of the 1980 high school seniors planned careers in professional and technical jobs despite the fact that such jobs comprised under 13 percent of the labor force (Wagenaar 1984), it is hardly surprising that the community college, which plays such a major role in the "cooling out" of unrealistic educational and occupational aspirations, serves more often as a shock absorber than as a platform for transfer to four-year institutions.

The low transfer rates of community colleges have, of course, always been in part a consequence of the different kinds of students attending them. Yet an extensive body of research now suggests that at least for students who wish to obtain a bachelor's degree, attendance at a community college independently lowers their prospect of success. Several major studies summarized by Dougherty (1987) reveal not only that two-year college students obtain bachelor's degrees at a lower rate than do their counterparts at four-year institutions but also that this pattern holds even when controls are introduced for factors such as individual ability, aspirations, and social origins. Attending a community college, according to these studies, reduces a student's chances of completing a bachelor's degree, by roughly 11 to 19 percent.

Because some of these results come from studies conducted before vocational programs were as dominant as they are today, it seems likely that the negative effects of community colleges on the attainment of a B.A. have become more pronounced in recent years. A number of factors have been suggested as the source of this negative effect—among them, the absence of residential facilities, the relative lack of supportive peer groups, the frequently nonacademic atmosphere at community colleges, and the tendency to track would-be transfer students into occupational programs (Dougherty 1987). But whatever the cause, the existence of such an independent effect has by now become a well-established and frequently replicated fact (Alba and Lavin 1981; Anderson 1981; Astin 1977, 1982; Folger et al. 1970; Velez 1985).

In an era in which a bachelor's degree is a prerequisite for entry into an increasing number of professional and managerial occupations, this negative effect must be a source of serious concern to those concerned about equality of opportunity. For it is precisely those groups in need of greater opportunities—minorities, women, and the economically disadvantaged—that are disproportionately con-concentrated in two-year colleges (Astin 1982, Karen 1980, Randour et al. 1982).[33]

Ties to Business

The states' responses to the fiscal crises of the mid-1970s are an important final element in the transformation of the community college. If the decline in the market for college graduates and the infusion of federal funds encouraged vocationalization, efforts to revitalize state economies pushed the transformation along distinctive lines. Nearly every state government suffered some degree of financial misery during the recession of 1974–1976. In its wake, officials throughout the country came to remarkably similar conclusions: given the dependence of state finances on economic prosperity, the states should try to attract new capital and to keep industries currently located in the state from leaving (Dougherty 1988a, Goodman 1979).

Government concern over capital flight spawned a variety of programs aimed at cultivating the business sector. Before long, the states were engaged in a furious competition with one another to provide the most attractive packages of benefits for businesses. "Tax holiday" packages were the centerpiece of the bonanza for business, but educational services were also important features of such programs. By the late 1970s, every state but Nevada had offered some form of subsidized industrial job training as an inducement to corporations contemplating relocation in their state (Goodman 1980). In states like North Carolina, Ohio, South Carolina, and Tennessee, community colleges became the center of these state-sponsored training programs for industry. In North Carolina, for example, Governor James B. Hunt made the community colleges "the presumptive deliverer" of state-subsidized skills training. With the state providing the principal financing, aided by $6 million worth of corporation-donated equipment, community colleges in North Carolina offered free training courses to thousands of employees and prospective employees of new and expanding industries in the state. The programs were designed to conform precisely to industry specifications. For example, if a company intended to build a new plant and said it would need fifteen additional machine operators by the time the factory opened, the local community college would provide the necessary training to prepare workers for the new jobs. According to a North Carolina community college official, more than four thousand workers from over eighty businesses were trained annually through these programs (Watkins 1982).

In California, the Worksite Education and Training Act authorized grants to community college districts for work in cooperation with local business and industry to provide entry-level training or skill upgrading in areas of industry needs. One program for the employees of the Fairchild Central System Company consisted of thirty-two weeks of classroom instruction and twenty additional weeks of on-the-job training intended to lead to promotions for employees in the field of computer-aided design and manufacturing. In these programs, the community colleges provided the instruction, and local business provided the necessary equipment (Cross and McCartan 1984).

South Carolina's Board of Technical and Comprehensive Education created a center for training in microelectronics as a means of attracting high-technology industries to the state. The center offered customized training for specific firms and teacher training for two-year college instructors at the state's sixteen technical colleges, with community college instructors encouraged to develop new courses in the area of electronics (Cross and McCartan 1984).

In Missouri, New Mexico, and California, funds for specific training programs and general increases in support of technical and skill training appeared in governors' budgets. These funds were earmarked for specific program areas most in demand in high-technology industries, typically business, computer science, and engineering (Cross and McCartan 1984). Still other states developed separate skill training corporations designed to channel funds to colleges that were able to obtain matching funds from local firms for customized training programs. Chapter 7 discusses an example of this approach developed in Massachusetts.

High Technology and the Growth of Business Influence

In general, the state economic development programs had two important effects on the community colleges. Because of the states' interest in attracting new capital, many of the plans emphasized training for high-technology industries, which were widely perceived as the most dynamic sector in the economy and also as particularly mobile. The governors of at least five states—Maryland, North Carolina, Florida, Indiana, and Connecticut—proposed establishing centers to promote research in science and technology programs, and many others targeted the development of human resources for high-tech industry as a priority (Cross and McCartan 1984). In many states, this enthusiasm led to the development of occupational programs in fields that provided only a small proportion of total employment (Bienstock 1981, Grubb 1984). Recent estimates suggest that high-tech industries have a significant presence in only nine states (Pollack 1983, p. 30). Even in California, one of the leading centers of high-tech development, the sector is expected to account for only one in every fourteen jobs by 1990. In Massachusetts, a smaller state but also a leader, the high-tech sector accounted for an even smaller proportion of all jobs. Nonetheless, the community colleges, under the influence of state officials, eagerly jumped on what Grubb has called "the high-tech bandwagon." As Grubb (1984, p. 440) demonstrated, the programs showing the fastest rate of growth (though not the highest absolute levels of growth) in the late 1970s and early 1980s were those most closely connected to high-tech employment: computer science, electronics technology, and health technology. By the early 1980s, the number of graduates in these fields was surpassing the number of available jobs.

The state programs also encouraged a wholly new approach to vocational training. Short-cycle training programs "custom tailored to meet the needs of specific firms" represented the beginning of a further structural change in the community colleges, for few of these programs required students to take any supplementary academic course work. The state plans emphasizing "customized" training legitimated efforts to expand in this area that community colleges had generated on their own initiative. In the new environment, cooperative arrangements between the colleges and local business, long a part of the community college "mission," grew in number and became more specific (Pincus 1986).

Many of these customized programs grew directly out of the colleges' long-standing commitment to identifying emerging occupational trends in their areas. In Atlantic City, New Jersey, for example, within months after voters authorized casino gambling, the local community college created courses to train dealers and slot machine mechanics. These courses proved so popular that the colleges added a culinary arts program to train chefs for the restaurants in Atlantic City's new hotels (Maeroff 1982). In similar California programs, officials in the San Mateo Community College District custom-tailored telecommunications programs to fit the local needs of that industry, and the Orange County Community College District developed short-cycle programs to provide technicians for local electronic and aerospace employers (Watkins 1982).

New programs were also sometimes developed at the employers' request. In one such program, forty community colleges across the country were given contracts by General Motors Corporation to retrain the company's dealer-based auto mechanics so that they could keep abreast of technological changes in automobile design (Maeroff 1982). In another, AT&T contracted with the community colleges to train telecommunications mechanics, paying the direct cost of training as an educational benefit for their employees (Watkins 1982).

In one of the most ambitious internally initiated efforts to provide specific training services for business, Portland Community College, long an innovator in community education, established its Institute for Community Assistance as an outreach program to local employers. The institute provides classroom facilities at the work site, awards college credits for training, and designed the curricula to meet the specific needs of the contracting organization. The director of the institute said: "We're really a partnership between the college and business. They have the employees, we have the curricula and the instructors, and we can offer college credits and facilitate customers' goals" (Fisher, quoted in McCabe and Skidmore 1983, p. 240). By 1977 some 85 percent of community colleges reported having developed occupational programs at the request of local employers (Abbott 1977). The trend toward closer relationships with local business continued: a study from the early 1980s revealed that the average community college had one hundred specific working arrangements with local organizations, mainly local businesses (Parnell 1982, p. 14).

The customized training programs enjoyed great popularity in state economic development offices and in many community college districts. State officials tended to view the programs as "good for everyone," providing industry with trained workers, workers with secure jobs, and the state with new taxpayers (Goodman

1980). Community college officials tended to share that view, believing that the programs were an extension of the natural cooperation between private industry and community colleges.

The promotion of Dale Parnell, former chancellor of the San Diego community college system, to president of the AACJC in 1981 provided a further boost to advocates of business service activities. Whereas his predecessor, Edmund Gleazer, had emphasized a broad community service identity, Parnell was more narrowly focused. He emphasized the community colleges' role as the provider of job-training services, working "in partnership with business and industry" (Vaughan and Associates 1983, p. 10). In one of his first acts as president, Parnell initiated a project aimed at building "public-private partnerships." The coordinator of the project said he was not worried that the community colleges would serve "too specifically the needs of business and industry"; the customized programs, he said, conformed to the mission of the community colleges and could coexist with the more traditional associate's degree curricula (Ellison, quoted in Watkins 1982, p. 4).

Not everyone agreed. Some educators asked whether highly specialized vocational courses were consistent with the ideals of providing equal opportunity and training for democratic citizenship (Aronowitz and Giroux 1985, Bastian et al. 1986, Pincus 1986). One critic quoted John Dewey's strong opposition to "whatever proposition, in whatever form advanced, to separate training of employees from training for citizenship, training of intelligence and character from narrow industrial efficiency" (Dewey, quoted in Goodman 1980, p. 39).

Just as the vocationalization project of the junior college vanguard was finally being realized, it thus became apparent that a new conflict was brewing over vocational education. The questions under debate, however, were not whether vocational programs should exist but whether they should be separated entirely from academic work, and not whether the community colleges should pursue contacts with business but whether they should entirely subordinate themselves to the needs of industry. The lines of division in the new debate indicated just how far the community colleges had traveled in their transformation from liberal arts colleges to vocational training institutions.

The Long Road from Joliet

By the early 1980s the junior colleges had come a long way from the small, often generally disdained preparatory institutions that banded together for self-defense in 1920. Indeed, they had come a long way even from the comprehensive colleges that constituted the dominant model in the 1960s. The leading colleges of the 1980s were predominantly vocational institutions, and many of them offered a growing number of short-term courses custom-tailored to meet the specific needs of local business.

A sense of the atmosphere of many community colleges in the early 1980s is captured by Saiter's[34] (1982) description of Triton Community College in River

Grove, Illinois: an amalgam of a research and development shop, an industrial factory, a shopping mall, and a suburban high school.

Art supplies crowded the shelves of the bookstore next to welding accessories; school tee shirts hung on a rack near the chef's aprons. The technical building housed expensive equipment loaned by such corporations as General Motors and Bausch and Lomb. Automotive parts posters—in both English and Japanese—decorated the walls.

In the many community colleges like Triton, vocational enrollments in the early 1980s far exceeded transfer enrollments, and some of the more popular vocational programs were over subscribed. In such programs—nursing was a good example at many schools—prospective students ironically had to be turned away and redirected into those liberal arts transfer courses which had once been the body and soul of community colleges.

Though initially oriented almost exclusively to the task of providing liberal arts transfer programs, the two-year college later embarked on a project to transform itself into a predominantly vocational institution. The logic of this vocationalization project, we have argued over the last three chapters, derived from the community college's vested organizational interest in establishing for itself a distinctive market niche in an organizational field dominated by four-year colleges and universities. We have shown also how the popularity of the colleges, based in part on their low cost and convenience, ultimately attracted outside sponsorship that helped make the vocationalization project a success. Above all, we have emphasized that it was the changing market for college students—and the changing perception of this market—that decisively eroded student opposition to vocational education, thereby allowing the vision of the early leaders of the junior college movement to become a reality after almost half a century of promotion.

The Ironies of Success

Paradoxically, community colleges now face problems created in large part by the very strategies they adopted in order to succeed. As they moved beyond their initial commitment to college-parallel transfer programs and drastically expanded their vocational offerings in the 1970s and early 1980s, enrollments and expenditures surged. Yet the triumph of vocationalism, and the concomitant weakening of academic transfer programs, has brought in its wake a serious crisis of institutional legitimacy. Among the correlates of this crisis are the first serious enrollment declines since World War II and a pronounced increase in state scrutiny of community college activities.

As recently as 1982, members of the AACJC, when discussing the status of their institutions, used such words as "thriving," "growing," and "expanding" (Middleton 1982). Despite all the talk in higher-education circles about the "baby bust" and its dire implications for college enrollments, community colleges continued to expand, growing by 56,000 between 1981 and 1982 to 4,772,000, while four-year institutions failed to grow for the first time in decades. In 1983, community college enrollments suddenly dropped, with most of the decline due to a decrease in the number of registered students in the state of California, the traditional bulwark of the junior college movement. But by 1984, the decline was clearly nationwide, with over 190,000 fewer students enrolled than in 1983 (U.S. Bureau of the Census 1987, p. 138). After years of burgeoning enrollments, the community college movement suddenly found that the supply of new "student markets" was finite after all.

To a considerable extent, the enrollment declines were due to forces beyond the control of the community colleges—declining unemployment rates (which tend to pull adults out of higher education and into the labor market), unfavorable demographic trends, and cutbacks by the Reagan administration in federal loans and grants. In addition, fiscally strapped state legislatures often imposed tuition and/or raised fees at community colleges—generally over the opposition of community college administrators and students alike. But the community colleges themselves also played a role in the decline; indeed, the very success of their vocationalization project placed them in increasingly direct competition with a growing number of proprietary institutions (Wilms 1987). Moreover, as the lower-tier four-year colleges came to model themselves less on the universities and more on the vocationalized community colleges, a number of occupational programs once monopolized by the two-year colleges began to be offered by four-year institutions. Thus the distinctive market niche that the vocationalization project had targeted—that of middle-level manpower—was now a bitterly contested one, with proprietary schools encroaching on it from below and four-year colleges from above.

While expanding their offerings in vocational and community education, many two-year colleges permitted their academic transfer programs to deteriorate. Sensing this, some potential full-time enrollees in community college liberal arts curricula have apparently chosen to enroll in four-year institutions, where they believe (correctly, in our view) that their chances of obtaining a bachelor's degree will be greater. Many lower-status four-year institutions, faced with a declining pool of recent high school graduates, have been more than delighted to receive these students.

Even the community colleges' emphasis on the economic benefits of vocational training has begun to be questioned by potential students. According to the president of Oregon's Mount Hood Community College, "A lot of folks say that now that they've got a job, they're not ready to go into a training thing that might not promise a better job in the end" (quoted in Meyer 1984). Moreover, some of the very government statistics that had revealed a decline in the relative economic advantage of college graduates were now showing an increase in this advantage. Indeed, the income of college graduates relative to the income of high school graduates turns out, by almost any measure, to have increased since 1974. By 1983, the adjusted earnings ratio of college to high school graduates for males aged 25 to 34 was 1.36—a figure that is slightly higher than the comparable ratio between 1967 and 1970 (Smith 1986, pp. 91–95).

In the changed political context of the 1980s—one which emphasizes "academic standards" and "accountability"—the vocationalized community college has found itself in a precarious position. In particular, legislators have begun to ask whether the state should support, as institutions of higher education, schools that actually provide relatively few persons with that most visible mark of a college education, the baccalaureate degree (Jaschik 1985, McCartan 1983a). With state rather than local governments now supplying the bulk of community college resources, state executives and legislatures are demanding that community colleges review their programs and justify their expenditures. From this perspective, the proliferation of recreational courses on such subjects as gourmet cooking, windsurfing, and bridge is hard to justify.

Traditional college-parallel transfer programs, in contrast, enjoy wide popularity with politicians and the public at large. Yet as legislative reviews in many states have revealed, community college transfer programs—once the junior college's *raison d'etre*—are frequently in a state of atrophy. If the community college is to address the crisis of legitimacy in which it now finds itself, it must strengthen its ties with four-year colleges and universities. For it is these ties that have historically distinguished junior colleges from trade schools and provided them with public legitimacy and support.

The declining transfer rates that have accompanied vocationalization have come under scrutiny as well from groups concerned that the community college may serve to reduce rather than enhance the educational and social mobility prospects of minority students. Black educators have been especially critical of the community colleges' failure to promote minority students toward higher levels of educational attainment (Maeroff 1983).[35] With minority students overrepresented not only in community colleges, but also in the vocational tracks within them (Olivas 1979), the issue of low transfer rates, particularly among black and Hispanic students, has taken on special political salience. Indeed, in 1982, the Ford Foundation–sponsored Commission on the Higher Education of Minorities explicitly endorsed a recommendation that had long been advocated by critics of community colleges: "In areas where senior institutions and community colleges are located close to one another, young people aspiring to a baccalaureate be encouraged to enroll in the senior institution" (Astin 1982, p. 191).

Yet whatever the difficulties faced by the community colleges today, their transformation has been one of the decisive developments in American higher education in recent years. In the late 1960s and early 1970s, educational policy-making elites such as the Carnegie Commission had proposed a two-pronged strategy to keep the system of higher education in relative harmony with the labor market: the drastic expansion of community colleges and the rapid growth of vocational programs within them. By the late 1970s, under the stimulus of a declining market for college-educated labor, both prongs of this strategy had become a reality. These changes constituted a realization of the dreams of the early leaders of the junior college movement; that they have also created in their wake perhaps the most serious crisis of institutional legitimacy and identity of the postwar era is one of the great ironies of the transformation of the community college.

PART II Community College Transformation at the State and Local Level: The Case of Massachusetts

In the first part of this book, we considered the forces encouraging the transformation of American community colleges from transfer-oriented institutions with links to the rest of academia into highly vocationalized institutions focused on an educational trajectory that ends at its own doors. We argued that this transformation cannot be accounted for by either the consumer-choice or the business-domination models. Rather, we suggested that vocationalization was pressed by the junior college leaders and their allies as the best available strategy for pursuing institutional interests in a context of powerful structural constraints.

In Part II of this volume, we provide a more detailed analysis of change by concentrating on one state system. By examining the birth, growth and subsequent vocationalization of the Massachusetts system—a relatively late-developing community college system—we try to document the actual processes that led to vocationalization. Moreover, our evidence regarding Massachusetts, based on extensive interviews as well as archival evidence, tends, we believe, to confirm our main thesis: that community colleges advocated vocationalization in the face of both business apathy and student resistance because of organizational interests rooted in their location in the complex ecological structure of American higher education.

Three concerns, in particular, led us to include a case study as part of our analysis of the transformation of two-year colleges. First, we believed it necessary to balance our emphasis on the influence of national-level events and actors with an emphasis on the specifically local influences bearing on community college development. Second, we wanted to illustrate how national influences concretely shaped local practices. Finally, we wanted to understand the concrete mechanisms through which vocationalizing policies were implemented on the campuses.

This last concern requires some amplification. In our view, analysts too often discuss patterns and rates of institutional change in education, without considering the actual dynamics of change. None of the major explanatory paradigms—neither neo-Marxist (Bowles and Gintis 1976) nor neo-Weberian (Collins 1971, 1977, 1979) nor functionalist (Clark 1962; Trow 1961, 1970) accounts—consider the precise mechanisms of organizational change.[1]

In the work of neo-Marxists and functionalists, for example, a correspondence is often postulated between very general social forces encouraging change and organizational response. One version of neo-Marxist theory hypothesizes a natural correspondence between the structure of the educational system and the structure of the economy (Bowles and Gintis 1976). With respect to the community colleges, therefore, the changing economy would be viewed by Marxists as the driving force behind the vocationalization of colleges and universities. In our case study of change in Massachusetts, however, we shall attempt to show that the partial correspondence that does exist between the system of higher education and the economy is a contingent outcome, constructed in large part by educational administrators seeking to rationalize the relationship between their institutions and the labor market. As such, there is no inherent correspondence between the educational system and the economy.[2]

Unlike the "correspondence" theorists, who generally take a tight fit between the school system and the labor market to be "natural," we see the strength of the connection as problematic and hence in need of explanation. In particular, we focus on an issue generally neglected by sociological theorists of education—the specific mechanisms through which educational institutions change and, on occasion, are brought into at least partial correspondence with the demands of the economy. The vocationalization of Massachusetts community colleges is one such case, and by focusing on the actual dynamics of change, we hope to show how leaders of educational institutions, acting in pursuit of their own organizational interests, can be the primary agents of change.

Several characteristics recommended the Massachusetts system as a site for the case study. Unlike many state systems, the Massachusetts system was both small enough (fifteen campuses) and young enough (the first college opened in 1960) to allow for a relatively comprehensive study. Moreover, our physical proximity to many of the system's main campuses facilitated such a study. The system, though unusually small for a state the size of Massachusetts (largely a consequence of the great number of private institutions of higher education), was also representative in the most important ways. The system was typical, for example, in the kinds of students it attracted. As in other states, community college students in Massachusetts were drawn from less privileged backgrounds than were four-year college and university students. In 1976, for example, only 16 percent of Massachusetts's community college students came from families earning $15,000 or more annually, compared with 24 percent of state college students and 40 percent of university students (Massachusetts Board of Higher Education 1978). Similarly, only about 30 percent of Massachusetts's community college students came from families headed by professionals or managers (Bunker Hill Community College 1977, Harris 1977, Tobin 1977), whereas two-thirds of the University of Massachusetts's students came from professional or managerial families (University of Massachusetts 1977). These figures closely parallel national patterns (American Council on Education 1976, 1977).

The governance of the system was also broadly representative of national patterns. As in over three-quarters of the states (Berdahl 1970), Massachusetts's community colleges were coordinated by a statewide board of appointed officials. Finally, the shift toward vocational education in Massachusetts's community colleges broadly paralleled national trends both in timing and extent.

Our case study is based on extensive interviewing of Massachusetts state government officials, community college central office staff and campus administrators, campus faculty, counselors, and students. We conducted over one hundred interviews in all. Most lasted between one and two hours. The study also included periods of observation at the central office of the Massachusetts Board of Regional Community Colleges (MBRCC) and at seven of the fifteen campuses in the system.[3]

The first chapter of the case study, Chapter 5, focuses on the years 1958 to 1970, covering the founding of Massachusetts's community colleges as predominantly liberal arts institutions and their move toward becoming technical training institutions. Chapter 6 departs from the chronology to discuss the mechanisms used on the campuses to implement vocationalizing policies. We return to the chronology in Chapter 7 with a consideration of the effects on community colleges of the labor market downturn of the early 1970s, the state fiscal crisis of 1975–1976, and the significance of corporate influence in the late 1970s and early 1980s. Chapter 7 concludes with a brief discussion of some of the theoretical implications of the case study, a discussion that sets the stage for our concluding chapter—Chapter 8—which places the transformation of the community college in historical and comparative perspective.

5 Designs for Comprehensive Community Colleges: 1958–1970

No analysis of the history of the community college movement in Massachusetts can begin without a discussion of some of the peculiar features of higher education in that state. Indeed, the development of all public colleges in Massachusetts was, for many years, inhibited by the strength of the state's private institutions (Lustberg 1979, Murphy 1974, Stafford 1980). The Protestant establishment had strong traditional ties to elite colleges—such as Harvard, Massachusetts Institute of Technology, Williams, and Amherst—and the Catholic middle class felt equally strong bonds to the two Jesuit institutions in the state: Boston College and Holy Cross (Jencks and Riesman 1968, p. 263). If they had gone to college at all, most of Massachusetts's state legislators had done so in the private system.

Private college loyalties were not the only reasons for opposition to public higher education. Increased state spending for any purpose was often an anathema to many Republican legislators, and even most urban "machine" Democrats were unwilling to spend state dollars where the private sector appeared to work well enough (Stafford and Lustberg 1978). As late as 1950, the commonwealth's public higher education sector served fewer than ten thousand students, just over 10 percent of total state enrollments in higher education. In 1960, public enrollment had grown to only 16 percent of the total, at a time when 59 percent of college students nationwide were enrolled in public institutions (Stafford and Lustberg 1978, p. 12). Indeed, the public sector did not reach parity with the private sector until the 1980s. Of the 15,945 students enrolled in Massachusetts public higher education in 1960 (see Table 5-1), well over 95 percent were in-state students. The private schools, by contrast, cast a broader net: of the nearly 83,000 students enrolled in the private schools, more than 40 percent were from out of state (Organization for Social and Technical Innovation 1973).

Table 5-1. Public Higher Education Enrollment in Massachusetts by Segment, Selected Years 1960–1970

Year	University of Massachusetts	Other Public Universities[a]	State Colleges	Community Colleges	Total
1960	6,030	2,557	7,207	151	15,945
1965	9,520	3,725	10,840	3,650	27,735
1967	12,835	6,370	15,792	7,930	42,927
1970	20,835	8,060	21,828	15,165	65,888

[a]Southeastern Massachusetts University and University of Lowell.

Source: Stafford and Lustberg 1978, p. 7.

The Origins of Community Colleges in Massachusetts

The opposition to public higher education began to recede in the late 1950s. Already by mid-decade, a large number of urban liberals had become members of the state legislature, and a new governor, Foster Furcolo, had been elected in 1956 on an activist platform. Democratic control of the legislature was solidified in 1958, with the election of a Democrat, Maurice Donahue, as majority leader of the senate, the first Democrat to hold that position in the commonwealth's history. According to Donahue, "Prior to 1958 . . . there simply was not much political support for the public colleges. When we got control in 1958, it was the first time in this century that there were enough people in the legislature sympathetic with the issue to do anything about it" (quoted in Stafford and Lustberg 1978, p. 17). Together, Furcolo and his allies in the legislature found an opportunity in the prosperity of the late 1950s to expand the state's economic development and welfare activities.[1] The governor pressed for the expansion of the University of Massachusetts (at the time a small, predominantly agricultural college with a single campus in Amherst) and the diversification of the state teachers colleges. He also introduced legislation to establish a system of regional community colleges.

Furcolo's Community College Bill

The community college idea in Massachusetts originated in the work of a special commission appointed by Furcolo in 1956 to "audit" the state's future needs. The Audit Commission Report of 1958, like many state master plans of the period, emphasized the immediate need to expand the state's higher education facilities. The commission's argument was based primarily on demographics, contending that the state's limited commitment to higher education would soon fall far short of the growing demand generated by the postwar baby boom (Massachusetts House of Representatives 1958, p. 8). Given the state economy's increasing need for educated labor, the commission suggested that this unmet demand would lead, in turn, to shortages of "technicians and specialists in medicine, engineering and the new 'high skill' industries" (Massachusetts House of Representatives 1958, p. 8).

As was the case in so many other states, the Audit Commission's report placed special emphasis on community colleges as an effective and economical solution to these problems. The commission emphasized the role that the two-year colleges could play both in "extending equality and opportunity" and in "training technical personnel" for business and industry (Massachusetts House of Representatives 1958, p. 8). The report also underscored the colleges' popularity in other parts of the country.

The Audit Commission's arguments regarding access, training, cost, and convenience all were staples of the promotional literature of the American Association of Junior Colleges. Indeed, the AAJC had a strong indirect influence on the report. John Mallan, Furcolo's aide who drafted the sections of the report on community colleges, remembered in an interview with us that his own interest in community colleges had developed several years before he read the work of Koos and Eells,[2] both prominent leaders of the junior college movement.[3]

Furcolo decided to press the Audit Commission's recommendations against the advice of most of his closest political aides, who feared that a community college bill would antagonize the fiscally conservative legislature. Thus in 1958 he introduced a bill calling for the introduction in the state of a system of regional community colleges. In his personal lobbying for the bill, Furcolo sounded themes familiar to the national debate over community colleges. He stressed the opportunities for social mobility and cultural enrichment that the colleges would provide and the role the colleges could play in training, at a low cost, workers for the state's economy. The governor supplemented his philosophical support for the community colleges with "considerable arm twisting" (Lustberg 1979). The combined force of these appeals proved convincing to many, and Furcolo was aided by an unexpected fiscal surplus in 1958, which did much to offset legislators' fears about increased state spending. Although the bill was initially contested by Republicans in both chambers, it eventually passed the senate by the comfortable margin of thirty-one to four, and the house by a decisive voice vote.

The new act (chap. 605, Acts of 1958) adopted the AAJC's formulation of the colleges' proper mission. Under the act, the community colleges were legally designated as "comprehensive" institutions combining "liberal arts, vocational-technical, and adult education." The law also required the colleges to be provided at low cost to both the students and the taxpayers and to be located close to regional population centers. Responsibility for the system was delegated to a statewide coordinating board of appointed trustees, designated the Massachusetts Board of Regional Community Colleges (MBRCC).

The Composition of the Board

In choosing his fifteen-member Board, Furcolo remembered looking for "active, energetic do-ers" who would "build confidence in the system" (Furcolo, quoted in Lustberg, 1979, p. 130). Thus Furcolo's Board was composed mainly of educational administrators, businessmen, and members of his own staff. Numerically, educational administrators dominated the first Board. The presidents of the University of Massachusetts, Salem State Teacher's College, New Bedford Institute of Technology, and Wellesley College were among the first appointees, as was the state's commissioner of education, Owen Kiernan. Three of the governor's close advisers were also selected: John Mallan, Kermit Morrissey, and Seymour Harris. Morrissey, a dean at Brandeis University, and Harris, an economist at Harvard University, had academic as well as governmental connections. The remainder represented other constituencies whose support Furcolo wanted to enlist for the community colleges: Robert Cutler, president of Old Colony Trust, William Belanger, president of the Massachusetts AFL-CIO, and Gwen Woods, executive secretary of the Massachusetts Congress of Parents and Teachers. Although Putnam and Kermit Morrissey remained influential board members for many years, many others served only briefly.[4]

Businessmen and educators on the Board worked closely together. As Furcolo had hoped, members of the Board tended to view one another as people capable of "getting things done." Members of the Board shared, above all, a strong commitment to the signature elements of managerial culture: efficiency and productivity. Even the chair did not escape the Board's impatience with those who failed to fit the prevailing style. "The Board really didn't need a genteel man like Roger Putnam as chairman," Morrissey recalled. High praise was reserved for those who were regarded as results-oriented, hard-headed and effective.[5] The only dissident member was Commissioner of Education Owen Kiernan, who wanted his office to coordinate many specific development activities, but he soon resigned (Lustberg 1979). Kiernan resigned from the Board after other Board members began to show impatience with his querulousness.[6] Interestingly, the Board's minutes reveal no disagreements on matters of educational substance and, indeed, few discussions of such matters.

The First Tasks of the Board

The Board's first tasks were to build support for the colleges and to arrange for the opening of the first campuses.[7] Legislative influence contributed to these first location decisions. Community representatives rarely approached the Board spontaneously with a proposal for founding a college. Nor were the Board's promotional efforts typically detached. Instead, powerful legislators on the House or Senate Ways and Means Committees bargained for campuses for their districts, and Board members followed through on these proposals by working to stimulate local interest in the legislators' districts.[8]

The location of the first college in the relatively isolated Berkshire mountain town of Pittsfield discharged the Board's debt to Pittsfield's representative, Thomas Wojtkowski, a member of the state house Ways and Means Committee, who had been helpful in the original debate on the community college bill. The next college went to the also sparsely populated Cape Cod region, a district represented by Edward Stone, the leading Republican on the state senate Ways and Means Committee. Most of the subsequent location decisions followed the same pattern, with the chair of the state senate Ways and Means Committee securing a college for his Worcester constituency, and other key senate committee members gaining commitments for their communities (see Lustberg 1979, p. 145).[9]

In the local communities, the Board's promotional efforts were usually channeled through the major economic interests and most often through the local chambers of commerce. There were practical political reasons for this: the leading businessmen were often the most influential forces in local political affairs. If they could be convinced of a project's usefulness, the project stood a good chance of acceptance. But the Board also saw the economic appeal the colleges might have for employers. The colleges were promoted for their potential not only to bring new customers to local business but also to provide better and more cheaply trained workers. The Massachusetts experience paralleled experiences in other states— educators sought business support far more than vice versa. In no case did local businessmen from the beginning identify community colleges as promising vehicles for training their workers. As Thomas Wojtkowski, who helped lead the Pittsfield campaign, put it: "The only way that community colleges could be sold in communities was by convincing business leaders that [they were] . . . an investment and not an expense . . . [that] there [would] be economic returns" (Wojtkowski, quoted in Lustberg 1979, p. 151).

Once convinced that it had an interest in community colleges, local business then became an active source of support. One study suggests that chambers of commerce were important to five of the first eight college foundings (Lustberg 1979, pp. 102–158). In two other cases, prominent business corporations or business families were the leading advocates.[10] By contrast, local educators, civic groups, and municipal officials, though rarely absent from the colleges' promotional and planning activities, usually played a secondary role.[11]

Defining a Philosophy

Only after the issues of financing and location were resolved did the Board pay much attention to matters of educational philosophy. On the few occasions when these issues were raised, the Board signaled its interest in moving toward a vocationally oriented program. All of those invited to speak at the Board's first formal meetings in 1959 were men closely associated with the meriotocratic philosophies of the Cold War era, philosophies revolving around the twin themes of expansion and differentiation of higher education.

At the Board's fourth meeting, for example, former Harvard president James B. Conant, whose views on community colleges we examined in Chapter 3, recommended the institution of the "California system" of higher education in Massachusetts. Conant said he recommended this system primarily because it had worked in California to increase access to higher education while keeping transfer from the lower tiers to a minimum. Under the California system, Conant noted approvingly, no more than 12.5 percent of high school students entering the community colleges would "end up in the third year of the university." The rest would be diverted through attrition or curricular tracking (Massachusetts Board of Regional Community Colleges, "Minutes" 1959). At the Board's fifth meeting, AAJC president Edmund J. Gleazer, Jr. spoke of the need for a "strong, adequate program in vocational and technical education" to feed the Massachusetts economy with a "continued supply of trained technicians and skilled workers" (Massachusetts Board of Regional Community Colleges, "Minutes" 1959).

Even at this early date, the Board indicated an interest in designing curricula to meet the labor demands of local businesses. The Board's emphasis on reaching out to business was perhaps most apparent in its 1959 "Guide Sheet to Preparation of a Regional Survey," which it distributed to all community groups interested in helping found new colleges (Massachusetts Board of Regional Community Colleges 1959). The guide proposed that representatives of a wide variety of local groups be included on working committees to explore community support for a new college, but it emphasized the priority of business representation. It also stressed the need for assessing the labor requirements of local businesses and industries. Once campuses were established, advisory groups composed mainly of local businessmen should be created to advise on the development of new programs and the administration of existing ones.

The late development of the Massachusetts system is perhaps largely responsible for the Board's apparent consensus on educational priorities. At the time the Board members were beginning to discuss educational planning, a national climate of opinion had already formed regarding the proper role and function of community colleges. By 1959, the battles in the AAJC between traditionalists and vocationalizers were well on their way to being resolved in favor of the vocational wing. The AAJC had not only gained a high degree of internal consensus regarding the need for more vocational programs, but it was also beginning to attract external sources of support for that view.

Gaining Respectability Through Liberal Arts

Given the Board's curricular preferences, it may seem surprising that the colleges themselves initially concentrated on developing liberal arts rather than occupational programs. Little real contradiction existed, however. Key Board members and campus officials understood clearly that the legitimacy of the colleges depended on their acceptance as institutions of higher education, which meant their offering liberal arts courses closely resembling those offered in four-year colleges and universities. As Kermit Morrissey recalled, "Liberal arts gave respectability—the stamp of legitimacy. The standards for higher education in Massachusetts were the standards of private colleges. . . . A six-week training program for secretaries would not have been regarded as higher education. The transfer part had to be nailed down first." [12] Others close to the Board at the time confirmed the members' awareness that transfer programs were a first priority in Massachusetts, where private liberal arts training had great prestige and students' images of college centered on the type of education offered at those institutions. [13]

Funding and facilities constraints served as a second brake on the development of the occupational programs. The temporary facilities in which the colleges were first located were not suitable for the laboratories and workshops required for vocational programs. The new colleges had to accommodate themselves to available spaces in converted high schools, abandoned college buildings, a former town hall, and a civil defense facility. In addition, the colleges' budgets during the first several years were low enough to discourage any ideas the Board might have had about buying expensive equipment for new occupational programs. Faced with the

Table 5-2. Enrollments in Vocational and Nonvocational
Programs, Massachusetts Community Colleges, Selected Years,
1964–1970

Year	Percentage Nonvocational[a]	Percentage Vocational
1964	85	15
1966	67	33
1968	60	40
1970	55	45

[a]The nonvocational column includes both transfer and general educational enrollment.

Sources: Interview with William Dwyer February 9, 1979; Putnam 1970; Massachusetts Board of Regional Community Colleges, "Enrollment Statistics" 1970.

constraints of low budgets and temporary facilities, the campus presidents found
transfer programs most economical. Arthur Haley, the first president of Mount
Wachusett Community College, recalled: "When I came in 1963, we were located
in an old high school in the city of Gardner. It was a small facility with high
ceilings and square classrooms. Under these circumstances, the cheapest, easiest
program to offer is transfer. . . . The lead time is small for liberal arts. . . . By
contrast, building new labs takes awhile."[14] The executive director of the Board's
central office staff recalled that the colleges had resources to allow for only a
handful of vocational programs: "a few secretarial and business programs, but not
much else."[15]

The students' preferences during this period reinforced the prevailing liberal
arts–transfer orientation (see Table 5-2). In the first few years, some 80 percent
of Massachusetts's community college students enrolled in transfer programs
(Massachusetts Board of Regional Community Colleges, "Enrollment & Statistics," 1960–1964).

The Board's minutes show no appeals by students or their parents for more
occupationally oriented curricula. Indeed, community college administrators recognized from the start that their students' high aspirations posed serious problems
for the future of the comprehensive program they hoped to develop. Thomas
O'Connell, the first president of Berkshire Community College, recalled many
early students requesting that he shorten the name of the college from Berkshire
Community College to Berkshire College, so as to make it seem more like a
"real" college: "The early students just didn't know what a career program was.
For them, college meant a baccalaureate. Every one of them assumed they would
be in a transfer program."[16] The students, according to O'Connell, suffered from
lack of direction: "A big percentage might really have been undecided, but all of
them thought their goals were transfer."[17] Another president recalled that "all the
students seemed to want to be doctors and lawyers."[18] In characteristic AAJC
phrasing, Gordon Pyle, a director of educational planning in the central office,
attributed early student resistance to a "cultural bias."[19] against occupational programs.[20]

If anything, the faculty in those years wanted the schools to resemble four-year institutions even more than the students did. Many of the staff at Berkshire, O'Connell remembered, thought of themselves as academic professionals, and they wanted their institutions and their students to resemble those they had known in graduate school. The community college faculty in Massachusetts were highly educated: in 1965–1966, 93 percent had advanced degrees, and 100 percent had at least bachelor's degrees. Nearly one-quarter either had a Ph.D or were actively working toward one (Deyo 1967, p. 13). It thus should come as no surprise that, in Gordon Pyle's words, "when we tried to introduce career programs, the staff reacted like we were tearing the ivy off their walls." [21]

The Dwyer Administration and the Rise of Vocational Education

Defoliation began in earnest in mid-1964. In May 1964, the Board requested that the assembly of campus presidents study the role of community colleges in technical and vocational education. The board specifically asked the presidents for recommendations from which it could "move toward further development in this important area" (Massachusetts Board of Regional Community Colleges, "Minutes" 1964). In the June meeting, the Board members received the AAJC's recommendations for building vocational education in the form of Norman Harris's guide, *Technical Education in the Junior College.*

During the spring of 1964, the Board also began its search for a new chief executive officer, and here too it indicated its growing interest in vocationalization. By July, it had decided on a candidate: William Dwyer, president of Orange Community College in New York. A graduate of Phillips Academy (Andover) and Dartmouth, Dwyer had worked in community college systems for twenty years, gaining a reputation as an energetic, vocationally oriented administrator.

Dwyer remembered thinking that his reputation would be held against him in Massachusetts:

> I had written some articles on the need for a comprehensive program. I gave them to the Board chairman and told him to have the Board read them. If the Board agreed unanimously (with the position presented in the articles), I said I would come up and talk with the Board. I thought that was the last I would hear from them. . . . [I was convinced that] they felt educational respectability came from the liberal arts. [22]

To his surprise, he was invited to speak to the Board and hired soon afterward. As the Board chairman Kermit Morrissey remembered it, there was no disagreement on Dwyer's appointment. "There was no dissension on hiring William Dwyer. It was a unanimous vote to bring him in. . . . We knew damn well that we needed career programs" [23]

The articles Dwyer submitted to the Board laid out the direction he could be expected to provide:

> The desire to emulate the first two years of a private liberal-arts college, the disregard for the implications of "post-secondary education," the struggle for

status on the terms of a four-year college rather than on those of a community college—all these are trends which our institutions must combat more effectively. . . . With expanded enrollments, great attention must be directed to the student who will terminate his college career after two years, and constant attention must be directed to qualification he needs for immediate employment. Since business and industry are rapidly eliminating the unskilled worker, post-secondary training and education will be more necessary in the future if the student is to qualify for the job or if he is to meet successfully the competition of the applicants who will be available. . . . The satisfying future of thousands of high school graduates rests with how effectively community colleges become truly comprehensive. The needs of industry and business on state and national levels, and the needs of human beings, can and should determine our programs. (Dwyer 1964, pp. 1–2)

Dwyer's statement encapsulated many of the themes of the community college movement during the mid-sixties. It adhered to the AAJC's strategy of avoiding direct competition with four-year colleges and accepting subordination in return for a distinctive function outside the academic hierarchy. It also pointed to a new type of society requiring training for increasingly complex technological jobs. Finally, it suggested a natural correspondence between business and human needs.

Although recognizing that the idea of vocationalization was already in the air, Dwyer credited himself with providing the necessary momentum to implement the policy in Massachusetts. "The Board wasn't necessarily opposed to a comprehensive program," he recalled, "I would say that it was more that they didn't know exactly what they wanted. They needed direction." [24]

Controlling the Presidencies

Dwyer clearly did not approve of some of the community college presidents that the Board hired during the first five years. For example, the president of Berkshire Community College, Thomas O'Connell, had been trained in English and had worked in the Dartmouth College administration. In his book, *Community Colleges: A President's View* (1968), O'Connell emphasized an image of community colleges as miniature liberal arts colleges for the socially disadvantaged. According to Dwyer: "Berkshire was academically oriented. This was because of the president. . . . We're friends now, but if you read his reminiscences . . . which helped give us a lousy reputation . . . you will see that his philosophy was very different. He didn't see the community colleges as service institutions." [25] Although the increasingly cooperative O'Connell remained at Berkshire, some presidents who were out of step chose to leave and were replaced by men from business or secondary school backgrounds. This happened, for example, at Cape Cod, where Carl Nickerson of the New Haven Railroad replaced the historian Irving Bartlett in 1965, and at Greenfield Community College, where former high school principal Lewis Turner assumed the presidency following the departure of Walter Taylor.

Most of the other presidents quickly fell into line. As Dwyer remembered it, this was due to a natural process of "emulation." "Enrollments grew very fast at the comprehensive institutions. I would have presidents call me and say, 'Hey, I feel I'm being outdone by this new guy. . . .' I would say, 'Get yourself some new deans who will go out and develop some programs.' " [26] Berkshire President O'Connell recalled that the "emulation" process was not quite as natural as Dwyer remembered: "Bill Dwyer was experienced and respected. . . . We picked up leadership from him in this respect. . . . If a president wasn't moving in the right direction, Bill would have moved them in the right direction." [27]

O'Connell and most of the other presidents soon became enthusiastic converts to the occupational programs: "One picked up quickly and became excited by the prospects of community colleges. . . . The impetus was to start (occupational programs). It was the exciting thing to do. We were starting programs as quickly as we could in the early and late 1960s." [28]

At meetings of the presidents' assembly, O'Connell recalled that Dwyer made a point of praising those presidents whose institutions were moving most rapidly toward building occupational programs. According to another president, Arthur Haley of Mount Wachusett, Dwyer used the presidents' assembly meetings and individual conferences to offer information on occupational programs, to talk about his experiences introducing occupational curricula into Orange County Community College, and to discuss his most recent meetings with vocationally oriented community college officials from other state systems. Sometimes Dwyer was more direct. His advice to James Hall, hired to head Cape Cod Community College, was unmistakable: "It's a marvelous little Harvard there," Hall recalled Dwyer saying. "Your job is to bring some balance." [29]

The Dynamics of Expansion

The Massachusetts community college system grew briskly in the 1960s. Eight colleges were opened in the first five years, and five more followed by 1970. Five of the colleges were located within commuting distance of Boston—one each in the northern suburbs of Beverly and Bedford, one in working-class Brockton to the south, and one in Plymouth County also to the south, and one in the western suburb of Watertown (see Figure 5-1). Other major population centers in the state— Springfield and Worcester—were also serviced by a community college and, in the case of Springfield, by two. Other community colleges were located in the Berkshire Mountains, Cape Cod, western rural Greenfield, the populous Merrimack Valley region of the northeast, and north central Gardner. Only the sparsely populated southwestern region lacked a community college.

Enrollments shot up in Massachusetts, just as they did in other parts of the country. The system opened with 151 day students at Berkshire in 1960 and grew to 3,650 students by 1965, after the first four schools had opened; this figure represented a 13 percent share of total public higher education enrollments in Massachusetts (Murphy 1974, p. 87). By 1971, the day enrollments were up to 21,300, or one-quarter of all public enrollments. Massachusetts community colleges were not entirely "open admissions." Because of budget restrictions, the colleges either squeezed in applicants or operated on a first-come, first-served basis (Asquino 1976, p. 28). But the admission requirements were not stringent. During a period when the state colleges doubled in size and the university grew

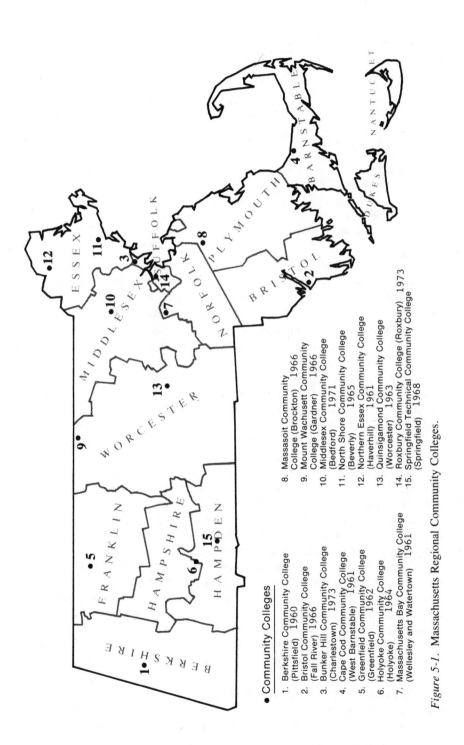

• Community Colleges

1. Berkshire Community College
   (Pittsfield) 1960
2. Bristol Community College
   (Fall River) 1966
3. Bunker Hill Community College
   (Charlestown) 1973
4. Cape Cod Community College
   (West Barnstable) 1961
5. Greenfield Community College
   (Greenfield) 1962
6. Holyoke Community College
   (Holyoke) 1964
7. Massachusetts Bay Community College
   (Wellesley and Watertown) 1961

8. Massasoit Community
   College (Brockton) 1966
9. Mount Wachusett Community
   College (Gardner) 1966
10. Middlesex Community College
    (Bedford) 1971
11. North Shore Community College
    (Beverly) 1965
12. Northern Essex Community College
    (Haverhill) 1961
13. Quinsigamond Community College
    (Worcester) 1963
14. Roxbury Community College (Roxbury) 1973
15. Springfield Technical Community College
    (Springfield) 1968

Figure 5-1. Massachusetts Regional Community Colleges.

153

Table 5-3. Background Characteristics of Students in Massachusetts Public Higher Education by Tier, 1976–1977 (in percentages)

Family Income (annual)	Community Colleges	State Colleges	University of Massachusetts
Over $15,000	16	24	40
Under $15,000	84	76	60
Father's Occupation[a]			
Professional/managerial	29	N.A.	66
Other white-collar	33	N.A.	18
Blue-collar	35	N.A.	14
Retired/unemployed	3	N.A.	2

[a]Community College data calculated from studies on three campuses: Bunker Hill, Middlesex, and Quinsigamond. All studies were from 1976–1977.

N.A.: Data not available.

by two and a half times, the community colleges' full-time enrollments multiplied sevenfold. Moreover, in many of the schools, the number of part-time and continuing education students equaled or surpassed the number of full-time day students. Several of the campuses quickly enrolled 1,500 and more.

There is little mystery regarding the colleges' popularity, given the increasing importance of higher education in occupational placement, the limited room available in the higher tiers, and the large number of people graduating each year from the state's high schools. At the same time, the community colleges clearly offered some special attractions to students. Annual fees remained at under $400 throughout the 1960s (OSTI 1973), and during the first six years, the tuition was only $200 (Deyo 1967). Aptitude tests were never required for admission, and campuses were located within commuting distance of nearly all Massachusetts's high school graduates. Many students also apparently approved of the colleges' tolerance of discontinuities in attendance and changes in status between full-time and part-time enrollment. Indeed, by the mid-1960s, more students were applying for admission than could be accommodated.

Most of the students who attended the Massachusetts community colleges were from lower white-collar and upper blue-collar families. Very few came from professional or higher managerial backgrounds, and few came from families headed by unskilled laborers. Minority enrollment was miniscule. Reflecting on his experience a teacher at a community college north of Boston, Richard Talbot (1978, p. 8) observed, "Contrary to popular belief, few lower-class individuals or minorities attended the college at all; mostly white . . . [ethnics] predominated." Another observer of the period noted that a large majority of community college students were "the first in their families to attend college" (O'Connell 1968). As Table 5-3 indicates, lower middle–class and upper working–class students continued to be characteristic of the community colleges in later years. In contrast, students enrolled in the University of Massachusetts came from markedly higher socioeconomic backgrounds.[30]

Charles Monroe's summary of national patterns is consistent with the data from Massachusetts:

Community college students are from the homes of neither the very rich nor the very poor. They tend to come from the lower middle–income homes, definitely lower than the homes of university students. Typical community college students in large urban centers are the children of third-generation Americans of European background who have become skilled laborers, low-level supervisors, and industrial managers, and who have aspirations that their children will become the first college graduates in their families. [These families] find it difficult to send their children away to college but want them to join the white-collar and professional ranks. (Monroe 1972, pp. 185–186)

As new campuses opened, Dwyer invited men who were friendly to his philosophy to join the system. When North Shore College College opened in 1965, Dwyer invited his former dean at Orange Community College, Harold Shively, to apply, and Shively was eventually offered the job. "I didn't guarantee jobs," Dwyer said, "but many of the people I contacted did receive offers".[31] The following year, two long-time acquaintances of Dwyer's, John Musselman and Jack Hudnall, also received offers. In later years, jobs were given to other community college and technical educators and to the retiring speaker of the Massachusetts House of Representatives. According to Dwyer, there was one important thread uniting these appointments—commitment to the vocationalizing philosophy: "The one thing that united all the presidents was that they all believed in a comprehensive community college. They were all sound philosophically. All had been in top positions—deans or top administrators. . . . At all of the campuses the presidents were committed to developing comprehensive institutions."[32]

Expanding the Options for Vocational Training

The Board's first major policy statement on occupational programs was drafted by Dwyer and passed by the Board in early 1965. The statement defined the community colleges' interest in "occupational education" as relating to "the 'upper' level of the total spectrum of vocational education, including technical and semi-professional programs in engineering, industry, business, service occupations (including government and public administration), agriculture/marine, and health-related occupations" (Massachusetts Board of Regional Community Colleges 1965).

The Board's master plan, written in 1965 and 1966, also called for the colleges' rapid vocationalization. The language here was relatively blunt: "The curriculum offerings of the state-wide community college system should reflect the occupational needs of the Commonwealth and of the placement market adjacent thereto." (Deyo 1967, p. 9).

In the forty-two page summary of the master plan (most of which concerned cost management and location decisions), four and one-half pages were devoted to occupational education and two paragraphs to liberal arts education (Deyo 1967).

With these guidelines on record, Dwyer and his staff moved quickly to develop vocational curricula. The first seven years of Dwyer's tenure as president of the Board were later described by the state's Board of Higher Education as a period of "indiscriminate expansion" of occupational programs by the community college Board (Massachusetts Board of Regional Community Colleges, "Minutes"

Table 5-4. Programs Approved by the Massachusetts Board of
Regional Community Colleges, 1965–1971

Year	Occupational Programs	Transfer Programs
1965	6	0
1966	13	1
1967	17	0
1968	33	2
1969	35	4
1970	22	3
1971	43	2

Source: Massachusetts Board of Regional Community Colleges, "Minutes," 1965–
1971.

1971). During this period, the Board aproved 169 "career" programs and 12
liberal arts–transfer programs (see Table 5-4), an average of 14 occupational programs approved to each liberal arts–transfer program (calculated from Massachusetts Board of Regional Community Colleges, "Minutes," 1965–1971).

Technician training programs comprised the largest part of the new vocational
offerings, accounting for 23 percent of the total number of occupational programs
by 1971. Business administration programs accounted for another one-fifth of
the total. The remainder of the programs were divided among five categories:
semiprofessional (9 percent of the 1971 total), government service (12 percent),
clerical (16 percent), craft (4 percent), and professionals' aides (16 percent).

Most of the presidents—at least those who had had community college experience—knew that the building of vocational programs started with a set of inexpensive, highly marketable programs, including business and accounting programs, secretarial programs, electrical technology programs, and, sometimes, nursing
and health technology programs. "These," said President James Hall of Cape
Cod Community College, "were the things you would start automatically." [33]
Once these "standard" programs were in place, the presidents began to look toward
developing technical programs related to new industries in their regions.

Dwyer emphasized the need for labor projections and for working with local
employers so as to develop programs that would lead to more employment opportunities. But most campuses paid relatively little attention to employers' suggestions or market projections. Mount Wachusett president Arthur Haley recalled that
the times encouraged the feeling that new programs "couldn't miss": "With enrollments burgeoning, we felt whatever we offered would catch on." [34] Only a
few areas were avoided: those in which there was no book-based learning tradition, in which markets were thought to be too small to support the costs of staff
and equipment or in which employers or labor unions already offered their own
training programs.

The community colleges advertised their commitment to "serving the needs
of the community" and welcomed program suggestions from all interested parties.
At many campuses, the presidents themselves helped create the programs. At others, program suggestions typically came from individual staff members and occa-

sionally from local businessmen. General Electric managers, for example, approached Thomas O'Connell about an electronics technology program for Berkshire, and the West Barnstable Chamber of Commerce talked to community college officials about initiating a hotel/motel management program.[35]

Whatever the source of the suggestion, if college officials sensed a market, they were usually quick to start the planning machinery. The openness of the process is apparent in Dean Frederick Viaux's description of the development of a new course in "packaging machinery technology" at suburban Middlesex Community College near Boston:

> A highly skilled person in our drafting department originally suggested it. He had worked in the field and felt there would be a market. We did a little initial investigating and found that there were 2,000 firms in the immediate area that used packaging machinery. We called up the biggest people in packaging and asked about employment opportunities. When we were satisfied that the opportunities were there, we went ahead and submitted our request to the Board to initiate planning.[36]

The expansion of the occupational programs, of course, was an essential first step in strengthening the colleges' vocational programs. Board members assumed that the students' preferences would eventually follow course offerings, rather than vice versa. Erroll Jacobsen, the long-time head of the Board's committee on educational policy, summarized the Board's outlook: "Students go to the programs that are there . . . if the programs are there, students will enroll in them."[37] Few statements indicate as clearly how little faith the Board had in consumer choice as a source of change.

Budgetary Incentives and Disincentives for Vocationalization

The administrators were impeded somewhat in their efforts to vocationalize by persistently tight budgets. The Commonwealth of Massachusetts provided a little over two-thirds of the costs per student, with the remainder paid by the students themselves as tuition. In the 1960s, state appropriations were low compared with both per-student expenditures in the state colleges and universities and expenditures in some other state systems. Per-student expenditures in the community colleges were only about one-third the sum received by the public universities and a little over half the sum received by the state colleges.

In the mid-1960s, a number of states supported community colleges at a rate of $900 or more per student. In Massachusetts, the rate was $635 (Deyo 1967, p. 15).[38] Although just below the national average at the time, this figure was even lower than it appeared, considering that the system was a new one, with new building and equipment requirements.

Restricted budgets limited the vocationalization project in obvious ways. Plans for new facilities were left on the drawing board, and much-needed equipment for the technical programs remained unpurchased. Between 1959 and 1966, for example, provisions were made to support only two professional staff positions in the central office: one executive director and one assistant to the director. No funds were authorized for positions pertaining to institutional resources, curricular development, business and finance, liaison with state agencies, planning, or personnel. Dwyer and his assistant handled each of these functions themselves in addition to routine administration. Thus the "system" was less a system than a federation of more or less autonomous regional facilities (see Deyo 1967, pp. 34–39).

At the same time, some state budget procedures may have encouraged vocationalization, at least indirectly. Unlike the situation in many state systems, community college budgets in Massachusetts were not explicitly enrollment driven. Instead, budget requests were based on student–faculty ratio guidelines sent to the colleges by the Massachusetts Board of Regional Community Colleges staff. In computing these ratios, central office staff assigned lower ratios to occupational programs than to liberal arts programs. Nursing programs, for example, were assigned a ratio of ten students to one instructor. Technical programs, like electronics technology, were assigned a ratio of fifteen to one, later dropped in some cases to thirteen to one. Liberal arts programs started at an eighteen-to-one ratio and gradually increased to twenty-one to one. These computations were meant to take into account the more individualized supervision expected in the occupational programs and also the higher costs of operating many of them.[39]

On some of the campuses, the program-based budgeting process provided a subtle incentive to develop occupational curricula, as additional resources could be most reliably guaranteed by offering new programs or expanding old programs with low assigned ratios. As one dean observed,[40] "That's the way things grew. You grew through new programs. The budgetary process encouraged you to add occupational programs."[41]

All new requests had to be justified, and the central office often refused to allow new resources if it doubted the strength of either student or employer demand.[42] Nevertheless, campus officials found budget requests to support growth in the occupational programs "easier to defend" than other requests were, because the decision makers accorded them special preference.

After appropriations were made, the colleges enjoyed considerable fiscal autonomy. This meant that funds could be transferred readily from surplus to deficit accounts. Administrators in most of the campuses used their fiscal autonomy to help build the more expensive occupational programs. Few state agencies enjoyed as much fiscal autonomy as did the higher educational institutions, and therefore few had as much potential for shaping their own environments.[43]

Yet despite the community colleges' strong record of growth and appealing programmatic goals, the legislature never treated the colleges as budgetary equals of the other two tiers. Moreover, throughout the 1960s and 1970s, community college administrators were unable to use their budgets as efficient rationalizing instruments because of the ability of powerful legislators to protect the budgeting interests of the community colleges in their districts. Legislators liked to see institutions in their districts well supported, regardless of the content of the programs offered. Budgeting provisions were taken as an indication of legislative clout, and so legislators worried about absolute levels of funding for their home colleges much more than they worried about how the funds were used. Colleges in districts represented by members of the senate and house Ways and Means Committees tended to obtain particularly generous appropriations (on this point, see the discussions in Coles 1977 and Stafford and Lustberg 1978, p. 11).

Although facilities and equipment appropriations remained difficult to obtain, by the end of the 1960s, permanent facilities were under construction at five of the colleges. The new campuses were, for the most part, both spacious and handsome, and indeed the Holyoke facility was noteworthy enough to receive an award for design. Most were set on rolling fields well outside the constricting urban corridors associated with traditional vocational-training institutions. If the community colleges were sold partly on the basis of promised mobility, the aesthetic impact of the campuses themselves were central to the success of the image.[44]

Compared with state appropriations, federal funds represented but a small fraction of the campuses' operating budgets, but they had an influence far out of proportion to their apparent contribution. The PL 90-156 (or vocational education) monies were the most important of these funds.[45] These "voc ed" grants were used as "seed money" to create new occupational programs. With state appropriations usually stretched tight to cover routine expenses, the federal funds quickly became the primary source of program innovation in the system. Their influence was based on the margin of discretion they afforded. Among the several sources of income for the campuses, they could be used exclusively for the kinds of programs that administrators needed to restructure their institutions.

For many years, the vocational education funds, though technically available for two-year colleges, were practically out of reach of the community colleges. Commissioner of Education (and erstwhile community college Board member) Owen Kiernan chose to channel voc ed funds to the state's secondary schools and vocational-technical institutes and away from the community colleges.[46] Kiernan's tight control began to loosen in 1966, when William Dwyer first publicly raised questions about the distribution of federal funds by the Department of Education. Dwyer characterized the subsequent maneuvering as a "tremendous battle for funds": "[In 1966], we got $200,000. I call it hush money. Then the *Globe* and the *Herald* (the major Boston daily newspapers) printed exposes on illegal spending of federal funds in '67. . . . I won't say I had anything to do with those stories. A couple of years after that we were getting over a million a year."[47]

The Quickening Pace of Change

Once Dwyer had secured the first federal monies, the community colleges quickly eclipsed the secondary schools and technical institutes in the competition for vocational education grants. By academic year 1969–1970, the colleges were receiving more than $840,000 in vocational education funds, and a year later they had passed the $1 million mark for the first time. Throughout the rest of the decade the colleges never received less than $1 million annually in vocational education awards (Massachusetts Board of Regional Community Colleges, "Summary," 1969–1979).

At many of the colleges, the development office soon became a magnet for the most energetic administrators. According to Dean Frederick Viaux of Middlesex Community College, the centrality and competitiveness of the work required virtually nonstop proposal writing. Viaux reported a backlog of twenty-five programs on his own shelf, some of which had no chance of approval. His main incentive, he said, was

> a self-protective function. You have to put [proposals] in, so you aren't shut out in case they decide to go ahead. We're in competition with vocational-technical schools, private junior colleges, our sister community colleges, the State universities, and with industry. You have to put a stake in. . . . If you don't do it, industry or some other organization will do it, and we'll be out of business.[48]

Administrators on several campuses estimated that between one-fifth and one-quarter of their occupational programs were developed with the help of federal funds.[49]

Class, Climate, and Consciousness

Although the administrators were often impatient for a more rapid advance, the shift in enrollments toward vocational programs was nevertheless dramatic in the mid- and late 1960s. In the five years between 1964 and 1968, for example, the proportion of community college students enrolled in vocational programs increased from 15 to 40 percent (see Table 5-2).

As was the case nationwide (Cross 1970, Karabel 1972, Pincus 1974), the enrollment in vocational programs in Massachusetts's community colleges was associated with social class background. For example, in a study of the 1972–1973 graduates of Northern Essex Community College, Talbott (1978) found that the children of unskilled and semiskilled blue-collar workers were twice as likely as were the children of professional or managerial workers to have graduated from vocational programs. Minority students were three times as likely as white students were to have graduated from vocational programs. By contrast, over 50 percent of the sons of professional/managerial fathers graduated in liberal arts at the community colleges and went on to four-year colleges (Talbot 1978, pp. 86–95).

Some of the most important differences between community colleges and other institutions of higher education are differences in academic "climate". In educational institutions, climates are largely shaped by differences in the expectations and life circumstances of the student population (Brookover et al. 1973, McDill and Rigsby 1973). A lower-than-average class composition often means that more students are working at least part time and come from less academically oriented backgrounds. Increasing vocationalization also means that more of the students have friends and acquaintances who are not pursuing academic studies.

The influences on the average student with a weak commitment to academic studies may therefore differ sharply in a community college environment from those in a university environment. In a community college, interests in jobs, dating, and family responsibilities—all interests that do not encourage academic concentration—are often the prevailing concerns. In a university, nonacademic interests may be important, but they are part of a larger institutional climate that also encourages academic study (see Boocock 1972, pp. 209–249). At a university, a student's friends are more likely to be committed to finishing school, and none will be studying for a terminal two-year degree. The typical social pressures (the influence of peer interest and activities) at four-year colleges, especially residential ones, are very different from those found in the community colleges. For the average students, institutional climates may weaken or strengthen commitments to serious study or to finishing school (Astin 1977).

In the Massachusetts community colleges, many of these climate factors probably served to weaken students' commitments to academic work. In the mid-1960s, the attrition rate between the fall and the spring term of the freshman year was about 20 percent. Of these who dropped out between semesters, about 65 percent did so because of academic problems, another 25 percent because of economic problems, and 10 percent for personal reasons (Deyo 1967, p. 14). Sophomore classes were typically only about half as large as freshman classes (Deyo 1967, p. 14). It is possible that economic pressures figure heavily in this freshman-to-sophomore-year dropout rate, along with a relative lack of academic interest.

When most students are from working-class and lower middle–class backgrounds, when many are doing poorly in their academic work, and when most are working full or part time, the climate factors are already strongly disposed against serious commitment to college (see London 1978). On top of these powerful influences, increasing vocationalization encourages a further climate change that weakens the average student's commitment to academic study.

The climate effects are somewhat more complex than a simple idea of across-the-board influence would suggest. Given the predominantly nonacademic climates in the colleges, a certain number of community college students will stand out as relatively good and industrious students and get a needed boost they might not have received in a more competitive university environment (Neumann and Riesman 1980). Similarly, a certain number of students in the university will find themselves demoralized by their peers' accomplishments and seriousness, when they might have fared better in a lower-pressure environment. For most students, however, nonacademic climates tend to depress achievement. Such climatic factors may be a major source of the recurrent finding (see Chapter 4) that when compared with four-year institutions, community colleges have negative effects on ultimate educational attainment even after differences in student background and measured ability are statistically equalized.

Patterns of Vocationalization

Not all of the Massachusetts campuses vocationalized at the same rate. By the early 1970s, six of the colleges had approached or surpassed the 50 percent vocational enrollment mark regarded as minimally acceptable by Dwyer and the Board, whereas five others remained under 40 percent vocational. Enrollments at the other colleges hovered around the system mean of 40 percent vocational (see Table 5-5).

No single difference among the schools explains their varying rates of change. Instead, it appears that the crucial factors varied somewhat on the different cam-

Table 5-5. Enrollments in Occupational-Vocational and Nonoccupational-Vocational Programs, Massachusetts Community Colleges, 1970 (as percentage of head-count enrollment)

Campus	Occupational Vocational	Liberal Arts and General Education
Berkshire	36	64
Bristol	45	55
Cape Cod	23	77
Greenfield	49	51
Holyoke	42	58
Mass Bay	37	63
Massasoit	35	65
Middlesex	32	68
Mount Wachusett	33	67
North Shore	53	47
Northern Essex	36	64
Quinsigamond	51	49
Springfield	78	22
Total (*n* = 18,911)	45	55
Total (excluding Springfield)	40	60

Sources: Deyo 1967; Massachusetts Board of Regional Community Colleges, "Enrollment Statistics," 1970.

puses. For example, Springfield Technical Community College was the most heavily vocationalized of the colleges, with a terminal occupational enrollment exceeding 75 percent. This heavy emphasis on vocational training was mandated by law. The law that permitted the absorption of Springfield Technical Institute into the community college system (chap. 273, Acts of 1967) required that the college retain a "primary emphasis" on postsecondary technical education. The Board's interpretation of "primary emphasis" is telling, however. When it joined the system, Springfield enrolled virtually 100 percent of its students in occupational programs, with an especially heavy emphasis on engineering technology. The college then diversified its technical curriculum to include allied health technologies and business administration, but it never achieved a significant liberal arts–transfer enrollment. Indeed, the proportion of liberal arts–transfer students fell gradually from a high of 22 percent in 1970 to just over 6 percent in 1977. Although the board members and central office officials were often critical of colleges they saw as lagging in vocational development, the proportion of transfer students declined at Springfield without a murmur of concern. The Board's treatment of Springfield indicates, perhaps better than any other measure, the willingness of officials to cast aside the rhetoric about comprehensiveness when enrollments tipped in the direction they preferred.

A host of other nonlegal factors shaped the vocationalization rates at the other schools. Energetic presidents working in poor rural or working-class areas were able to build the occupational programs with some dispatch. By 1970, Lewis Turner in rural Greenfield had achieved a high (49 percent) vocational enrollment, and Jack Hudnall in industrial Fall River had also achieved a high (45 percent) vocational enrollment. Indeed, very determined presidents could have an effect, even in schools with relatively high SES student bodies. This appears to be what happened at North Shore (53% vocational in 1970) and Quinsigamond (51% vocational). Less determined presidents with high SES student bodies were less likely to restructure their curricula as quickly. This situation seems to fit the cases of Massasoit in Plymouth County, Berkshire in the Berkshire Mountain resort region surrounding Pittsfield, and Massachusetts Bay in Boston's western suburbs.

Where SES did not have an important effect, local labor market conditions could help depress the vocational enrollment. Cape Cod, for example, had low SES students but unfavorable labor market opportunities. The Cape is essentially a two-industry region, relying on fishing and tourism, and, of the standard community college offerings, only hotel and motel management (and perhaps the business and secretarial programs) complemented local economic strengths.

Yet the differences among the schools should not obscure the impressive uniformity in the direction all were moving. Year by year, the enrollment ratios for virtually all the schools came close to meeting the Board's objectives. By 1970, with the abrupt shift in the college labor market, seven of the colleges had already placed a plurality of students in occupational programs, and two had already placed a clear majority in them.

These changes were created on the campuses through the concerted efforts of top administrators and in the outcomes of thousands of face-to-face encounters between students and staff members. Most of the change up to this point had occurred without significant market pressure. Chapter 6 looks at the mechanisms used by campus administrators and their staffs to build the occupational enrollments before the change in the labor market made it possible to complete the transformation.

6 The Process of Vocationalization: Mechanisms and Structures

An atmosphere of amiable routine now surrounds North Shore Community College in the Boston suburb of Beverly. Still located on a main downtown thoroughfare, as it has been since it opened in 1965, the college serves an economically varied region, including both the affluent oceanside towns of Marblehead, Swampscott, and Gloucester to the north and the chronically depressed old mill towns of Lynn and Peabody to the southwest. By the mid-1980s, enrollments were heavily occupational, and both staff and students seemed to like it that way. "There's more demand than there are seats in the technical programs," said one counselor. "In allied health, there's a very heavy demand—three or four to one. But generally in liberal arts, we can accept people until the first week of classes."[1] The staff tended to view the history of their college as a natural unfolding. "The original intent," observed one dean, "was to provide something for everyone, and that's what we've done."[2]

But vocational education did not always predominate at North Shore. Indeed, in 1965, the college's first year of operation, over 80 percent of North Shore's students were enrolled in liberal arts–transfer programs, and many of the faculty were committed to keeping the college's distinctively academic image. According to one long-time member of the faculty, "At first, some of the faculty . . . had the idea that we were some kind of elitist thing. For them, the important thing was having the smartest students. . . . Quite of few of them were from universities. They didn't know anything about community colleges."[3] "Yes, there were some internal battles," one dean acknowledged. "The occupational programs were a concern to some liberal arts faculty."[4]

The faculty's grumbling had little effect on Harold Shively, the first president of North Shore. Shively, a long-time associate of William Dwyer in New York, shared Dwyer's commitment to building a vocationally oriented system, and he did not wait long to press his plans for transforming North Shore in the direction

164

suggested by this commitment. To the faculty, he repeated the maxims of vocationalization: most students were terminal in fact if not in aspiration; the college had the responsibility to do something for these students; not everyone could be a professional, and most two-year college students would not be; the college should provide something useful to them; and occupational programs were practical and well suited to the abilities and interests of most students. To believe otherwise, Shively argued, was to accept an "elitist" model of the community college that had no place in this most democratic of higher education institutions.

Shively's arguments worked on many. According to one instructor, "Shively was a great leader. He convinced many of those who were initially opposed."[5] Shiveley's friend Bill Dwyer remembered that his former dean "promoted the hell out of career programs. He promoted them for a full year with the faculty and guidance counselors. His attitude was 'I'm going to show those academic birds.' "[6]

Despite the absence of student demand for vocational programs in the early years, Shively worked as aggressively outside the college as inside in his quest for an expanded vocational wing. He spent much of his time evaluating opportunities for new occupational programs and lobbying the legislature to ensure support for his plans. Shively did much of the developmental work himself, relying on the regional economic survey and his experiences in New York as guides to program planning. The head of the Beverly Chamber of Commerce recalled that "Shively knew the needs and demands of the area. He picked courses needed by the community."[7] He also drew in local industrial people. During the first few years, most of the large employers in the area were approached either by Shively or by the Beverly Chamber of Commerce for advice on training needs or course design. The new electronics and research firms on Route 128 to the north and east of Boston were at the time beginning to flourish, and Shively closely followed their progress, consulting with representatives of firms like Bomac, Sarton Engineering and Sylvania, and Ventron, all Route 128 firms.[8]

Gradually, the money to support new programs arrived. "I had good success with the legislature," he said.[9] Building on the standard business and secretarial programs, he soon added curricula in electronics technology, aviation science, and health sciences technology. A key factor contributing to Shively's success was his ability to bring in new faculty. The new faculty contributed not simply by operating the new programs but also by helping shift the balance of opinion toward those sympathetic to vocationalization. In all of his new hiring—for both vocational and nonvocational faculty—Shively looked for people who accepted his philosophy. Willingness to endorse the principles of a comprehensive program thus became an implicit criterion for hiring.[10] Shively further encouraged philosophical consensus by combining liberal arts and occupational functions in the administrative structure and avoided naming separate deans of technical and liberal arts education. Instead, all divisions mixed the two emphases. "You don't get them thinking like rivals that way," he said.[11]

But there was never a real battle against vocationalization at North Shore. Although some of the faculty disagreed with Shively, none mounted an active protest against him. Indeed, those who disagreed did not stay at North Shore for long. Once they understood that the administration's view of the functions of a two-year college differed from their own, they simply departed for what they hoped would be more congenial jobs. According to mathematics instructor Henry Hammerling, the dissidents "didn't last long in the community college environment. Once we shook the faculty down . . . all of us started to take great pride in our occupational programs. . . . It just took a while to get the faculty acclimated." [12]

Many of those who were not happy at the time were Ph.D.s and Hammerling recalled that many divisions created informal policies to discourage their hiring: "The doctorate [got] to be almost a detriment. . . . We wouldn't blackball a guy because he had a Ph.D. We hired one or two, but we'd rather have a guy who had a master's and really wanted to teach and counsel students." [13]

According to Dwyer, "After the first year, [Shively] couldn't beat the system average [for occupational enrollment], but he turned over the soil." [14] Before long, Shively's North Shore campus was a system leader in occupational enrollment, and Shively himself had gained a reputation among his fellow presidents as a top-performing activist to be emulated. [15] In the first five years after 1965, the college increased its occupational enrollment by 30 percent. By 1971—before the decline in labor market opportunities for graduates of four-year colleges—nearly half of its students were enrolled in the technical programs (Massachusetts Regional Board of Community Colleges, "Enrollment Statistics," 1971).

Without Shively's efforts, it is unlikely that vocationalization could have progressed as rapidly or as far as it did at North Shore. His program additions were carefully researched, and he worked hard to gain the respect and cooperation of local business people. Oscar Olsen, head of the Beverly Chamber of Commerce, recalled that "there was a lot of enthusiasm from the beginning" for the college, and that Shively was "very aggressive" in building on that support by expanding "to include [programs in] areas where there was a need for more personnel." [16] Shively also introduced counseling and academic advising programs to inform students about the new programs, and he made sure that his appointments included persons committed to the vocationalizing policy.

In many ways, Shively's techniques were representative of those used by top administrators throughout the Massachusetts system in their efforts to transform their campuses. Few schools showed changes as dramatic as those at North Shore in the years before 1971, but nearly all used similar practices to move in the same direction.

The Dynamics of Vocationalization

Several mechanisms helped expand the number and size of vocational programs in Massachusetts's community colleges. At the state level, as we showed in Chapter 5, these mechanisms included control of the presidencies of the individual campuses and the use of budgetary instruments favoring the occupational programs. At the campus level, there were five important mechanisms: (1) Presidential powers governed hiring and staff socialization and eventually led to a climate favorable to vocationalization on all campuses. (2) Guidance counseling helped channel students into the new programs created not in response to student demand but to administrative initiative. (3) Enrollment ceilings and other structural barriers were imposed on at least a few campuses to limit movement from program to program or to limit enrollments in liberal arts–transfer programs. (4) Vocational education was promoted on some campuses to rescue marginal programs and also to help build support for the programs in general. And (5) the establishment of exchange relationships with local employers raised the status of vocational programs and held out the promise that jobs would be available to students after they graduated.

The Use of Presidential Powers

The example of Shively illustrates that executive director William Dwyer's emphasis on controlling the campus presidencies was not misplaced. The presidencies were strategically located for the transmission of influence from the central office to the campuses, and they were also invaluable sources of local information and expertise. The Board wanted men (no women were appointed president) who could become experts on the needs of their local communities. Over the first several years, they hired men who shared Dwyer's philosophy and then gave them more or less free rein (within budgetary limits) to implement that philosophy as they saw fit.

The president's powers were extensive and were used to promote the Board's policy. Perhaps most importantly, the presidents had the power to decide the direction of program development by encouraging or vetoing program ideas and by putting together new programs themselves. Not all presidents were as aggressive as Harold Shively was in canvassing the community for marketable ideas, but virtually all used their powers to speed planning and development activity. Some did so by hiring aggressive new deans, others by consulting with their advisory boards, and still others by drawing on their own experience.

The new programs alone could not ensure the staff's commitment to the colleges' mission, and indeed they could have encouraged a hostile reaction among some academically oriented faculty. To build staff commitment, therefore, the presidents used their powers of recruitment and their ability to influence the faculty's values.

The power to hire new staff was particularly critical. Because the presidents of the campuses approved the hiring of all new faculty and administrative staff, they were often able to avoid internal conflict simply by hiring men and women who were willing to go along with the vocationalizing plans generated at higher levels. Like Shively, several of the presidents used the hiring interviews to test the applicants' educational philosophies. As John Musselman, the first president of Massasoit Community College, recalled, 'I employed all of the faculty. This was a great advantage. . . . I could sound them out first to see if they were really interested in being in a community college setting.''[17] As in many other states, many applicants to the community colleges in Massachusetts were high school teachers desiring ''to upgrade themselves'' and consequently happy ''to say whatever they thought would go over well.''[18] The tight college teaching market in

Massachusetts may also have helped ensure compliance with administrative policies.

The presidents emphasized both the economic demand for occupational training and the students' interest in an education that would prepare them for work. They drew on their faculty members' hesitations about the academic preparation of students to contend that only a few students could compete effectively in the senior colleges. Using an argument made, ironically, by critics of the community colleges, some presidents also reasoned that if the colleges refused to provide curricula suitable to the students' real interests, the open-door colleges would become "revolving-door" colleges.

These were already standard elements of the AAJC's vocationalizing ideology. In Massachusetts, some less standard elements were also used. Perhaps because of the state's history of class and ethnic antagonisms, the charge of elitism was an especially important feature of the campaign to vocationalize. Indeed on many campuses, this charge was used against any member of the staff or faculty suspected of not identifying with the vocationalizing policy. For example, Dwyer's education-planning director, Gordon Pyle, used it to criticize academically oriented faculty in two of the campuses: "At Cape Cod and Berkshire, there's a lot of Harvard grads, and they don't like greasy hands-on programs."[19] Anthony Cotoia, a dean of continuing education, used the hint of elitism to question the goals of some administrators: "At Mass Bay, they felt courses on how to buy a house were below their dignity."[20] Others used anti-elitism to sanction the community colleges' alternatives to the standard curriculum: "We took the opposite approach to the elitist schools," said one former counselor, "we gave the customer what he wanted and what he needed."[21]

In the absence of a well-developed counterideology, the presidents' time-tested messages could hardly help but sound convincing. The traditional academic ideology, with its emphasis on the capacity-building benefits of a liberal arts education, briefly served as a plausible alternative. But the teachers' meritocratic commitments soon ran into conflict with their humanistic ideals. In his ethnography of Bunker Hill Community College, Howard London (1978) captured much of the sense of disappointment that prevailed among liberal arts teachers at many of the community colleges. Many of the teachers spoke of a conflict between their initial hopes for their students and the realities of their academic performances in the community college environment. One social science teacher explained: "I think I didn't quite anticipate what I call morale problems among the students. Their absenteeism is greater than I expected and they have a lot more difficulty tuning in" (quoted in London 1978, p. 121). A science teacher expressed the same kind of disappointment more bluntly: "It's not easy for me to relate to them as people. If I met them on the street or any place else the problem would still exist. There is a gap between the intellectual academic community and the way that they operate" (quoted in London 1978, p. 120).

As it became apparent that many students were either unable or disinclined to spend much time in school, liberal arts teachers sometimes reluctantly began to see positive virtues in the seemingly practical orientation of the comprehensive model. As one said: "I do not think that the primary purpose of the community college is to get these kids ready for a job. I think that that is a secondary purpose, but an important one. But I think that the primary purpose is to prepare them to be willing to take a job and to work with it but not as an end in itself'' (interview with a Bunker Hill English teacher, quoted in London 1978, p. 123). Other teachers had still lower expectations:

> I think one job of the community college is to enrich the community by providing vocational jobs which would enrich it economically and by giving back to the community people who are just a little bit more capable of filling community needs; and so that we send people back . . . with an understanding of what the issues are, or what to ask the candidate running for office, or why it's a good idea to help the policeman on the beat . . . or what they should ask for their children in the way of child care, or health care or school care. And I think we're capable of doing that. (interview with Bunker Hill history teacher, quoted in London 1978, p. 122)

By contrast, to many the liberal arts model appeared increasingly impractical and utopian.

One other aspect of the presidential role encouraged staff compliance as well. In Massachusetts, a good deal of uncertainty always surrounded state appropriations. Consequently, the faculty had reason to fear capricious legislative actions, even though the colleges were growing. The presidents typically did not use their own budgetary powers, as they might have, to encourage austerity. Instead, they tended to adopt the role of staff advocate, which had the unintended consequence of encouraging identification with presidential aims in a way that enthusiasm for budget trimming certainly would not have had. The staff were grateful that the presidents stood up for them in negotiations with the legislature.

Nonetheless, community college administrators still had to contend with the strong preferences of students and their parents for the higher-prestige liberal arts courses. Implementing the policy of vocationalization took a long time and required more than the exercise of presidental powers alone.

Guidance Counseling

Guidance counseling proved a key element in the rechanneling process. Through formal counseling, most of which took place in the form of admissions interviews, large numbers of "marginal" and "unrealistic" students were encouraged to reconsider their plans by scaling down their aspirations. Buttressed by performance records and test scores, this advice convinced many students.

It should be emphasized that most of the counselors were sincerely interested in helping the students succeed at the highest level they felt to be consistent with the students' abilities and motivations. They did not deliberately try to steer the students away from the universities and toward lower middle–level jobs. Counselors simply acted in ways that they perceived as rational and humane, given a competitive system of educational and social selection. A basic assumption was that the students should adjust to the market. Few, if any, counselors believed that the students' aspirations should be taken as seriously as market needs, and certainly very few felt responsible for "heating up" rather "cooling out" the students' mobility aspirations. As one dean from Bunker Hill commented, "Conflicts between students' desires and the needs of the community are resolved in favor of the community." [22] "[The] idea is to placate them, not to motivate them," a counselor at the same school observed unhappily. "We're giving the American Dream in a watered-down version." [23]

Counselors justified their actions by urging the students to be "realistic" about their options and, by implication, to give up unrealistic ideas about achievements that were beyond their grasp. In this way, counselors were able to place themselves in a position of moral strength as mature adults capable of squarely facing unpleasant facts while subtly questioning the psychological fitness of their younger charges. The dean of students at Bunker Hill explained: "Many of the students have unrealistic ideas. When they make a decision, they should base it on information that will help them make wise decisions. They must know what they can expect." [24]

None of the campuses followed precisely the same counseling and guidance practices. Some favored a psychological approach, paying close attention to the students' feelings. Others favored a "hard" quantitative approach and displayed little interest in the students' feelings. Some of the colleges used elaborate batteries of tests and interest inventories to help rank the students; others de-emphasized these instruments. Some required that students take a freshman orientation course on the "world of careers"; others did not.

Yet a set of similar assumptions lay beneath this apparent diversity. At all the schools, the counseling staffs assumed that most students should be in occupational programs and that these programs were in the students' best interests. Most counselors were accustomed to encouraging the occupational programs and discouraging the liberal arts programs.

Two styles seemed to predominate. Counselors tended to favor either a consultative, emotionally supportive approach or a prescriptive, emotionally neutral approach. The consultative counselors often disliked ability testing but used psychological testing and vocational interest inventories. They took into account the students' feelings and tried to let the students decide their own courses. These counselors encouraged the students to take whatever courses they wanted, suggesting alternatives only when the students returned with mediocre or low grades. Then the students were encouraged to take remedial courses or less demanding programs.

Thomas O'Connell explained how this process worked in the early years at Berkshire: "Very few of our students thought a two-year program was what they wanted. . . . We'd let them try whatever they wanted to try. . . . If they could handle the level of abstraction involved, good. . . . If they had their hands full, maybe we'd suggest some other options. . . . If they just limped through with a 'C', we'd tell them about other options." [25] The idea, said O'Connell, was to help students "see the light" through "persuasion rather than closing doors." Counseling at Berkshire continued to adhere to a supportive, consultative style in later years. Jeff Doscher, the director of counseling, described himself as "not a testing type of person" and emphasized the importance of talking to students at length to understand their motivation. If students wanted to take programs for which they were not prepared, Doscher said he would suggest remediation or some alternative programs, but ultimately the decision was left up to students.[26]

Although this "consultative" approach was perhaps the more common in Massachusetts, some counselors relied on a more directive style, which was part evaluative assessment of the students' abilities and interests, part negotiation, and part recommendation. Don Rininger, admissions director of Massachusetts Bay Community College, said that before meeting with a student, he made an initial assessment of him or her on the basis of high school performance, standardized test scores (when available), and grades in courses related to the student's expressed program preference. Sometimes his assessment did not coincide with the student's aspirations. In these situations, Rininger said he felt responsible for directing the student into a "less demanding" program. On the same grounds, students were "occasionally" directed into more demanding programs. His decisions, he said, were not forced on students: "I don't make the decision for them. I present them with a given body of facts, then they come to their own conclusion."[27] In these conversations, the students were made aware of weaknesses in their preparation. They were asked if they felt they could handle the course they had requested, and they were given "objective evidence" that they could not, if Rininger's estimate was decidedly different from the student's.

Rininger said he could not think of a single student who had failed to accept his final recommendations. "Through a comprehensive accumulation of data, we try to have the total mosaic. . . . Education is open-ended, but performance-based. . . . It becomes evident in conversation that they should follow the proper course."[28] The element of negotiation helped encourage compliance. Riniger said he made some adjustments in his decisions on the basis of subjective estimates of desire, "maturity," and work experience. He felt that the psychological effects of past schooling were most important to encouraging compliance among applicants. Rininger explained, "You have to remember—these kids are all experts on schooling. They all know what's required."[29] There is another way of putting it. For many community college students, past academic performance was associated with the pain of failure. Students may not have been entirely reconciled to their fates, but many of them felt, at some level, that they deserved them.

The prescriptive approach was followed also at Mount Wachusett where students were placed in "challenging, but not too challenging" courses on the basis of their performance record and where programs were sometimes "modified" without consulting students.[30] According to the counselors, students only rarely objected to being placed in programs they had not requested. According to Barbara Landry of Mount Wachusett: "We would tell them, 'We have modified your program. If you have any questions, please consult with us.' Very few argued. Underneath it, students knew we were doing it in their best interest. . . . Students feel that we are concerned."[31]

On most campuses, counselors used "general education" programs as their primary means of testing students' resolve and of reorienting "marginal students" toward the occupational programs. At some campuses, as many as one-third of entering freshman were assigned to the general education programs (Massachusetts Board of Regional Community Colleges 1980). General education was a sort of limbo category between liberal arts–transfer and vocational programs. Although the courses covered the same fields as did the liberal arts–transfer courses, they were less demanding, and credit for them typically would not transfer to four-year institutions. By taking general education courses, students who had been identified as "marginal" could either prove they belonged in transfer curricula or could give themselves and the staff further evidence that they should reconsider their academic plans.

Francis P. Roman, the long-time admissions director at Massasoit, described the use of general education programs at his school as a catchall category allowing both students and counselors maximum flexibility for subsequent adjustments. "The students who could not get into liberal arts transfer," he said, "could begin in general liberal arts and go from there."[32]

Enrollment Ceilings and Other Structural Barriers to Transfer

Enrollment in general education courses presented a structural barrier to transfer-oriented students. In order to become eligible for transfer, students were required to repeat liberal arts courses taken in general education at a higher level in the liberal arts–transfer curriculum. Similarly, courses in the occupational programs generally were not accepted by four-year colleges. Thus if students asked to change in midstream from occupational to transfer programs, they were forced to start virtually from the beginning, no matter how good their grades. For many years, this led to a "locking in" of occupational students in the "career" programs.[33] Whatever the community colleges might say about their dedication to maximizing "flexibility" and student choice, movement from the occupational to the transfer curriculm was not designed to be fluid, especially during the early years of community colleges in Massachusetts.

Although most counselors attempted to make clear to students the rules for transferring credits, uncertainty about transfer requirements was pervasive on most campuses. Despite the firm rules for transfer between the community colleges and the University of Massachusetts, agreements with the state colleges and private institutions frequently changed. In many cases, students were forced to negotiate directly with these schools to determine which of their credits would transfer.

This confusion engendered a general climate of uncertainty on campus about the transferability of credits. Counselors recognized the problem, but did not see it as a serious obstacle. "It might take them a little longer than they thought," said one, "but they could still do it, if they wanted to."[34] For the students, though, the discovery of mistaken understandings could be discouraging.

The confusion over credit requirements is only one difficulty presented by the physical break between institutions. It is not simply that misinformation flourished behind institutional walls. Students who are not physically present in an institution are often (usually unintentionally) treated as "second-best" in administrative decisions. In Massachusetts, the most important area where this occurred was in decisions on financial aid. In a state study of transfer students in the early 1970s,

Ernest Beales, found that "transfer students [were] definitely discriminated against by many four-year colleges in the area of financial aid awards." The typical practice in Massachusetts was for transfer students not to be accepted until very late spring or early summer, and by then "all fall semester awards [had] already been granted to newly enrolled upperclassmen" (Beales 1974, pp. 8–9). Because community college students are more frequently from lower SES families, this kind of institutional disregard presents an especially formidable obstacle. The general point warrants emphasis. The physical separation of tiers, though it may be rational from an administrative point of view, also creates conditions in which misinformation, articulation problems, and institutional disregard for students can flourish. This is one reason why separate tiers serve in many instances as clear hierarchical dividers despite their explicit intentions of fostering mobility.

If the credit system (and the confusion surrounding it) impeded transfer, enrollment quota systems, which were introduced on some of the campuses, were still greater barriers. Through quotas, several of the schools limited the number of students they would accept in any given program. If the demand exceeded the number of designated places in a particular program, students would be assigned to their second-choice curriculum or to general education for those who requested placement in the liberal arts–transfer program.

At Massasoit, all programs had quotas, which were filled on the basis of students' high school records. Those applying for the transfer programs were also required to take standardized tests of academic aptitude. Admissions director Francis Roman recalled that the liberal arts–transfer program had seventy-five openings in the late 1960s and early 1970s. Students who applied for the transfer program were placed on a waiting list and told that they could begin in general education. The president and his staff periodically adjusted the quotas on the basis of demand and placement statistics. Some of the most rigidly controlled programs, to be sure, were in occupational areas—nursing was an example—but the quota system also served to lower enrollments in the liberal arts–transfer programs. A similar system was implemented at Bristol by its first president, Jack Hudnall, and in the early 1970s, Middlesex Community College also adopted a quota system for some its programs, including liberal arts.

In later years, Bunker Hill Community College adopted the most rigid quota system. In the late 1970s, president Harold Shively, who had moved to Bunker Hill from North Shore when the new campus opened in 1973, limited liberal arts–transfer enrollments to 25 percent of all matriculants. Upon admission, students were asked to write down their first several program preferences. The first 25 percent who chose liberal arts–transfer programs were accepted, and the others were given their second or third choices. This procedure was justified to students as necessary owing to limited space and resources.[35] Shively explained that, despite student preferences, he couldn't "justify" a larger transfer program: "There are so many liberal-arts programs in the area, we can't justify a larger one here . . . We would rather funnel resources into other programs, like hotel/motel management or office work, here . . . Students can get liberal arts elsewhere."[36] The dean of students, Patricia Chisholm, admitted that there were some conflicts between the desires of students and the administrative objectives. "Yes," she said, "we are structuring things. . . . But the liberal arts degree isn't negotiable anymore." [37]

What is perhaps most striking about the course assignment practices in Massachusetts is how incompatible they were with the "consumer-choice" model of community college vocationalization. Strict ceilings on the number of students enrolled in liberal arts transfer programs, for example, can hardly be interpreted as expressions of "consumer sovereignty," yet enrollment quotas were commonly used by Massachusetts community colleges. Similarly, the common practice of channeling nonvocationally oriented students into "general education" courses was a response not to student demands, but rather to the institution's administratively defined need to sort and classify students. Finally, the existence of important structural barriers to transfer, such as the failure to accord any transfer credit to courses taken in occupational programs and the widespread confusion as to which liberal arts courses would receive credit at four-year colleges, cannot be understood as a response to the preferences of largely transfer-oriented students. Instead, these barriers (which did not, it should be emphasized, exist at all of the campuses) may be seen as an expression of the willingness of community colleges to override "consumer choice" when it conflicted with administrative definitions of organizational and student interest.

Public Relations and Recruitment of Students

Despite the efforts of counselors and admissions directors, some of the occupational programs did not attract as many students as had been expected. In these cases, presidents and their staffs were forced to promote the programs on campus and to recruit actively in the local high schools for future enrollees. The promotional efforts typically involved "informational" campaigns. Thomas O'Connell, the former president of Berkshire Community College, described what would happen in these efforts: "If a program was not filling properly, faculty members would keep their eyes open for students. In advising sessions, they might say, "According to your record, you're not necessarily talking about transferring. Here's a new program in a growing field. Maybe you ought to give this a try." [38] Eventually, he said, some of the students approached in this way would be willing to "give it a try." [39]

These special on-campus recruiting campaigns were rare. Most of the other schools concentrated instead on building stable future enrollments by working with local high schools. Thomas O'Connell, the former president of Berkshire Community College, remembered that electronics technology at Berkshire had enrollment problems from the start. In cases like these, he said, faculty members in charge of the program joined admissions officers in recruiting talks at local high schools. The incentives for faculty were quite compelling: "Sometimes we would have to go out and talk it up. Some of the faculty had their jobs on the line. If there weren't enough students, they couldn't continue. This provided them with a real incentive to promote it." [40] Francis Roman, the long-time admissions director of Massasoit, remembered a similar episode: "Engineering technology never filled properly," he said. "I must have visited every single high school to get people for the program, and we still had trouble."[41]

Students were not the only ones recruited for the new programs. Some of the presidents, like John Musselman of Massasoit, invested extra time in hiring experienced and dynamic instructors for the new occupational programs in the hope that attractive teachers would help sell the new programs. Musselman recalled going all the way to California to hire a commercial artist for one new program and aggressively pursuing the director of a prominent private secretarial school in Boston for another.[42]

Promotion also sometimes took the form of public relations innovations designed to make the occupational programs more palatable. At Cape Cod, many students were strongly opposed to the programs, which they identified with high school vocational education and, according to president James Hall, regarded as "a dirty thing." Hall's solution was to invent a new name for the programs; once called "technical education," they were now called "collegiate technical education." This, said Hall, helped students gain the kind of prestige they needed. "There's a lot in a name," he observed. "A rose is not always a rose by any other name."[43]

It would be misleading, however, to suggest that administrators spent a great deal of time promoting the occupational programs; in fact, promotional campaigns were only occasionally necessary. The colleges had more reliable means of ensuring stable enrollments in programs, through surveys of demand, counseling, and, sometimes, course assignment. At the same time, in those cases in which intensive promotion and recruiting campaigns were used, they represented an effort to shape, rather than to respond to, consumer choice.

The Establishment of Exchange Relationships with Employers

Community college officials believed that the occupational programs' success depended not only on the creation of a stable student demand but also on the availablity of jobs for students once they completed the programs. Instead of urging local employers directly to hire occupational students, the colleges studied labor force projections and surveys of regional economic needs until they were convinced that a demand existed for proposed new programs. They assumed that if the market studies were correct, the students would be able to find jobs on the basis of the demand for their skills. But the colleges also attempted to supplement these impersonal means with personal contacts, that is, close relationships with local employers.

The local advisory committees were especially helpful in this regard. Following Board policy dating from 1960, the colleges formed advisory committees to consult on "community needs." These committees were composed mainly of local business people. At Berkshire, for example, the advisory committee helped develop the first electronics technology program. At Cape Cod, they took an active interest in the hotel/motel management program.[44] At Massasoit, the advisory committee helped provide necessary information to get a chemical technology program started. Indeed, on most of the campuses, the advisory committees were instrumental in creating at least one of the occupational programs, and sometimes many of them.[45]

The committees also sometimes provided advice on how course work could be coordinated with current industry practices. In the technology areas, in particular, college administrators consulted widely with both the advisory committees and outside sources for information on designing proper curricula. As one president put it, "Before you go into robotics, you better get some advice."[46]

By creating the advisory committees, the colleges conferred a degree of prestige on local employers in return for their help in protecting and developing the colleges. In many communities, business people looked on their involvement with the local community college as a symbol of their civic pride and responsibility. The colleges hoped that the members' concern for the colleges would translate into a willingness to hire students from the colleges. According to one placement director, "Hopefully, members of the advisory committee will do some hiring. I would say their first purpose is informational. But their second may be hiring."[47]

There were other types of exchanges as well. Some colleges purchased equipment from companies, hoping that those companies would, in turn, establish close training relationships with the colleges. Holyoke Community College, for example, bought several computers and other advanced equipment from Digital Electronics Corporation in the hope that Digital would look to Holyoke when hiring its technicians.[48] "Co-op programs" also became increasingly popular in the colleges. These were work–study programs in which students worked part time in a local firm as part of their formal training. They received little pay for their work, but some did find permanent jobs through the programs.[49]

The colleges also brought in managers and skilled workers from local industries to teach in the continuing education programs. And the expertise flowed in the other direction as well, with faculty from the colleges occasionally serving as consultants to local business people.

For all their efforts to build strong ties with employers, the colleges were surprisingly passive in their actual placement activities. Placement offices were small and usually headed by one person who, in addition to placement work, often had other counseling responsibilities. In most offices, placement officers advised students on how to write résumés and conduct interviews. They also distributed handouts about local employment opportunities. Only rarely, however, did they bring employers to campus for "career fairs" or employment interviews. Moreover, they usually did not aggressively seek to place particular students in firms they knew to have openings. Given the colleges' strong need to prove the marketability of the occupational programs, the limited activities of the placement officers in this regard and their general reticence are noteworthy.

In fact, the weakness of the placement offices reflected the presence of powerful constraints. Employers did not like to feel that they were being badgered into taking students who might not be suited to their needs. Moreover, the colleges themselves did not want to be blamed for students who failed to perform to company expectations. Thus the college chose to stand behind the programs rather than the individual students who graduated from them. In addition, some administrators feared the potential for lawsuits: " 'We can't guarantee placement,' said one administrator. 'If students are buying a contract, we're liable. If they start thinking they're investing X amount of money to get a job, and they don't get the job, we'd have law suits on our hands.' "[50]

Under these circumstances, the colleges' approach to linking student and jobs seems quite sensible. By concentrating on building friendly relationships with local business people and by studying labor projections, the colleges hoped to enhance the marketability of their graduates without actually making a commitment to them.[51]

The Exception That Proves the Rule: The Case of Roxbury

All but one of the colleges followed essentially the same course, using similar mechanisms to implement the Board's vocationalizing policy. Roxbury Community College, located in Boston's largest black neighborhood, was the sole exception. It was this college that most actively questioned the occupational programs. Administrators and faculty at Roxbury tended to encourage students to go as far as they could in higher education, and the students themselves were skeptical about the returns from anything other than traditional liberal arts education.

Roxbury administrators felt that strong academic programs reflected the particular needs of their community. "We had to be a strong transfer college," said one former president, Kenneth Haskins. "There was a strong recognition that since over 50 percent of all black and Hispanic students [in higher education] were in two-year colleges, our two-year colleges had to serve a greater purpose. It's not that we had anything against occupational programs. . . . But there was a recognition that we had to train people that [some] would call frivolous, such as philosophers and even poets."[52]

This attitude contrasted with that of the central office, and the central office deplored the difference. According to educational policy chief Gordon Pyle, Roxbury has "held to the myth of the four-year degree. They feel the career programs are not designed to help them up. Instead, they see it as a continuation of keeping them in their place."[53]

The informal policy of the staff at Roxbury encouraged both high aspirations and alternatives to the usual career programs. The career programs at Roxbury were sometimes unconventional, relating more to the staff's perception of community needs than to the central office's emphasis on new technologies and business occupations. There were, for example, programs in community organizing and urban renewal at Roxbury that existed nowhere else in the system (Massachusetts Board of Regional Community Colleges, "Career Programs," 1977). Moreover, Roxbury did not have a general education curriculum, and far from imposing limits on liberal arts enrollments, the faculty fought to retain and expand the liberal arts and transfer programs. The occupational programs were designed from the beginning to allow transfer into higher-level programs. The electronics technology program, for example, was designed to dovetail with the electrical engineering program by providing the same basic core courses. When students had difficulty in courses, they were placed in special "developmental" (remedial) courses, rather than being assigned to nontransferable curricula. The emphasis was on going as far as possible and on leaving options open for transfer to four-year colleges.

In some ways, the case of Roxbury highlights the dilemmas of vocationalization. The occupational programs were less popular at Roxbury than were the transfer programs, for example, but they were not actively opposed. Some teachers at Roxbury felt that the occupational programs served primarily to track low-income students into low status-jobs, but many also felt that the programs could lead to better jobs than the students might otherwise expect. According to one of these teachers: "In the long term, most of these jobs are lower level. But sometimes high skills are needed in 'career' programs. Secretaries need good grammar and spelling. The program is difficult for many students, and those who graduate can do fairly well."[54] "The 'career' programs are a step in a positive direction," said a counselor. "To go beyond the high school level is something important."[55]

Although it remained a comprehensive community college, Roxbury favored a student-centered model of development over the employer-centered model favored by the other colleges and by the board. The difference was in emphasis, not in basic structure. By concentrating on providing remedial courses and as many academic courses as the students desired and could handle, Roxbury's administrators signaled their commitment to student achievement rather than "manpower development." "We didn't want just the chance to pattern ourselves after everyone else," said Roxbury's Kenneth Haskins. "We wanted to create institutions that were in the best interest of our community."[56]

It would be a mistake to attribute the relative weakness of vocational programs at Roxbury solely to an administrative policy that diverged from that of other Massachusetts community colleges. Roxbury is located in a highly race-conscious black community, and most of its students had come from this same community. As such, these students were, like their counterparts elsewhere, especially sensitive to what they perceived as the racial implications of tracking in higher education.[57] More politically active than their white working-class counterparts and far more sensitive to any educational structures that smacked of segregation, the Roxbury students themselves were an important source of resistance to the policy of the central office.

Patterns of Faculty and Student Response to Vocationalization

The Faculty Response

The liberal arts faculty at some of the schools did raise concerns about the rapid shift toward occupational training. Humanities and social science instructors, in particular, sometimes considered a traditional liberal arts education to be the only appropriate training for college students. The most persistent objections were raised at Cape Cod and Berkshire, two campuses that, perhaps because of their idyllic locations, at first attracted relatively large numbers of instructors from Ivy League and other prestigious universities. At all schools, presidents recognized that humanities and social science teachers were less enthusiastic than the others were about the employer-oriented colleges they proposed to develop.

Some presidents dismissed their faculty critics as "elitists" whose status insecurities prevented them from recognizing the proper goals and mission of community colleges. At the same time, most also tried to keep the liberal arts faculty happy by providing employment security and regular budget increases. The tremendous growth of enrollments no doubt facilitated the easing of tension. This growth meant that faculty in the occupational programs could be hired without jeopardizing the jobs of the liberal arts faculty. None of the schools was forced to dismiss faculty to finance growth in occupational fields. As Cape Cod's James Hall observed: "It wasn't an either/or situation. While we were building the technical programs, we also tried to make liberal arts stronger."[58]

The presidents also tried to emphasize the differences between community colleges and more strictly vocational institutions. A few of them even highlighted the importance of liberal arts courses for broadening and improving the cultural range of vocational and nonvocational students alike. "I wanted the faculty to appreciate that they had a great responsibility for providing humanities to vocational students," Hall said. "[Those students] might never get it [exposure to the humanities] again. . . . That's gotten through."[59] Some presidents encouraged joint courses between faculty from occupational and liberal arts divisions, such as "The Criminal in American Literature" offered jointly by a law enforcement and an English instructor at Bristol Community College.

Ultimately, however, the most important causes of faculty support for vocationalization may have been based on experience with community college students as it compared with their own college experiences. To most faculty members, including those in liberal arts programs, higher education was legitimately a sorting process, in which the most able and highly motivated were separated from their peers on the basis of academic performance. Most felt that some common core of liberal arts training should be widely shared, but that only the few were fit for intense exposure to the liberal arts tradition. In a sense, the faculty's commitment to academic excellence overwhelmed its commitment to the idea of a common curriculum. Time and time again, faculty members spoke glowingly of one or two shining stars among the hundreds of students they had taught. In the teachers' telling, these students alone justified the many sacrifices they made. As a psychology instructor at Massasoit put it, "The students are either good or lousy. . . . I don't want you to misunderstand me—there are some who are top notch, but most of them don't belong in college."[60]

Virtually all the teachers wanted to talk about the few students who had won full scholarships or academic prizes or who had become college professors, doctors, or scientists. All seemed to have at least one Horatio Alger story to share, and some had as many as two or three. As for the rest of the students, many of them were "good kids," but they were "lazy" or "immature," "had family responsibilities," "lacked desire," "didn't want to do the work," "wanted to get by the easiest way possible," or, for some other reason, did not measure up. Thus, many of the liberal arts faculty tended to adopt the Jeffersonian view that their task was to identify and foster the development of America's "natural aristocracy of talent.'' This focus on selecting and cultivating an intellectual elite was a far cry from John Dewey's emphasis on liberal arts instruction as the best guarantee of democratic citizenship and as the best hope for a broadened appreciation of life. It was farther still from the view that community college students should be taught intellectual skills as a means of overcoming class differences. In practice, it translated into a receptivity for differentiated curricula that would have been present even without the active intervention of administrators or the exclusive admissions policies of many four-year colleges. At the same time, there is little doubt that the intervention of administrators and the policies of higher-level institutions strongly reinforced these predispositions, lending an air of institutional inevitability to the elements of moral virtue that most faculty saw in the hierarchical practices of academic life.[61]

The Student Response

Disorganized, poorly informed, and transient, community college students were hardly in a better position than the faculty to challenge the vocationalization of their institutions. Even so, given their strong general preference for the higher-status academic programs, their failure (with the partial exception of Roxbury) to challenge this transformation requires an explanation. To understand the students' reactions to occupational and liberal arts programs and to obtain better impressions of student life and culture, we conducted some thirty interviews with community college students at two campuses, Bunker Hill and Massasoit. In addition, we also used material from interviews conducted by Howard London at a Massachusetts community college and reported in *The Culture of a Community College* (1978).

The students' insecurity about intellectual activity is surely a key factor in understanding their response to vocationalization. Most students did not feel comfortable talking about abstract ideas. Many did not come from homes in which such ideas were commonly discussed, and they often associated past school experiences with the risk—and reality—of failure. Consequently, although most students longed for the upward mobility that college could lead to, they were uncertain about their ability to do the intellectual work necessary to succeed in college. Many of the students we interviewed at Bunker Hill and Massasoit complained about the difficulty of the course work and the high expectations of their teachers. Occasionally, the students revealed their doubts: ''I wanted to go into data processing,'' said one Massasoit student, ''but I didn't like it. It might have been the professor—it was like he expected everyone to know what he knew already—but I had a hard time learning two computer languages at once. Maybe it was too hard for me.''[62]

Many students hoped to move into the higher white-collar ranks, but most were unsure they could reach this level or that they truly belonged there. For many, the academic pressures were constant. As one of London's students commented, ''Every time you screw up, you know you're closer to being out.'' In this context, the generally less demanding occupational programs were attractive and were promoted by administrators as marketable alternatives to liberal arts. By enrolling in the vocational programs, students were freed from this perhaps threatening intellectual work. Indeed, London's respondents indicated that they often found the occupational courses to offer relative freedom, marked by a relaxed classroom atmosphere, easy relations between teachers and students, and usually much less demanding work.

If our interviews were representative, perhaps as many as 25 to 30 percent of community college students had so weak an image of their future in the labor market that to portray them as in any way job conscious would be mistaken. Rather, these students enrolled at a community college mainly because it was a social gathering spot away from full-time work, a place to be with others and to enjoy the social life. This attitude was epitomized by a liberal arts student at Massasoit who objected to our interview questions, which were heavily weighted toward education and labor market issues: "I really don't have that many opinions about the kinds of questions you're asking," he said. "Now, if you want to know about the social life at this school, I can tell you all about that."[63]

No doubt some of these students had hopes for the future but none so firm as to constitute a commitment. Instead, one has the sense of these students living more or less unplanned lives, embracing and abandoning plans in relation to whatever new opportunities might arise. Asked about his reasons for entering the community college, one of these students replied, "I didn't like high school. I didn't know about getting a degree. I wasn't necessarily planning to transfer at all. I just came with the idea of seeing what it was like."[64] Another said: "I'm a liberal arts float. I'm just drifting now, sampling a little of everything. . . . My intention is to transfer to a four-year college depending on my job."[65] Asked about her plans after graduation, another of these uncommitted students replied, "I really can't say. I'll just have to see what comes up."[66]

All together, students with serious intellectual insecurities and students whose backgrounds—both social and academic—left them with weak attachments to educational and occupational objectives probably made up a majority of the liberal arts student body. Neither group was a likely opponent of vocationalization, and both were highly susceptible to the various mechanisms used by community college administrators in pursuit of vocationalization.

7 The Final Transformation in Massachusetts: Market Pressures, Fiscal Crises, and Business Influences, 1971–1985

The focus of this chapter is on the shift toward predominantly vocational enrollments in the 1970s, brought on by the combined pressures of market decline, state fiscal crisis, and the political ascendance of conservative business leaders. Nevertheless, it would be misleading to suggest that contrary forces were not in evidence at least in the first few years of the 1970s. The most important of these contrary pressures was the sheer growth of the community college and university systems, which, for a time, encouraged an increase in the absolute numbers of transfers.

The community colleges in Massachusetts proved to be at least as attractive in a period of economic retrenchment as they had been in better times. Low-cost, close-to-home two-year colleges were a practical alternative to more expensive higher education. Between 1970 and 1973, the community colleges' full-time enrollment increased by over one-third, and the other two tiers grew slightly less rapidly (see Table 7-1).

As the system became more vocational in the late 1960s, it also grew. Because of this growth, the absolute number of community college students who transferred to four-year colleges increased, even though the transfer enrollment rates were slowly declining. The number of community college students transferring to the University at Massachusetts at Amherst, for example, increased from just 80 in 1964, when only seven community college campuses were open, to 425 in 1970 and then to 950 in 1972, when twelve campuses were operating at full capacity.[1] In 1973, at the peak of transfer enrollments, 1,165 public two-year college students enrolled at the University of Massachusetts; 680 enrolled in the state colleges; and 525 enrolled in four-year private colleges in Massachusetts.[2] Although never more than a small fraction of total community college enrollments, transfer rates did rise dramatically, from approximately 12.5 percent of the sophomore

Table 7-1. Public Higher Education Enrollments[a] by Fiscal Year and Sector, Selected Years, 1960–1977

Fiscal Year	University of Massachusetts Head Count	FTE	State Colleges Head Count	FTE	Community Colleges Head Count	FTE	Total Head Count	FTE
1960	6,030	—	7,207	—	—	—	15,794	—
1965	9,520	—	10,840	—	3,650	—	27,735	—
1967	12,835	—	15,792	—	7,930	—	42,927	—
1970	20,835	—	21,828	—	15,165	—	65,888	—
1973	26,729	—	27,148	—	21,126	—	85,453	—
1976	—	29,146	—	31,078	—	27,305	—	99,160
1977	—	28,678	—	30,064	—	28,098	—	97,747

[a]Enrollment figures before FY 1973 are taken from the governor's budget recommendation of that year and reflect student head count. Enrollment figures for FY 1973 reflect actual full-time equivalent (FTE) student enrollment in the fall semester. Enrollment figures for FY 1976 and FY 1977 reflect actual average full-time equivalent student enrollment in both semesters.

Source: Massachusetts Board of Regents 1980.

class in 1964 (a rate congenial to the original planners) to nearly 30 percent of the sophomore class in 1973 (Beales 1974).[3]

The New Market Hits Massachusetts

The nationwide decline in the market for college-educated labor in the early 1970s hit Massachusetts with slightly greater force than in other states, being reinforced by a recession in the newly emerging high-technology belt around Boston that was related to the winding down of the war in Southeast Asia. Many of Massachusetts's hopes for a prosperous future had been predicated on these science-based industries. As labor economist Richard Freeman noted:

> The sudden collapse of the science market . . . made a mockery of the forecasts, analyses and national concern (about manpower shortages in scientific fields). Employment and salaries of researchers tumbled; the number of R & D workers dropped; real starting salaries declined—a stark transformation from the previous decade. (Freeman 1976, pp. 100, 106)

As in the rest of the country, the more competitive market for college-educated labor shifted demand away from liberal arts programs and toward more practical types of training. This shift occurred at both the four-year and two-year colleges, but the change was most noticeable in the community colleges. Between 1970 and 1974, enrollment in the occupational programs in community colleges grew rapidly, but liberal arts enrollments remained virtually stable (U.S. House of Representatives, 1975b, p. 449).

At the same time, it bears emphasizing that the increased interest in occupational training at the community college level could not have found expression without vigorous efforts on the part of the community colleges themselves to develop new vocational curricula.

Between 1968 and 1971—largely before the market shift—new laboratories and technical facilities were constructed on all of the campuses, and new career programs were approved. Community colleges knew what they wanted students to study, and when the changing labor market for college graduates softened the students' resistance to occupational education, a broad variety of vocational programs were already in place to receive them.

State Policy and the Growth of Vocationalism, 1971–1978

State funds kept pace with the new demand for practical training. Although the colleges were never entirely satisfied with their appropriations, tensions between higher education and the legislature eased somewhat in the early 1970s. The colleges could look forward to predictable annual increases and could also begin to feel confident that their building needs would eventually be met. Looking back over the period, William Dwyer, testifying before Congress, lauded Massachusetts's "strong commitment and financial support of the comprehensive community college and the occupational-education student" (U.S. House of Representatives 1975a, p. 449).

The legislature further aided the colleges by adopting new budgetary procedures that encouraged the growth of the occupational curricula. Beginning in 1970, administrators were asked to calculate their personnel needs using a formula that allocated faculty–student ratios differently across programs. The formula called for one full-time faculty member for each twenty-one liberal arts students, one faculty member for each fifteen occupational students, and one for each ten nursing students. This reflected a realistic appraisal of the supervisory demand of the three types of programs. However, the formula also helped ensure that new development would be mostly in the career programs, as the personnel budgets were not subjected to the same political considerations as were the requests for new capital outlays.

Ironically, the community colleges' problems during this period were for the first time mainly problems of increased competition, in part because of the very success of their vocationalization project. The community colleges were well positioned to take advantage of the new market situation, but the new market also encouraged other educational institutions to mimic the community colleges. In the vocational sphere, the Massachusetts state colleges in the 1970s became major competitors for both students and new training markets. Once almost exclusively teacher-training institutions, the state colleges in Massachusetts had been reorganized as comprehensive institutions by the 1965 Willis–Harrington Act. At the first evidence of a labor surplus for jobs requiring college degrees, state colleges began to consider instituting explicitly job-related training. Increasingly, the community colleges, not the university, served as their model. Beginning in about 1970, therefore, the state colleges gave up what one administrator termed their "ten-year flirtation with liberal arts" and moved, sometimes haltingly, into developing occupational programs of their own (Boucher, quoted in Lustberg, 1979, p. 182).

The state colleges first began to express their new sense of "mission" in meetings with the staff of the state's Board of Higher Education (BHE), the coordinating body nominally responsible for public higher education in Massachusetts. BHE staff members agreed that new market and demographic pressures required that the state colleges move away from liberal arts toward becoming multipurpose institutions. As program analyst Richard Offenberger recalled, "Parents and students were becoming more utilitarian . . . [and] you didn't have the same military draft pressures keeping students in school."[4]

First Attempts at Rationalization

A new concern for the survival of the state colleges led the Massachusetts Board of Higher Education to try to slow down the growth of the community colleges' occupational programs and to increase such programs in the state colleges. Charging the community colleges with "indiscriminate expansion" during the previous six years, the Board of Higher Education implemented a procedure for program development in June 1971 that paradoxically encouraged even more vocationalization in the community colleges. According to the Board's plans, all new proposals were required to show that they would meet present and projected local and regional "job needs." Colleges were expected to mention specific industries or agencies that would be served by each new program and to demonstrate that the proposed program did not duplicate or overlap with courses already offered elsewhere (Massachusetts Board of Regional Community Colleges 1971).

Ironically, the new policy, far from slowing down the development of vocational programs in the community colleges, led to an average of forty-five new vocational programs every year between 1971 and 1976, far more approvals than in the years of "indiscriminate expansion." Though the BHE tried to coordinate program development with consideration for the state colleges' interests, its inherent legal and jurisdictional weaknesses forced it merely to reward the most enterprising institutions under its nominal control (Stafford 1980). As a result, according to BHE staff analyst Richard Offenberger, "the best entrepreneurs" received BHE approval.[5] The community colleges, with their years of experience in locating markets and justifying programs, were, not surprisingly, often the best entrepreneurs; over three-quarters of the programs they proposed were given BHE permission to proceed (calculated from Massachusetts Board of Regional Community Colleges, "Minutes," 1971–1976).

Thus the new competition intensified the pressures for community colleges to develop new programs before other competitors could. Vocationalization was often perceived both on campus and in the central office as necessary for the defense of organizational interests. Speaking of the community college system as a whole, one dean said, "If we don't do it, industry or some other organization will do it, and we'll be out of business."[6]

Increased competition also encouraged credential inflation. Many of the programs that the state colleges added merely prolonged the community colleges' course work. The BHE approved a number of programs at the B.A. level that were intended as upper-division supplements to programs the "community colleges already had at the lower division."[7] New upper-division law enforcement and social-service programs were especially popular, for example, but this inflationary pattern extended also to such areas as horticulture, culinary arts, and even industrial repair.

Efforts were made, also beginning in 1971, to rationalize the distribution of federal vocational-education monies as well. These efforts were somewhat more successful than the efforts to rationalize program development. In 1971, the control of vocational-education funds shifted from the Department of Education to the Community College Board. Each year the Board was given a set aside sum to distribute as it pleased. This sum reached slightly over $1.5 million annually during the mid-1970s (Massachusetts Board of Regional Community Colleges, "Summary of Federal Aid Awarded," 1975–1977).[8]

Fiscal Crisis and Response

By the early 1970s, educational administrators in Massachusetts, as elsewhere, increasingly thought in terms of a rationalized system, that is, a hierarchically arranged system of centrally coordinated institutions of public higher education developed along lines dictated by labor market opportunities. During the next decade, educational practice caught up with educational rhetoric, as a serious crisis in state finances provided budgetary incentives for the state to think about new ways of maximizing its "tax investment" in higher education.

The first signs of serious fiscal trouble in Massachusetts came in 1973, when the state found itself caught between an eroding tax base and an increasing financial commitment to state services. The erosion of the tax base could be traced largely to the high levels of unemployment and the business closings brought on by the recession of 1970–1971 and compounded by the energy crisis of 1973. While these economic shocks threatened the tax base, the continued climate of liberalism encouraged increased spending on social and welfare programs.

In this era of tight budgets, the colleges began to be criticized as increasingly irrelevant to the job market. Like other citizens around the country, Massachusetts voters had become aware, through the news media, of "Ph.D.'s driving taxicabs and a surplus of teachers and engineers" (Asquino 1976, pp. 8–9). Calls for accountability focused, accordingly, on proposals for more "practical, market-relevant" educational programs.[9] In several speeches, the Massachusetts senate majority leader, Kevin Harrington, a man with close ties to the higher education establishment, emphasized that the golden age of higher education in the commonwealth was over (Harrington, quoted in Asquino 1976, p. 248). He warned that colleges and universities could no longer expect automatic increases in their budgets each year and that the legislature would be looking for more documentation to support requests and much more evidence of accountability. True to Harrington's prediction, higher education budgets for fiscal year 1974 were sharply questioned in the legislative committee meetings. Still, the budgets were for the most part passed at the anticipated levels.

These were just the early warning signals. In 1974, a new recession hit Massachusetts at a time when it still had not fully recovered from the 1970–1971 recession. By the time the new governor, Michael Dukakis, took office in January 1975, the gap between state revenues and outlays had reached crisis proportions. "Massachusetts today faces the most serious budgetary crisis in memory," said Dukakis in his budget message to the legislature, ". . . the largest current budget deficit of any state in the nation and an economic base that is stagnant and eroding" (Dukakis 1975, p. 1). Dukakis reported a budget deficit of $350 million, an unemployment rate of 9 percent (nearly 3 percent above the national average), and a gap of $125 million between expected and actual state revenues for fiscal year 1976.

Instead of running still larger deficits, Dukakis chose to pursue the politically difficult task of sharply reducing expenditures while borrowing to finance the debt. "I believe that you and I," he told the legislature, "must make a Herculean effort to reduce expenditures; to eliminate waste; to reexamine old programs and priorities; and to do everything humanly possible to match expenditures with revenue" (Dukakis 1975, p. 2). With no clear end in sight to the state's fiscal problems, Dukakis found the legislature receptive to his injunction. Dukakis immediately imposed a freeze on state hiring and proposed to cut or level-fund virtually all discretionary programs. For fiscal year 1976, Dukakis proposed a 30 percent budget cut for education (McCartan 1983b, p. 5), a proposal that was strenuously opposed by the colleges and eventually was lowered to a more manageable but still uncomfortable 2 percent loss to the inflation rate.

This cut signaled the true end of the golden age of higher education in the state. College officials who had previously counted on annual real increases in their operating budgets would henceforth struggle (and usually fail) to keep budgetary levels in line with the inflation rate. Higher education budgets also declined in relation to those of other state programs. After having increased from 4 to 7 percent of the total state budget between fiscal years 1960 and 1975, higher education expenditures dropped to 6 and then 5 percent of the state budget in the late 1970s (see Table 7-2).

Like the rest of higher education, the community colleges had fewer real dollars for fiscal year 1976, and they won only modest increases in the following two fiscal years (Massachusetts Board of Regional Community Colleges, 1980). State appropriations, which had tripled between 1970 and 1975, leveled off at about $40 million for the next two years. As these figures indicate, the community colleges did not fare better than did the other higher education institutions in the budgeting process, despite their widely publicized "practical orientation." Given the state's intense concern about economic development, this pattern may at first seem anomalous. But in a context in which all organizations and programs are supported by interest groups and powerful representatives, defining priorities among state functions threatens to become too time-consuming and conflict ridden to pursue seriously. Incremental gains and losses therefore become the norm, which is violated only under truly extraordinary circumstances (Padgett 1981, Wildavsky 1974). Thus budgets were tightened but not rationalized.[10]

These were difficult years in Massachusetts higher education. "Roofs leaked, and we couldn't fix them," recalled one state office administrator. "At Boston State, we had to sell old books from the library to buy new ones. . . . There

Table 7-2. Annual State Appropriations for Public Higher Educational Institutions, Selected Fiscal Years 1960–1979

Fiscal Year	Total Higher Education Appropriations (in millions)	Percentage of State Budget
1960	$ 17.1	4
1965	35.8	6
1970	98.7	5
1975	215.3	7
1976	219.8	6
1977	236.0	6
1978	250.5	6
1979	271.2	5

Source: Commonwealth of Massachusetts, Office of the Governor, Governor's Budget Requests (House 1), Fiscal Years 1960–1979. Appropriations represent amounts originally authorized by the General Court for annual operating expenses.

might have been a computer revolution in the country, but I don't think you would have been able to find one computer in the public colleges."[11]

For the most part, the community colleges were able to adapt to the leaner budgets and the increased uncertainty without reducing their commitment to the occupational programs. Most of the colleges reduced the number of part-time faculty in order to bring expected costs into line with appropriations. Long-promised technical facilities were put on hold, and the colleges scrambled for donations of old equipment; plans to buy new equipment were temporarily shelved. Some inviting new markets were ignored because the budgets could not support new program development.

The Maturation of the System

Despite the budgetary uncertainties of the first Dukakis term, the colleges continued to grow in size, and they became for the first time predominantly vocational institutions. The vocational programs looked increasingly attractive to students, compared with the seemingly more risky liberal arts–transfer curricula. As Tables 7-3 and 7-4 show, the shift toward vocational programs was most dramatic between 1972 and 1976, although it continued somewhat more erratically through the end of the decade.

By 1976, two-thirds of the schools were over 50 percent vocational, and nine of these schools were closer to three-fifths vocational than one-half. By 1977, nearly 150 different career programs were offered by at least one of the fifteen community colleges. Secretarial, accounting, nursing, law enforcement, and fire protection programs were offered by all or nearly all of the colleges. Business, marketing, electronic technology, data processing, medical technology, early childhood education, and specialized secretarial programs were offered by a ma-

Table 7-3. Percentage of Career Enrollments, Fall Semester, Massachusetts
Community Colleges, 1970–1978

	1970	1972	1974	1976	1978
Berkshire	36	42	41	38	48
Bristol[a]	45	46	60	55	33
Bunker Hill	—	—	60	70	70
Cape Cod	23	26	36	47	42
Greenfield	49	56	60	60	62
Holyoke	42	51	60	64	66
Mass Bay	37	44	49	58	58
Massasoit	35	44	63	59	56
Middlesex	32	38	45	57	68
Mount Wachusett	33	43	51	57	53
Northern Essex	39	39	41	48	50
North Shore	47	50	56	57	53
Quinsigamond	51	41	36	36	34
Roxbury	—	—	15	38	34
Springfield	78	64	70	73	72

[a]For purposes of comparability, students in the general education classification adopted by Bristol in 1977 are not counted in the 1978 calculation.

Source: Massachusetts Board of Regional Community Colleges, "Enrollment Statistics," 1970–1978.

jority of schools. These were the mainstays of the occupational track—the first developed and the most popular of the programs.

More specialized curricula could also be found at one or more of the colleges. These ranged from the down-to-earth, blue-collar world of construction and building to the Buck Rogers world of laser electro-optics technology and diagnostic medical sonography. There were courses primarily for women (culinary arts, horticulture, cosmetology) and courses primarily for men (motor freight, machine and tool design technology, turf management). There were programs for the socially conscious (air quality, social welfare, land use planning) and programs for the money-minded (banking and finance, real estate, agricultural business). If we count programs repeated at more than one school, there were more than 400 separate "career" programs at the fifteen community colleges, an average of roughly twenty-seven programs for each institution.

When he retired as president of the Massachusetts Board of Regional Community Colleges in 1976, William Dwyer could look back with satisfaction on the transformation of the liberal arts colleges he had inherited in 1964. In an interview with the *Boston Globe* at the time of his retirement, he indicated that he was proudest of the shift in emphasis that he had helped to engineer. Noting that ten years before most students studied the liberal arts, he proudly claimed "at the present time, 65 percent are in programs that train them for jobs" (Cohen 1976). Dwyer was exaggerating slightly. The figure was actually closer to 60 percent (if sophomores alone were counted), but the shift was remarkable nonetheless. Nine years before, just over one-third of sophomores had been enrolled in "career" programs (see Table 7.4).[12]

Dwyer was replaced by Jules Pagano, formerly dean of Florida International

Table 7-4. Career Enrollments As Percentage of Total
Enrollments, Massachusetts Community Colleges, 1967–1980

Year	Total Sophomore FTE Enrollment	Career Students	Career/ Total
1967	4,012	1,414	0.35
1968	4,751	1,779	0.37
1969	5,866	2,622	0.45
1970	6,523	2,841	0.44
1971	7,697	3,256	0.42
1972	8,390	3,776	0.45
1973	8,544	4,359	0.51
1974	10,218	5,525	0.54
1975	11,174	6,298	0.56
1976	11,166	6,812	0.61
1977	10,893	6,528	0.60
1978	10,422	6,381	0.61
1979	10,112	6,354	0.63
1980	9,897	6,371	0.64

Sources: Massachusetts Board of Regional Community Colleges, "Enrollment Statistics," 1967–1979; Massachusetts Board of Regents of Higher Education, "Enrollment Statistics," 1980–1981.

University. The arrival of Pagano marked the movement of community colleges from an entrepreneurial to a mature stage of development. Most of the colleges were by this time solidly vocational. Central office coordination had advanced, so that planning efforts routinely involved consideration of offerings at the other campuses and contributions to the system as a whole. Henceforth, growth would be slower. The pattern set during Dwyer's tenure would continue, but the spirit of "indiscriminate expansion" would gradually disappear. The men who administered the now-developed system encouraged more careful planning and a prudent approach to growth. Pagano described the process as involving "discussion, review, and research"—and then more of the same:

> Every new program has an assessment of need, both in terms of the student as well as the economy, and [a] job market survey has [to have] been done, so we're talking about some potential reality. That gets reviewed after the first graduates [finish], . . . so that we're not producing something that shouldn't be at the postsecondary level, or that's not viable to our economy. There are some fads; . . . everybody now is interested in solar energy. A year ago everybody was interested in ecology. You have to have a process that can at least flag a potential fad.[13]

Although community colleges were ultimately creatures of the state, with the great majority of their funds coming from state appropriations, they continued to operate through the mid-1970s with a remarkable degree of autonomy, guided less by the state than by the AACJC's vision of "comprehensive" colleges. Their concerns often coincided with state interests, to be sure, but they were not directed by those interests. The colleges typically justified themselves in terms of practical benefits to the state, but after the annual appropriation hearings, they went along their own way.

Yet, as the system matured and the health of the state economy remained delicate, this "relative autonomy" was to be drastically reduced as the colleges were gradually pulled into the orbit of a state government increasingly coordinated for purposes of economic recovery and growth.

The Development of a State Economic Strategy

The first efforts to fashion a state economic strategy were made by the Dukakis administration following the fiscal crisis of 1975. Like so many mayors and governors during this period, Governor Dukakis concluded that the state's long-term fiscal stability depended on attracting new businesses and encouraging their success. With high levels of unemployment and business failure plaguing the state, the identification of state interests with private-sector profitability seemed inescapable. Long-term stability in state revenues depended on high levels of employment and comparatively attractive levels of corporate net profitability. Dukakis thus concluded that the state had to attract new industry and to improve the climate for businesses already there.

The community colleges were involved only peripherally in the governor's economic development plan. The new job-training programs promised to businesses locating in the state were, for example, administered chiefly through the high schools and vocational institutes. The state did, however, begin to identify the community colleges as business-service institutions coordinated by state economic development plans. In a guide for employers on training resources, the governor noted the "innovative courses and programs" found in the state's community colleges. These included a CETA-funded training program for the unemployed at Northern Essex, a Western Electric–sponsored course on the "fundamentals of commercial and industrial lighting" in the Greenfield area, and job-retraining and -upgrading courses offered through the continuing education program at Bunker Hill.

The increasing talk about the high-technology future in Massachusetts had a more important implication for community colleges, however, than did any of the governor's specific programs. Although most of the colleges offered electrical and electronics technology programs, many had been slow to move into other advanced technology areas. These programs required more sophisticated (and expensive) equipment and teaching expertise than the colleges could easily afford. But the state's economic image-making stimulated the colleges to action in these areas. Between 1975 and 1978, numerous new high-technology programs appeared, representing the bulk of the new career programs in colleges (Massachusetts Board of Regional Community Colleges, "Minutes," 1975–1978).

The state's emphasis on economic development also narrowed administrators' thinking about the community colleges' purposes. They increasingly looked at the students as so much fuel for the state's economic machinery. In the view of Board member Robert Simha, campus presidents were like "division managers" whose performance could be assessed in input–output terms, with the number of degrees granted as one indicator of performance and placement rates in program-related jobs as another. In Simha's view, students could be described without embarrassment as "products" that could be assessed in terms of their acceptability to their consumers, local industry. Community college officials also increasingly justified their programs on the basis of returns to the state's "tax investment." Charles Hamilton, a management consultant who was appointed MBRCC chairman by Dukakis in 1976, said he tried to emphasize this "economic component" in his financial appeals to the state legislature: "To me, we are a training institution . . . we can affect the state economy by dealing with underemployment, unemployment and upgrading. . . . We have increasingly sharpened our strategies since I've been chairman . . . [concerning] how to talk about . . . [this] impact. . . ."[14]

The Declining Number of Transfer Students

During the period of rationalization, the enrollment of community college transfers in four-year colleges decreased abruptly in the mid-1970s fiscal crisis and only gradually rose in the late 1970s. Despite the larger size of the community college system, the number of transfers never reached the level attained in the early 1970s. Our only reliable trend data on transfer rates come from the University of Massachusetts at Amherst, which was, as noted earlier, the state's most popular transfer institution for community college students. The data for the university show community college transfers falling below 300 in 1975 and rising gradually to nearly 700 in 1978. In the 1980s, community college transfers to the university stabilized at between 450 and 500 annually—half as many as transferred between 1972 and 1974. This change reflects the special impact of the fiscal crisis as well as the general impact of market forces, both of which led to declines in application rates. It also represents the stabilization of acceptance rates at about 65 percent of applicants, a somewhat lower rate than in the later 1970s.[15]

The Era of Business Dominance, 1979–1984

The Dukakis economic strategy antagonized liberals and conservatives alike. Liberals found his budget cutting and responsiveness to the private sector more consistent with Republican philosophy than Democratic ideals. Conversely, conservatives felt that the governor's policies failed to move either far enough or fast enough in those directions. Caught between the two camps, Dukakis lost the 1978 Democratic primary to Edward J. King, a conservative businessman who had most recently served as head of the state's transit authority.

The King administration represented the apogee, at least in the modern era, of direct business influence over Massachusetts state government and, in particular, of business influence over the state's systems of higher education, including its community colleges.

King was an early convert to the idea of a high technology–dominated future in Massachusetts, and the new governor was particularly attentive to the concerns of high-tech industry in the state, a sector then employing one out of nine Massachusetts workers.[16] He spoke frequently at meetings of the Massachusetts High

Technology Council and drew many of his policy ideas and much of his top executive manpower from the industry's leadership.

The state's promotional materials clearly expressed the new emphasis on high tech. Under the leadership of former high-tech entrepreneur George Kariotis, later secretary of economic affairs under Governor King, the state claimed to position itself at "the cutting edge of the technological venture." The administration's publicity brochures emphasized three bases for the "exceptional opportunities" open to "sophisticated industries" in Massachusetts: a large and progressive financial center, a highly competitive "tax holiday" package, and a vast pool of educational and human resources capable of contributing to technological advance (see, for example, Massachusetts Board of Commerce 1982). The brochures even began to adopt the slick, full-color style of corporate annual reports, a sharp departure from the low-grade bond paper and often uninspiring prose of the Dukakis administration.

Under King, the state's Division of Employment Security participated in the promotional campaign extolling the contribution of high-technology employment to the state's economic health. Its reports showed that of the ten industrial states, Massachusetts had the greatest proportion of manufacturing employment in high-technology industries,[17] a trend that would accelerate in the later 1980s and 1990s (Commonwealth of Massachusetts, Division of Employment Security 1979). The reports also highlighted the ties between high-tech industry and higher education. "From the beginning, these industries had close ties to the academic community. Massachusetts colleges and universities attracted the talented, inventive genius and trained the technical and professional men and women needed for . . . industrialization" (Commonwealth of Massachusetts, Division of Employment Security 1979, pp. 3–7).

The High-Tech Regents and the Rise of Corporate Control

The reorganization of higher education in 1980 provided an opportunity to tie the community colleges more closely to the state's economic development plans. Pleas for reorganization had been in the air for years. Many educators were dissatisfied with the system's weak coordination provided by the Board of Higher Education, and many had grown impatient with the rivalry between the BHE and the state's secretary of education. With the new governor's support, the legislature finally agreed in the summer of 1980 (after nearly two years of hearings and debate) on a plan for reorganization. Under this plan, the segmented boards that had separately administered the three tiers of higher education in Massachusetts and the coordinating Board of Higher Education were disbanded, and a single board, the Massachusetts Board of Regents of Higher Education, was created to take their place.[18]

Not surprisingly, three of the first regents appointed by Governor King were executives from the high-technology sector, whose interests were expressed through their influence over the Board's fiscal mechanisms. The Regents established guidelines for campus budget preparations, guidelines that included several features that shaped development efforts along lines of the Regents' design. The budget was divided into two components: maintenance requests and new requests. If maintenance requests conformed to established procedures, they were approved virtually automatically. Decisions on new requests, however, were entirely at the Regents' discretion. Each year, the Regents established "request priorities" for deciding among these new requests. For the first three years, the highest-priority items were always the same: new instructional programs in engineering, computer science, and allied health.[19] Requests related to instructional support, management and administrative support, data processing, and plant improvement were listed as successively lower-priority areas. New library materials were typically listed last if at all, and new programs outside high-tech fields were not listed among the Regents' priorities.

The Regents' "high-cost course adjustments" provided a further incentive for the colleges—if one was needed—to organize new high-tech curricula. As part of the formulas used in the maintenance budgets, funds were allocated to the campuses "in recognition of (the) additional costs associated with certain courses in (the) Regents' targeted program area" (Massachusetts Board of Regents of Higher Education 1984). In the first three years, allocations for high-tech programs were substantially above the base allocations.

The Board's control over appropriations meant that its priorities would carry weight, for the Regents' financial powers were extensive. When it created the Board, the legislature abandoned its past practice of distributing appropriations on a campus-by-campus basis. Instead, the legislature decided on one sum for all of public higher education and then turned over campus-level allocation decisions to the Regents.[20]

The more politically attuned campus presidents quickly understood the implications of the new authority structure. For example, when three Regents visited Northern Essex Community College in their initial site visitations in December 1980, President John Dimitry listed his top four priorities as construction of a high-tech building, personnel exchanges with high-tech industry, expansion of corporate training programs, and a new budgeting system. Dimitry also showed his appreciation of the new power structure by suggesting that Massachusetts consider adopting the governance structure of the Southern Carolina community college system, in which board members were simultaneously appointed by the governor to two boards: the economic development board and the community college board (Massachusetts Board of Regents of Higher Education 1981).

Throughout the system, curriculum development fell into line with the new emphasis. Between 1978 and 1982, the community colleges more than doubled their enrollments in electronics and computer technology programs, and the number of degrees awarded in these areas increased by some 50 percent (Useem 1982, p. 37). In all, eighty different programs in advanced technology fields were introduced in the three years following reorganization.[21]

During the first year of operation, the Regents also introduced a five-year planning system, which required the colleges to chart their proposed development. These plans were then reviewed by the Regents' staff for their conformity to the Regents' priorities and for any unnecessary duplication of programs in nearby institutions. The community colleges, like the state colleges and the state university, were asked to describe and justify the curricula they proposed to develop in the succeeding five years and the "linkages" they planned to develop with local business and industries. Once approved (and the process was arduous for some schools), these documents were treated as contracts between the colleges and the Regents: any modification in the plans required justification in budget narratives, and a new review by the Regents' staff.

A review of the community colleges' planning documents from 1981 shows just how well the Regents' control succeeded. Of the fifteen campuses, only seven had plans for any development of liberal arts–transfer programs. Even this figure overstates intentions, however, as four of these seven planned just one new transfer program. Thus, twelve of the fifteen schools planned development of no more than one liberal arts program over the next four to five years. Conversely, of the fifty-six new career programs mentioned in these planning documents, half were in the Regents' high-tech priority areas, including word processing and applied energy technology at Bristol; electronics technology and petroleum technology at Cape Cod; microelectronics technology and computer-aided design technology at Mass Bay; electronic biomedical technology and technical graphics at Middlesex; and microprocessor technology and numerical control technology at Springfield (Massachusetts Board of Regents of Higher Education 1983).

The colleges' cooperation was rewarded by the Regents' advocacy of their interests. With the expansion of high-tech planning under way, the Regents were able, by 1982–1983 to persuade the governor to recommend a 10 percent increase in his higher education budget, the first significant increase for higher education in three years. Part of the increase was designed to cover faculty salary increases and the remainder to finance new programs (Useem 1982, p. 42).

During the King era of direct business influence, the community colleges were transformed from a confederation of more or less autonomous educational entrepreneurs into a relatively coordinated system of business-service organizations. For the first time, rationalizing authorities had both the fiscal mechanisms and the organizational acumen to shape the colleges in the image they desired. It is possible, of course, that impersonal market forces might have generated similar efforts, but it is likely that the rate of change would have been somewhat slower. Although the high-tech sector was the most dynamic business sector in the state, it was not the only important sector. Consequently, impersonal market forces alone would almost certainly have led to a somewhat more diversified vocationalization. The Regents' direct instrumental control allowed for a much greater concentration of vocationalizing activities in particular occupational fields than would otherwise have occurred.

Bay State Skills Corporation: Harbinger of a "Corporatist" Model

The Regents were not the only vehicle of coordination that the King administration used; the Bay State Skills Corporation (BSSC) also had some influence. The BSSC, the brainchild of Governor King's secretary of economic affairs, George Kariotis, provided grants to train workers to the specifications of the contracting industries. In return for this training, industries were required to provide a matching grant of equipment, instructors, materials, and/or curricular advice. BSSC sought to tailor the training to "individual industry needs" and to pay particular attention to the needs of companies in high-growth fields. Indeed, BSSC heralded itself as "the catalyst uniting industry and education in training today's workforce for the jobs of tomorrow. By encouraging its technologically successful companies, Massachusetts controls the transition from declining industries to its future—computers, robotics, numerically controlled machines, biotechnology, and others which are coming upon us so suddenly" (Bay State Skills Corporation, 1984).

All educational institutions were eligible as training sites, and ideas for proposals typically originated with the schools. After the schools secured local industry involvement, they prepared a proposal for the BSSC outlining the scope and nature of the proposed training. Successful proposals could receive a matching grant of up to $200,000, although most of the grants were in the range of $40,000 to $80,000. The Bay State Skills Corporation was designed to be independent of the state government, except during negotiations regarding its annual appropriations. According to BSSC officials, this quasi-public status allowed it to avoid "many of the complications traditionally considered an obstacle to business working with government." Strong corporate representation on the BSSC's board of directors further ensured its relevance "to the real problems industry faces" (Bay State Skills Corporation, 1984).

The community colleges were avid participants in the new scheme proposed by BSSC. For example, Northern Essex received grants to train electronics technicians for the Gould-Modicom Company and licensed practical nurses for three regional hospitals; Middlesex received a BSSC grant to train nurses and another to train technical interns; Mount Wachusett trained cable-television installers for a local company; and Roxbury trained computer-aided drafters and design technicians for four Boston companies. Other community colleges provided training for printed-circuit technicians, respiratory therapy technicians, graphics-printing technicians, energy-sales people, clerical and banking operations assistants, and machine operators (Bay State Skills Corporation 1984). The training for machinists offered at North Shore was considered so successful in terms of cost and placement that the college received an award from the BSSC for exceptional involvement.

Each of these programs originated in the colleges' continuing education divisions. By 1984, however, the nursing courses, the computer-aided drafting at Roxbury, and the printed-circuit technology at Northern Essex were moving toward inclusion as day division/associates' degree offerings.[22] BSSC grants functioned much like federal vocational education grants, but with "quality control," as BSSC's George Denhard put it, resting more with the corporations than with the colleges. "The employer input is important as a quality control input. The process encourages production-quality training. . . ."[23]

In the summer of 1984, BSSC added a set of special institutes to its programs which were designed to allow Massachusetts faculty to "exchange information" with industrial experts in new technologies. The institutes concentrated on high-tech industry and were planned by BSSC and industry officials. Provided at little or no cost to the faculty, the institutes limited enrollment to those "who intended to return to their classrooms and directly apply their new-found knowledge to their curricula" (Bay State Skills Corporation 1984). The high-tech focus is evident in seven of the eight topics chosen for the first series of institutes: robotics and flexible information, spectral estimation, computer-integrated manufacturing, artificial intelligence, biotechnology, computer-assisted drafting, and the use of microcomputers in chemical laboratories. (The eighth topic was international business).

Many observers regarded BSSC as an experiment in European and Japanese-style "corporatism": "American managers have long complained that when they go head-to-head with Japanese and European competitors, the margin of victory is often the government support and cooperation they receive. . . . We are just beginning to understand the exciting possibilities created by the interaction of educational institutions, private industry, and the Bay State Skills Corporation" (Bay State Skills Corporation 1984).[24] But, in fact, the program was business dominated in both conception and design. The "skills corporation" idea represented a small, but distinct reduction in the autonomy of Massachusetts higher education institutions. Few complained; in an era of intense competition for limited resources, the dangers of state subordination to the special interests of private industry seemed a remote concern to most Massachusetts educators. Indeed, by 1984, BSSC has become a model for emulation. Three other states had adopted the idea, and the U.S. Congress had even briefly considered the establishment of a "United States Skills Corporation" based on the Massachusetts model.

Organizational Tensions and Market Competition

Although relations between business and the two-year colleges grew increasingly close during the King years, they were not without strain. First, there were practical problems in building closer ties. Frequent turnover among corporate officers and difficulties in locating key personnel were persistent barriers to coordination. Corporate arrogance was also a problem. Community college officials continued to have the most to gain from cooperative arrangements, and they often resented the ingratitude they sense in the business officials.

Many community colleges officials accurately perceived that corporate interest tended to focus on four-year college engineering and computer science programs and also felt some resentment on this count (Useem 1982). Moreover, most community college administrators believed that firms were not truly interested in using their services to train or upgrade their employees. "Once a company hires a training director, all is lost," said one administrator (Useem 1982, p. 44). Some traditional tension between academic and industrial goals was also apparent, although these tensions were only infrequently expressed. One continuing education director, for example, criticized programs that required avoidance of controversial topics, such as labor relations or occupational safety issues. This same administrator also remarked on the limitations of highly specific job-training programs, which he felt steered employees away from the kind of broad theoretical training that could give them more career flexibility. Another administrator expressed alarm at the prospect of complete vocationalization. "I am always fighting attempts to make this a technical institute," he said, "We want to leave some room for the liberal arts" (anonymous administrator quoted in Useem, 1982, p. 41).

Yet despite some episodic strains, virtually all college administrators were eager to adjust their curricular offerings to fit employment opportunities in high-growth areas, and nearly all of them approved of the far-reaching influence of high-tech executives on higher-education curricula (Useem 1982, pp. 43–44). Not surprisingly, the community colleges were often the most vocal in their enthusiasm for these developments.

Institutional Rivalries and the Struggle for a Market Niche

While relations between the community colleges and business moved closer, relations between the two-year colleges and their closest market rivals, the state colleges, deteriorated somewhat. In search of a stable market niche, the state colleges found themselves pressed to choose between the successful community college strategy of occupational training and the higher-prestige, but economically risky, strategy of liberal arts upgrading. Under the press of market forces and the state's interest in job training, most chose to vocationalize their curricula in an effort to stabilize their enrollments and incomes. The sudden interest by the state colleges in the later 1970s in career program development had become by the early 1980s an ever-swelling enthusiasm. "If you look at a state-college catalogue now," said one amused but slightly rueful administrator, "you think you're reading the catalogue of a community college." [25]

The situation created chaos out of efforts to coordinate the programs of the two- and four-year schools. [26] The two-year colleges usually did not mind if the state college offered upper-division courses in their program areas, but they objected to courses at the freshman and sophomore levels. This limitation, in turn, was not acceptable to the state college officials, who had vested interests in full four-year programs.

In keeping with their own curricular development goals, the state colleges sometimes refused to accept lower-division courses completed at community colleges. Debates in the Council of College Presidents often revolved around the appropriateness of topics covered in specific courses. Although many suspected that institutional rivalry was responsible for most of the friction, the issues were not easily resolved because of the element of judgment involved in categorizing levels of course work. The contretemps sometimes reached bizarre resolutions. "I teach exactly the same course in labor relations at Bridgewater (State College) and at Bristol Community College," said one administrator/part-time instructor, "but Bridgewater will not accept for transfer credit the course I teach at Bristol. . . . They say it doesn't have enough on grievance, but it's exactly the same course I teach for credit there." [27]

As one approach to the problem, community college presidents began to demand that agreements be worked out before any new occupational programs were adopted by a state college. These agreements would state that community college students would be eligible for automatic acceptance as first-semester juniors if they had completed their associate's degree in a program paralleling that in the state college they wished to enter. Parallel programs already in existence, however, remained open to seemingly endless wrangling over transfer requirements. These disputes continued to be settled on a case-by-case basis through the early 1980s.

Observers agreed that the "turf conflicts" between the community and the state colleges led to great confusion among students, as the students often could not know before they attempted to transfer whether their courses at the community college would be accepted.

In addition, the market-centered institutional rivalries added fuel to the "credential inflation" (see Collins 1979) that had been increasing in recent years. By the mid-1980s, courses like law enforcement and electronics technology that had previously required only two years of college (and, in come cases, no college at all) for entry-level certification were often requiring four. Such prolongation of the educational process undoubtedly served vital organizational interests for the colleges, whose flow of resources from the state was partially dependent on maintaining enrollment levels. But it is hard to see how this pattern of credential inflation served the interests of the state's "consumers" of education.

The Community College As a Business-Service Institution

Massachusetts voters again opted for change in 1982, replacing Governor King with his predecessor, Michael Dukakis. For the most part, the second Dukakis administration adopted most of the programs of the King administration, moderating only King's sometimes stridently conservative rhetoric. After Dukakis's election, two of the "high-tech" Regents left the Board. Dukakis replaced them with new people from outside the high-tech world—a pattern he continued throughout the second term—but the original Regents' educational policies were left essentially unchanged. Indeed, nothing in the second Dukakis Administration altered the course of the community colleges' development into business-service institutions.

The concentration on vocational programs in some ways even increased during the second Dukakis administration. Whereas the Board of Regents had still received at least a few requests for new liberal arts programs during the King administration, it received none in Dukakis's second term (compared with five to six new requests per year in vocational fields). The Board approved an average of three new vocational programs per year, mainly in office management and applied technology areas—computer sciences, lab technology, applied energy technology, business administration, and word-processing management.

For the most part, this lack of change represents the increasingly self-regulating character of the educational machinery. Nearly all of the campus presidents of the 1980s had been appointed during the campaigns to build occupational education. They owed their careers to the success of the comprehensive model, and they were ideologically committed to the vocational orientation. Moreover, the key lieutenants in the system were often younger men, trained in labor projection, market research, cost–benefit analysis, research methodology, and other tools of policy planning. These young technocrats frequently saw the organizational interests of the community colleges with even greater clarity than did their elders. Having little close contact with students or parents, they concentrated on constructing institutions tailored to the state's avowed interest in economic development.

Most of the efforts of these men went into designing programs attuned to emerging employment opportunities and into developing partnerships with business. All the schools eagerly chased federal vocational education funds and Bay State Skills Corporation grants. All designed customized training programs for local industries under the auspices of their continuing education programs. Most introduced increasing numbers of short-term "certificate" programs to train workers at or below the associate's degree level. Neither the continuing education nor the certificate programs required any arts or sciences courses. Perhaps because of this, even more people enrolled in these programs than in the associate's degree vocational programs. Most of the schools also continued to plan their futures with the high-tech labor market foremost in mind. The five-year plans emphasized the training of technicians in robotics, biotechnology, technical writing, scientific laboratory technology, computer-aided manufacturing, and other technological areas.[28]

Conflicts between the state colleges and community colleges were, for the time being, resolved by defining the state colleges as centers for "professional occupational programs" and the community colleges as centers for "vocational occupational programs." The professional programs encompassed business, nursing and teaching careers, and the vocational programs focused on technician training. Problems with transfer credits, however, remained as confusing as ever.

In spite of their best efforts to turn themselves into service stations for the growth sectors of the corporate economy, the Massachusetts community colleges could not be compared in the mid-1980s with other community college systems elsewhere either in the intensity or the volume of their involvements with business and industry. The dozen or so direct involvements of most of the Massachusetts community colleges paled in comparison, for example, with the 100 or so separate business-partnership arrangements at the De Anza College District in California's Silicon Valley during the same period. Low budgets and equipment deficiencies made comparable efforts in Massachusetts impractical (Useem 1982). But the trajectory was clearly in the de Anza direction. As one young administrator put it "It's in the back of everybody's mind. . . . We all know where our bread is going to be buttered."[29]

In Massachusetts, the last major opportunity for change occurred with reorganization in 1980. The reorganization did bring into prominence new high-tech priorities, but, since that time, few new interests. The largely self-regulating character of Massachusetts's community colleges in the years after reorganization can be seen in the declining role played by the Regents and also by the AACJC itself. The current situation was captured in an offhand remark by one of the Regents' staff members regarding the AACJC. "A few of the college presidents may be involved," he said. "Others may not even know it exists."[30]

The Vocationalization of Community Colleges in Massachusetts

In looking back on the development of Massachusetts community colleges, what is perhaps most striking is the considerable degree of autonomy they enjoyed for much of that time, not only from business, but from the state itself. Although dependent on state resources, Massachusetts community colleges were not—at least for the first fifteen years of their history—harnessed to a coherent state plan. Instead, they were relatively free to pursue their interests as they themselves defined them. For their first decade, this meant, as was the case with community colleges nationwide, an emphasis on the liberal arts transfer function. As we have argued in Chapter 2, it was only via their link to established four-year colleges and universities that community colleges could hope to gain respectability by claiming to enhance access to "higher education' as traditionally defined.

While they were trying to establish their status as a bona fide part of higher education via their emphasis on transfer, community colleges were also actively engaged in pursuing their function as comprehensive institutions. Especially when William Dwyer became president of the Massachusetts Regional Board of Community Colleges in 1964, the community colleges turned considerable energy toward increasing the proportion of their students enrolled in vocational programs. This vocationalization project, we believe, illustrates in detail our theoretical point that the two-year colleges were driven by internal organizational exigencies to try to monopolize a distinctive function in higher education—and, in so doing, to secure a stable market niche for themselves in the competition among institutions for "training markets." Certainly, the movement toward vocationalism in the second half of the 1960s in Massachusetts cannot be understood in terms of consumer demand; on the contrary, our evidence reveals that community college students in Massachusetts, as elsewhere, were initially quite resistant to institutional policies that threatened to divert them from four-year institutions.

The various mechanisms used by community colleges in pursuit of their vocationalization project are described in Chapter 6; for our purposes here, what is perhaps most noteworthy is that many of these at times rather blunt-edged mechanisms were put into effect *prior to the decline in labor-market opportunities for graduates of four-year colleges.* These efforts, our study reveals, were not without effect; by the early 1970s, the proportion of students in vocational programs was already growing. Nonetheless, it was not until the changed labor market conditions of the post-1970 period became evident that the community colleges' longstanding vocationalization project really gathered momentum.

Yet if the consumer-choice explanation of community college vocationalization leaves much unaccounted for, the business-domination model is at least as inadequate. Indeed, throughout the 1960s, businessmen, far from seeking to impose their will on Massachusetts community colleges, showed a striking lack of interest in them. Needing business far more than business needed them, the community colleges engaged in an at times pathetic quest to convince employers that they could be of use to them. Thus, far from being subject to the direct "instrumental" control of business in their first decade, community colleges had difficulty convincing business to pay attention to them. That they nonetheless shaped themselves in their efforts to meet corporate needs in the absence of business intervention is, to be sure, testimony to the extraordinary structural power of business.

When William Dwyer left office in 1976, the community colleges' vocationalization project was a success. Greatly facilitated by an objective change during the early 1970s in the employment prospects of graduates of four-year colleges, this project had succeeded in putting an elaborate network of vocational programs in place even before there was substantial demand for them. Whereas under one-third of the Massachusetts community college students had enrolled in vocational programs in the mid-1960s, well over half of these students were in the vocational track by 1976. Had the programs not been there for them already, the students would not, quite simply, have had the opportunity to choose them.

In the years after Dwyer's departure, there was a rapid acceleration in direct business involvement in community college affairs. Especially after Edward King's election to the governorship in 1978 and the associated creation in 1980 of a new Board of Regents, big business became intensely interested in the structure and content of Massachusetts public higher education. As we have shown, the rise of direct business influence over community colleges was consequential in harnessing these institutions to the needs of the state's increasingly influential high-technology corporations. Yet this said, it remains true that business domination became a reality only after vocationalization was already in place.

CONCLUSION

8 The Community College and the Politics of Inequality

Since its origins at the turn of the century, the junior college has had a complex, and at times uneasy, relationship with a public that has looked to the educational system as a vehicle for the realization of the American dream. Despite its self-portrayal as "democracy's college" and its often heroic efforts to extend education to the masses, the two-year institution has faced widespread public skepticism. For to most Americans, college was a pathway to the bachelor's degree, and the junior college—unlike the four-year institution—could not award it. Moreover, the early public junior colleges were often tied administratively and even physically to local secondary schools, a pattern that compounded their problems in gaining legitimacy as bona fide institutions of higher education.

The two-year institution's claim to being a genuine college rested almost exclusively on its promise to offer the first two years of a four-year college education. Yet the junior college was never intended, despite the high aspirations of its students, to provide anything more than a terminal education for most of those who entered it; indeed, at no point in its history did even half of its students transfer to a four-year institution. Nonetheless, for at least the first two decades of its existence, almost exclusive emphasis was placed on its transfer rather than its terminal function. As the early leaders of the movement saw it, the first task at hand was to establish the legitimacy of this fragile institution as an authentic college. And this task could be accomplished only by convincing the existing four-year institutions to admit junior college graduates and to offer them credit for the courses that they had completed there.

If the pursuit of academic respectability through emphasis on transfer dominated the junior college movement during its first decades, by the mid-1920s a countermovement stressing the role of the junior college as a provider of terminal vocational education began to gather momentum. Arguing that most junior college students were, whatever their aspirations, in fact terminal, proponents of this view saw the institution's main task not as providing a platform for transfer for a minority but, rather, as offering vocational programs leading to marketable skills for the vast majority. This debate—between the forces seeing the junior college as a primarily academic institution dedicated to the democratic ideal of mobility through equality of educational opportunity and the forces looking on the junior college in more economic terms as a training ground for middle-level manpower—was to mark a recurrent tension within the community college movement.

By 1940, the two-year college had come to occupy a distinct position in the system of higher education. Attended by students of generally lower socioeconomic status and measured academic ability than their counterparts at four-year colleges and sending well under half of their entrants to bachelor's degree–granting institutions, the junior colleges constituted the bottom track of the system of higher education's increasingly segmented structure of internal stratification. But tracking within the junior college had not yet crystallized on the eve of World War II, with only about one-fourth of the students enrolling in the vocational programs so enthusiastically supported by Walter Crosby Eells, Leonard Koos, Doak Campbell, and other leaders of the national junior college movement. The students' resistance to the vocationalizing efforts of the junior college vanguard was strong at this time and remained so for the next three decades. Yet the vocational wing of the junior college movement was, after years of assiduous effort, ultimately triumphant. In the following section, we shall attempt to explain the causes and consequences of this transformation.

From Liberal Arts to Vocational Training

Like all other American institutions of higher education, the community colleges' survival is dependent on its capacity to attract students in a competitive educational marketplace. Moreover, two-year colleges have in common with all other colleges and universities a need to win a share of the market for educated labor from which employers, especially the major corporations and large public bureaucracies, hire their higher-level employees. Success in the competition for these "training markets" is arguably the single most important determinant of a college's status. An institution that is closely linked to a wealthy and powerful training market—for example, as a medical school is linked to the medical profession—will become a prestigious one. Conversely, an institution tied to a more modest training market—for example, as a state teachers college is tied to the teaching profession—is likely to acquire, at most, moderate status.[1]

From its inception, the junior college's biggest problem was that the most lucrative and high-status training markets were already occupied by existing higher education institutions. Head-to-head competition for these markets with established colleges and universities, especially the more powerful and prestigious, was futile. Much of the history of the junior college—the ceaseless debate over "mission," the persistent ambiguity of "identity," and the constant search for new markets (both training and student)—can be understood as a process of gradual and uneven adjustment to this reality.

If the four-year colleges dominated the best training markets, so too did they dominate the competition for the most desirable secondary school graduates. The junior colleges' response to the reality of its structural subordination to established four-year institutions was to attempt to become "feeder schools" for the upper division of universities in much the same way that the public high schools had become feeder schools for the freshman and sophomore years in the nation's colleges and universities. Indeed, in its early years, the junior college movement dreamed—with the encouragement of the administrators of some of the country's leading universities—of establishing a monopoly over entry into the upper division, much as the nation's secondary schools had established, by the early twentieth century, a monopoly over college entrance.

The problem with this strategy was that four-year colleges, especially the leading ones, already had a generally adequate supply of freshmen and sophomores, and for the most part, neither wanted nor needed the types of students likely to attend junior colleges. Some of the nation's top universities—among them, Chicago, Stanford, and Berkeley—did, to be sure, dream in the first years of the century of divesting themselves of their lower divisions altogether and becoming pure universities on the German model. But these institutions were in no way dependent on the junior colleges to provide them with students. During World War I, when the loss of tens of thousands of young men to the military cut into the enrollments of the nation's colleges and universities, many less prestigious institutions became convinced that they needed their freshman and sophomore classes in order to be economically viable. This realization, coupled with the awareness in the state legislatures of the enormous political outcry likely to accompany cutting off the state's youth from access to the freshman and sophomore years of taxpayer-supported state universities, was sufficient to defeat the cause of those who wished the junior college to be the locus of all lower-division education.[2]

Although the junior colleges never became the sole route to the junior and senior years of college, most of them retained a strong emphasis on the liberal arts–transfer function. This emphasis reflected a shrewd, if not entirely conscious, assessment of organizational interests. For in the absence of an institutional linkage to four-year institutions (and, indirectly, to the professional and managerial positions to which they often led), the junior college would have enjoyed no more status than that of a technical institute or a proprietary school. That the junior college came to be considered an authentic part of higher education, rather than a mere extension of secondary school, was due in large part to its professed function of serving as a platform from which students could transfer, with credit, to an established four-year college.

Before embarking on any other projects, the two-year institution thus had to establish itself as a "genuine" college. The import of this task was appreciated by the earliest leaders of the junior college movement who chose to pursue academic respectability through the only available path—emphasis on the liberal arts–transfer function. This same pattern was repeated several decades later in Massachusetts, where, as we showed in Chapter 5, the founders of community colleges concentrated almost exclusively in the early 1960s on transfer programs as a way of convincing a skeptical populace that two-year colleges really were part of higher education.

If the two-year colleges were supported by the public because they were viewed as way stations on the road to four-year institutions, the sponsorship that they received from their allies in the major universities was based on a different vision of their proper role. Fearing that they would be "overrun" by hordes of unqualified students and yet recognizing the powerful political pressures for more open access to universities in a society emphasizing upward mobility through education, the elite universities saw the junior college as an essential safety valve that would satisfy the demands for access while protecting their own institutions.[3] From the perspective of William Rainey Harper, David Starr Jordan, Alexis Lange, Robert Gordon Sproul, and other university administrators who did who much to spur the growth of the junior college, the two-year institution existed less to offer new opportunities to obtain a bachelor's degree to excluded segments of the populace than to divert them away from four-year colleges and universities. If only a minority of junior college students wanting a B.A. ever transferred to a four-year institution (and many fewer still to a prestigious one), this was of little concern. On the contrary, the fact that only a select few of two-year college students gained access to their institutions was, in their view, a sign that the junior colleges were successful in performing their assigned sorting function.

The early growth of public junior colleges tended to be strongest where they had vigorous sponsorship—as in California and Illinois—from the leaders of prestigious universities. They tended to be weakest where the organizational field in which they were located was dominated by unfriendly competitors, whether private institutions (as in New England and the Mid-Atlantic states) or state universities that had a tradition of relatively open access (as in Ohio and Indiana). But wherever they developed, the public junior colleges faced two contradictory tasks: the democratic one of bringing new populations into higher education and the exclusionary one of channeling them away from the four-year institutions that they hoped to attend.

Locked into a subordinate position in the academic hierarchy from which they had no real prospect of escape, some leaders of the two-year college movement began to develop in the 1920s and 1930s an alternative strategy to enhance their institutions' low status. These men, whom we have referred to as the junior college vanguard, recognized that most of their students would never transfer to a four-year college and were deeply concerned about these students' fate in a highly competitive labor market. Their solution—one that, in their view, served both student and institutional interests—was to transform the junior college from a predominantly transfer-oriented institution into one principally dedicated to providing terminal vocational education.

Noting that there were only a limited number of professional and upper-managerial positions and that far more junior college students aspired to these positions than could ever attain them, such men as Koos, Eells, and Campbell saw the two-year college's task as the firm but gentle rechanneling of these students toward middle-level jobs commensurate with their presumed abilities and past accomplishments. Seen through this prism, the educational and occupational aspirations of most junior college students were "excessive" and therefore in need of "adjustment." The appeal of the leadership's vocationalization project resided in its promise to provide "latent terminal" students with at least short-range upward mobility at the same time that it would satisfy the junior college's organizational interests by capturing for them the best training markets still unoccupied by their four-year competitors.

The vocationalization project aroused widespread, if not uniform, enthusiasm among junior college administrators. For what a drastic increase in vocational education promised to do was to move the two-year colleges from the bottom of the liberal arts–oriented academic hierarchy to the top of the occupational training hierarchy. The junior college would thus be removed from an academic competition that it could never win at the same time that its new emphasis would connect it to training for emerging occupational fields. Furthermore, the move toward terminal vocational education could be expected to receive the enthusiastic approval of powerful outside sponsors. This approval seemed likely to come from the elite universities, which saw the junior college's proper function as one protecting them from unqualified students. But it also was likely to be welcomed by cost-conscious state and local governments, which tended to look favorably on practical, job-oriented training that promised to avoid the problem of "overproducing" graduates.

Whatever else might be said about the community colleges' vocational programs, it cannot be claimed—and this is corroborated by both our analysis of national trends and our Massachusetts case study—that they were initiated in response to mass demand. On the contrary, administrators repeatedly noted the resistance of junior college students (and their parents) to increased vocational training. Yet despite this resistance, which persisted from the 1930s through the 1960s, key junior college administrators and researchers remained committed to the project. Indeed, much of the discussion about vocational education in the junior college literature of this period was devoted precisely to the issue of how to expand these programs despite the lack of student interest in them. The students' preferences—far from being sovereign, as in the consumer-choice model—thus became socially defined as a problem to be overcome.

The consumer-choice model of educational change discussed in Chapter 1 therefore cannot explain either the origins of this vocationalization project or its pursuit by junior college leaders in the face of persistent, albeit usually passive, student opposition.[4] Nor can the business-domination model explain the long-standing movement to vocationalize the junior college. For big business, although it had actively tried to shape community colleges to its own purposes in Massachusetts and other states since the late 1970s, was for decades generally indifferent to the entire junior college movement. Far from exerting over the two-year colleges the kind of "instrumental" control suggested by some Marxist analysts, big business for decades thought them unworthy of attention. The community colleges, instead of having to fight off threats to their autonomy from domineering corporate giants, spent years unsuccessfully trying to convince large firms that they could be of use to them.

Yet if large corporations showed little interest in the community colleges and only rarely intervened in their internal affairs, they nonetheless exerted considerable influence on the direction of the junior college movement. By their very location in the social structure, the large firms controlled what was, from a community college point of view, a critical resource: the capacity to hire the student "products" of the nation's colleges and universities. Thus, even in the absence of any active interest whatsoever, business—unlike labor—simply had to be taken into account. This capacity of business to influence the actions of other institutions in the absence of any direct intervention has been referred to as its *structural power*.

Recognizing that no institution of higher education can prosper if it fails to form links with employers, junior colleges set about trying to convince business that its graduates were worth hiring. But the major business firms did not need the community college; they already had well-established relations with higher-status colleges and universities and, in any case, trained many of their employees themselves.[5] Still less did a largely indifferent business community demand that the community college vocationalize itself. Indeed, although community college journals in the 1950s and 1960s were full of ideas about how to "sell" the two-year college to big business, one searches the business press of this period almost entirely in vain for any references to two-year as opposed to four-year colleges. If, by the 1970s, a marriage of sorts was finally consummated between the corporate community and the junior college, it was a radically unequal one and one that, like most asymmetrical unions, was realized only after an ardent courtship by the more eager partner.

After decades of strenuous effort, the vocationalization project finally began to yield dividends in the late 1960s. By this time, outside sponsors—among them, major private foundations and the federal government—had joined the push for expanded occupational training in the community college. These outside interests adopted the community colleges after they had proved themselves to be popular institutions. Thus it was primarily after the two-year colleges had become successful as low-cost, convenient alternatives to four-year institutions that outside elites became interested in them. With the assistance of external sponsors, administrators gradually improved their capacity to effect change through the mechanisms of enrollment redirection—among them guidance, testing, recruitment, and job linkages. By the late 1960s, the percentage of students in vocational programs began to rise for the first time since the 1930s. And even in Massachusetts, where the community college movement was young and vocational programs faced especially difficult status problems, the proportion of students in the occupational track started to rise around 1968.

What is striking about the increase in the relative size of vocational programs during these years is not its magnitude, which was modest, but that it occurred before the much-publicized decline in the early 1970s in employer demand for college graduates. The rapid multiplication of vocational programs in this period was not a response to "consumer choice"; in Massachusetts, in fact, the new programs were created first and students sought for them only afterward. Both nationally and in Massachusetts these programs were initiated in the hope that creating a diverse and attractive array of vocational offerings would finally "cure" students of their fixation on bachelor's degrees. Aided perhaps as much by large infusions of external support as by an increase in popular demand, the community college vocationalizers, after years of frustration, were finally having an impact.

The abrupt downturn in 1970–1971 in the labor market for college graduates gave the forces favoring the vocationalization of the community college a new justification for expanding occupational training. Much like the executives in the so-called "garbage-can" model of decision making (Cohen and March 1974, Cohen et al. 1972) who are full of favored "solutions" but in search of "problems" to which they can attach them, community college administrators proffered their preexisting vocational solution to the emergent problem of underemployment. Under the changed market conditions of the early 1970s, the old arguments in favor of junior college vocational programs took on unprecedented force. Faced with a barrage of media images of Ph.D.s driving taxis and college graduates waiting in long lines in unemployment offices, community college students began to view the college transfer programs not as way stations on the road to success but as gateways to nowhere. For the first time in the junior colleges' seventy-year history, the status of vocational programs began to rival—and, in some cases, even to surpass—that of the liberal arts–transfer programs.

The objective decline in the labor market for college graduates that occurred in the early 1970s was a principal reason why, after decades of frustration, the vocationalization project of community college administrators finally took off. As long as holders of a B.A. were manifestly doing well, the much-bemoaned "degree fixation" of most junior college students was impossible to dislodge. In the context of a strong market for graduates of four-year colleges, vocational programs looked, if not dead-end, then decidedly second-best.

Yet if the objective deterioration in the labor market situation of college graduates in the 1970s was undeniably a powerful force behind the expansion of community college vocational education, it nonetheless remains the case that students make decisions on the basis of subjective perceptions of their prospects. Beliefs about available opportunities are, of course, connected to one's "objective chances" in the labor market (Bourdieu 1974); at the same time, however, there is no logical reason to believe that the former are a direct function of the latter.[6] And in the case of community college students in the early 1970s, there is reason to believe that the disjuncture between objective economic trends and subjective perceptions of these trends was quite sizable. From the analysis of news media images of the market for college graduates during this period that we reported in Chapter 4, we concluded that the public—including community college students—in all likelihood had an exaggerated view of the seriousness of the plight of the college-educated.

Reports in the mass communication media virtually never mentioned the continuing advantages of those who completed four years of college—their higher salaries, greater chances of promotion, and lower rates of unemployment. At the same time, the media presented an image of high economic returns to community college occupational training that was incompatible with available evidence on the more modest results of these programs. This is not, of course, to deny that there was a significant decline in the fortunes of college graduates in these years. Nor is it to claim that all community college vocational programs yielded low returns.

But it is to suggest that the student influenced by the reports then appearing in the mass media was likely to have a far rosier view of the results of vocational programs than was warranted by their performance. Although there is no reason to believe that this was its intent, the effect of this media reporting was to facilitate the efforts of the forces wishing to vocationalize the community college.

If our investigation of media images of the market for college graduates suggests that students may not have had access to the "perfect information" essential to models of rational choice, our study of the vocationalization of Massachusetts community colleges raises questions about the extent to which genuine freedom of choice was a reality. A variety of mechanisms were used to increase the proportion of students in terminal vocational programs in Massachusetts community colleges. Some of these—such as the disproportionate allocation of institutional resources to occupational education and the selection for the presidencies of individual campuses only of men committed to vocationalization—helped shape student choices, but could not entirely control them. Guidance and testing were also used to help shape student choices. At times, more radical steps were taken, such as several instances of quota setting on the size of liberal arts programs at Massachusetts community colleges. Although such practices may not have been representative, they suggest that at least some community colleges, in their eagerness to increase their vocational enrollments, not only sought to structure incentives, but went so far as to violate the freedom of choice of their supposedly sovereign student "consumers."

As was the case nationally, the declining market for college graduates in the early 1970s was a major factor behind the increase in Massachusetts in the proportion of students enrolled in community college vocational programs. Interestingly, however, at institutions at which the administration adopted a neutral posture toward vocationalization—as, for example, at the predominantly black Roxbury Community College—occupational enrollments expanded at a slower rate. Had more community colleges taken a neutral stance rather than sponsoring expanded occupational training, vocational enrollments would no doubt have increased substantially, but the magnitude of the increase might not have been the same. Indeed, had two-year college administrators and major outside forces such as the federal government and key private foundations been as vigorous in promoting liberal arts transfer programs as they were in channeling students away from them, it is entirely possible that the community college today would be balanced more evenly between its transfer and its vocational functions.

Yet if the active pursuit of vocationalization was a choice, it was certainly not a random one. In reflecting on the development of two-year colleges both nationwide and in the state of Massachusetts, a common pattern emerges. In both cases, the first objective of the junior college was to establish itself as a bona fide institution of higher education—a task pursued in both instances by an almost exclusive initial reliance on the development of college-parallel transfer programs. Once this task was basically accomplished—by the 1920s in California and parts of the Midwest, but not until the mid-1960s in Massachusetts—attention then turned to the expansion of terminal vocational programs. In neither instance was vocationalization pursued in response to either student demand or the insistence of business. On the contrary, the community colleges tenaciously pursued their vocationalization project in the face of student opposition and business indifference.

Although community colleges were agents of their own vocationalization, their transformation was strongly supported by other key institutions. The university, which from the era of Harper and Jordan to that of Conant and Kerr consistently saw the junior college as a crucial buffer between itself and a populace clamoring for access to college, was delighted at a policy that promised to strengthen the junior college's sorting function and thereby to channel students away from its gates. The state, perennially concerned about budgets and in later years frightened by the prospect of masses of "overeducated" workers, saw terminal vocational training as a means of limiting enrollment and providing students with practical skills that could be harnessed to larger state economic development strategies. Business, after decades of neglecting the junior college, finally recognized around 1970 the advantages of vocational programs that could provide private training at public expense. And the great private foundations, especially Carnegie, grasped the potential of terminal vocational education as a means of rationalizing the relationship between a burgeoning system of higher education and an economy that remained highly stratified.

The genius of vocationalization was that, in addressing a particular organizational problem faced by the junior college, it simultaneously addressed a far broader societal problem: that of managing ambition in a society that generates far higher levels of aspiration for upward mobility than it can possibly satisfy. Faced with unprecedented numbers of students clamoring for access to a traditional four-year college education (and implicitly, to the types of professional and managerial jobs to which such an education was supposed to lead), the system of higher education responded by channeling many of these students into two-year community colleges. Once there, however, the majority of students held onto their dreams of individual advancement and continued to reject terminal vocational education as incompatible with their goal of transfer to a four-year college. Rather than enroll in vocational programs which constituted an implicit admission of failure, many of these students—at least until the labor market downturn of the early 1970s—chose to leave the junior college altogether.

What the junior college vanguard and their successors proposed to these students was, in effect, that they renounce their goal of gaining access to the higher rungs of the occupational ladder in exchange for short-range mobility and the security of stable employment in middle-level jobs. By offering vocationalization as a solution to the problem of the gap between the aspirations of junior college students and the opportunities available to them, community college administrators were pursuing their own organizational interests in finding a distinctive function and a secure market niche for their institutions. But they were also, it must be stressed, expressing a genuine concern for the welfare of the large numbers of students who entered the community college only to emerge with neither the credits necessary for transfer nor any marketable skills. If this dilemma continues to be with us, it is because it is woven into the fabric of a society that is striving still to reconcile the democratic promise of upward mobility through education with the stubborn reality of a class structure with limited room at the top.

The Institutional Model and the Problem of Change

The transformation of the community college from a transfer-oriented institution to one emphasizing terminal vocational training is one of the most fundamental changes to have taken place in the history of twentieth-century American higher education. Having rejected models of this change that focus primarily on either consumer choice or business domination, we have proposed instead an *institutional* explanation. In the section below, we shall attempt to identify some of the features of an institutional approach to structural change. Although we shall focus on how we applied the institutional perspective to the specific case of the transformation of the community college, we hope our ideas will be of interest to those who are concerned with the dynamics of change in institutional domains other than education.[7]

A core element of the institutional approach is that it recognizes that organizations can take on a logic of their own and pursue their own distinctive interests.[8] These interests cannot be reduced—as they are in most pluralist and Marxist accounts of politics—to those of competing groups in civil society.[9] It follows from this that institutional policies and structures—whether in education or in other domains—do not reflect in mirrorlike fashion the distribution of power in the larger society. On the contrary, such policies and structures may, under some circumstances, embody less the interests of external groups than the logic of the organization itself.

To paraphrase Karl Marx's famous remark in the *Eighteenth Brumaire*, organizations may make their own history, but they do not make it just as they please. An adequate theory of structural change must, accordingly, emphasize the constraints under which organizations operate. As Paul Starr noted in reference to medicine, the development of institutions "takes place within larger fields of power and social structure" (Starr 1982, p.8). A key task of the institutional analyst is to specify these fields of power and social structure and to show how they shape and constrain the pattern of development of organizations operating within a particular institutional domain. Because organizational forms develop over time, such an analysis will almost necessarily be historical.

In the case of the junior college, the specification of the constraints it faced required an analysis of the *organizational field* in which it was located. This field—which we defined in Chapter 1 as a set of organizations constituting a recognized area of institutional life—already included a substantial population of four-year colleges and universities from the moment that the two-year college was born, and this fact decisively shaped the junior colleges' development. From the beginning, four-year colleges and universities already virtually monopolized the training markets for the higher-status occupations, placing the junior college in a structurally subordinate position. Much of the trajectory of junior college development—including the tireless pursuit of a strategy of vocationalization—cannot be understood without grasping this subordination.

Within the institutional framework, special attention is directed to the interests, beliefs, and activities of the managers and administrators who set organizational policy and devise strategies to ensure the institution's survival and prosperity within particular organizational fields. In contrast with models of structural change that see business and labor as the only major social actors, the institutional approach thus accords an autonomous role to a third major social group—the full-time professionals, typically unpropertied but highly educated, who have administrative responsibility in such organizations as the community college. In emphasizing the strategic position of credentialed professionals in the life of modern bureaucratic societies, the institutional approach has points of convergence with the "new class" theories of such analysts as Gouldner (1979) and Konrad and Szelenyi (1979).[10]

The emphasis in the institutional model on organizational interest is therefore logically connected to a focus on the role of a new middle class of professionals and managers in defining these interests.[11] Indeed, one way of viewing the small-town Protestant men who shaped the development of the junior college is as members of a larger Progressive movement that brought the new middle class to a position of unprecedented prominence in American life.[12] For the early leaders of the junior college movement shared more with the Progressives than a similar social background; they shared as well their belief in an orderly and stratified society in which a rationalized educational system would play an increasing role in separating the talented from the less able and in filling the nation's manpower needs. In their vision of the nation's future, knowledge and expertise would take their place alongside property as the basis of authority in a society at once more efficient and more just than the disorderly one that then existed.

Yet if the early leaders of the junior college were in many ways idealists who were almost missionary in their zeal to spread the blessings of education to the masses, they were also practical men who faced the difficult task of guaranteeing institutional survival in the complex organizational ecology of American higher education. In situating their activities, our analysis suggests an image of constrained entrepreneurs.[13] Like other entrepreneurs trying to sell a new product, community college administrators wished to establish for their institutions a distinctive market niche that would ensure a stable—and, if possible, an expanding—flow of resources. The problem, however, was that the market for students seeking higher education was not an entirely open one; on the contrary, it was already densely populated by colleges and universities with established ties to both students and employers.

But the organizational entrepreneurs who shaped the development of the junior college movement were constrained not only by the structure of their own organizational field but also by the relation of this field to other major institutions. A fundamental tenet of the institutional approach—whether it is applied to education, the media, or medicine—is that patterns in one societal domain cannot be understood apart from their relation to other key domains. In advanced capitalist societies, the most commanding of these institutional domains are typically the state and major private corporations.

Throughout the twentieth century, governmental bodies have been a powerful constraining force on junior college development. Even for private junior colleges, state governments have played a key role through their accreditation procedures.

And for the public junior colleges—which by the mid-1920s already enrolled a majority of junior college students—state and local governments supplied most of their resources.[14] Although the community colleges enjoy, as do other institutions of higher education, a certain degree of autonomy from the state, they tend not to stray too far in pursuing their interests from the preferences of those on whom they depend for resources.

It would be a mistake, however, to see the state as simply imposing its will on institutions of higher education. In the case of community colleges, there were, certainly, instances of pressure from the state to expand vocational training. For example, the Texas legislature required in 1949 that one-third of junior college students be enrolled in vocational programs, but perhaps more typical is the state's allocating resources in a way that encourages the implementation of preferred policies. The creation of special funds for postsecondary vocational education at both the state and federal levels is a characteristic example of such policies.

Even more common, however, than either direct imposition by the state or the use of fiscal incentives is a pattern in which institutions of higher education curry favor with the state by pursuing policies that, they believe, will gain approval. Such behavior—especially when manifested by one institution toward another, usually more powerful institution—may be referred to as *anticipatory subordination*. In this sense, the responses of the community colleges to state officials and major private corporations are similar. In both cases, they have recognized the state's and corporations' structural power and thus have channeled their development along lines that would appeal to them. For example, in attempting to gain the approval of key state officials, the community colleges were well aware that presenting themselves as committed to providing students with vocationally relevant training could usually be counted on to elicit a positive response.[15]

Yet relations between the community colleges and governmental bodies were more complex than simple models of resource dependency would suggest (Pfeffer and Salancik 1978). The interests of legislators in higher education go beyond—and sometimes conflict with—their interests in providing trained workers for industry. As elected officials, they must take into account not only the logic of a capitalist economy but also the demands of a democratic polity. In particular, legislators are under strong pressure to expand opportunities to attend college, for the public has come to see higher education as the principal pathway to success in an increasingly credentialized society. In light of the popular view of the junior college as a steppingstone to a four-year institution, any attempt to abolish transfer programs and to transform the comprehensive community college into a terminal vocational institution was unlikely to win much support from the democratic state.[16]

The extension of educational opportunity was, to be sure, not the only reason that junior colleges proved so popular with local and state governments. State officials also looked to two-year institutions to provide new employment opportunities for those who built and worked in them, to attract business into their areas, to provide community-service activities, and to raise the cultural level of their communities. But above all, the community college was a relatively low-cost means of extending opportunities to attend college to a populace with a seemingly insatiable demand for more higher education.[17]

Yet if the state supported the growth of junior colleges for a variety of reasons, there was nonetheless an underlying logic to its pattern of sponsorship. From the adoption of the first state "master plan" for higher education in California in the 1930s to the present, statewide planning agencies have generally stood in the way of those junior colleges that, spurred on by both popular demand and the quest for higher status, have wished to transform themselves into four-year institutions. Often more insulated from popular control than state legislatures are, state coordinating bodies have mainly adhered to a technocratic vision in which a hierarchy of institutions, each with a distinct function, channels its "products" into appropriate slots in the division of labor.[18] In this scheme, there was no more room for junior colleges striving for upward mobility into the next tier of higher education's tracking structure than there was for students whose "excessive" ambitions outran the objective possibilities afforded them by the class structure.

Always a force for rationalizing the relationship between the system of higher education and the labor market, state planning agencies viewed with special alarm the rise in the 1970s of what James O'Toole (1975a, 1975b) referred to as the "reserve army of the underemployed." As the supply of college graduates increasingly outstripped the demand for them, state coordinating bodies—often with the encouragement of state legislatures and the federal government—called for the rapid expansion of community college vocational programs.[19] With the decline of the civil rights and student movements of the 1960s and the emergence in the mid-1970s of a fiscal crisis of the state, those who viewed the liberal arts–transfer programs as central to the community colleges' democratic mission found themselves more and more on the defensive. In this new political and economic context, the initiative had shifted to those who emphasized the community colleges' economic function as suppliers of trained middle-level workers over their social function of extending opportunities for upward mobility to previously excluded working-class and minority students. If in past years the state had acted to prevent junior colleges from moving up in the tracking system by becoming four-year institutions, by the 1970s it was asking in effect that they weaken their already-tenuous links to the higher tiers of the tracking structure and solidify their position at the base of this system by expanding their terminal vocational programs.

If an institutional perspective emphasizes the ways in which the state shaped the trajectory of junior colleges' development, so too does it underscore the enormous influence of business. For in a capitalist society, educational institutions feed their students directly into a structure of jobs that is predominantly controlled by private business firms. Institutions of higher education must, quite simply, be able to place at least some of their graduates in these firms, or they will not be viable in the long run. Rather than stressing—as do analysts in what we have called the instrumentalist (or business-domination) model[20]—the preponderance of university trustees who are businessmen or those dramatic (but, in our view, relatively isolated) cases of direct corporate intervention, the institutional framework leads us to focus instead on the structural power of business. From this perspective, large corporations, owing to their position in the American social structure, profoundly influence the behavior of other institutions—including institutions of higher education—without having to do anything active at all.[21]

Faced with the tremendous resources controlled by big business, colleges and universities have exerted vigorous efforts to convince major corporations that they could be of use to them. Even a casual reading of the history of American higher education makes clear that community colleges were not the first in their campaigns to "sell" their graduates to large firms; thus, in 1903, the Moseley Education Commission quoted a college administrator who reported: "It took 15 years to persuade manufacturers of the value of our men. It was a long hard struggle. But they know it now" (quoted in Wyllie 1954, pp. 111–112). Far, then, from business demand always preceding the "production" of graduates, colleges and universities often train students for reasons of institutional self-interest and then seek to create demand for them.

By virtue of its control over jobs, business possesses a type of veto power over college administrators.[22] Business need not actively exercise this power for it to be effective; the mere threat that it might do so is usually more than sufficient to assure that others comply. Thus, colleges compete with one another for the right to form "partnerships" with industry and in many cases seek to tailor their curricula to the specific needs of private firms.

In emphasizing the structural power of business, we do not wish to suggest that large corporations never attempt to impose their will on colleges and universities nor that they lack the capacity for collective action. On the contrary, our own study of Massachusetts's community colleges revealed that high-technology firms in that state ultimately were able not only to agree on a corporate agenda for public higher education but also to make much of this agenda a reality. Yet such instances of direct corporate control of higher education policy are the exception rather than the rule. The power of business over institutions of higher education is at once more subtle and more profound than the instrumentalist approach would suggest. Whereas active corporate intervention is rare, those who preside over institutions of higher education can never long ignore what Charles Lindblom (1977) has referred to as "the privileged position of business."[23]

Within the institutional framework, the structural power that business exerts over colleges and universities resides less in the active interventions of major corporations than in the ordinary workings of the capitalist labor market.[24] Indeed, normal market processes may be seen as embodying underlying power relations in which the buyers of labor power shape both institutional and individual action (Offe 1985). In the case of the community college, the decline in the market for college graduates that occurred in the early 1970s was crucial to the triumph of vocationalism. Such ordinary market processes, within which millions of students pursue their economic interests in a relatively uncoordinated way, are among the principal regulative mechanisms by which the educational system tends to accommodate itself to the structure of economic power.[25]

Yet although the economic logic of politically democratic societies does limit the autonomy of colleges and universities, it does not, of course, eliminate it. Even in a capitalist society, a tight correspondence between the educational system and the economy is by no means inevitable; the examples of Italy (Barbagli 1982) and Sri Lanka (Dore 1976), where the number of graduates produced by the system of higher education has persistently exceeded the demand for them, makes this quite clear. Though capitalism may therefore preclude certain educational outcomes, it by no means dictates which among many possible policies will be chosen.

Within the broad boundaries set by the economic system, the question of educational policy is thus a preeminently political one.[26] Sometimes group struggle—sometimes among classes and other times among races and ethnic groups—is a source of structural change in education. Especially in politically democratic capitalist societies such as the United States in which the publicly proclaimed openness of the nation's class structure is an important source of legitimation, the struggle for equal opportunity through education takes on a special force. This has been manifested over the course of American history in the bitterness of the struggles over such issues as vocational education, quotas in college admissions, busing, and affirmative action.

As educational administrators pursue their own professional and organizational interests, they are thus constrained not only by the structure of the economy and the state but also by the power of politically mobilized social groups. This is a point not always grasped by institutionally oriented analysts (who sometimes emphasize structure over action), but it has been made forcefully by revisionist scholars of educational history (Collins 1979, Hogan 1985, Katznelson and Weir 1985, Nasaw 1979, Wrigley 1982) who have insisted on the role that group struggle—among both classes and status groups—has played in shaping American education.[27] We are indebted to this perspective and believe that it has made a major contribution to understanding educational history. But in the specific case of the junior college, our research disclosed relatively little conflict of this sort.[28]

Yet if politically overt struggles over fundamental issues of educational policy were rare in the junior college, popular resistance, manifest in the refusal of students to enroll in terminal vocational programs, was nonetheless a major force in shaping the two-year institution.[29] To note the general absence of overt collective struggles over junior colleges is not, therefore, to say that resistance failed to play an important role in the history of these institutions. On the contrary, student opposition to the vocationalization project of the junior college vanguard and their successors was for decades the main obstacle to its imposition. This resistance was usually not active and not, for the most part, even conscious. Yet until it disintegrated, vocationalization could not succeed.

The institutional model of change that we propose thus takes into account both the pursuit of organizational interests and the role of group struggle, overt and covert, in determining educational policy. In contrast with "externalist" models of educational change that view state policy as registering in almost barometer-like fashion the pressure exerted by contending groups in civil society, the starting point of the institutional approach is an analysis of the institution's problems in trying to establish itself in a particular organizational field. Within this framework, the pursuit of distinct organizational interests by managers and administrators is central. Yet administrators are by no means free to pursue any policy they please; on the contrary, their autonomy is sharply bounded by the environment in which they operate and, in particular, by the structural power of such key institutions as major private corporations and the state.

Moreover, the pursuit of organizational interests is also limited by group conflict and resistance. Even in the case of the community colleges, in which the resistance that did take place broke down in response to changed market conditions, it was the unwillingness of the students of lower middle– and working-class backgrounds to be "cooled out" into terminal occupational programs that long frustrated the administrative push for vocationalization.[30]

Major shifts in educational policy sometimes occur in direct response to group conflicts: the rise of Jewish quotas in the Ivy League in the 1920s (Karabel 1984, Wechsler 1977) and the adoption of affirmative programs for blacks in the 1960s (Weinberg 1977; Wilson 1978, 1987) are particularly graphic examples. Yet even in those instances in which the demands of external groups—whether dominant or subordinate—are made forcefully and self-consciously, they are nonetheless refracted through a prism of organizational self-interest. Seen from the institutional perspective, the educational system that has emerged is thus more than a compromise between dominant and subordinate groups; it is also a system that bears the imprint of educators themselves. Although operating within the constraints set by political and economic forces beyond their control, educators have nevertheless managed to pursue professional and institutional interests of their own.[31]

American Education, Meritocratic Ideology, and The Legitimation of Inequality

The unique system of education that has developed in the United States—a system of which the community college is an essential component—has had a great influence on the texture of American social and political life. This impact does not, to be sure, lend itself to precise measurement; indeed, our remarks on the effects of the educational system on American life will necessarily have a somewhat speculative quality. Nonetheless, a case can be made that some core aspects of what observers, both foreign and domestic, have referred to as American "exceptionalism"[32]—the egalitarian tenor of daily life, the relative weakness of class consciousness, the felt fluidity of class boundaries, and the persistent national preoccupation with equality of opportunity as opposed to equality of condition—are both embodied in the peculiar structure of American education and constantly reinforced by this same structure. To understand why this might be so requires a grasp of just how distinctive the American educational system has been in comparative and historical perspective.

Compared with the educational systems of other advanced industrial countries, American education has been characterized by striking levels of openness and fluidity. The first nation to offer access to secondary education to the entire population, the United States was also the inventor of the comprehensive high school, in which academic and vocational curricula were taught under the same roof. In Europe, in contrast, secondary education was typically divided into separate institutions offering distinct programs of academic, technical, and vocational training. The academic sectors in these systems—in France the *lycée*, in Germany the *gymnasium*, in England the grammar and "public" schools—were attended by only a small proportion of the population and had a decidedly elite character. As recently as 1950, for example, only about 5 percent of French and German young people—most of them from privileged backgrounds—received academic secondary school diplomas. In the United States during the same period, where about 60 percent of its young people completed what was admittedly a less rigorous secondary education, roughly 11 percent of the population graduated from college (Ringer, 1979, p. 252).

The differences in sheer numbers do not, however, convey a full sense of the depth of the dissimilarities in structure and cultural atmosphere between American and European schools. For it was not simply a matter of more Americans being enrolled in secondary education; what was of greater social and political import was that students of diverse backgrounds were enrolled in the same school. In Europe, the typical pattern was markedly different; secondary students from the same community attended separate schools of sharply divergent statuses, where they studied distinct curricula with students from broadly similar social backgrounds.[33] Moreover, in the elite sectors of the European systems, a cultural ideal of the classically educated "cultivated man" generally held sway; such an ideal, with its implicit emphasis on the cultural superiority of the elite over the masses, tended to magnify the social distance between classes that the American comprehensive high school, with its emphasis on the democratic mixing of students in lunchrooms, school assemblies, and extracurricular activities, was expressly designed to reduce.

If the characteristic American pattern of educational organization was a unitary one, then the typical European pattern was one of segmented schooling—a pattern Fritz Ringer (1970, p. 29) has defined as "one in which parallel courses of study are separated by institutional or curricular barriers, as well as by differences in the social origins of their students." American education has not, of course, been free of segmentation; indeed, as George Counts (1922) had already documented in the years after World War I, there was curricular tracking by social class within American high schools. Nevertheless, the barriers that did exist between the various segments of American education were neither as sharp nor as visible as those in Europe.

One of the most distinctive features of the American educational system—and one that is fundamental to its openness—is that it gives students with undistinguished academic records multiple chances to succeed. Whereas in England and many other European countries, allocation to a nonacademic track took place as early as age eleven and thenceforth had a virtually irreversible character, the "late bloomer" in the United States could reveal his or her talents in high school or even later (Turner 1966). Indeed, after World War II, equality of opportunity in the United States increasingly came to mean that everyone—even those with poor academic records—had a right to enter higher education. As a consequence, as Burton Clark (1985, p. 315) has noted, students graduating from secondary school in the United States "have second, third, and fourth chances in a fashion unimaginable in most other systems of higher education."

The rapid rise of the junior college in the postwar years made the American system of higher education, which already enrolled a far higher proportion of young people than did the system of any other country,[34] more accessible than it had ever been. From a comparative perspective, what was new about the community college was not that it did not charge tuition or that it enabled people to attend college while living at home; after all, many European universities had long been free of charge (indeed, some offered students stipends for living expenses) and possessed no residential facilities whatsoever. The community college's innovative character instead resided in three of its other features: it offered two rather than four (or more) years of higher education; it provided both academic and vocational programs within the same institution; and it was open to the entire population, including adults (and, in some states, even those who had not completed high school). In a sense, the public two-year college brought to higher education the comprehensive model that Americans had introduced to secondary education: universal access, relatively weak boundaries between curricular offerings, and an orientation of service to the entire community. As part of this service orientation, the two-year institution was geographically dispersed so as to provide maximum accessibility. By 1980, over 90 percent of the population was within commuting distance of one of the nation's more than nine hundred community colleges.

In its very design, the junior college was an expression of the long-standing American pattern of avoiding sharp segmentation between different types of institutions. Whereas the typical pattern in European and other countries has been to draw a sharp line between the "university" and other forms of "postsecondary" education, such barriers have been consciously rejected in the United States. Instead, boundaries between institutions of different types are relatively permeable, with transferable course credits being the "coin" that makes exchange possible (Clark 1983, p. 62). Although the community college is the lowest track in America's highly stratified structure of higher education, it nonetheless is connected—through the possibility of transfer with credit—to the system's most prestigious institutions. Thus a student from East Los Angeles Community College, a predominantly Hispanic institution in a poor urban neighborhood, can transfer to UCLA and even, at least in principle, to Harvard.[35] Imagining a comparable move from a British polytechnic to Oxbridge or from a French *institute universitaire de technologie* to the *Ecole Normale Supérieure* conveys a sense of just how different the American system is from some of its European counterparts.

In offering both academic and vocational subjects in the same institution, the community college was continuing an already well-established pattern in American higher education of refusing to create strong institutional boundaries between traditional and new fields of study. This tradition first became institutionalized in the late nineteenth and early twentieth centuries in the nation's great land-grant universities, which were pioneers in introducing such fields of study as agriculture, business, and education. If European universities were slow to integrate into their curricular offerings subjects other than the classical ones of law, medicine, and divinity, the American university eagerly embraced new fields of study such as the social sciences and readily provided training for a wide variety of scientific, technical, and professional occupations. (Ben-David 1966, 1972). The community college extended this pragmatic and utilitarian educational tradition by refusing to exclude virtually any field of study for which there was—or might be—popular demand. And in both community colleges and four-year institutions, students retained the right to change their field of study, sometimes switching from liberal arts to vocational subjects or vice versa.

Even the seemingly rigid boundary between student and nonstudent has been eroded by the fluidity of the American system. With the rise of the community college, students could easily enroll in higher education on a part-time basis, often retaining full-time jobs while obtaining student status. In recent years, four-year colleges and universities in search of new student markets have also increased their part-time offerings, following the community college pattern of enrolling growing numbers of adult students.[36] But it is the community college that is the quintessential open-door institution, and the proliferation of opportunities for part-time attendance at any point in the life cycle has powerfully reinforced the belief that it is never too late for individual talent to reveal itself—and to be rewarded.

From a comparative and historical perspective, the distinctiveness of American education is therefore apparent. What is less clear, however, is what effect, if any, this peculiar structure has had on the political and ideological tenor of American life. It is our contention that the perceived "classlessness" of American society is integrally associated with the character of its educational system.

By their very mode of organization, educational systems may tend to promote a sense that the boundaries between social groups are clearly defined and formidable or that they are fluid and easily traversed. In Europe, segmented systems have historically segregated dominant and subordinate groups in separate institutions, where they instructed them in distinct curricula.[37] Unintentionally or not, such segmented structures are powerful instruments of class socialization, for they are crucibles in which distinctive class cultures may be forged and recreated from generation to generation (Cookson and Persell 1985). If the effect of segmented systems is to reinforce the level of experienced social distance between groups, nonsegmented systems tend to reduce such distance (Ringer 1979, pp. 267–268). In the United States, the relative lack of such segmentation in both secondary and higher education has highlighted the seeming permeability of class boundaries.

The structure of the American educational system may thus be seen as both an institutional embodiment of the ideology of equal opportunity and a constant source of its reinforcement. By avoiding early selection and providing numerous opportunities to show one's talents, the educational system reaffirms the national belief that any individual, no matter how humble the circumstances of his birth, can rise as far as ability and hard work will take him.[38]

The American educational system has thus been a powerful instrument for the dissemination of meritocratic ideas. For if the system offers opportunities for success to all who show talent and industry, then failure must reflect a deficiency of individual ability and/or effort (Piven and Cloward 1980).[39]

Part and parcel of these meritocratic ideas is an emphasis on individual mobility rather than group solidarity. Class consciousness, of course, has never been especially pronounced in the United States when compared with Europe. Many factors militated against the development of a sense of common fate among the American working classes, including the exceptional salience of racial and ethnic cleavages, the early extension of the franchise to all adult white males, and wide-spread geographic mobility. Yet among those features of American life hindering the growth of class sentiment must be counted its education system. As it developed over the course of the last century, the American education system—with its rejection of early selection, its openness, its lack of segmentation, its sheer size, and its commitment to the provision of multiple chances to succeed—almost certainly reinforced the national emphasis on individual rather than collective advancement.

An institutional embodiment of the national preoccupation with upward mobility, the educational system in its normal daily operations gave renewed vigor to the traditional American belief that, as James Conant (1940, p. 598) put it, "each generation may start life afresh and . . . hard work and ability . . . find their just rewards."[40] By providing the "ladders of ascent," for which Carnegie and others had called a century ago and multiple opportunities to climb them, the schools infused the American dream of individual advancement with new life.[41]

As in other societies, the educational system in the United States plays an important role in the transmission of inequality from generation to generation.[42] In spite of the apparent openness of the system, a wide body of empirical evidence shows substantial gaps in educational attainment among students of different social backgrounds and a significant underrepresentation in the system's upper tiers of minority students and students from modest socioeconomic backgrounds. The qualities that lead to success in the education system are no doubt partly personal, but they are also to a considerable degree linked to advantages of birth and especially to family cultural resources.[43]

In addition to its role in transmitting inequalities, the American educational system may well contribute to the legitimation of these inequalities. The very structure of American schooling has the effect of obscuring the substantial level of transmission of privilege that actually does occur. And it probably does so more effectively than segmented systems on the European model, for the workings of these systems are socially transparent. It is difficult, for example, to miss the social-class implications of the traditional division of British secondary education into secondary modern technical, grammar, and "public" schools; the class implications of such a system are relatively obvious. In comparison, the American educational system conveys a strikingly democratic appearance, and its contribution to the transmission of inequality from generation to generation is, accordingly, rather opaque. As a general proposition, it seems likely that the more opaque the mode of transmitting inequalities, the more effective it is likely to be in legitimating these inequalities.

The American educational system and the vast network of community colleges that comprises one of its most distinguishing features may thus be seen as integral elements of a social order that emphasizes individual advancement over collective advancement, personal success over group solidarity, and equality of opportunity over equality of condition. In a way that was not entirely intended, this system may also be important for veiling some of the gaps between American ideals and American practice.[44]

Although the United States is, compared with other advanced capitalist countries, exceptionally generous in its allocation of resources to higher education, it is unusually ungenerous in its expenditures for social welfare (Heidenheimer 1973, 1981). In a comparative study of patterns of public expenditure in twenty-one countries, Wilensky (1975, pp. 7, 122) reports a negative correlation of −.41 between spending for social security and rates of enrollment in higher education; strikingly, the United States ranks twentieth in the former but first in the latter.[45] Although there are important exceptions (the Netherlands and Belgium, for example, exhibit relatively high expenditures in both categories), for the majority of countries, one kind of expenditure seems to substitute, to some degree, for the other.

In the United States, the extraordinary level of national resources invested in higher education has helped to keep the American dream of individual advancement alive under drastically changed circumstances. But this national commitment to equality of opportunity may be the other side of a relative lack of concern with equality per se—a lack of concern that distinguishes the United States from many other advanced societies where powerful labor unions and working-class parties have been instrumental in the creation of genuine social "safety nets" below which vulnerable individuals may not fall.[46]

The Community College and Democratic Ideals

As an organizational innovation, the community college has been one of the great success stories in the history of American higher education. In less than a century, the two-year institution has moved from being no more than a fantasy in the minds of a few educational visionaries through a period of rapid, if uneven, growth into its current status as a major component of the world's largest system of higher education. Still something of a regional phenomenon as recently as 1940, the public junior college had by 1970 spread to every state in the union. During these same years, the idea of "short-cycle" higher education spread—with some help from the AAJC and the Organization for Economic Cooperation and Development (OECD)—beyond the United States and become institutionalized to varying degrees in nations as diverse as France, Yugoslavia, Canada, Norway, and Japan (OECD 1973). As relatively undifferentiated university systems in Europe and elsewhere face the problems posed by mass higher education, the junior college— or something like it—may well become even more of a presence on the world scene.

As an institution centrally involved in what we have called the *management of ambition*, the community college—however firm its ideological commitment to democratization—has had little choice but to participate actively in the "cooling-out" process.[47] The role of the public junior college as a place where a large number of students will be channeled away from four-year institutions and the professional and managerial occupations to which these institutions have historically provided access is thus not a matter of administrative preference but, rather, is built into the nature of the institution.[48]

Required by virtue of its location at the intersection between popular aspirations and structural constraints to serve as a gatekeeper for both the universities and the larger society, the junior college has nonetheless taken seriously its task of democratizing higher education. No one familiar with the history of the two-year college movement can fail to be impressed by the energy and the dedication with which thousands of junior college teachers and administrators have tenaciously pursued—often under extremely difficult conditions—their mission of bringing higher education to the people. This effort, which continues today in institutions across the nation, has yielded some impressive results: in opportunities provided, in horizons expanded, in academic deficiencies remedied, and, in a not inconsiderable number of cases, ambitions "heated up" rather than "cooled out." Lest there be any misunderstanding, we wish to make our position clear: in the absence of community colleges, many highly motivated and able individuals—among them, workers, immigrants, minorities, and women—would never have entered, much less graduated from, an institution of higher education.

The very real contribution that the community college has made to the expansion of opportunities for some individuals does not, however, mean that its *aggregate* effect has been a democratizing one. On the contrary, the two-year institution has accentuated rather than reduced existing patterns of social inequality. Indeed, in both the social origins and the occupational destinations of its students, the community college clearly constitutes the bottom tier of a class-linked tracking system in higher education. As a growing body of evidence accumulated over more than two decades demonstrates, the very fact of attending a two-year rather than a four-year institution lowers the likelihood that a student will obtain a bachelor's degree. Similarly, entering a two-year as opposed to a four-year college has a negative effect on adult occupational status, even controlling for individual differences in socioeconomic background, measured mental ability, and other variables.

To be sure, the growth of community colleges has brought some individuals into higher education who would otherwise never have attended college; at the same time, however, this growth has also meant a diversion to the two-year sector of large numbers of students—disproportionately of modest social backgrounds—who would otherwise have attended four-year institutions. Finally, a fundamental (and by no means entirely unintended) effect of the rapid extension of community colleges has been to enable public four-year colleges and universities to tighten their admissions requirements and thereby to exclude on meritocratic grounds many students who, in the absence of community colleges, might have felt entitled to a place in the freshman class of what are, after all, public institutions.

If the junior college has been beset from its beginning by contradictory pressures both to extend opportunity and to ration it, its transformation in recent years into a predominantly vocational institution should be seen as strengthening its diversionary function. Hailed for their "democratic" character, vocational programs appeal to pragmatic and utilitarian elements in American culture; above all, they are said to yield excellent economic returns and to provide great opportunities for upward mobility. Yet the reality of the situation is quite different. Most vocational programs, the evidence reviewed in Chapter 4 suggests, offer at best modest returns, and many of them fail even to place their students in the fields for which they were ostensibly trained. Some individuals no doubt benefit from enrolling in these programs; this seems especially likely for occupational training in the health sciences and certain technical areas for which there is a strong market demand. But for most community college students, some notable exceptions to the contrary notwithstanding, placement in vocational education constitutes relegation to the bottom rung of higher education's tracking system.

Yet our reservations about the expansion of community college vocational education extend beyond their frequent failure to deliver the economic returns that they promise; they extend beyond even their role in reinforcing rather than weakening existing inequalities of class, race, and gender. Indeed, our primary reservation about occupational programs concerns not their effectiveness in producing workers for private industry. Rather, it concerns the impact that such programs have on educating citizens for a democratic polity. Our fear, in short, is that vocational training, especially of the narrowly specialized sort that is often found today in community colleges, fails to prepare students for life in a democratic society whose highest ideals call for a citizenry that is fully capable of administering its own affairs.

Our reservations about vocational education hearken back to an indigenous American tradition of commitment to the ideal that the educational system should be as devoted to the formation of democratic citizens as it is to the training of workers and that one of its principal tasks is to empower ordinary people. This venerable tradition is now in retreat, and it may seem outmoded and even utopian in an era when policymakers are obsessed with transforming the schools into instruments for restoring the United States to its former position of preeminence in international economic affairs. Yet this tradition, which we shall call the *democratic mode*, has deep roots in American history and earlier in this century was a central concern among both working-class organizations and middle-class reformers concerned with educational policy.[49] A 1915 report about vocational training in secondary education presented to the American Federation of Labor's national convention remains strikingly timely:

> We hold the child must be educated not only to adapt to his particular calling . . . but that they should be educated for leadership as well; that they should have the power of self-direction and of directing others; the powers of administration as well as ability to assume positions of responsibility.
>
> It is not only essential that we should fit our boys and girls for the industries, but it is equally essential to fit the industries for the future employment of our young men and women. (quoted in Wirth 1972, p. 60)

Without safeguards, the report warned, industrial education could be made so subordinate to commercial interests that "the opportunities of the worker's children for a general education will be limited, which will tend to make the workers more submissive and less independent."

The recent trend of providing contract training for private corporations raises anew the long-standing issue of the domination of educational programs by commercial interests. Approximately seven in ten community colleges now offer customized training on a contract basis (Deegan and Drisko 1985). To an even greater extent than ordinary junior college vocational training, these programs are likely to offer narrow, firm-specific training that threatens both the institutional integrity of the community colleges and the interest that employees have in obtaining the kind of broad, general skills that will maximize their bargaining power with employers at the same time that it will enable them to adjust with the greatest possible flexibility to a rapidly changing economy.

The main issue raised by vocational education, however, is whether the principal task of the educational system is one of adapting students to the existing economic order. John Dewey touched on this in a letter to *The New Republic* protesting a bill in the Illinois legislature (the Cooley bill) that, in his view, would have created a system of secondary education segmented along class lines:

> The kind of vocational education in which I am interested is not one which will "adapt" workers to the existing industrial regime; I am not sufficiently in love with the regime for that. It seems to me that the business of all who would not be educational time servers is . . . to strive for a kind of vocational education which will first alter the existing industrial system, and ultimately transform it. (quoted in Lazerson and Grubb 1974, p. 37)

As Dewey elsewhere makes clear, he is not opposed to vocational education per se; the question is what kind of vocational education the schools will teach.[50] For him, as for others committed to training a democratic citizenry, the key question is whether a particular form of vocational education will foster in individuals "the ability to become master of their industrial fate" (Dewey 1966, p. 320).

The problem with community college vocational education is not, therefore, that it attempts to connect the educational system with the world of work. On the contrary, the democratic mode in American educational thought is, in our view, correct in its belief in the desirability of linking, where possible, the process of education to the activities of work and community. Work–study programs at institutions such as Antioch College have alternated education with participation in the labor market and have been justifiably hailed by educational progressives. But such programs are distinct from the narrower forms of vocational education, in that the experience in work is designed to have primarily an educative rather than an economic function. In those instances in which vocational programs in community colleges perform this task and do not close doors to further educational and occupational advancement, it would be inappropriate for those who are committed to the two-year institution's democratic mission to object.

That most vocational programs in community colleges (or, for that matter, four-year institutions) fall short of these ideals seems clear. It does not follow, however, that college-parallel liberal art programs are in all cases preferable. For these programs, too, have been plagued by enormously high rates of attrition, and they all too frequently neither enhance the life chances nor expand the horizons of those who enroll in them. Nonetheless, the current movement to revitalize transfer programs is, we believe, more compatible with democratic ideals than is further vocationalization. Yet several cautionary notes are in order.

First, and perhaps foremost, community colleges moving to strengthen their transfer programs must be careful in creating a more coherent and rigorous college-parallel curriculum that they do not unintentionally reinforce their role as agents of diversion rather than democratization. In an era in which many students emerge from the nation's secondary schools with academic deficiencies in one or more areas, a simple tightening of standards at community colleges will not do; if opportunity is to be genuine, strong remedial programs must be in place for those students—many of them from minority backgrounds—whose past handicaps place them at a serious disadvantage. Despite their self-characterization as "people's colleges," two-year institutions have throughout their history been less likely to send on to four-year institutions their less socially and culturally advantaged students. Unless forceful measures are undertaken to counteract this tendency, the current effort to reinvigorate the transfer function of the community college may have the unintended consequence of reducing rather than increasing the educational and occupational mobility of minority and working-class students.[51]

Those who wish to revitalize community college transfer programs must also be aware that the "articulation" problems with four-year institutions which they constantly bemoan have deep structural roots. For the truth of the matter is that junior colleges have historically been supported by the major universities less to supply them with students than to insulate them from the masses clamoring at their gates. The language used by university administrators when describing junior colleges reveals clearly what they perceive to be their proper function; to them, junior colleges are "shock absorbers," "sieves," "bumpers" or, for those of a more military temperament, "lines of defense" and "moats." It is unlikely that these same institutions will make major efforts to articulate their offerings with those of community colleges. Change, if it is to come at all, is likely to result not from the initiative of the major universities, but rather from the pressure that state legislatures and planning bodies place on public institutions to coordinate their programs with those of the two-year institutions.

In their relations with less selective four-year colleges and universities, community colleges that wish to strengthen their transfer programs face a different problem: direct competition for students. With the number of high school graduates projected to drop as much as 25 percent in the early 1990s from the peak years of the 1970s and with the market for adults showing signs of saturation, it is possible that there will be an increasingly ferocious battle between the community colleges and the lower-tier four-year institutions for promising students. Both community colleges and four-year colleges have powerful vested interests in keeping enrollments from dropping, for lower enrollments generally mean fewer resources.

Yet as our case study of Massachusetts suggests, a growing number of institutions are responding to this problem by in effect dividing the market; through the creation of $2 + 2$ occupational programs, students in formerly terminal occupational community college curricula have an opportunity to transfer to enrollment-hungry four-year institutions. It is an open question whether such programs, which contribute to the twin processes of educational inflation and growing credentialism, further the well-being of community college students. Indeed, the proliferation of such programs may be a classical instance of a clash between organizational interests and the public interest. For in pursuing what is unquestionably beneficial to them, institutions of higher education are not, we must remember, inevitably following policies that are of maximum benefit to either individuals or the larger society.

If the policy of strengthening community college transfer programs is not without serious difficulties, the alternative—which is to permit them to languish and, in some cases, to wither away altogether—seems to us even more problematic. Historically, the public has looked to the two-year college less for vocational education than for the opportunity to transfer to a four-year college; even in the career-obsessed climate of the 1980s, according to a poll published by the AACJC, 48 percent of the public sees the community college's chief function as providing academic training so that students can transfer to a four-year institution and earn a bachelor's degree, compared with only 28 percent who view vocational training as its principal task (AACJC 1981, p. 25).[52] In a society in which the best jobs are increasingly monopolized by college graduates, we should be clear about what the continued weakening of links between two- and four-year colleges really means: a cutting off of opportunities for upward mobility for those millions of students who are now enrolled in the community college sector.

Although community colleges now serve as the principal gateway to higher education for the nation's minorities and in many states constitute the primary point of college entry for the great majority of all students, the policy of further eviscerating their transfer function is not without influential supporters.[53] Breneman and Nelson (1981, pp. 211–212), for example, in a widely read study of community college finance sponsored by the Brookings Institution, stated that they "favor an educational division of labor among institutions that would result in community colleges enrolling fewer full-time and transfer students of traditional college age." Community colleges, they added, should "continue to evolve away from the junior-college emphasis on transfer programs toward service to new clienteles"; moreover, "state education officials" should "play an active role in supporting these natural directions of development through statewide planning that encourages and strengthens institutional division of labor" (Breneman and Nelson 1981, pp. 211–212).

Former AACJC president Edmund J. Gleazer, Jr., a vigorous advocate of the "community education" mission of the community college, goes even further than Breneman and Nelson, suggesting that community colleges deemphasize their identification with higher education altogether and reconsider their use of the term "college," which "may get in the way of what really needs to be done in the community" (Gleazer 1980, pp. 4–5). To such proposals, the response of those who remain committed to the democratic tradition in American education is clear and unequivocal: without strong and accessible transfer programs, the community college will have effectively abandoned its historic dream of bringing higher education to the people.

Yet for many students, however successful the effort to revitalize transfer programs may be, the community college will be their final point of contact with the system of formal education. For these students, the task is not simply to help them acquire a marketable skill, though that is desirable; it is also to assist them in developing the capacities that will prepare them for life as citizens in a democratic society, where the gap between leaders and the general population may be growing ever more profound. According to the precepts of classical democratic theory, the citizenry of a democratic society must be able not only to participate in the governance of its own affairs, but to do so in a thoughtful and informed fashion. Yet the American educational system—its elementary schools, its high schools, its colleges—has over time come more and more to abandon even attempting to fulfill its mission of cultivating an active and enlightened populace. No less than other segments of the educational system, and perhaps more, the community college has been guilty of this pattern of neglecting its responsibilities for the training of citizens as well as workers.

The centrality once assigned to education in realizing the American democratic project is vividly captured by an 1830 statement by a committee of Philadelphia working men:

> The original element of despotism is a monopoly of talent, which consigns the multitude to comparative ignorance, and secures the balance of knowledge on the side of the rich and the rulers. If then the healthy existence of a free government be, as the committee believe, rooted in the will of the American people, it follows as a necessary consequence . . . that this monopoly be broken up, and that the means for equal knowledge, (the only security for equal liberty) should be rendered . . . the common property of all classes. (quoted in Welter 1962, p. 47)

Knowledge, the committee realized, is a form of power; as such, its concentration poses a grave threat to the promise of democracy.

A sign that at least some community colleges are beginning to address this issue may be found in discussions of the role of the two-year institution in fostering *critical literacy,* a knowledge of reading and writing that "involves high levels of independent thinking" (Richardson et al. 1983, p. 5). We define the cultivation of critical literacy as "the capacity and inclination to think critically and act on the basis of informed judgment" (see Katz 1982, p. 194), and we believe that it is an essential goal for the entire school system. Community colleges, which are uniquely accessible to the adult population, should foster its development in all students, transfer and nontransfer alike.

A more democratic community college would not, it should be emphasized, be a place where the "cooling-out" function has been abolished. As long as American society generates more ambition than its economic structure can absorb, the community college will be actively involved in channeling the aspirations of students away from four-year colleges and universities. Yet this said, there is something deeply troubling, especially in a society that prides itself on its openness, about the covertness of the cooling-out process as it now operates. If the community college is, by and large, going to remain, as Burton Clark put it more than a quarter of a century ago, "a place where students reach undesired destinations" (1960, p. 165), then this reality should be known to all who enroll in it.

We are thus in favor of measures that would increase the transparency of the role that institutions of higher education play in processes of educational and social selection. The exact form that such measures should take is, of course, a matter for public debate and discussion. One suggestion that warrants serious examination is Astin's proposal that all institutions of higher education, two-year and four-year alike, publish figures on their rates of attrition, transfer, and graduation (1983, pp. 122–138).[54]

As the history of the junior college clearly reveals, those who have struggled to make its democratic promise a reality have faced formidable obstacles. Today, powerful forces both inside and outside the community college are pushing to move it still further away from its popular function of serving as a pathway into four-year colleges and universities; indeed, some would like the two-year institution to withdraw even more thoroughly from the mainstream of higher education, focusing its energies instead on terminal vocational programs. Yet those who are unhappy with the transformation of the community college into a predominantly vocational institution over the past two decades should nonetheless acknowledge the powerful organizational logic behind this development, for vocationalization has provided a more stable market niche than transfer programs ever did. Furthermore, terminal vocational programs spoke—and speak—to an obdurate truth in the history of the junior college: that most of their students in fact never transfer to a four-year institution. That this high rate of attrition, however painful to individual students, may very well be functional for the existing social order is a possibility that those who wish to reform the community college must squarely face.

If present trends continue, the community college may well become increasingly isolated from the rest of the system of higher education. Barely functioning transfer programs may break down altogether; already astronomical attrition rates may increase; and private corporations may, through contract training, transform into virtual trade schools what were not long ago comprehensive colleges.

Yet this scenario, though possible, is not inevitable. For the community college has been buffeted throughout its history by the contradictory pressures of capitalism and democracy, efficiency and equality, and diversion and democratization, and it continues to be an arena of conflicting forces today. Although constrained both by organizational interests and the logic of the larger society in which it is embedded, the community college faces a future that is, to a considerable extent, a matter of choice. It is our hope that these choices will be made after vigorous and far-ranging public debate and that they will remain faithful to the vision of creating a genuinely egalitarian system of education that fosters the development of a citizenry fully equal to the arduous task of democratic self-governance.

Notes

CHAPTER 1

1. The Lincoln quote is from his July 4, 1861, Message to Congress in Special Session, reprinted in Williams (1943, pp. 124–142).

2. On the centrality of the image of Lynn (1955) the self-made man in American history, see Wyllie (1954), Lynn (1955), Cawelti (1965), and Wohl (1966). For data suggesting that, even in the putatively egalitarian Jacksonian era, men of wealth tended in fact to be born into relatively privileged families, see Pessen (1971).

3. In 1890, only 3.5 percent of young people were graduated from high school; a decade later, in 1900, the proportion had almost doubled, reaching 6.3 percent (U.S. Bureau of the Census, 1975, p. 379).

4. An impressive body of scholarship has chronicled the process by which this transformation occurred. Among the scholarly works that trace the transformation of a disorganized set of loosely associated educational institutions into a coherent, sequential system are Perkinson (1977), Collins (1979), and Nasaw (1979). Discussions on the development of the high school—a crucial bridge between the traditional common school and the emergent national system of colleges and universities—are contained in Cremin (1961) and Krug (1964). The classic work on the transformation of higher education in this period is Lawrence Veysey's *The Emergence of the American University* (1965); other important works include Rudolph (1962), Jencks and Riesman (1968), Brubacher and Rudy (1976), Bledstein (1976), and Barlow (1979). The development of specific curricular prerequisites for admission into public universities (with the University of Michigan as a case study) is discussed in Wechsler (1977); the transformation of requirements for admission into medical school is examined in Starr (1982); the question of why large corporations finally began to hire college graduates in the late nineteenth century is addressed by Chandler (1977). Gorelick (1981), in a study of the role of the City College of New York in the lives of Jewish poor between 1880 and 1924, explicitly argues that educational channels of opportunity did not exist in the late nineteenth century, but needed to be constructed; at the beginning of this period, both new educational and occupational opportunities (as well as

233

mechanisms linking them) had to be created if higher education was to offer effective avenues of upward mobility (see also Barlow 1979). An important recent addition to the literature on the history of higher education, focused on the growth of differentiation in higher education between World War I and World War II, is David O. Levine's *The American College and the Culture of Aspiration* (1986).

5. The unusual emphasis in the United States on giving everyone a chance in the race for success—and the accompanying emphasis on upward mobility through education—was noted by Lipset in *The First New Nation* (1963); interestingly, a former U.S. colony, the Philippines, whose culture has been shaped in part by American values, in 1956 had a much higher proportion of its twenty-to-twenty-four-year-old population in higher education than a number of far more economically advanced European nations, including England, France, and Germany. Similarly, Lipset notes that Puerto Rico, which has been under American hegemony, enrolled 11.9 percent of its twenty-to-twenty-four-year-olds in higher learning, compared with only 0.7 percent in Jamaica, a former British colony at a roughly comparable level of economic development (Lipset 1963, pp. 296–298). Perhaps the most extensive bodies of scholarly work specifically focused on setting American higher education in comparative perspective, however, are those of Ben-David (1966, 1972, 1977) and Clark (1983, 1984, 1985). Other key works that help set America's distinctive system of colleges and universities within a comparative framework include those of Ringer (1979), Touraine (1974), Ashby (1971), and, from an earlier era, Flexner (1930).

6. For the first four decades of its history, the two-year institution was referred to almost exclusively as a *junior college*. This term, which implicitly emphasized the subordination of the two-year college to the *senior college*—the institution to which junior college graduates would have to transfer if they wished to receive a bachelor's degree—was gradually replaced in the decades after World War II by the term *community college*. The new appellation tended to direct attention toward the two-year institution's relationship to the local population and to the provision of functions such as terminal vocational education that were not dependent on the granting of recognition by senior colleges; at the same time, the term community college deflected attention away from the two-year college's subordinate position within the stratification structure of higher education. A detailed discussion of the meaning of the shift from *junior* to *community* college is included in Chapter 3; for our purposes here, it suffices to note that the terms junior college, community college, and two-year college will be used interchangeably throughout the book. Moreover, these terms will refer to both public and private two-year institutions, although our emphasis will be placed on the former, especially in the postwar period. Students from public junior colleges, it should be noted, comprised the majority of two-year college students as far back as 1926; by 1947, the public proportion was well over three-quarters, and by 1967, it had surpassed 90 percent (Eells 1931a, p. 70, National Center for Educational Statistics 1970, p. 75).

7. The idea that all educational systems, capitalist and socialist alike, face a problem in the management of ambition is borrowed from Hopper (1971). Hopper's attempt to create a general theory of the relationship between systems of education and systems of mobility is, in turn, inspired by Ralph Turner's classic article on "sponsored" and "contest" mobility. According to Turner, all societies face a "conspicuous control problem . . . of ensuring loyalty in the disadvantaged classes towards a system under which they receive less than a proportional share of society's goods." Crucial to the system of social control in the United States, Turner suggests, is a "folk norm" in which "mobility may be viewed as most appropriately a *contest* in which many contestants strive . . . restricted only by a minimum set of rules defining fair play and minimizing special advantage to those who get ahead early in the game." A "contest system," Turner notes, "must avoid

any absolute points of selection for mobility and immobility and must delay clear recognition of the realities of the situation until the individual is too committed to the system to change radically" (Turner 1966, pp. 452, 458). Although we do not endorse all the particulars of Turner's portrait of American education, we have been influenced by his idea that national folk norms of mobility shape the educational system and may play a role in securing the consent of subordinate social groups by legitimating existing inequalities.

8. The belief that America remains a land of opportunity is a recurrent finding of sociological studies of American communities (see, for example, Warner and Lunt 1941, and Hollingshead 1949). Even in the midst of the Great Depression, Robert and Helen Lynd reported in *Middletown in Transition* that the typical community resident continued to believe that a man "really gets what is coming to him in the United States" and that "any man who is willing to work hard and to be thrifty . . . can get to the top" (Lynd and Lynd 1937, p. 409). The centrality of equality of opportunity to the "American creed" has also been a theme of a number of foreign social scientists who have written about the United States, including Myrdal (1944) and Ossowski (1963).

9. White youths, especially those from the most disadvantaged segments of the urban working class, may also withdraw from the competition to get ahead. For a powerful portrait of "leveled aspirations" in a low-income neighborhood, see Macleod's ethnographic study of youths in a public housing project, *Ain't No Makin' It* (1987).

10. Kluegel and Smith (1986), for example, in a nationally representative survey of 2,212 Americans, find that economic differences among groups are often attributed to individual differences in such qualities as "hard work" and "talent." Moreover, many of the survey respondents view economic inequality as being legitimate in principle (Kluegel and Smith 1986, pp. 75–142).

11. The argument that working people were enthusiastic and influential supporters of the early expansion of education in the United States was first made by Carleton (1911) and has been a staple of "Progressive" educational history ever since. In 1968, in a pathbreaking "revisionist" work, Katz challenged this thesis and, based on evidence from Beverly, Massachusetts, argued that educational expansion was imposed from above on a hostile working class. Katz's argument has, however, been brought into question in recent years, and a number of scholars have found evidence of broad popular support for the expansion of schooling (Kaestle and Vinoskis 1980; Meyer et al. 1979; Wrigley 1982; Katznelson and Weir 1985; Rubinson 1986).

12. The idea that education in the United States is pulled in contradictory directions by the logics of capitalism and democracy is discussed in Shapiro (1982; 1983) and developed at length in Carnoy and Levin's book, *Schooling and Work in the Democratic State* (1985). Katznelson and Weir (1985), in their historical study of education and the urban working class also develop this theme, focusing in particular on the conflicting pressures inherent in preparing students for life as both democratic citizens and workers in a highly inegalitarian division of labor.

13. Interestingly, this fear seems to have been most pronounced in those regions—the West and the Midwest—where the egalitarian impulse and the ideology of equal opportunity were strongest; perhaps not coincidentally, it was in California, Michigan, and Illinois that the junior college first rose to prominence.

14. The sources of the powerful impact that the ideology of vocationalism has had on American education are explored in Lazerson and Grubb (1974) and Kantor and Tyack (1982). Hogan (1985, pp. 139–193) offers an excellent account of the triumph of vocationalism in the public schools of Chicago during the early decades of the twentieth century; other major works that focus on the case of Chicago include Counts (1928) and Wrigley (1982). On the more recent phenomenon of "career education," a form of vocational

education that exerted considerable influence during the 1970s, see Grubb and Lazerson (1975).

15. Estimating changes in the number and percentage of community college students enrolled in vocational programs poses a number of serious methodological issues. First, states are sometimes inconsistent in their categorization of transfer and occupational enrollments. Second, new enrollment categories, neither occupational nor transfer, have become significant in total enrollment and, in some states, even exceed the number of students enrolled in traditional transfer and occupational curricula. These categories vary by state, but usually involve students who are either "unclassified," pursuing "general studies," "undecided," "developmental," or enrolled for a short-term "vocational skills" program. Finally, because of funding formulas, states sometimes find it desirable to show high enrollments in occupational programs. They may classify as occupational those students who take at least one occupational course, whether or not they are enrolled in occupational programs. With these complications in mind, it is not surprising that studies in the same years frequently find different proportions of occupational enrollments. In presenting estimates of occupational enrollments, no single source can be regarded as consistently reliable. For statistics on vocational enrollments over time, we have scrutinized all of the standard, and some of the nonstandard, sources: AACJC (1977), Blackstone (1978), Bogue (1950), Brunner (1962), Eells (1931a, 1941a), Lombardi (1978), Cohen and Brawer (1982), Grubb (1984), Medsker (1960), Medsker and Tillery (1971), Monroe (1972), NCES, *Digest of Educational Statistics* (1963–1985), Olivas (1979), Parker (1974, 1975), Pincus (1980), U.S. Office of Education (1930–1958), and Venn (1964). We have drawn most heavily on Blackstone, Brunner, NCES, Parker, and the USOE, which we believe are the most reliable sources.

16. Data documenting that the era prior to vocationalization was no "golden age" are examined in a 1972 article by one of the authors that describes the community college as "the bottom track of the system of higher education both in class origins and occupational destinations of its students" (Karabel 1972, p. 526). At the same time, however, the article acknowledges that educational expansion *"has* been critical in providing upward mobility for many individuals" (1972, p. 526, emphasis in original). The movement to vocationalize the community college was then visibly gaining momentum and received considerable attention (see 543–552); the trend toward increasing enrollments in vocational programs was not, however, discernible in 1972. For a discussion of developments in research on the community college since 1972, see Karabel (1986).

17. As we will attempt to show in Chapter 4, the lower educational and occupational attainment of community college students compared to those who attend four-year colleges is at least in part a consequence of *institutional* effects. There are, of course, overall differences in the individual characteristics of students at two- and four-year colleges, with students at two-year institutions generally of somewhat lower socioeconomic status (SES) and measured academic ability; moreover, these differences are doubtless associated with the higher educational and labor market attainments of students who attend four-year institutions. At the same time, however, it is important to note that there is considerable overlap in the academic and social characteristics of students at two- and four-year colleges, with the former enrolling significant numbers of high-ability and high-SES students and the latter enrolling considerable numbers of students of modest social origins and poor prior academic performance. Nonetheless, a growing body of empirical evidence strongly suggests that *organizational* characteristics—especially the relatively nonacademic climate of community colleges and the sheer availability of large numbers of terminal vocational programs—tend to depress the occupational and, especially, the educational attainments of community college students, independent of the characteristics of the students themselves.

This is why community college students who are matched to four-year college students similar in background and ability have been significantly less likely to obtain a bachelor's degree and, consequently, the boost in life that obtaining the B.A. often provides. (For a summary of this evidence, see Dougherty [1987].)

We are thus skeptical of those analyses of stratification in higher education that see it as a simple reflection of differences in individual ability and motivation. To be sure, such differences do exist, and they are, moreover, correlated with an individual's position within the structure of inter-institutional stratification. But even if the entire population of community college students consisted of highly able and highly motivated individuals, there would still be a need for differentiation in higher education, for the simple reason that the hierarchical division of labor which employs college-educated manpower offers only a finite number of high-status professional and managerial positions. Accordingly, the system of higher education must find a way to allocate at least some students to less desirable positions in the division of labor. The community college—or, for that matter, any institution or program located toward the bottom of higher education's system of tracking—would thus face powerful pressure to allocate its "products" into the middle levels of the class structure, even if all its students were brilliant and hard-working. How this structurally based pressure to channel students away from a limited supply of high-status professional and managerial jobs has affected the trajectory of community college development will be one of the main subjects of this volume.

18. Freeman (1976, p. 205), for example, summarizes his well-known study *The Over-Educated American*, by concluding that: "the major factor determining enrollment of college graduates (during the 1960s and early 1970s) . . . was the state of the labor market. Enrollment decisions appear to be highly sensitive to market incentives." David Riesman (1980), with his emphasis on the role that "student consumerism" has played in shaping American higher education in recent decades, could be considered a proponent of a more sociological version of the "consumer-choice" model.

19. The classical expression of the Marxist "instrumentalist" perspective has been offered by Miliband (1969). Important criticisms of the viewpoint, many of them from a more "structuralist" perspective, have been offered by Poulantzas (1973), Offe (1973, 1974, 1984), Block (1977, 1980), and Skocpol (1979). With respect to higher education, two representative expressions of the "business-domination" model are Smith (1974) and Aptheker (1972).

20. Although Bowles and Gintis' (1976) work may be considered the most influential general application of the business-domination model, there are aspects of their approach—particularly the emphasis on class conflict as well as class domination—that distinguish it from many "instrumentalist" versions of Marxism. Moreover, there are elements of Bowles and Gintis' theory of educational change (1976, pp. 224–241)—notably the emphasis on "pluralist accommodation" and the partially autonomous role of professional educators—that constitute advances over more orthodox Marxist interpretations of the educational system (see also Bowles and Gintis [1981] for a useful, if rarely cited, elaboration of their theory of education).

21. Among the key works on organizations that have informed our approach are Robert Michels' *Political Parties* and Max Weber's *Economy and Society*, especially the sections on "Domination and Legitimacy" and "Bureaucracy." In addition to Weber and Michels, we are also indebted to the work of a number of scholars who have contributed to the institutional tradition of organizational analysis, including Selznick (1949), Gouldner (1954a; 1954b), Mills (1956), and Lipset et al. (1956). Among many noteworthy recent contributions that embody an institutional perspective, our approach has been particularly influenced by the historically grounded work of Chandler (1977) on business, Starr (1982) on medi-

cine, Larson (1977) on professions. Tyack (1974) and Tyack and Hansot (1982) on education, and DiMaggio (1982b, 1982c) on culture. Perrow's (1984, 1986) writings on organizations, with an emphasis on the role of power in organizational life, have also shaped our institutional framework. For a survey of the new "institutionalism"—a term which covers a number of perspectives, not all of which are entirely compatible with our own—and its impact on social science, see March and Olsen (1984).

22. Our concept of "organizational field" is similar to Meyer and Scott's (1983, pp. 137–139) concept of a "societal sector" which, while building on the economists' concept of "industry," is broader in that it includes organizations that contribute to or regulate the activities of a focal industry group.

23. But we also emphasize, drawing on Bourdieu (1971, 1975, 1984), that fields are arenas of power relations, with some actors—generally those possessing superior material and/or symbolic resources—occupying more advantaged positions than others. The concept of "structural power" used here is indebted to the illuminating discussion of the relationship between power and participation in Alford and Friedland (1975). Our formulation differs somewhat from theirs, however, and is in fact closer to their concept of "systemic power."

24. For the national study, we have conducted original archival research on convention reports, institutional research studies, and other materials provided by the American Association of Community and Junior Colleges. In addition, we have drawn extensively on the available secondary literature, both quantitative and qualitative. Finally, we have supplemented this evidence with a systematic examination of governmental documents and other materials from the key state of California.

25. The study of community college development in Massachusetts is based almost exclusively on primary research. Much of the data are drawn from interviews we conducted with persons involved in the development of the Massachusetts community colleges. Over 100 interviews were conducted, with most lasting between one and two hours. During the field study, we visited seven campuses—one in western Massachusetts and six in the eastern part of the state. The field study included periods of observation of campus life at each of the seven campuses visited. We also observed activities at the Massachusetts Board of Regional Community Colleges, and examined minutes of its Board meetings between 1959 and 1984. In addition, we inspected documents on state and campus policy, including budget data, enrollment figures, and educational policy planning documents.

CHAPTER 2

1. Enrollment data on junior colleges prior to 1915 are sparse and unreliable. According to McDowell (1919, p. 41), there were fewer than ten junior colleges in existence in 1907; Eells (1931a, p. 74), however, reports thirty-two junior colleges—all but one of them private—by 1905. Koos (1925:3) reports approximately fifteen junior colleges by 1906 but, like McDowell and Eells, provides no enrollment figures. Despite competing definitions of what constituted a junior college in those years and diverse estimates of the number of institutions, two things nonetheless seem clear: first, that more students were enrolled in private junior colleges than in public ones in the years before World War I and, second, that junior college students comprised well under 1 percent of all college students (calculated from U.S. Bureau of the Census, 1975, p. 383).

2. Lange had been a student at the University of Michigan when its president, Henry Tappan, first proposed separating the lower and upper division studies. Lange saw himself

as carrying Tappan's ideas toward realization in a more receptive environment than Tappan's own state proved to be (Eells 1931a, pp. 91–92).

3. For illuminating biographical and intellectual portraits of Harper, Jordan, and Lange, see Chapter 2 of Goodwin (1971, pp. 19–92). All three of these sponsors of the junior college movement were believers in the core "Progressive" values of efficiency and order, and all three, according to Goodwin, were skeptical of the intellectual capabilities of the masses. Jordan, a prominent figure in the peace and anti-imperialist movements of his time, was also a believer in the genetic superiority of the Anglo-Saxon race. The author of *The Blood of the Nation: A Study of the Decay of Races Through the Survival of the Unfit* (1910), Jordan believed that wars tended to kill off the finest specimens of the race and therefore should be opposed (Goodwin 1971, p. 3).

4. The figures in Table 2-2 are based on data gathered by the AAJC rather than the U.S. Office of Education. In general, the AAJC figures show somewhat higher enrollments than figures from the Office of Education because they include some lower divisions of four-year colleges and universities as well as students who are in "special" or "adult education" programs in two-year institutions. Although the Office of Education figures are consistently lower than those of the AAJC, it is important to note that the trends they reveal are always in the same direction. Because the U.S. Office of Education (and later the National Center for Educational Statistics) has no vested institutional interest in inflating junior college enrollments, we have relied on government figures where possible. For a detailed discussion of the two sets of data arguing that they should be viewed as complementary, see Fields (1962, pp. 35–41).

5. There were some strictly vocational colleges such as John Tarleton Agricultural College and the Grubbs Vocational College in Texas—both maintained as branches of the Agricultural and Mechanical College of Texas (Koos 1925, p. 362). Most of the first junior colleges in Mississippi also took root as agricultural training schools (Eells 1931a, p. 139).

6. The one institution in the Northeast classified in 1930 as a public junior college was in fact a program at Central High School in Springfield, Massachusetts, that offered only one year of college work and enrolled only thirty-five students (Eells 1931a, pp. 24, 137). By 1938 this institution, which arguably should never have been classified as a bona fide junior college, had ceased to exist (see Eells 1940a, p. 83).

7. Accreditation requirements also focused administrative attention on the college-parallel curricula. Accrediting boards, made up primarily of university faculty, were often skeptical of the junior colleges' ability to provide adequate college-level instruction. Because accreditation was critical for institutional legitimacy, administrators were forced to focus much of their energy on upgrading their standards for college preparatory work (Eells, 1931a). Although the standards for college instruction were clear, the standards for vocational programs were frequently murky. The cost of setting up vocational programs also acted as an obstacle in some of the small institutions. Laboratory equipment and practice machinery cost much more to install than the chalkboard and lectures that were sufficient in a liberal arts classroom.

8. Aldridge, in a study of "ideas and theories" concerning junior colleges during 1900–1935 and 1945–1960, found that the principal figures during the early decades of the century were (in rank order): Leonard V. Koos, Walter C. Eells, William R. Harper, Alexis F. Lange, David S. Jordan, and Doak S. Campbell (Alridge 1967, p. 12). Of these figures, Harper, Lange, and Jordan were, of course, administrators at leading universities and are therefore best viewed as "external" to the junior college movement in a way that Koos, Eells, and Campbell—all of whom were extremely active in the affairs of the AAJC—were not. Although Aldridge (1967, p. 13) derived his rank ordering of junior college leaders from a survey of "fifty-five professors of junior college education and specialists in junior

college education in the state departments of education as well as the U.S. Office of Education,'' Goodwin's 1971 study of the historical development of the junior college ideology reached a similar conclusion based on an analysis of works on junior colleges cited in the *Educational Index* and *Reader's Guide* (Goodwin 1971, p. 10). In an illuminating metaphor borrowed in part from George Zook (see page 35), Goodwin suggests that "if Harper, Jordan, and Lange can be considered the prophets of the junior college movement, then Koos, Eells, and Campbell can be considered its generals in the field" (Goodwin 1971, p. 115).

9. Graduate school was another matter, with Koos and Eells receiving their doctoral degrees from Chicago and Stanford, respectively. Perhaps reflecting his more humble origins, Campbell's doctoral degree was awarded at George Peabody College in Tennessee (Goodwin 1971, pp. 95–112).

10. Campbell remained an active Sunday School teacher throughout his life and was active in local, state, and national Baptist affairs (Goodwin, 1971:112). As for Eells, it is perhaps noteworthy that he described himself in the 1944–1945 edition of *Who's Who in America* as a Congregationalist and a Republican.

11. Several smaller studies in Kansas, Iowas, and Arizona found a similar pattern of preferences (Eells 1931a, p. 223). Clearly, students liked the convenience, size, and cost of the two-year colleges and also the opportunities they afforded for movement into higher level institutions. But they were much less likely to see vocational programs as a major source of attraction to the junior college.

12. In the Koos study (1924, p. 123–125), 59 percent of parents also mentioned as a reason for sending their children to junior college that it was close to home, thereby allowing the home influence to be extended.

13. In spite of the large proportions of students enrolled in college preparatory programs, junior colleges never sent most of their students on to four-year colleges and universities. In the 1930s, estimates on the proportion transferring ranged from 30 to 35 percent (Goodwin 1971, p. 188). The remaining students who were enrolled in transfer programs either dropped out before completing their programs or graduated but did not transfer. Many in the movement interpreted these figures as highlighting the gaps between student aspirations for college degrees and their actual achievement. In this view, many students who said they were transfers were actually latent terminal students, and their expressed aspirations should consequently not be taken seriously. Another way of looking at the figures, however, would be to emphasize the extent to which junior college students faced a more formidable task than four-year college freshman in making their way through the full four years of college. Indeed, the chances that junior college transfer students would receive a bachelor's degree were only about half of those of four-year college freshman, in spite of the high attrition rates among college freshmen during the period. Studies in the late 1920s suggest that just over one in four students who transferred from junior colleges graduated from college, compared with just over one-half of four-year-college freshmen (Eells 1931a, pp. 249–254). How much of this was due to differences in ability and motivation, how much to financial differences in the climates of the junior and senior institutions cannot be known, but there is reason to believe that the latter two factors played some role, perhaps a substantial one.

14. Not all of the articles on the California colleges were panegyrics; several cautionary notes were sounded. For example, in ''Misconceptions Regarding Junior Colleges,'' Weersing (1931) was particularly critical of the practice of labeling ''recommended'' and ''nonrecommended'' students that prevailed in the California colleges at the time. He also criticized the strict segregation of terminal and transfer courses, arguing that all qualified students should be allowed to take transfer-level academic courses if they were so inclined.

15. The remaining two members of the Commission of Seven were Orval R. Latham (president of the Iowa State Teachers College) and Albert B. Meredith (head of the department of administration of the school of education at New York University).

16. This national and state policymaking elite in higher education was in many ways analogous to what Tyack and Hansot (1982, pp. 105–167) have referred to as the "educational trust" that shaped American elementary and secondary education during the early decades of the twentieth century. In both groups, institutional elites from the major universities (including their schools of education), key federal agencies, state departments of education, and a handful of large private foundations, notably Carnegie and Rockefeller, formed a network that supplied much of the personnel to major policy commissions and influenced patterns of hiring and promotion in the educational bureaucracy. For an analysis of interlocking networks of influence among elites in higher education policymaking today, see Scott (1983, pp. 64–111).

17. Consistent with its view of the junior college as part of secondary rather than higher education, the Commission of Seven recommended that the junior college be "included within the common school system and should continue to be managed as local schools under the general supervision of the State Board of Education, along with other common and local schools." Indeed, lower-division college work, whether in the University or the two-year college, should be considered part of secondary education, because secondary work "terminates general education" and higher education begins "specialization" (Carnegie Foundation 1932, pp. 25–26). Toward the objective of sharpening this distinction between lower-division and upper-division education, the report recommended that the University of California itself award a certificate at the end of the second year of college as a means of marking the completion of general education—and of encouraging students to terminate their education.

18. As Goodwin (1971, p. 146) points out, the term *social intelligence* was first used by some educators in the Progressive education movement to mean the type of thinking that would allow citizens to question and analyze social issues and government policies. In the course of its incorporation by junior college administrators and educational policy boards, however, its meaning shifted to denote thinking that would lead average citizens to accept their place in society and to be loyal to governmental and business authorities.

19. The history of higher education in the United States suggests that concerns about the strength of shared values often emerge during periods of extraordinary stress. The influence of the Depression era was apparent in the Carnegie Foundation's own diagnosis of the need for the "social intelligence" curriculum. "Failure of citizens to understand many of our current problems and their tragic inability to cooperate in the solution of them constitute one cause that has led to breakdowns in our current civilization" (Carnegie Foundation 1932, pp. 17–18).

20. That the outlines of a class-linked structure of tracking were already visible in California before the publication of the Carnegie report is apparent from the results of a 1929 study by Eells and Brand showing that the proportion of lower-class students in California junior colleges was more than three times greater than their proportion at the state's four-year institutions (cited in Levine 1986, p. 181).

21. In 1914, for example, the Illinois State Federation of Labor (ISFL) vigorously opposed the Cooley Bill, a business-sponsored proposal to establish a separate vocational track (in the form of new vocational schools) at the secondary level. The ISFL's special committee on vocational education, headed by Victor Olander, insisted that all children must be given a broad and general education "so that class distinctions in our public schools such as practiced in the German system of education could be avoided." Moreover, any attempt by employers "to limit the opportunities of the workers for obtaining a general

education and thus render them more submissive and less independent should be resisted"
(quoted in Hogan 1985, p. 179). For a contemporary account not only of the controversy
over the Cooley bill, but of school politics in Chicago during the early decades of this
century, see the classic work by Counts (1928).

22. To overcome what it perceived as massive overenrollment in college-parallel transfer programs, the Carnegie panel advocated "the reeducation of both students and parents,
and much rearrangement and reorganization of junior college offerings, accompanied by
more effective educational guidance, curricula-making, and teaching." Only then will the
junior college be "giving in each case the right kind of education to each of its different
groups" (Carnegie Foundation 1932, p. 39).

23. Seven years earlier, in 1934, Doak S. Campbell made a similar point when he
remarked in a speech at Arkansas State College that "education is the strongest and cheapest social insurance that can be employed, and the nation that neglects it is inviting disas-
ter" (quoted in Goodwin 1971, p. 146).

24. Koos's commitment to the idea that junior colleges were *not* a part of higher education was so intense that when, in 1926, the University of Minnesota offered him the
opportunity to become the nation's first professor of higher education, he declined on the
grounds that the junior college movement, with which he was becoming increasingly identified, was a part of secondary rather than higher education (Goodwin 1971, p. 102).

25. In many institutions, separate terminal programs were maintained, but rarely did
they reach the dominant position suggested for them in the Carnegie study of higher education in California. In 1938–1939, about one-quarter of all terminal enrollments were in
general cultural programs, which were especially popular in the Northeastern and Middle
Atlantic states, at private women's colleges, and in the larger public colleges (Eells 1941a,
pp. 56–57). This fact suggests that they appealed mainly to relatively well-to-do female
students and to middle-class students who rejected the vocational programs as stigmatized
but had difficulties with or lacked interest in the more demanding academic preparatory
programs.

26. A small number of Eells's respondents did raise concerns about the potential negative effects of vocationalization on students' life chances. One private college president,
for example, wrote, "I am not in favor of the junior colleges because I think a larger
number of students who have finished two years in junior colleges stop there than is the
case of students who have finished the first two years of a four-year college." (Cottingham,
quoted in Eells 1941b, p. 128). Concerns like these were raised, however, by fewer than
one in fifteen of the respondents quoted by Eells (calculated from Eells 1941b, pp. 88–
244).

27. In spite of the specification in the Smith-Hayes and George-Deen acts that vocational education funds could be used only for programs "of less than college grade," some
junior colleges, particularly those administratively connected to secondary schools, were
able to obtain vocational education money. In 1940, for example, sixty-two junior colleges
in fourteen states received at least small amounts of federal vocational education assistance.
Efforts to obtain this funding from state allocating boards were, however, often unsuccessful, and the funds obtained were trivial in contrast to the support given to high schools
(Eells 1941a, pp. 29–30).

28. With the outbreak of war, general education programs gained a new significance
as vehicles to ensure loyalty to the state and to safeguard American values against competing ideologies. Leland Medsker, who replaced Eells as director of the Terminal Education
study during its final year, became a particularly strong advocate of values-oriented general
education. Winning the conflict, Medsker stated, would involve understanding "not only
how to fight a war but why it should be fought" (Medsker 1943, p. 19). Other wartime

leaders of the Association agreed that "citizenship training" had priority in the junior colleges. (For additional statements on the war aims of the junior colleges, see Goodwin 1971, pp. 238–245).

CHAPTER 3

1. On the issue of discrimination, for example, the Truman Commission militantly denounced violations of equal opportunity on the basis of race or religion and, remarkably, for the time, included a brief section repudiating "anti-feminism in higher education" as another form of "arbitrary exclusion." Not surprisingly, *Higher Education in American Democracy* provoked a vigorous public debate, with a strong attack from conservatives and an energetic counterattack from liberals (this debate is ably summarized in a volume edited by Kennedy [1952]). For useful discussions of the Truman Commission's recommendations and impact, see Henry (1975) and Dougherty (1980).

2. In a similarly populist vein, the report categorically rejected the view that financial factors did not constitute a major obstacle to college attendance: "The old comfortable idea that 'any boy can get a college education who had it in him' simply is not true. Low family income, together with the rising costs of education, constitute an almost impassible barrier to college education for many young people" (1948, vol. I, p. 28).

3. Because of the expanded state systems, the high-cost, low-prestige, private junior colleges began to lose out in the competition for students. The number of private colleges fell from a peak of 350 in the early 1940s to 259 by 1955 (Hillway 1958, p. 18). Private enrollments also fell after experiencing a surge in the immediate postwar era. By the mid-1950s, private colleges constituted only a small portion of the national association, enrolling under one-seventh the number of students enrolled in the public colleges.

4. For a systematic analysis of the political and organizational dynamics that led some states to expand junior colleges rapidly, others more gradually, and still others (at least for a time) not at all, see Dougherty (1988b), who has examined the cases of Indiana, Illinois, Washington, New York, and California. For a detailed treatment of the cases of Illinois and Washington, see Dougherty (1983).

5. It may be that fewer incentives to regulate patterns of student enrollment exist in times of plenty. We are thus not entirely convinced by those analysts who have suggested that the entrance of large numbers of working-class students automatically encourages strenuous efforts to differentiate curricula tracks (see, e.g., Zwerling 1976, Bowles and Gintis 1976, and Nasaw 1979). Although this is a general tendency, market conditions can moderate the curricular effects of changes in student body composition.

6. An earlier study by Eells (1943) found that the small number of terminal students who managed to transfer to four-year colleges performed well. Nearly half of these students received above average grades, and only 16 percent received marks that were below average.

7. A careful study of 200 colleges surveyed by Medsker indicated that 30 percent of junior college students in 1952 scored above the mean for college students on a standardized test of intelligence. Only 16 percent had scores considered below average, compared with about 7 percent of four-year college students. In other studies, terminal students received slightly lower average scores than transfer students on standardized tests of intelligence. Interestingly, the scores of female terminal students were quite similar to those of transfer students, and the scores of men also indicated a substantial overlap in aptitude scores between the two tracks (Medsker 1960, pp. 30–40).

8. Remarkably, when Gleazer became executive director (the title had been changed,

at his request, from executive secretary) of the AAJC in 1958, he was the third of four executives of the Association to come from a devoutly religious background. A minister in the Reorganized Church of Jesus Christ of the Latter-day Saints (the Mormon Church), Gleazer was the first AAJC executive to have graduated from a junior college (Graceland College, a Mormon institution in Lamoni, Iowa). From there, he went on to UCLA, from which he received the B.A. in 1938. After several years of working in Philadelphia as a Mormon minister, Gleazer completed his M.Ed. at Temple University in 1943. Following three additional years of church work, Gleazer returned to his alma mater, Graceland, and served as president until 1957. While at Graceland, he managed to earn an Ed.D. from Harvard in 1953, and in 1958, having served as elected president of the AAJC the year before, accepted a full-time position as executive director of the organization (Goodwin 1971, p. 220). The 1977–1978 edition of *Who's Who in America* lists him as a member of the Cosmos, Harvard, and Rotary clubs. In 1980, after a record tenure of 22 years, Gleazer retired as executive director of the Association.

9. A 1957 national ranking of graduate programs found that the University of California at Berkeley was the second ranked institution of the country, behind only Harvard and ahead of such institutions as Yale, Chicago, Michigan, Columbia, Stanford, and Princeton. In 1925, Berkeley had ranked ninth (Harris 1972, p. 401).

10. Crucial background to the California Master Plan of 1960 is provided by its postwar precursors, *A Report of a Survey of the Needs of California in Higher Education* (the so-called Strayer Report of 1948) and *A Restudy of the Needs of California in Higher Education*, a 1955 report written by T. C. Holy and H. H. Semans. All these reports were written under the auspices of the Liaison Committee of the Regents of the University of California and the California State Board of Education. On the origins of the Liaison Committee, see State of California (1957) and Condren (1960). Finally, for additional background materials on the politics of public higher education in California, see the useful study by Coons (1968).

11. Robert Sproul, in a 1958 article entitled "Many Millions More," also acknowledged the "shock absorber" function of the two-year institution when he wrote that "the University of California . . . would hardly have been able to establish and maintain its present standards" in the absence of "the excellent junior colleges that have developed" (Sproul 1958, p. 101). But it is David Riesman, an astute observer of higher education and a fellow member of the Carnegie Commission with Clark Kerr, who has perhaps put the matter most graphically: "In that state [California], community colleges were seen as a kind of moat built by the Master Plan of 1960 . . . around the University of California, protecting it from having to take inept students in as freshmen" (Riesman 1980, p. 185).

12. A number of other studies, including follow-ups of the state's graduating high school classes of 1966 (Tillery 1973) and 1975 (University of California Systemwide Administration 1978), confirm the existence of a powerful relationship between social class and tracking in California higher education. Yet in California, according to data from the National Longitudinal Study of the High School Class of 1972, there is significantly less stratification by class than in some states. Calculations made by Dougherty (1988b) reveal that college freshmen in California from the lowest socioeconomic quartile are 14 percent more likely to be enrolled in a junior college than students from the top quartile, compared with gaps of 30 percent in Illinois and 21 percent in New York.

13. Attrition in the California system of higher education, several studies suggest (Knoell and Medsker 1984, Coordinating Council 1969), was unusually high; according to official state figures, fewer than 30 percent of all college entrants would ever receive a bachelor's degree (Joint Committee on Higher Education 1969, p. x). Although rates of college entry in California were higher than average, they were apparently not accompanied by higher

rates of college graduation. Indeed, there is some evidence that the California model may have provided four or more years of college to an unusually low percentage of its population; the Pacific division of the U.S. Census Bureau (of which the state of California accounts for 75 percent of the population, with Washington, which also has a large community college system, providing almost 15 percent more), although among the highest of nine census divisions in rates of high school graduation and college entry, has the second lowest proportion of younger age cohorts completing four years of college (Jaffe and Adams 1972, pp. 229–231).

14. For an assessment of the evidence available in the early 1970s on the effects of attendance at a community college on the likelihood of obtaining a bachelor's degree, see Karabel (1972, p. 530–536).

15. Information on foundation and corporate support to the junior college movement was kindly provided by Jack Gernhart, former national secretary of the AAJC.

16. Ideological resistance among businessmen on fiscal grounds is clearly in evidence, for example, in the U.S. Chamber of Commerce's opposition to federal funding for community colleges in the early 1960s. Chamber officials repeatedly argued that federal aid to higher education was both improper and unnecessary and that instead it should continue to be financed from state, local, and private sources (Dougherty 1980). The other cause of business distance, its historical commitment to private institutions, is well documented (Jencks and Riesman 1968), and it is in evident in patterns of giving to two-year colleges as well. Corporate gifts and grants to private junior colleges in the 1960s, though modest, were more than twice as large as their gifts to the far more populous community colleges (O'Neill 1973).

17. It should be noted that given the tremendous growth in enrollments during the decade, changes in the *absolute* number of students enrolled in the vocational programs were impressive in spite of small percentage changes. The best studies show approximately a tripling of the absolute number of junior and community college students enrolled in occupational programs between 1960 and 1970 (Medsker 1960, Medsker and Tillery 1971, Blackstone, 1978).

NOTES TO CHAPTER 4

1. A number of attempts have been made by analysts close to the community college movement to explain the decline of transfer education and the rise of occupational programs during the 1970s; among the most useful are Lombardi (1978, 1979), Friedlander (1980), Cohen and Brawer (1982, pp. 200–207), and Baron (1982). For a detailed discussion of the many complexities involved in estimating the number of students enrolled in transfer programs, see Cohen (1979).

2. In 1967, Pifer also became president of the far wealthier Carnegie Corporation, a position which had also been occupied by his predecessor as chief of the CFAT, John Gardner (who left to become the U.S. Secretary of Health, Education, and Welfare in August 1965). The CFAT, while legally independent of the Carnegie Corporation, was in fact financially dependent on it; had the latter foundation not subsidized the former, it is doubtful whether the activities of the Carnegie Commission and its successor group, the Carnegie Commission on Policy Studies in Higher Education, would have been possible. Together, it is estimated that the two groups spent roughly $12 million between 1967 and 1979 (Lagemann 1983, pp. 122, 129–130, 226).

3. The choice of Kerr as director of the Carnegie Commission was apparently not a difficult one; when asked why Kerr had been selected, Alden Dunham, a program officer

for higher education at the Carnegie Corporation, responded, "There was just nobody better known in American higher education at that point." Asked the same question, Alan Pifer said simply, "He was always number one on the list" (Stuart 1980, p. 274).

4. In the view of many foundation officials, assaults from the right as well as the left threatened the stability of American society. Indeed, the announcement to the press of a forthcoming Carnegie study of higher education was in fact made much earlier than had been scheduled as a public protest by the liberal Pifer over Clark Kerr's Ronald Reagan–assisted ouster as president of the University of California on January 20, 1967. Four days after his dismissal, Pifer proclaimed the existence of the Kerr-led Commission as a gesture of both public and personal support (Lagemann 1983, p. 132). One of the great ironies of the Regents' dismissal of Kerr was that it, if anything, enhanced his already enormous national stature at the same time that it made him available to work full-time in a position from which he could exert an even greater influence on the shape of American higher education.

5. Of the Commission's nineteen members, only two were women (Katherine McBride, president of Bryn Mawr College, and Patricia Harris, a black Washington attorney and later Secretary of Commerce in the Carter Administration), and only two were members of minority groups (Ms. Harris and Kenneth Tollett, the dean of the law school at predominantly black Texas Southern University). Among the best-known members of the Commission were Theodore Hesburgh, president of the University of Notre Dame; Carl Kaysen, director of the Institute for Advanced Study at Princeton; Nathan Pusey, the president of Harvard University; Kenneth Keniston, professor of psychology at Yale Medical School and author of books on student alienation and radicalism; David Riesman, the prolific writer on higher education and professor of social science at Harvard; William Scranton, the former Republican governor of Pennsylvania; and Norton Simon, the California businessman and former Regent of the University of California. Though the Commission proposed policies for the entire system of higher education, only one of its members was associated with the two-year movement; Joseph Cosand, president of the St. Louis Junior College District. For discussions of the membership of the Carnegie Commission, see Stuart (1980, p. 273–282) and Lagemann (1983, p. 136–138).

6. Carnegie Commission Chairman Clark Kerr's view that advanced industrial economies, whether capitalist or socialist, necessarily generate a hierarchical, occupationally based class structure is visible in Kerr's major scholarly work (with Harbison, Dunlop, and Myers), *Industrialism and Industrial Man* (1960) and is implicit in his classic *The Uses of the University* (1963). For radical critiques of the social and political vision underlying the various reports of the Carnegie Commission, see Wolfe (1971, 1974) and Darknell (1975, 1980).

7. Some of the inherent difficulties involved in attempts to use the educational system as a tool of manpower planning in state socialist societies are well described in Lane and O'Dell's *The Soviet Industrial Worker: Social Class, Education and Control* (1978). Useful historical studies of the Soviet case include Lapidus (1978), Bailes (1978), and Fitzpatrick (1970, 1979).

8. The classical cross-national study of university "overproduction" of graduates is Walter Kotschnig's *Unemployment in the Learned Professions* (1937). Barbagli's meticulous historical study of the Italian case, *Educating for Unemployment* (1982), shows how organizational and political factors can contribute to the production of a disequilibrium between the education system and the labor market that may become chronic, especially in societies with relatively undifferentiated structures of schooling. For an analysis of the sources of educational overproduction in the Third World, see Dore's *The Diploma Disease* (1976).

9. The information in this section on foundation and corporate support for the AAJC/AACJC in the 1970s was kindly provided by AAJC secretary Jack Gernhart.

10. The change in terminology from junior to community college was partly, to be sure, a genuinely populist effort by important segments of the two-year college movement to be responsive to the needs of the entire local population. But like the linguistic shift from "vocational" to "career" education, it also obscured, albeit perhaps unconsciously, the realities of tracking in a society in which educational credentials are closely linked to individual life chances. When in 1972 the AAJC became the American Association of Community and Junior Colleges (AACJC), the two-year college movement in effect withdrew a step further from the traditional academic hierarchy of higher education institutions at the same time that it symbolically legitimated its new thrust toward vocationalism.

11. Labor economist Richard Freeman has corrected the conventional wisdom about the supply of college graduates in the 1960s, by noting that between 1958 and 1968 the absolute number of male bachelor's degree graduates increased substantially, but the "net" number seeking work (the number of graduates minus the number enrolling in graduate and professional programs), relative to the total male civilian work force, was halved. Thus, he concludes, "the 1960s were a period of declining relative supply of new college workers, not—as is often thought—a period of increasing supply" (Freeman 1976, pp. 67).

12. In the decade between 1957 and 1967, the number of annual births in the United States declined from 4,300,000 to 3,521,000. This decline continued until 1973, when the number of births reached a low of 3,137,000 and then began a gradual climb, reaching 3,681,000 by 1982 (U.S. Bureau of the Census 1987, p. 58).

13. A bachelor's degree recipient working full time was defined by the National Center for Education Statistics as "underemployed" if he or she was "in a job that was not professional, technical, managerial, or administrative and when asked, responded that the job did not require a college degree" (NCES 1979, p. 242).

14. Among women with 1976–1977 bachelor's degrees in the humanities, social sciences and public affairs, and psychology, rates of underemployment were 32.5, 40.4, and 32.0 percent, respectively; among men, the comparable figures were 32.9, 36.3, and 36.8 percent. Women working full time earned an average of only 88 percent of what men earned: $10,300 versus $11,700 per year (National Center for Educational Statistics, *The Condition of Education 1979*, p. 242).

15. Because most junior college students never attain a bachelor's degree, the labor market experiences of individuals in the category of "some college" frequently used by researchers is of special interest. The most extensive analysis of the some-college category (also defined as individuals with one to three years of college) was carried out by Jencks et al. (1979, pp. 159–190) who found that, at least into the early 1970s, college graduates had substantially higher earnings than those who had never received a bachelor's degree, even when controls were introduced for prior differences in ability, socioeconomic status, and other factors. In addition, an analysis of the independent "credential effect" on earnings and occupational status showed that it went above and beyond the effect that would be yielded by a fourth year of college. Along similar lines, an analysis of U.S. Census Bureau data from the late 1960s found that only 32 percent of the young men with five to seven terms of college were employed in professional and managerial jobs, compared with 82 percent of young men who had completed eight or more terms (Jaffe and Adams 1972, p. 249).

16. This section is based on a study of the mass media's presentation of the changing labor market for college graduates as revealed by a systematic review of all stories on the subject that appeared in the following sources between 1969 and 1978: CBS morning and evening news programs and special reports, *Time* magazine, *Newsweek* magazine, the *Wall*

Street Journal, Fortune, Business Week, and *Nation's Business.* Transcripts of CBS stories were obtained through the assistance of Michael Lehrman of CBS News. For a more extensive treatment of this data, see Strong (1980).

17. Writers for the business press were particularly enthusiastic about the growth of community colleges, which they saw as a means of relieving the problem of "overeducation" and providing corporations with trained yet contented workers. As a businessman quoted in the December 10, 1968 issue of the *Wall Street Journal* put it, junior college graduates have "sufficient education to do a good job and insufficient education to become dissatisfied quickly" (quoted in Strong 1980, p. 6).

18. Student classification practices varied considerably between states, as did the basis of measuring enrollment (some used head counts, others unduplicated head counts, and still others full-time equivalent measures). As funding patterns began to place a premium on vocational education enrollments, some colleges began to classify as vocational many programs that had previously been classified as general education or liberal arts (Lombardi 1978, Cohen and Brawer 1982, p. 202). In one attempt to redefine classifications, the state of Washington increased academic enrollments by 4 percent and decreased vocational enrollments by 4 percent (Price, cited in Cohen and Brawer 1982, p. 202).

19. Although some associate's degrees are awarded by four-year institutions, the National Center for Education Statistics data reveal that between 1970–1971 and 1975–1976, two-year colleges awarded from 85.0 to 87.6 percent of all associate's degrees (Malitz 1978, p. 9).

20. The educational aspirations of all community college students (including part-time students) may, it should be noted, be considerably lower than the ACE-based estimate that seven to eight in ten aspire to a bachelor's degree. For a fuller discussion of this issue, see Dougherty (1987, p. 187).

21. In its annual report of 1975, the AACJC acknowledged the impact of the mass media in helping to boost occupational enrollments: "Not for many years has there been such an emphasis on job education as during 1975. Syndicated columnists, government leaders, and a writer of a nationally-touted book underlined the decreasing need for baccalaureates . . . and the better job prospects for those trained in technical and semi-professional training" (AACJC 1976, p. 3). The "nationally-touted book" referred to is Caroline Bird's *The Case Against College* (1975).

22. In a more recent analysis which simultaneously controlled for a broader array of variables than did the earlier study, Wilms and Hansell (1982, p. 57) again emphasized that the vocational programs that are seemingly linked to the highest status jobs are the least successful: "Post-secondary vocational education, despite its historical promise, has little economic payoff for students who train for professional technical-level jobs. . . . To the extent that vocational education has an economic payoff, it seems to be limited to training for lower-status occupations."

23. In an unpublished article, Monk-Turner found significant income as well as occupational penalties associated with enrollment at two-year rather than four-year institutions. Analyzing the earnings of young men and women 10 years out of high school who were employed full time, Monk-Turner reported returns of 5.4 percent a year for an additional year at a community college, compared with 7.9 percent for an additional year at a four-year college, controlling for ability, race, gender, work experience, years of education, and other variables.

24. Noting that attendance at a community college rather than a four-year institution has a depressing effect on educational attainment, Monk-Turner has suggested that community colleges may have indirectly contributed to occupational sex segregation by increasing the number of women who do not complete college. According to 1970 U.S. Census

Bureau data, 44.9 percent of women with one to three years of college were clerical workers, compared with 10.9 percent of similarly educated men. For college graduates, however, the gender gap was much narrower, with only 14.8 percent of women employed in clerical work, compared with 6.3 percent of men (Monk-Turner, 1985:94).

25. A number of important gaps remain in research on the effects of community vocational education, among them the long-term economic effects of occupational programs. Because the gap between college graduates and those with some college tends to increase over the course of the life cycle (O'Neill and Sepielli 1985, p. 53), we suspect that studies covering a longer period may make the returns to terminal vocational programs look even more modest. At the same time, such programs may well improve the life chances of those students who would otherwise never have attended college; accordingly, properly controlled studies comparing the income and occupational status of the alumni of community college vocational programs with those of high school graduates would be useful.

26. Because community college vocational programs are, in principle, designed to meet the needs of employers and to produce high payoffs to their graduates, the question arises as to how one can explain their apparently modest economic returns. Part of the answer may reside in the inability of community college vocational programs to monopolize particular training markets effectively. In contrast, for example, to professional schools that train students for occupations with state-enforced licensing requirements that can be met only through the acquisition of educational credentials from duly accredited institutions, most community college vocational programs send students out into labor markets in which a variety of alternative pathways to entry exist, including on-the-job training, proprietary schools, and other postsecondary institutions. In a fashion that is structurally similar to some of the most closed professions, craft unions monopolize the training markets for entrance into certain skilled jobs; where such unions are strong, individuals who have acquired the relevant skills through other means are not allowed to practice their trade. What these observations suggest is the possibility that the relatively low returns of community college vocational programs may reflect not a failure to impart technical skills, but rather an inability to monopolize particular training markets and thereby to boost incomes by restricting the supply of aspirants.

27. With its influence and resource base expanding and its vocationalization program beginning to be realized, the Association leadership felt confident enough to provide a forum for its internal critics. In 1972, Edmund Gleazer recommended an expanded and diversified board of directors designed to guarantee representation for faculty members, students, and minorities. The proposal passed the 1972 convention, and the new groups were included, although community college presidents remained the single largest voting bloc on the board (Dudley 1974).

For the first time since the early 1950s, the pages of the *Junior College Journal* were opened to criticisms of the leadership's emphasis on occupational programs, and some were written by minority group faculty members and administrators (Dow 1973, Love 1973, Pasqua 1974). Others were written by white liberal staff members concerned about the gap between the colleges' promises of opportunity and what the programs actually delivered (Furniss and Martin 1974). Even Gleazer himself sometimes appeared in the guise of an old-fashioned Populist. In one article, he criticized those who argued that the country had too many college graduates and Ph.D.s. "Tell that," he wrote, "to the millions of people in this country who are still wanting a basic education" (Gleazer 1973:3).

28. Community colleges, however, continued to practice "community-based education" successfully, especially in their noncredit night divisions or "continuing" or "adult" education courses. By 1978, 3 million people were enrolled in their largely "civic, cultural and recreational" courses (Cohen and Brawer 1982, p. 259; Friedlander, 1980).

29. For students entering college immediately after high school graduation, the proportion entering two-year as opposed to four-year institutions is significantly lower than for all first-time college freshmen. Among graduates of the high school class of 1980 who entered college in the fall of 1980, roughly 37 percent entered two-year rather than four-year colleges (calculated from High School and Beyond data reported in the National Center for Education Statistics, *The Condition of Education 1985*, p. 224). For *all* first-time freshmen (a figure that includes large numbers of older students), however, the proportion enrolled in two-year colleges was 53.9 percent in 1980 (calculated from Monk-Turner 1985, p. 92).

30. These figures are rough estimates of the proportion of all students, including adults, who transfer to a four-year institution. For those students who enter a community college immediately after high school, transfer rates are somewhat higher. Analyses of the transfer rates of cohorts of recent graduating seniors such as the High School and Beyond study of the high school classes of 1980 and 1982) would thus yield higher figures than those based on the community college student body as a whole.

31. In New York state in 1977–1978, only 7,716 out of 156,096 students transferred to a four-year institution, for a rate of 4.9 percent. In Washington state, the figures for 1977–1978 were 3,852 of 171,068 students, for a rate of 2.3 percent. Five years earlier in Illinois (in 1972–1973), 10,145 community college students out of a possible population of 183,286 transferred to four-year colleges and universities, yielding a rate of 5.5 percent (Baron 1982, p. 79–80).

32. In a system such as California's, in which over 40 percent of recent high school graduates become freshmen in community colleges, compared with roughly 9 and 6 percent at CSUC and UC, respectively, the issue of who ultimately transfers is of special interest. Although evidence on the class composition of transfers is not easily available, data on the racial composition of transfers have been gathered. Whereas blacks and Chicanos constituted 10.1 and 16.7 percent, respectively, of first-time CCC freshmen under the age of nineteen in 1981, they comprised only 6.6 and 9.7 percent of the transfers to CSUC, and 4.2 and 8.9 percent of transfers to UC, in 1983. At some institutions, the racial discrepancies in rates of transfer reached striking proportions; at Laney College in Oakland, for example, whites constituted only 18.9 percent of freshmen but comprised 38.9 percent of transfers to CSUC and 74.2 percent of transfers to UC (California Postsecondary Education Commission 1984).

33. According to data from a nationally representative study of the high school class of 1980, 32 percent of seniors from low socioeconomic backgrounds enrolled in college in the fall of 1980, compared with 74 percent of their counterparts from high socioeconomic backgrounds. Of the students of high socioeconomic origins, however, only 26 percent were enrolled in two-year as opposed to four-year institutions, compared with 47 percent of those of low social origins (calculated from National Center for Education Statistics, *The Condition of Education 1985*, p. 224).

34. Saiter, Susan. 1982. "No Belltower or Fraternities, Little Football, Lots of Serious Study." New York Times, August 22, pp. 32, 33, Section 12.

35. The Ford Foundation's recent project on improving minority transfer rates is a notable outcome of this type of questioning. In 1983, the Ford Foundation invited seventy urban community colleges to develop projects to assist more students to transfer to four-year colleges after completing their two-year programs (Maeroff 1983). In 1984, ten of these colleges received grants of up to $250,000 to continue their projects. Alexander Astin, the author of the Ford Foundation–sponsored report, *Minorities in American Higher Education*, observed that the project was designed to counteract the tendency of the community colleges' open door to lead "to a dead end" (Astin, quoted in Maeroff 1983). For

more information on the Ford project, see Center for the Study of Community Colleges (1985) and Donovan et al. (1987).

PART II INTRODUCTION

1. For a more detailed discussion of neo-Marxist, neo-Weberian and functionalist theories of education as a social institution, see Karabel and Halsey (1977, p. 8–44).

2. This point is illustrated by the case of American higher education in the early 1970s (Freeman 1976) or, more strikingly still, by the case of the Italian system, which has consistently "overproduced" graduates (Barbagli 1982).

3. During the course of the field study from 1978 through 1983, seven of the fifteen campuses were visited (Bunker Hill, Cape Cod, Greenfield, Massachusetts Bay, Massasoit, Middlesx, and Roxbury). Of the interviews, six were with current or former board members; seven were with current or former central office staff; eight were with campus presidents; seventeen were with campus administration; twenty-one were with counselors and placement officers; ten were with faculty; three were with state legislators; two were with high-ranking state government officials; six were with businessmen or labor officials; two were academic experts on the Massachusetts community colleges; and the remaining forty were with students. All minutes of Board meetings between 1959 and 1980 and other public documents relating to Board policy were made available thanks to the assistance of Helen Genereau and other members of the central office staff.

CHAPTER 5

1. Expanding public higher education was a particularly high priority for Furcolo, who like many liberals tended to see higher education as a social equalizer: "It had always bothered me," he recalled, "that some students could not go to college just because they couldn't afford it." (Furcolo quoted in Lustberg 1979, p. 113)

2. Interview with John Mallan. For a full list of interviews, dates, and the titles of those interviewed, please see pages 300–303.

3. The Audit Commission also engaged the services of S. J. Martorana, an educational research and community college administrator long associated with the AAJC leadership (Goodwin 1971). Martorana's influence, however, appears to have been limited primarily to arguing the case for local funding, a proposal that was eventually not included in the Commission's report.

4. Indeed, some of the most important Board members were named after resignations by original members of the Board. Among the most influential new appointees were Raymond Swords and Asa Knowles, the presidents of Holy Cross College and Northeastern University, respectively, and corporate attorneys Joseph Mulhern, Henry Foley, and Theodore Chase. Several businessmen were also appointed to fill vacated seats in the early 1960s. These men included architect Nelson Aldrich of Campbell, Aldrich and McNulty; Daniel England of England Brothers; Meyer Jaffe of J & J Corrugated Box Corporation; Henry Morgenthau of television station WGBH; and Richard Philbrick of ITEK Corporation.

5. Interview with Kermit Morrissey.

6. Ibid.

7. These tasks were temporarily impeded by a political crisis. One year after approving

the governor's community college bill, the legislature chose to block capital outlay for the first college in retaliation for the governor's efforts to pass a new sales tax to finance his social programs. The sales tax had virtually no support in the legislature, and it looked as if the community colleges would be caught in the crossfire between the governor and the legislature over the tax. Kermit Morrissey described the battle for the first appropriation as "a terrible fight." Following an initial defeat of the bill, several members of the Board met with the governor and his aide to chart a strategy for passing the appropriations. The key decision made in these sessions was to ask Roger Putnam to step down as chair and to recruit Joseph Mulhern, a former lobbyist for the railroads and utilities, as a replacement. Mulhern agreed to work closely with the legislature to pass the appropriations, while Morrissey, the new vice-chair, agreed to take responsibility for the administrative end of the Board's affairs. This division of labor worked well. The sales tax issue blew over, and Mulhern, a skillful political operator, drew on his personal friendships and lobbying experience to help secure adequate appropriations. Morrissey, meanwhile, supervised the hiring of the central office staff, helped arrange an articulation agreement with the University of Massachusetts, and spent many hours promoting community colleges in places targeted as potential sites for the first colleges.

8. Local support was necessary because Board policy required that local communities donate temporary facilities for the colleges and that they also donate land on which permanent facilities could eventually be built. In addition to these donations, the Board required other signs of community support, including letters of endorsement from business, education, and political leaders and regional surveys of employment needs (interview with John Costello, March 15, 1983).

9. There were, however, a few exceptions to this pattern. Community groups in Gardner and Beverly initiated the processes leading to the founding of colleges in these cities. Nor were powerful legislators inevitably successful in their efforts to secure colleges for their districts; several members of the state Ways and Means Committees tried to obtain colleges and failed (see Lustberg 1979, p. 145).

10. Businessmen were uninvolved in the founding of Massachusetts Bay Community College in Boston, where the relative economic impact of a community college would be slight and hard to measure. In Boston, the mayor and the city's Redevelopment Authority played the leading role.

11. Generally, all potentially important interest groups were at least consulted. In Pittsfield, for example, Representative Wojtkowski recalled discussing the college with members of parent-teacher associations, the Rotarians, the Kiwanians, the city council, the school committee, the Chamber of Commerce, the League of Women Voters, and the mayor. Thomas O'Connell, who later became president of the college in Pittsfield, spoke also to managers of the local General Electric facility and to editors of the *Berkshire Eagle* (Lustberg 1979, p. 147).

12. Interview with Kermit Morrissey.

13. Interviews with John Costello, October 17, 1978, and Theodore Chase.

14. Interview with Arthur Haley.

15. Interview with John Costello, March 15, 1983.

16. Interview with Thomas O'Connell.

17. Ibid.

18. Interview with Arthur Haley.

19. This "cultural bias" was analyzed at some length in the Board's 1967 "Master Plan," written by Donald Deyo. According to the report: "All groups are agreed, including parents, that the community college ought to offer a wide variety of occupational programs. However, these are always for 'other people's' kids; my own are going to _____; or to

medical school or law school.' This universal recognition of the necessity of occupational education, coupled with the inconsistent reluctance to consider it for one's own children, is almost entirely a matter of prestige. It is difficult for parents to confess to neighbors, to professional associates, or to social acquaintances that one's son is learning to be an electronics technician; it is so much more prestigious to announce that 'my son is studying electrical engineering'. Until social attitudes can be changed regarding occupational education, it is not likely that the community college, even though dedicated to its responsibility in this field, will be able satisfactorily to fulfill this function" (Deyo 1967, p. 8).

20. Interview with Gordon Pyle, July 10, 1978.

21. Ibid.

22. Interview with William Dwyer, February 9, 1979. Interview dates are cited for individuals who were interviewed on more than one occasion.

23. Interview with Kermit Morrissey.

24. Interview with William Dwyer, February 9, 1979.

25. Ibid.

26. Ibid.

27. Interview with Thomas O'Connell, February 15, 1978.

28. Ibid.

29. Interview with James Hall.

30. For additional data on patterns of stratification in Massachusetts higher education, see the longitudinal study of the state's high school class of 1966 reported in Tillery (1973).

31. Interview with William Dwyer, February 9, 1979.

32. Ibid.

33. Interview with James Hall.

34. Interview with Arthur Haley.

35. Interview with John Costello, October 17, 1978.

36. Interview with Frederick B. Viaux.

37. Interview with Erroll Jacobsen.

38. This figure includes costs of instruction, plant operation, campus administration, and special capital outlays for equipment and library resources. It does not include central office costs and operating funds (so-called seed money) spent before a college opened for classes (see Deyo 1967, p. 15 for details on the computation of per student costs and variations among the campuses).

39. Interview with Patrick Capeci.

40. Interview with Donald Zekan.

41. Not all campus officials gave in to what one called the "temptation" to grow through concentration on the occupational curricula. Administrators at Berkshire and Cape Cod, for example, insisted that all requests were "demand-driven," that is, based on a combination of enrollment pressures and labor market opportunities (interviews with Pat Capeci and Dan Asquino).

42. Campus and MBRCC budget-makers habitually added enough "fat" in their budgets to cover the standard reduction made by the staff in the governor's office and in the House. Cuts in excess of 25 percent were not uncommon in particular accounts. The deans of administration on the campuses knew this and planned their budgets accordingly. The strategies of budget makers in this highly ritualized environment are well described by Asquino (1976).

43. For a fuller discussion of this point about the consequences of fiscal autonomy, see Asquino (1976).

44. Not all the facilities were equally inviting, however. Four of the campuses—North Shore, Springfield, Middlesex, and Roxbury—remained in their original quarters, and these

were among the least pleasant in appearance. Middlesex was housed in an old Veteran's Administration building on the grounds of a VA hospital complex in Bedford. Students sometimes complained that they wanted a campus where they could tell "who were the students and who were the patients." At least two of the other campuses—North Shore and Bunker Hill—were clearly identifiable from the outside as "blue-collar" colleges. Though Bunker Hill was modern in architectural style, both campuses were located within sight of the freeways and factory-dominated skylines of industrial Beverly and east Boston.

45. The community colleges also received federal funds from eighteen other programs. The largest of these were the student loan and work-study programs and the facilities construction and developing institutions programs. Through the early 1970s, vocational education funds made up about one-third of the total federal aid (Massachusetts Board of Regional Community Colleges, "Summary of Federal Aid Awarded," 1969–1974). After 1974, education opportunity grants and work-study funds made up a much larger proportion of total federal aid.

46. The Federal Vocational Education Act of 1963 made vocational education funds available to community colleges for the first time. The Massachusetts plan for disbursing vocational education funds, however, emphasized expansion at the high school level, mainly in the area vocational schools (Deyo 1967, p. 8). Some observers, including the executive director of the community college system, speculated that the state plan reflected Commissioner of Education Owen Kiernan's resentment over his treatment while a member of the community-colleges' Board of Trustees.

47. Interview with William Dwyer, February 9, 1979.

48. Interview with Frederick B. Viaux.

49. Still there were problems in persuading the state to pick up costs once the federal seed money stopped. The legislature did not always wish to assume the costs for the often expensive vocational programs. Because of this, presidents were forced to juggle continuously—giving up some pet projects, diverting funds from the prosperous continuing education programs to the day division, and gradually working program costs into their annual budgets. Facilities and equipment appropriations were often particularly difficult to obtain. James Hall of Cape Cod remembered the president of Springfield Technical Community College as the envy of others in the system for his special access to old navy equipment in the Springfield armory, which allowed Springfield to expand more cheaply than the other colleges. In light of the tight budgets, community college administrators tended to see the legislature as the chief constraint on their activities. As James Hall, president of Cape Cod, said in our interview, no doubt speaking for many of the campus presidents, "You start to sympathize with whoever said, 'Everybody's life is a danger as long the legislature is in session.' "

The theoretical point to be made here is that even state agencies with important economic development (or business service) functions are not immune to budgetary austerity. Legislators must balance taxpayer concerns, fiscal limitations, particularistic interests, and official state priorities. Even high-priority agencies may suffer in this calculus, and community colleges were not high-priority institutions in Massachusetts before 1970.

CHAPTER 6

1. Interview with Bernard Rotundo.
2. Interview with Anthony Cotoia.
3. Interview with Henry Hammerling.

4. Interview with Anthony Cotoia.

5. Interview with William Rowe.

6. Shively himself could not recall much disharmony on campus. ''The faculty,'' he insisted, ''were very eager to assist with the career programs'' (interview with Harold Shively, October 5, 1984).

7. Interview with Oscar Olsen.

8. Ibid.

9. Shively was forced to spend more time than he would have liked lobbying for the approval of the funds required to hire new faculty and purchase facilities and equipment: ''Each college had to honcho its own budget. . . . You had to have the ability to fight for the money. The Board's reluctance to go after it left the presidents on their own with the legislature'' (interview with Harold Shively, June 25, 1984).

10. Interview with Allan Saval.

11. Interview with Harold Shively, October 5, 1978.

12. Interview with Henry Hammerling.

13. Ibid.

14. Interview with William Dwyer, February 9, 1979.

15. Interview with Thomas O'Connell.

16. Interview with Oscar Olsen.

17. Interview with John Musselman.

18. Interview with Allan Saval.

19. Interview with Gordon Pyle, July 10, 1978.

20. Interview with Anthony Cotoia.

21. Interview with Francis P. Roman.

22. Interview with Patricia Chisholm.

23. Interview with Bob Ross.

24. Interview with Patricia Chisholm.

25. Interview with Thomas O'Connell.

26. Interview with Jeff Doscher.

27. Interview with Don Rininger.

28. Ibid.

29. Ibid.

30. Interview with Barbara Landry.

31. Ibid.

32. Interview with Francis P. Roman.

33. Interview with Bob Ross.

34. Interview with Francis P. Roman.

35. Interview with Harold Shively, October 5, 1978.

36. Ibid.

37. Interview with Patricia Chisholm.

38. Interview with Thomas O'Connell.

39. Ibid.

40. Ibid.

41. Interview with Francis P. Roman.

42. Interview with John Musselman.

43. Interview with James Hall.

44. Interview with John Costello, October 17, 1978.

45. In some communities, the Chamber of Commerce played a role analogous to that of the advisory committees. In Beverly, for example, the Chamber of Commerce conducted

a communitywide survey to determine developing employment fields and helped to bring together industrial people to discuss their needs with the North Shore Community College's president.

46. Interview with James Hall.

47. Interview with Richard Murphy.

48. This particular exchange worked out poorly for Holyoke. One year after the machines were purchased, Digital imposed a hiring freeze and for several years did not hire a single student trained at Holyoke. (Interview with John Costello, March 15, 1983).

49. On some of the campuses, the co-op programs were less successful than job placement services. At Bristol, for example, only about 10 percent of the co-op students received permanent jobs through their participation in the program, and CETA-sponsored programs hardly ever led to jobs. (Interview with Jack Hudnall.)

50. Interview with Paul Buckley.

51. The work of John Meyer and Brian Rowan (1977, p. 1978) suggests that the colleges' relative indifference to placement might derive less from potential embarrassment or legal complications than from the colleges' proper performance of its most central activities, the ritual classification of people into categories that have an institutionalized meaning. For Meyer and Rowan, the creation of certified vocational graduates would presumably be at the heart of the community colleges' mission. In a highly institutionalized system, they argue, the credential itself implies that work will be available. However, this analysis may not fit the particular case of the community college very well, because the system's ritual categories were only weakly institutionalized.

52. Interview with Kenneth Haskins.

53. Interview with Gordon Pyle, July 10, 1978.

54. Interview with Bob Krim.

55. Interview with Gail Cody.

56. Interview with Kenneth Haskins.

57. For one of many examples of the resistance of black students to tracking in higher education, see Karabel's analysis (1983) of the conflict over open admissions at the City University of New York.

58. Interview with James Hall.

59. Ibid.

60. Interview with Robert Casik.

61. The teachers' private doubts about their own competence may have been another important reinforcing influence. Many teachers were, in a sense, downwardly mobile; most had at one time hoped to pursue academic careers in higher level institutions. All but a few were effectively able to rationalize their failure to achieve this goal, but, for many, private doubts probably remained. Howard London (1978) had argued that these doubts tended to heighten the sensitivity of many teachers to the academic deficiencies of their students. He argues that teachers were tempted to displace their own sense of failure onto their students, leading to less acceptance and appreciation than would otherwise have been possible. This argument strikes us as plausible, albeit a difficult one to prove. Certainly, the fact that many community college teachers were themselves "cooled out" of their primary occupational goals adds an element of pathos to the often tense relationship between liberal arts teachers and community college students.

62. Interview with a B.M., student, Massasoit Community College, May 8, 1984.

63. Interview with S. P., student, Massasoit Community College, May 8, 1984.

64. Interview with T. L., student, Massasoit Community College, May 8, 1984.

65. Interview with J. H., student, Bunker Hill Community College, April 26, 1984.

66. Interview with D. G., student, Massasoit Community College, May 8, 1984.

CHAPTER 7

1. Data on transfers to the University of Massachusetts were kindly provided by Kathy L. Ryan, director of transfer affairs.

2. For a full flow analysis of transfers in Massachusetts, see Beales (1974, p. 17). Nearly 300 students transferred to other public four-year schools like Lowell Tech (later the University of Lowell) and Southeastern Massachusetts University.

3. The total transfer rate is known only for 1973. The 1964 rate is an estimate based on the assumption of a constant ratio of total transfers to the University of Massachusetts at Amherst, and the margin of error is therefore considerable. Fortunately, however, trend data are available on the number of transfers to the University of Massachusetts at Amherst, far and away the first choice of Massachusetts community college students (Beales 1974, pp. 14–15).

4. Interview with Richard Offenberger.

5. Ibid.

6. Interview with Frederick B. Viaux.

7. Interview with Richard Offenberger.

8. The Board tended to administer the funds somewhat more impartially than the Department of Education. Although the Department of Education tended to reward the best entrepreneurs, the Board tended to use the funds to stimulate vocational program development at colleges that were lagging behind in vocationalization. By the early 1970s, the Board had no reason to use money to reward those moving in the direction it favored. All the campuses (with the partial exception of Roxbury) were committed to the goals the Board espoused, and the funds were therefore used most often in a compensatory fashion. Thus, in the mid-1970s, Cape Cod, Massasoit, Mass Bay and Northern Essex all began to receive annual awards of $100,000 or more in vocational education funds, as did the two new campuses, Bunker Hill and Roxbury. Previously, Bristol, North Shore, and Springfield, all highly vocationalized campuses, had tended to receive very disproportionate shares of these funds. They continued to receive large grants, but by the mid-1970s they ceased to be favored above other campuses (Massachusetts Board of Regional Community Colleges, "Summary," 1969–1977).

9. The backlash problems of the period may have further contributed to the mood of increased skepticism about higher education budgets. The colleges were seen by many working people as havens for such unpopular groups as anti-war protestors, student radicals, black militants, and counterculturalists. Many politicians found it politically profitable to attack higher education as a culturally alien force.

10. Indeed, during the Dukakis years, the budgetary process grew ever more unpredictable, as weak appointments and frequent turnover allowed for the reemergence of campus-by-campus budget negotiations. Under the newly decentralized system, colleges with politically adept presidents and those with powerful legislative representatives fared comparatively well, whereas those with neither fared less well (Coles 1977, Lustberg 1979, interview with Daniel Asquino). Interestingly, legislators were, if anything, less interested during this period in the colleges' arguments about their contributions to the state economy. Legislative thinking focused instead on how to keep the institutions functioning without undue disruption. More abstract discussions of purpose were treated as irrelevant to the much more fundamental task at hand. Budget expert Daniel Asquino found this to be consistent with the general trend: "In surplus years, the legislature is more creative. . . . more receptive to arguments about rationality. In bad years, when there's pressure for a tax increase, no matter how persuasive or logical your arguments are, they're going to fall on deaf ears" (interview with Daniel Asquino).

11. Interview with John Weston.

12. Dwyer was perhaps counting continuing education enrollments in this calculation. In fact, the systemwide average for "career" enrollments in the day division, including both sophomores and freshmen, was just over 56 percent in 1976 (Massachusetts Board of Regional Community Colleges, "Enrollment Statistics," 1976).

13. Interview with Jules Pagano.

14. Interview with Charles Hamilton.

15. Data provided by Kathy L. Ryan, director of transfer affairs at the University of Massachusetts, Amherst.

16. Though still a small sector in terms of total employment, high-tech industry was clearly the fastest growing manufacturing sector in the late 1970s and early 1980s. By 1981, high-tech firms accounted for over 40 cents of every dollar of capital spending by manufacturing companies in New England (Useem 1982).

17. The "Massachusetts definition" of high-technology industry used Standard Industrial Classification (SIC) codes and broadly covers the manufacture of drugs; ordnance and accessories; computing and accounting machines; electric and electronic machinery, equipment and supplies; guided missiles and space vehicles; measuring, analyzing and controlling instruments; and photographic equipment and supplies (Commonwealth of Massachusetts, Division of Employment Security, 1979).

18. The reorganization found many supporters as a cost-cutting measure. Indeed, the new Board was budgeted at a rate equal to that of one of the four previous boards, and the number of functions it performed was also proportionately decreased. For years after reorganization, basic statistics on enrollment patterns were uncollected, and no studies were commissioned on planning or evaluation. The Board of Regents was a shoestring operation. Yet it was a shoestring operation with a paradoxically high level of clout because of its centralized control. The new legislation also established campus-level boards of trustees for each of the institutions. These boards were responsible for most immediate operational issues. For a further discussion of the reorganization, see McCartan (1983b) and Stafford and Lustberg (1978, pp. 35–50).

19. "Hard science" was another priority field, but one typically reserved for the four-year colleges.

20. Gifts, too, played a role, although perhaps a minor one, in furthering the Regents' objectives. These gifts—such as An Wang's donation of new computer equipment to each of the campuses—most likely added an element of gratitude to the natural responsiveness of administrators to higher level authorities.

21. Interview with James Carifio.

22. Interview with George Denhard.

23. Ibid.

24. For a discussion of European efforts to foster cooperation between government and business so as to facilitate capital accumulation, see Phillipe Schmitter's work on "corporatism" (1974, 1977).

25. Interview with Daniel Asquino.

26. By the mid-1980s, more than one observer suggested that entrepreneurial energy had shifted from the community colleges to the state colleges, but this observation is not clearly demonstrated by development patterns. The community colleges continued to be unmatched in their access to training markets through continuing education. In these areas, which were self-supporting and outside the control of rationalizing state officials, low prices and unabashed opportunism kept the community colleges preeminent. Although the state colleges offered continuing education courses, their programs were small, and few saw them as ever likely to capture the community colleges' popularity.

27. Interview with Daniel Asquino.

28. Some observers argue, however, that the number of positions available in the high-tech segments of the labor force will be far fewer than is generally believed. According to them, while the *rate* of growth will be highest in high-tech occupations, the occupations with the highest *absolute* levels of growth will be in relatively low-skilled service sectors of the economy (see Levin and Rumberger 1983, Grubb, 1984).

29. Interview with James Yess.

30. Interview with John Weston.

CHAPTER 8

1. This link may be direct, as in the case of leading graduate and professional schools, or it may be indirect, as in the case of preparatory secondary schools that provide pathways to institutions directly tied to elite labor markets. For an interesting historical analysis of the prestige hierarchy among preparatory schools and its relationship to the larger class structure, see Levine (1980).

2. Another factor that played a role in the defeat of efforts to shift lower-division education to the junior college was the adverse impact that this was thought likely to have on the nation's major college athletic teams (Zwerling 1976, p. 26). Rudolph (1962, pp. 373–393) and Riesman and Denney (1951) offer colorful discussions of the role of football in American collegiate life in the early twentieth century—a time when the legendary Alonzo Stagg coached the highly ranked University of Chicago football team, and a number of Ivy League teams were major national powers.

3. The vision of the junior college as a kind of "safety valve" for the university was well expressed by University of California President Robert Gordon Sproul who, in a major 1937 address entitled "Before and After the Junior College," stated that "university administrators the country over complain of the hordes who invade their courses, and urge that something be done, and done soon." The expansion of junior colleges was crucial, in Sproul's view, to the resolution of this problem. But care must be taken, he noted, to enroll the great majority of junior college students in appropriate terminal programs, for "85 percent of their students are not of college caliber and certainly should not go on to a university." The remaining 15 percent, Sproul suggested, should be discovered "early enough to prevent their being trampled in the mass," and efforts should be made "to encourage them to prepare themselves for higher training" (Sproul 1938, p. 15).

4. So, too, does the consumer choice model fail to explain one of the major structural changes in American higher education after World War II—the radical increase in the proportion of students attending two-year rather than four-year colleges. Throughout the postwar era there has, to be sure, been strong popular demand for low-cost, geographically accessible, open-access colleges. But there is no convincing evidence that the public was demanding the expansion of two-year as opposed to four-year colleges; on the contrary, there were many controversies at the community level over the failure to convince state authorities of the need to build bachelor's degree–granting institutions.

The appeal of junior colleges to state legislatures and planning agencies—especially their relatively low cost per student and their promise to provide practical training for occupations below the professional and upper-management levels—is apparent. But it would be misleading to see the drastic shift upward in the decades after World War II in the ratio of students starting college at two-year rather than four-year institutions as a response to consumer choice. Instead, this shift was a consequence of a series of decisions made by state authorities as numerous "master plans" consciously attempted, especially after the late 1950s, to divert the bulk of the tidal wave of baby-boom students away from four-year colleges. What we have here is neither a structural necessity nor a response to the wishes of educational "consumers," but rather a *policy choice*. Where such a choice was not made—as, for example, in Indiana or Utah—the proportion of students in two-year institutions remained low.

5. In contrast to major national corporations, local businesses showed somewhat more interest in junior colleges, especially in institutions located in their own communities. But even local businesses were courted by the junior colleges and needed to be convinced to hire their graduates. In Massachusetts, it was not until the late 1970s that local businesses had anything resembling a coherent vision of what community colleges should be doing, much less a plan for putting this vision into practice.

6. As the historian Joseph Kett (1982, pp. 79–109) points out in his penetrating analysis of the rise of vocational education in American high schools during the first decades of the twentieth century, there is no reason whatsoever to believe that the assumption of "rational" choice in vocational decision making—if by "rational" we mean a decision to maximize economic gain over the long run—can withstand empirical scrutiny. Rejecting the notion the "workers shopping for jobs behaved like scientists," Kett (1982, p. 101) cites the classic study by Reynolds and Shister (1949) showing that security-conscious workers, far from trying to locate the jobs that promised the greatest opportunities for promotion, instead were inclined to choose the first available job. The problem with rational choice models which see individuals as trying to gain the greatest net advantage, he argues, is that they ignore the role of structurally rooted cultural conditioning or, in Bourdieu's term, *habitus* (1984).

Decision makers, too, often act in ways not consistent with rational choice models. A key problem in focusing on objective causes of the rise of vocational education, Kett suggests, is the "tendency to neglect subjective values and cultural norms." He continues:

> As anyone knows, *policy decisions have often been based on misperceptions of reality.* Those who seek to explain the vocationalization of education are actually trying to explain a vast range of decisions—to prolong education, to build more secondary schools, to build more vocational schools. Why should we assume that all or even most of these decisions are based on an accurate reading of objective conditions and why, as a corollary, should we then search only for those objective conditions? (Kett 1982, pp. 105–106, emphasis ours).

7. For a more detailed discussion of our particular version of "institutional analysis" and of its relationship to recent developments in the sociology of organizations, see Brint and Karabel (forthcoming).

8. The *locus classicus* of the argument that organizations can take on interests that are distinct from—and sometimes in conflict with—the goals that they are ostensibly designed to serve is Robert Michel's *Political Parties* (1962).

9. In emphasizing that organizations, including state organizations, have their own institutional interests and that these interests do not simply reflect the balance of power among external forces, we are drawing on a theoretical tradition associated with the work of Max Weber on the state and bureaucracy. Interestingly, recent Marxist scholarship on the role of the state in capitalist societies has tended to emphasize its "relative autonomy" from the capitalist class (see Carnoy 1984) and hence has shown a surprising degree of convergence with traditional Weberian themes. For a recent expression of this tendency to draw on both Weber and Marx in analyzing the roots of state policy, see Evans et al. (1985) and Alford and Friedland (1985).

10. Two models of the determinants of state policy with some affinities to the institu-

tional approach—the "managerial perspective" described by Alford and Friedland (1985) and the "organizational" perspective discussed by Tyack (1976)—also focus attention on the autonomous role played by professionals and managers in shaping political outcomes. Such a focus need not, of course, be accompanied by an uncritical endorsement of "new-class" theory; Brint (1984), for example, presents evidence suggesting that a "new-class" framework does not adequately explain the relatively liberal political attitudes of American professionals.

11. In using the term *organizational interest,* we do not wish to suggest that there is a single best path for pursuing such goals as organizational survival and prosperity; on the contrary, organizational interests are often worked out through a long historical process of conflict and experimentation. Moreover, what is in the interest of the managers and administrators who tend to define organizational interests may not coincide with the interests of employees or with those of consumers or clients; thus, the growth of community college vocational programs may have done more for the administrators of two-year institutions than for the students who attended them. Although recognizing that some policies do benefit an entire organizational field (e.g., increased federal spending on defense is presumably good for the military as well as for the contractors associated with it), we must be attentive to those instances in which organizational interests are little more than the particularistic interests of managers that have been generalized to the whole.

12. The growth of large organizations that brought the new middle class to prominence and that set the stage for the emergence of the Progressive movement is discussed in Wiebe (1967). With respect to the relationship between Progressivism and education, see the wide-ranging discussion by Cohen and Lazerson (1972). The powerful impact of Progressivism on the ideology of the early leaders of the junior college movement is documented in Goodwin (1971).

13. The metaphor of the college administrator as an entrepreneur is not, we should note, our own creation; to take but one example, it informs the analysis offered in Jencks and Riesman's *The Academic Revolution* (1968). The underlying idea—that the university could be viewed as a "business concern" subject to the laws of "competitive enterprise"—was developed at length in Thorstein Veblen's brilliant and bitter indictment of American universities, *The Higher Learning in America* (1918). It was in this work that Veblen, in a memorable phrase, referred to the chief executives of colleges and universities as "captains of erudition."

14. Over the years, state and local governments have provided between two-thirds and three-fourths of the revenues of public two-year colleges, with states replacing localities as the largest single source of support during the late 1960s (O'Neill 1973).

15. Especially in the context of the "overproduction" of college graduates during the politically tense years of the early 1970s, the self-presentation of the community college as a down-to-earth alternative to ethereal—if not outright subversive—university liberal arts programs was a valuable symbolic resource in dealing with fiscally strained state legislatures.

16. Efforts to turn the two-year college into an exclusively terminal vocational institution failed, we believe, for much the same reason that attempts to establish separate vocational high schools in the early decades of this century generally foundered: separate vocational institutions were unpopular with a public that viewed sharp educational segmentation as undemocratic and as a threat to the mobility prospects of its children. Communities thus adopted a "comprehensive" model of both the high school and the community college which embodied a compromise between the demands of the masses for opportunity and pressures from the economic system for selection and curricular differentiation. For an

analysis of the sources of the triumph of the "comprehensive" high school over models of secondary education that would have created separate academic and vocational institutions, see Nasaw (1979, pp. 114–156).

17. Another factor that should not be overlooked in what made community colleges palatable to state legislators is the inertial tendency in the state budgetary process (Wildavsky 1974). Once community colleges became an accepted step in what Riesman (1956) has called the "academic procession," close scrutiny of their activities was rare. The key for community colleges was to create an accepted meaning and place for themselves in a chain of institutions with specified relations to another; once this task was accomplished, their value became taken for granted.

18. Even more insulated from popular control than state coordinating bodies—and arguably even more influential in shaping higher education policy—have been the nation's major private foundations. In the United States, where the educational system is controlled by states and localities, the great foundations have performed many of the functions carried out in other countries by national ministries of education. In fact, foundations such as Rockefeller, Ford, and especially Carnegie have historically played a central role in defining the boundaries of legitimate debate about alternative models of educational organization and in developing coherent plans for rationalizing the relationship between the system of higher education and the labor market. In addition, the foundations have funded some of the major commissions—among them, the state of California's Commission of Seven and the AAJC's Commission on Junior College Terminal Education—that have given shape to higher education's system of tracking and impetus to the junior college movement's vocationalization project. Private foundations have, in short, been major actors in the shaping of the nation's colleges and universities, and no analysis of the institutional dynamics of American higher education can afford to ignore them.

19. In recent years, a number of neo-Marxist works on the role of the state in democratic capitalist societies have argued that there is a fundamental division in the state's economic function of encouraging the accumulation of private capital and its more political function of legitimating the social order (O'Connor 1973, Offe 1974, Habermas 1975, Wolfe 1977, Carnoy 1984). As applied to education, the implication of these theories is that the schools are often subject to two contadictory logics: the political logic of democracy encouraging more high-status education and the economic logic of capitalism encouraging job-relevant education. According to Bowles and Gintis (1976, p. 237) the salience of the two logics varies, depending on economic conditions. When state budgets are ample and the demand by employers for the products of the school system is high, educators may exercise a relatively free hand in developing new programs and approaches to instruction. Students are also freer to choose as they desire. But a budget squeeze and a threat of unemployment "serve to weed out both the opportunity and the student demand for educational experiences that do not contribute directly to employability."

The theme of contradictory functions has been applied to the educational field by Carnoy and Levin (1985), as well as by Bowles and Gintis (1976). Other recent works on education within the Marxist tradition that see the state as a contested arena rather than a simple "instrument" of the dominant class include Centre for Contemporary Cultural Studies (1981), Barbagli (1982), Connell et al. (1982), Apple (1982), and Katznelson and Weir (1985).

20. Despite the powerful influence of large corporations on American colleges and universities, it is not our view that "big business" *controls* American higher education. We are thus in disagreement with that long tradition of social scientific and journalistic commentary on American universities that portrays them as directly controlled by corporate capital. Veblen's *The Higher Learning in America* (1918) provided the first major work to

lay out this viewpoint (see note 13 above), and it remains unsurpassed as a literary document. But a number of other such analyses, some of them sober academic treatments and others more in the muckraking style, have appeared since; among the more important are Sinclair (1922), Beck (1947), Ridgeway (1968), and Smith (1974).

21. Our argument that power may exist in the absence of overt conflict and may be exercised by institutions as well as individuals and groups is indebted to the lucid discussion by Lukes (1974), and in particular, to his "three-dimensional" view of power. Lukes argues that "groups and institutions succeed in excluding potential issues from the political process . . . in ways that are neither consciously chosen nor the intended result of particular individuals' choices." The three-dimensional view of power, Lukes suggests, focuses on "the many ways in which *potential* issues are kept out of politics, whether through the operation of social forces and institutional practices or through individuals' decisions" (1974, pp. 21, 24). For an interesting application of Lukes's three-dimensional view of power, see Gaventa's (1980) study of quiescence and rebellion in an Appalachian valley community.

22. The dilemmas posed to higher-education administrators by the structural power of business may be likened to those faced by *state managers*. In an influential essay on the theory of the state, Block (1977) defines state managers as the leading figures in the executive and legislative branches, including top civil servants as well as appointed and elected politicians. State managers, according to Block, characteristically pursue the distinct organizational interests of the state, but in ways that are consistent with the expansion of their own power. But because business controls the process of capital accumulation, state managers are constrained. They are reluctant, for example, to pursue policies that might improve the position of subordinate social groups while simultaneously increasing the resources under their own control, if to do so threatens to undermine "business confidence." For in a predominantly capitalist economy, the state is dependent on private investment to keep the economy functioning and, in so doing, to provide it with indispensable fiscal resources. Even in the absence of direct political mobilization, the very possibility of an "investment strike" by private capital imposes a powerful constraint on the activities of state managers.

23. Our own formulation closely parallels Lindblom's (1977, p. 175) when he writes:

> To understand the peculiar character of politics in market-oriented systems requires . . . no conspiracy theory of politics, no theory of common origins uniting government and business officials, no crude allegation of a power elite established by clandestine forces. Business simply needs inducements, hence a privileged position in government and politics, if it is to do its job.

24. In emphasizing the structural power of business, we do not wish to suggest that business is the only institution that exerts structural power over the community college. For the university itself, by virtue of its domination of the most privileged training markets, constrains the activities of the two-year college and relegates it to a subordinate niche in the ecology of higher education, even in the absence of direct intervention. Because of this structural relationship, the community college may therefore be viewed as subject to "dual structural subordination"—a pattern deriving from its subordinate relationship to both business and the university.

25. Perhaps the boldest attempt to identify the place of the market in larger patterns of educational change is contained in Bowles and Gintis' *Schooling in Capitalist America,* which views the normal workings of the labor market as integral to processes that involve a "more or less automatic reorientation of educational perspectives in the face of a changing economic reality" (Bowles and Gintis, 1976, p. 236). In a more recent contribution, they have argued that "the requirements for economic success expressed in the labor mar-

ket . . . structurally delimit the forms of change open to the educational system, whatever the desires of educational reformers" (Bowles and Gintis 1981, p. 232). This process of "structural delimitation," they claim, sets boundaries on the range of possible educational outcomes and puts pressure on the educational system to bring itself into at least some degree of "correspondence" with the economy.

26. In state socialist societies as well, the economic system sets broad boundaries on the range of possible educational policies. To the extent that these societies are themselves stratified and stress manpower planning, educational policies in them often reflect attempts, sometimes heavy-handed, to establish correspondence between schooling and work through the expansion of vocational training and strict control over the number of university graduates. But within the constraints of a planned economy, politics often plays a key role in the determination of the specific form that the educational system will take. For the Soviet case, see Fitzpatrick, (1970, 1979), Lapidus (1976, 1978), Bailes (1978); for China, see Pepper (1980), Shirk (1982), and Unger (1982).

27. The body of scholarship to which we are referring was developed in part in reaction against an earlier version of "revisionist" scholarship that tended to portray educational policy as an imposition by elites on a powerless working class. The more recent revisionist works, however, emphasize not imposition, but struggle as a key factor in the determination of educational outcomes. Some of these works (see, e.g., Katznelson and Weir 1985) stress that divisions over educational policy in American history have often been along racial, ethnic, and religious rather than class lines.

A widely publicized, but in our view intemperate and distorted, critique of the earlier body of "revisionist" scholarship is contained in Ravitch (1978). A response to Ravitch by some major revisionist scholars, including Katz, Feinberg, and Violas is contained in Feinberg et al. (1980).

28. Insofar at there has been overt conflict over the social function of the community college, it has had, as we noted in both our national and Massachusetts studies, much more of a racial than a class character. Although segments of the white working class have at times engaged in a kind of passive resistance (e.g., their refusal to enroll in vocational programs and their participation in the kind of cultural opposition documented by London [1978]), the limited active political resistance to the tracking function of community colleges that has occurred has been carried out almost exclusively by blacks. The fact that the struggle over junior colleges has had more of a racial than a class character may reflect the greater political salience of racial cleavages in the United States in recent years, as well as the historic American pattern in which racial consciousness has often been stronger than class consciousness.

29. Resistance to the initiatives of elites, it must be emphasized, may take a variety of forms; to have an impact, such resistance need not always be highly conscious or even visible. To be sure, sometimes resistance is both active and collective, as it was in the case of the fight of the Chicago labor movement in the early twentieth century against separate vocational schools (Counts 1928) and the struggle of blacks and Puerto Ricans in 1969 for open admissions at the City University of New York (Karabel 1983). But at other times, this resistance may be passive and basically individual, as it was in the case of those junior college students who, rather than being channeled into vocational programs, opted for academic training or left the junior college altogether.

30. The class character of the resistance of community college students to vocational education was emphasized in a 1972 work by one of the authors (Karabel 1972). What was missing from this analysis, however, was an adequate understanding of the autonomous role of organizational interests in shaping institutional policy. Consequently, the 1972 article, although correctly identifying the pressure to vocationalize that powerful external

forces were placing on the community college by the early 1970s, did not take fully into account the extent to which the community college was trying to vocationalize itself. Moreover, although the assertion that "there was little popular clamor for community college vocational programs" was accurate, as was the argument that various institutional elites favored vocationalization, the article somewhat inflated the active role of major corporations in pushing for expanded vocational training and underestimated the structural power of business. For later analyses of the sources of structural change in higher education that attempt to take into account both class and organizational factors, see Karabel (1983, 1984).

31. The idea that educational policy, although shaped by class and other group conflicts, is powerfully influenced by organizational and managerial factors has been a long-standing theme in the work of Tyack (1974, 1976). Tyack has further developed this theme in his important recent work with Hansot (Tyack and Hansot 1982; Tyack, Lowe, and Hansot 1984). Interestingly, a number of scholars working primarily within the Marxist tradition, while continuing to emphasize class conflict, have also come to insist on the importance of the role of professional educators and organizational interests in determining the character of educational change (Center for Contemporary Cultural Studies 1981, Barbagli 1982, Katznelson and Weir 1985). Recent Marxist work on education shows many points of convergence with traditional Weberian themes about the autonomous role of state bureaucracies and the political centrality of the administrators and managers who run them.

32. The starting point for most discussions of American "exceptionalism" is the 1906 work by the German sociologist, Werner Sombart, *Why Is There No Socialism in the United States?* Sombart's question has been a lifelong concern of Seymour Martin Lipset (1950, 1963, 1977, 1983) and has also been examined in recent years by Katznelson (1978, 1981), Karabel (1979), Davis (1986), Howe (1985), and Mink (1986).

33. The shift toward comprehensive secondary education that has taken place to varying degrees in a number of European countries during recent decades has reduced, though by no means eradicated, the differences between European and American secondary schools. Although all American high school graduates (roughly 75 percent of the age group) are eligible to attend "open-door" colleges, only about 29 percent of French young people and fewer than 20 percent of their British counterparts are eligible for entry into higher education (see Rhoades 1987, p. 5). For a useful overview of the dilemmas facing secondary education systems in western Europe as they attempt to move to less segmented structures, see Levin (1978).

34. In 1934, for example, the number of students per 10,000 inhabitants was 83.3 in the United States, compared with 31.3 in the Soviet Union, 20.8 in France, 12.4 in Italy, 11.3 in Great Britain, and 10.9 in Japan (Ben-David 1966, p. 464). That this pattern has by and large persisted in the period since World War II is documented in Poignant (1969) and OECD (1983).

35. The number of students who actually transfer from a community college to an elite four-year college or university is, of course, very small. For an analysis of some community college students who did manage to transfer to private four-year institutions—some of them elite—in the state of Massachusetts, see Neumann and Riesman (1980).

36. Between 1968 and 1983, the number of students enrolled in American higher education on a part-time basis more than doubled from 2.3 million to 5.3 million (U.S. Department of Education 1986, p. 103). In 1983, these part-time students comprised more than 40 percent of all students in higher education nationwide and well over half of all community college enrollees.

37. The role of German secondary schools, universities, and state examinations in the formation of "status groups" (as opposed to "classes") was commented on by Max Weber, who wrote in 1917:

> Differences of "cultivation" are nowadays undoubtedly the most important specific source of *status group* differentiation. . . . Differences of cultivation are . . . one of the very strongest purely psychological barriers within society. Especially in Germany, where almost all privileged positions inside and outside the civil service are tied to qualifications involving not only specialized knowledge but also "general *cultivation*" . . . All our diplomas also—and principally—certify the possession of this important *status* qualification (from Ringer 1979, p. 16, italics and quotation marks from Weber).

38. In this regard, the provision of opportunities for success well into adulthood is an effective means of keeping hopes for individual mobility alive long after they would have been extinguished in a less open system. Former president of the Carnegie Corporation and Secretary of Health, Education, and Welfare John Gardner (1961, p. 137) put the matter bluntly: "our principle of multiple chances is not a sentimental compromise with efficient procedures but a measure well calculated to reduce the tensions to which our system is subject."

Expressing sentiments similar to those put forward by Gardner in 1961, the famous anthropologist W. Lloyd Warner, writing in a 1944 collaboration with Robert J. Havighurst and Martin B. Loeb, put the matter in *Who Shall Be Educated?* as follows:

> The educational system promotes social solidarity, or social cohesion, partly through its provision for social mobility. A society has social solidarity when its members believe that they have a substantial common ground of interest—that they gain more than they lose by sticking together and maintaining intact their political and social institutions. A certain amount of social mobility seems necessary to maintain social cohesion in our class-structured society. The possibility of rising in the social scale in order to secure a larger share of the privileges of the society makes people willing to "stick together" and "play the game" as long as they believe it gives them a fair deal (Warner et al., 1944:157).

"Educators," Warner and his colleagues suggested, "should try to adjust the educational system so that it produces a degree and kind of social mobility . . . which will keep the society healthy and alive" (Warner et al. 1944, p. 158).

Warner and his colleagues, it should be noted, also expressed a concern about "too much" social mobility, which in their view could produce a "chaotic society" (Warner et al. 1944, pp. 157–158). But the main thrust of Warner's work, in his well-known "Yankee City" series and elsewhere, was that American society was threatened by a decline in social mobility that could make it dangerously difficult to carry out the Durkheimian task of "social integration." Thus Warner warned the readers of his book, *American Life: Dream and Reality:*

> When those who compete for the prizes of life find that the rules of the games have been changed and no longer permit the rise of those who strive to advance, then the systems of free enterprise and equal opportunity are doubted, and the common people seek other ways to get what they want (Warner 1962, p. 143).

Emile Durkheim, whose concern with the sources of social solidarity exerted a great influence on Warner, echoes this theme in a little-cited passage in *The Division of Labor in Society* in which he states that "the division of labor produces solidarity . . . only if society is constituted in such a way that social inequalities exactly express natural inequalities" (Durkheim 1964, p. 377). As Durkheim makes clear in his extended discussion of the "forced division of labor," greater equality of opportunity is necessary if modern societies are to be able to maintain themselves without the use of force.

39. Although theories of legitimation usually focus on the conditions under which members of subordinate groups accept their lot in life, Weber emphasized the need of

dominant groups to justify their privileges to themselves. In *Economy and Society* (1978, p. 953), he writes:

> The fates of human beings are not equal. . . . Simple observation shows that in every such situation he who is more favored feels the never ceasing need to look upon his position as in some way "legitimate," upon his advantage as "deserved," and the other's disadvantage as being brought about by the latter's "fault." That the purely accidental causes of the difference may be ever so obvious makes no difference (quotation marks in original).

Consistent with Weber's perspective is Scully's (1982) finding, based on an extensive review of the empirical literature, that while all groups in American society believe that opportunities for individual advancement are abundant, the privileged are far more likely to see the distribution of opportunities as equal. Moreover, members of upper socioeconomic groups are considerably more likely to attribute personal wealth to such factors as "ability" and "hard work" than are the poor and blacks (Centers 1949, Huber and Form 1973).

40. Conant's hope was that the schools, by providing equality of opportunity and thereby avoiding the inheritance of position, would produce a "classless society." In characteristic American fashion, Conant made clear that the "classless society" he had in mind was compatible with substantial inequality; indeed, he explicitly described it in his 1940 article, "Education for a Classless Society," as characterized by a "differentiation of labors with a corresponding differentiation in types of education" (Conant 1940, p. 594). One of the fundamental objectives of such a society would be to avoid assiduously the "continuous perpetuation from generation to generation of even small differences." For such intergenerational transmission of privileges "soon produces class consciousness" (Conant 1940, p. 598).

41. One way in which American education has, however, promoted strategies of collective rather than individual advancement has been through the ease with which the university has opened itself to new and emerging "professions" which elsewhere remained outside the system of higher education. The openness of the American university to new fields of study has encouraged the widespread pattern whereby people in middle-class occupations were able to upgrade themselves into "professions" through collective action, often involving the enactment of state licensing laws. This is a very different pattern of collective action than the European one in which middle-class occupational groups often drew inspiration from the more solidaristic strategies of a politicized labor movement (Larson 1977, p. xviii). Indeed, it may not be an exaggeration to say that the willingness of the American university to provide training for middle-status occupations was a major factor in the historic pattern whereby these occupations adopted collective strategies for advancement more oriented to professionalization than unionization and, in so doing, reaffirmed the peculiarly "middle-class" character of American society (see also Bledstein 1976).

42. There is little evidence that the American educational system, despite its enormous size, is less an agent of transmission of inequality than the educational systems of other societies (Husen 1972, 1979; Passow et al. 1976). In examining this issue, Ringer (1979, pp. 22–25) makes a useful distinction betwen inclusiveness (the proportion of the population that is enrolled in school in various age groups) and progressiveness (the degree to which a system draws a large proportion of its advanced students from the lower-middle and lower classes). Interestingly, Ringer's own historical data, although confirming that American higher education has been unusually inclusive, suggest that it has not been more progressive (Ringer 1979, pp. 253–254).

Furthermore, an extensive body of research on mobility suggests that, contrary to popular belief, the amount of intergenerational movement up and down the system of stratification may not in fact have been historically higher in the United States than elsewhere. Although the issue is not settled, studies dating from Lipset and Bendix's *Social Mobility in Industrial Society* in 1959 to more recent investigations by Heath (1981) and Grusky and Hauser (1984) reveal broadly similar rates of exchange (or "circulation") mobility in industrial societies; the United States, however, may be characterized by slightly higher rates of structural mobility. The issue of why the expansion of the educational system in advanced countries has apparently not led to an increase in rates of social mobility has been addressed by Boudon (1974), who uses a mathematical model to show how even a successful reduction of inequality of educational opportunity will not necessarily lead to a reduction in inequality of social opportunity (i.e., inequality in access to positions in the class structure), and by Bourdieu and Passeron (1977, 1979), who argue that the school's role as a transmitter of class-based cultural capital necessarily makes it a major agent of cultural and social reproduction.

43. Documentation of a strong link between social background and academic performance has been a staple of twentieth-century social science, constituting a major theme in such classic works as Counts (1922), Warner et al. (1944), and Hollingshead (1949). Among the more important studies of the past quarter century, a period which has seen the introduction of vastly more sophisticated quantitative methods, are Coleman et al. (1966), Blau and Duncan (1967), Jencks et al. (1972), Bowles and Gintis (1976), Featherman and Hauser (1978), Jencks et al. (1979), and DiMaggio (1982c). The history of racial inequalities in American education is ably discussed in Weinberg (1977) and Ogbu (1978), and ethnic inequalities are examined in Cohen (1970) and Steinberg (1981).

44. Our arguments here may, we are well aware, trigger ideological reflexes. Some people will find them obviously true, whereas others will consider them dubious and perhaps even offensive. The relative merits of alternative social arrangements—between, for example, individual and collective orientations and between different degrees of equality— have to be debated on their own grounds. Certainly a case can be made for a meritocratic social order emphasizing equality of opportunity and rewards for individual achievement. Similarly, a forceful case can be made for an orientation to the collective welfare and to greater equality of condition. Although we have our own views on these matters, our argument here is essentially empirical: social orders vary, we believe, in their degree of emphasis on individual mobility versus equality and in their level of class consciousness; in explaining where they are located along such dimensions, the nature of their educational system is one of many important factors.

45. It should be noted as well that the United States has one of the most unequal income distributions in the advanced industrial world. Sawyer (1976), in a survey of data from the mid-1970s on ten major capitalist countries, found that only France had a more inegalitarian income distribution than the United States. According to Reich (1983), developments since that time have increased inequality in the United States while decreasing it in France, leaving the United States as the least egalitarian of a comparison group of nations that includes England, Japan, West Germany, Italy, Norway, Canada, Australia, and the Netherlands.

46. From a comparative perspective, evidence from a variety of sources suggests that societies with high degrees of working-class organization (as measured, e.g., by unionization and/or strength of electoral support for socialist, social democratic, and other left-of-center political parties) tend to have strong welfare states (Hibbs 1976, 1977; Cameron 1978, 1982; Korpi 1978, 1983; Esping-Andersen 1984). Within this framework, the relative lack of class consciousness and organization among American workers may be viewed as causally connected to the weakness of the American welfare state.

47. In emphasizing that there is a large-scale gap between aspirations and opportunities in the United States, we do not wish to imply that this is a phenomenon peculiar to capitalist societies; indeed, state socialist societies, which remain highly stratified despite their official ideology of "classlessness" (Ossowski 1963, Parkin 1979, Lane 1982), face their own problems in the management of ambition. For a discussion of some of the educational mechanisms used in the Soviet Union to "cool out" the mobility aspirations of its industrial workers, see Lane and O'Dell (1978).

48. In *The Open-Door College,* Burton Clark also emphasized the centrality of diversion to the mission of the community college, referring to "the specific operation of transforming transfer students into terminal students" as its "most important feature" (Clark 1960, p. 146). Elsewhere in the same volume he states that the "student who filters out of education while in the junior college appears to be very much what such a college is about" (Clark 1960, p. 84).

49. A detailed discussion of the *democratic mode* in American educational thought is contained in Shapiro (1978). According to him, a defining feature of this tradition is the conviction that education should be committed to providing a wider social awareness and consciousness; as such, it must be primarily nonvocational and direct itself to broad humanistic aims. Unlike classical or liberal arts education, with which it otherwise has much in common, the democratic mode in educational thought rejects the rigid separation of education and other human activities. In addition, this tradition in American educational thought looks on school reform as part of a larger process of social change, which would involve the extension of democratic ideals to the workplace. Shapiro historically locates the main social base of support for the democratic mode in the urban, industrial working class. Rubinson, in a synthetic analysis of American educational history, finds that characteristic working-class educational demands were for the expansion of publicly funded, unstratified schools offering a common curriculum that would provide "a liberal, not just a technical or vocational, education" (Rubinson 1986, p. 527). Among intellectuals, John Dewey was the major figure in the elaboration of the democratic mode, and his *Democracy and Education,* first published in 1916, remains perhaps the best single expression of it. The importance of popular education to American democratic thought through the 1950s is traced by Welter (1962). Among the more important contemporary efforts to revive the democratic mode in American educational thought are Bastian et al. (1986), Aronowitz and Giroux (1985), and Carnoy and Levin (1985).

50. Virtually all education is, as Dewey (1966, pp. 312–313) noted, in some sense vocational; thus, though "education which has to do chiefly with preparation . . . for teaching, and for literary callings, and for leadership, has been regarded as non-vocational and even as peculiarly cultural," it, too, is training for particular callings. Today, a community college program in cosmetology or dental hygiene is certainly no more vocational in character than a law or medical program in a prestigious professional school.

51. The low transfer rates of minority students from community colleges has recently been an object of concern to the Ford Foundation, which has funded programs at a number of urban, two-year institutions for the purpose of increasing the flow of minority students into four-year colleges and universities. For discussions of these programs, see the reports published by the Center for the Study of Community Colleges (1985) and Donovan et al. (1987).

52. The figures presented are from a poll taken in 1981; in a similar poll taken in 1977, the transfer function was favored over the vocational function by a margin of 45 to 22 percent. Another poll conducted in 1984 by the Group Attitudes Corporation revealed that 46 percent of the public strongly agreed with the statement that an A.A. degree from a community college is very helpful in transferring to a four-year college or university, com-

pared with only 32 percent who strongly agreed that an A.A. from a community college is very useful in obtaining a job that requires "some expertise or training" (AACJC, 1984, pp. 20–24).

53. In addition to the sources discussed below, our discussion of the dilemmas currently facing community colleges has been informed by the policy discussions contained in Vaughan (1980), Cohen and Brawer (1982), Vaughan and Associates (1983), Deegan, Tillery, and Associates (1985), and Zwerling (1986). Of particular help to us were the lucid analyses offered by Clark (1980, pp. 15–31), Cohen (1983, pp. 159–185), McCartan (1983b), and Cross (1985, pp. 34–50). For an interesting sociology-of-knowledge perspective on community college research, see Oromaner (1984).

54. Because institutions differ enormously in the kinds of students they enroll, their actual dropout rates would, according to Astin's proposal, then be compared to their expected rates, leaving open the possibility that institutions with high rates of attrition might nonetheless be shown to offer unusually effective educational programs.

Bibliography

Abbott, William. 1977. "College and Labor Union Cooperation." *Community and Junior College Journal* 47 (April): 48–51.

Alba, Richard D., and David E. Lavin. 1981. "Community Colleges and Tracking in Higher Education." *Sociology of Education* 54: 223–247.

Aldridge, Jack H. 1967. "A Comparative Study of Ideas and Theories, Concerning Junior Colleges, of Educational Leaders: 1900–1935 and 1945–1960." Ph.D. diss., Stanford University.

Alford, Robert R., and Roger Friedland. 1975. "Political Participation and Public Policy." *Annual Review of Sociology* 1: 429–479.

———. 1985. *Powers of Theory.* New York: Cambridge University Press.

Allison, A. A. 1928. "Junior Colleges." *Texas Outlook* 12: 10.

American Association of Community and Junior Colleges. 1976. "The New Boom: Annual Report of the American Association of Community and Junior Colleges." *Community and Junior College Journal* 46(5): 15–35.

———. 1977. "Types of Programs Offered in Two-Year Colleges." Washington, D.C.: AACJC.

———. 1978. "AACJC Annual Report 1977." *Community and Junior College Journal* 48 (February): 29–38.

———. 1979a. "Enrollment in Two-Year Colleges." Washington, D.C.: AACJC.

———. 1979b. "Policies and Proposals: 1978 Annual Report." *Community and Junior College Journal* 49 (February): 21–32.

———. 1979c. "Programs in Progress at AACJC." Washington, D.C.: AACJC.

———. 1981. *A Gallup Study of the Image of and Attitudes Toward America's Community and Junior Colleges.* Washington, D.C.: AACJC.

———. 1984. *American Attitudes Toward Community, Technical, and Junior Colleges.* A Report by Group Attitudes Corporation. Washington, D.C: AACJC.

American Association of Junior Colleges. 1965. "Junior College Student Personnel Programs—Appraisal and Development." Washington, D.C.: AAJC.

———. 1967. "AAJC Annual Report, 1967." Washington, D.C.: AAJC.

272   Bibliography

——. 1968. "AAJC Annual Report, 1968." Washington, D.C.: AAJC.

——. 1969. "AAJC Annual Report, 1969." Washington, D.C.: AAJC.

——. 1970. "Crisis in the Country: Statement by Black Junior College Leaders." Washington, D.C.: AAJC, May 26.

American College Testing Program. 1966–1981. *College Student Profiles: Norms for the ACT Assessment*. Iowa City, Ia.: Research and Development Division, American College Testing Program, Annual Report.

American Council on Education. 1966–1985. *The American Freshman: National Norms*. Washington, D.C.: American Council on Education, Annual Report.

——. 1982. *1981–1982 Fact Book for Academic Administrators*. Washington, D.C.: ACE.

"America's New Jobless: The Frustration of Idleness." 1975. *Time,* March 17, pp. 20–26.

Anderson, C. Arnold, et al. 1972. *Where Colleges Are and Who Attends*. New York: McGraw-Hill.

Anderson, Kristine L. 1974. "College Effects on Educational Outcomes: A Comparison of Two- and Four-Year College Entrants." Unpublished paper, University of North Carolina, Department of Sociology.

——. 1981. "Post-High School Experiences and College Attrition." *Sociology of Education* 54 (January): 1–15.

Apple, Michael W. 1982. *Education and Power*. Boston: Routledge & Kegan Paul.

Aptheker, Bettina. 1972. *The Academic Rebellion in the United States: A Marxist Appraisal*. Secaucus, N.J.: Citadel Press.

Aronowitz, Stanley. 1973. *False Promises*. New York: McGraw-Hill.

Aronowitz, Stanley, and Henry Giroux. 1985. *Education Under Siege*. South Hadley, Mass.: Bergin and Garvey.

Ashby, Eric. 1971. *Any Person, Any Study*. New York: McGraw-Hill.

Asquino, Daniel M. 1976. "Budgeting As a Possible Aid to Better Policy: The Community Colleges in Massachusetts." Ph. D. diss., University of Massachusetts.

Astin, Alexander W. 1972. *College Dropouts: A National Profile*. ACE Research Reports, vol. 7, no. 1. Washington, D.C.: American Council on Education.

——. 1977. *Four Critical Years: Effects of College on Beliefs, Attitudes and Knowledge*. San Francisco: Jossey-Bass.

——. 1982. *Minorities in American Higher Education*. San Francisco: Jossey-Bass.

——. 1983. "Strengthening Transfer Programs," pp. 122–138 in George B. Vaughan and Associates, *Issues for Community College Leaders in a New Era*. San Francisco: Jossey-Bass.

Bachrach, Peter, and Morton S. Baratz. 1962. "The Two Faces of Power." *American Political Science Review* 56: 947–952.

Bailes, Kendall E. 1978. *Technology and Society Under Lenin and Stalin*. Princeton, N.J.: Princeton University Press.

Baird, Leonard L. 1969. *Patterns of Educational Aspirations*. ACT Research Report no. 32. Iowa City, Ia.: American College Testing Program.

Barbagli, Marzio. 1982. *Educating for Unemployment*. New York: Columbia University Press.

Barlow, Andrew L. 1979. "Coordination and Control: The Rise of Harvard University, 1825–1910." Ph.D. diss., Harvard University.

Baron, Robert F. 1982. "The Change from Transfer to Career Education at Community Colleges in the 1970s." *Community/Junior College Research Quarterly* 7: 71–87.

————. 1984. "Why the Big Change in Student Program Selection at 2-Year Colleges?" *Educational Record* 65(1): 35–36.

Bastian, Ann, et al. 1986. *Choosing Equality.* Philadelphia: Temple University Press.

Bay State Skills Corporation. 1984. "Summer 1984—Special Institutes." Boston: BSSC.

Beales, Ernest W. 1974. *College Transfer Students in Massachusetts: A Study of 20,000 Transfer Applicants to 48 Massachusetts Colleges and Universities for Fall, 1973.* Boston: Massachusetts Board of Higher Education.

Beck, H. P. 1947. *Men Who Control Our Universities.* New York: Kings Crown Press.

Becker, Gary Stanley. 1983. *A Treatise on the Family.* Cambridge, Mass.: Harvard University Press.

Bell, Daniel. 1973. *The Coming of Post-Industrial Society.* New York: Basic Books.

Ben-David, Joseph. 1966. "The Growth of the Professions and the Class System," pp. 459–472 in Reinhard Bendix and Seymour Martin Lipset, eds., *Class, Status, and Power,* 2nd ed. New York: Free Press.

————. 1972. *Trends in American Higher Education.* Chicago: University of Chicago Press.

————. 1977. *Centers of Learning.* New York: McGraw-Hill.

Bender, Louis. 1973. "Middle Manpower Utilization Through Career Education." *Community and Junior College Journal* 43 (May): 16–17.

Berdahl, Robert O. 1970. *Statewide Coordination of Higher Education.* Washington, D.C.: American Council on Education.

Berkenkemp, Fred J. 1977. "More on the Federal Impact on Colleges and Universities." *Community and Junior College Journal* 48 (November): 7–9.

Bienstock, Herbert. 1981. *New and Emerging Occupations: Fact or Fancy.* Columbus, Ohio: National Center for Research in Vocational Education, Occasional Paper no. 77.

Bigelow, Karl W. 1951. "Report on Discussion Groups." *Junior College Journal* 21 (May): 494.

Binzen, Peter A. 1974. "Portland Community College," pp. 185–190 in Lawrence Hall and Associates, *New Colleges for New Students.* San Francisco: Jossey-Bass.

Bird, Caroline. 1975. *The Case Against College.* New York: McKay.

Birenbaum, William. 1971. "The More We Change the Worse We Get." *Social Policy 2* (May–June): 10–14.

Bishop, Curtis. 1950. "Inventory." *Junior College Journal* 20: 501–504.

Blackstone, Bruce. 1978. *Summary Statistics for Vocational Education Program Year 1978.* Washington, D.C.: U.S. Department of Health, Education and Welfare.

Blair, Larry, Michael Finn, and Wayne Stevenson. 1981. "The Returns to the Associate Degree for Technicians." *Journal of Human Resources* 16: 459–467.

Blau, Peter, and Otis Dudley Duncan. 1967. *The American Occupational Structure.* New York: Wiley.

Bledstein, Burton. 1976. *The Culture of Professionalism.* New York: Norton.

Block, Fred. 1977. "The Ruling Class Does Not Rule." *Socialist Revolution* 3 (May–June): 6–28.

————. 1980. "Beyond Relative Autonomy: State Managers As Historical Subjects," pp. 217–242 in Ralph Miliband and John Saville, eds., *The Socialist Register.* London: Merlin Press.

Block, N. J., and Gerald Dworkin. 1976. "IQ, Heritability and Inequality," pp. 410–540 in N. J. Block and G. Dworkin, eds., *The IQ Controversy.* New York: Pantheon.

Blocker, Clyde B. 1959. "Philanthropy and the Public Community College." *Junior College Journal* 30 (September): 6–7.

Blocker, Clyde B., Robert H. Plummer, and Richard C. Richardson, Jr. 1965. *The Two-Year College: A Social Synthesis.* Englewood Cliffs, N.J.: Prentice-Hall.

Blocker, Clyde B., and Richard C. Richardson. 1964. "Human Relations Are Important." *Junior College Journal* 34 (April): 19–22.

Bogue, Jesse P. 1950. *The Community College.* New York: McGraw-Hill.

———. 1953. "From the Executive Secretary's Desk." *Junior College Journal* 23 (January): 292.

———. 1957. "The Functions of Good Public Relations in Junior Colleges." *Junior College Journal* 28 (December): 223–228.

Boocock, Sarane S. 1972. *An Introduction to the Sociology of Learning.* Boston: Little-Brown.

Boren, F. J. 1928. "The Junior College: A Community Asset." *Teachers' Journal of Northern California* 3: 4.

Boudon, Raymond. 1974. *Education, Opportunity, and Social Inequality.* New York: Wiley.

Bourdieu, Pierre. 1971. "Intellectual Field and Creative Project," pp. 161–188 in Michael F. D. Young, ed., *Knowledge and Control: New Directions for the Sociology of Education.* London: Collier-Macmillan.

———. 1974. "Avenir de classe et causalité du probable." *Revue Française de Sociologie.* 15: 3–42.

———. 1975. "The Specificity of the Scientific Field and the Social Conditions of the Progress of Reason." *Social Science Information* 14: 19–47.

———. 1977. "Cultural Reproduction and Social Reproduction," pp. 487–511 in Jerome Karabel and A. H. Halsey, eds., *Power and Ideology in Education.* New York: Oxford University Press.

———. 1984. *Distinction.* Cambridge, Mass.: Harvard University Press.

Bourdieu, Pierre, and Jean-Claude Passeron. 1977. *Reproduction.* Beverly Hills, Calif.: Sage Publications.

Bourdieu, Pierre, and Jean-Claude Passeron. 1979. *The Inheritors: French Students and Their Relation to Culture.* Chicago: University of Chicago Press.

Bourdieu, Pierre, et al. 1973. "Les stratégies de reconversion: les classes sociales et le système d'enseignement." *Social Science Information* 12: 61–113.

Bowles, Samuel, and Herbert Gintis. 1976. *Schooling in Capitalist America.* New York: Basic Books.

———. 1981. "Education As a Site of Contradictions in the Reproduction of the Capital–Labor Relationship: Second Thoughts on the Correspondence Principle." *Economic and Industrial Democracy* 2: 223–242.

Brandy, Norman J. 1979. *Financial Statistics of Institutions of Higher Education, Fiscal Year 1979, State Data.* Washington, D.C.: U.S. Government Printing Office.

Bremer, Fred H., and Floyd S. Elkins. 1965. "Private Financial Support of Community Colleges." *Junior College Journal* 36 (September): 16–19.

Breneman, David W., and Susan C. Nelson. 1981. *Financing Community Colleges: An Economic Perspective.* Washington, D.C.: Brookings Institution.

Brick, Michael. 1964. *Forum and Focus for the Community College Movement.* New York: Bureau of Publications, Teachers College, Columbia University.

Brint, Steven. 1984. " 'New Class' and Cumulative Trend Explanations of the Liberal Political Attitudes of Professionals." *American Journal of Sociology* 90: 30–71.

Brint, Steven, and Jerome Karabel. Forthcoming. "Institutional Origins and Transformations: The Case of American Community Colleges," in Walter Powell and Paul DiMaggio, eds., *The New Institutionalism in Organizational Analysis.* Chicago: University of Chicago Press.

Brookover, Wilbur, et al. 1973. *Elementary School Social Environment and School Achievement*. East Lansing: College of Urban Development, Michigan State University.

Brown, Scott Campbell. 1979. "Educational Attainment of Workers—Some Trends." *Monthly Labor Review* 102: 54–59.

Brubacher, John, and Willis Rudy. 1976. *Higher Education in Transition*. New York: Harper & Row.

Brunner, Ken August. 1962. "The Training of Subprofessional Personnel in the United States." Paper presented at the International Conference on Middle Level Manpower, San Juan, P.R.

Bunker Hill Community College. 1977. "Cooperative Institutional Research Program— Summary of Data on Entering Freshmen, 1977." Washington, D.C.: American Council on Education.

Burawoy, Michael. 1979. *Manufacturing Consent: Changes in the Labor Process Under Monopoly Capitalism*. Chicago: University of Chicago Press.

Burk, J. E. 1939. "Cultural Curriculum at Ward-Belmont." *Junior College Journal* 9: 486–487.

Bushnell, David. 1973. *Organizing for Change: New Priorities of Community Colleges*. New York: McGraw-Hill.

Butts, R. Freeman. 1939. *The College Charts Its Course*. New York: McGraw-Hill.

California Committee on the Needs of California in Higher Education. 1957. "The Origin and Functions of the Liaison Committee of the State Board of Education and the Regents of the University of California." Berkeley and Sacramento: University of California and State Department of Education.

California Postsecondary Education Commission. 1979. *California Community College Students Who Transfer*. Sacramento: California Postsecondary Education Commission.

————. 1984. *Update of Community College Transfer Student Statistics*. Sacramento: California Postsecondary Education Commission.

Callahan, Raymond E. 1962. *Education and the Cult of Efficiency*. Chicago: University of Chicago Press.

Cameron, David R. 1978. "Expansion of the Public Economy: Comparative Analysis." *American Political Science Review* 72(4): 1243–1261.

————. 1982. "On the Limits of the Public Economy." *Annals of the American Academy of Political and Social Science* 459 (January): 46–62.

Campbell, Doak S. 1930. *A Critical Study of the Stated Purposes of the Junior College*. Contribution to Education, no. 70. Nashville: George Peabody College for Teachers.

————. 1932. "The Purposes of the Junior College." *National Education Association Journal* 21: 221–222.

————. 1933a. "From Within." *Junior College Journal* 4: 109–110.

————. 1933b. "Junior College Standards." *Junior College Journal* 3: 416–419.

————. 1936. "After Sixteen Years." *Junior College Journal* 7: 109–110.

Campbell, W. V., et al. 1952. *Current Operating Expenditures and Income of Higher Education in the United States: 1930, 1940, 1950*. New York: Columbia University Press.

Carleton, Frank Tracy. 1911. *Economic Influences upon Educational Progress in the U.S. 1820–1850*. Madison: University of Wisconsin Press.

Carnegie, Andrew. 1886. *Triumphant Democracy*. New York: Scribner.

————. 1889. "Wealth." *North American Review* 148: 653–664.

Carnegie Commission on Higher Education. 1970. *The Open-Door Colleges*. New York: McGraw-Hill.

———. 1973. *College Graduates and Jobs*. New York: McGraw-Hill.

Carnegie Council on Policy Studies in Higher Education. 1975. *The Federal Role in Post-secondary Education*. San Francisco: Jossey-Bass.

———. 1976. *The States and Higher Education*. San Francisco: Jossey-Bass.

———. 1980. *A Summary of Reports and Recommendations*. San Francisco: Jossey-Bass.

Carnegie Foundation for the Advancement of Teaching. 1932. *State Higher Education in California*. Sacramento: California State Printing Office.

Carnoy, Martin. 1984. *The State and Political Theory*. Princeton, N.J.: Princeton University Press.

Carnoy, Martin, and Henry Levin. 1985. *Schooling and Work in the Democratic State*. Stanford, Calif.: Stanford University Press.

Carson, Peter. 1974. "The Intellectual Taxicab Company." *Newsweek*, June 3, p. 15.

Cawelti, John G. 1965. *Apostles of the Self-Made Man*. Chicago: University of Chicago Press.

CBS Reports. 1972. "Higher Education: Who Needs It?" May 25.

Center for the Study of Community Colleges. 1978. "Science and Humanities Instruction in Two-Year Colleges." Unpublished report. Los Angeles: Center for the Study of Community Colleges.

———. 1985. *Transfer Education in American Community Colleges*. Los Angeles: Center for the Study of Community Colleges.

Centers, Richard. 1949. *The Psychology of Social Classes*. Princeton, N.J.: Princeton University Press.

Centre for Contemporary Cultural Studies. 1981. *Unpopular Education*. London: Hutchinson.

Chandler, Alfred D., Jr. 1977. *The Visible Hand*. Cambridge, Mass.: Harvard University Press.

Charles, R. F. 1978. *Survey Results for Participating Colleges: Classes and Programs for the Aged in California Community Colleges, 1978*. Cupertino: California Community College Continuing Education Association.

Chinoy, Eli, 1955. *Automobile Workers and the American Dream*. Garden City, N.Y.: Doubleday.

Clark, Burton. 1960. *The Open Door College: A Case Study*. New York: McGraw-Hill.

———. 1961. "The 'Cooling-Out' Function in Higher Education," pp. 513–521 in A. H. Halsey et al., eds., *Education, Economy, and Society*. New York: Free Press.

———. 1962. *Educating the Expert Society*. San Francisco: Chandler.

———. 1977. *Academic Power in Italy: Bureaucracy and Oligarchy in a National University System*. Chicago: University of Chicago Press.

———. 1980. "The 'Cooling-Out' Function Revisited." *New Directions for Community Colleges* 8(4): 15–32.

———. 1983. *The Higher Education System*. Berkeley and Los Angeles: University of California Press.

———. ed. 1984. *Perspectives in Higher Education*. Berkeley and Los Angeles: University of California Press.

———. ed. 1985. *The School and the University*. Berkeley and Los Angeles: University of California Press.

Cohen, Arthur M. 1971. "Stretching Pre-College Education." *Social Policy*, May–June 1971, pp. 5–9.

———. 1979. "Counting the Transfer Students." *Junior College Resource Review.* Los Angeles: ERIC Clearinghouse for Junior Colleges.

———. 1983. "Leading the Educational Program," pp. 159–185 in George B. Vaughan and Associates, *Issues for Community College Leaders in a New Era.* San Francisco: Jossey-Bass.

Cohen, Arthur M., et al. 1971. *A Constant Variable.* San Francisco: Jossey-Bass.

Cohen, Arthur M., and Florence Brawer. 1982. *The American Community College.* San Francisco: Jossey-Bass.

Cohen, Arthur M., and John Lombardi. 1979. "Can the Community College Survive Success?" *Change,* November–December, pp. 24–27.

Cohen, David K. 1970. "Immigrants and the Schools." *Review of Educational Research* 40 (February): 13–28.

Cohen, David K., and Marvin Lazerson. 1972. "Education and the Corporate Order." *Socialist Revolution* 2(March–April): 47–72.

Cohen, Michael D., and James C. March. 1974. *Leadership and Ambiguity.* New York: McGraw-Hill.

Cohen, Michael D., et al. 1972. "A Garbage Can Model of Organizational Choice." *Administrative Science Quarterly* 17(1): 1–25.

Cohen, Muriel. 1976. "William Dwyer Resigns." *Boston Globe,* August 18, p. 25.

Coleman, James S., et al. 1966. *Equality of Educational Opportunity.* Washington, D.C.: U.S. Government Printing Office.

Coleman, Richard, and Lee Rainwater, 1979. *Social Standing in America.* New York: Basic Books.

Coles, Ann. 1977. "The Dynamics of Non-Planning in the Massachusetts Community College System, 1958–1972." Unpublished paper, Graduate School of Education, Harvard University.

"College, Who Needs It?" 1972. *Time,* June 12, p. 37.

Collins, Randall. 1971. "Functional and Conflict Theories of Educational Stratification." *American Sociological Review* 36: 1002–1019.

———. 1975. *Conflict Sociology.* New York: Academic Press.

———. 1977. "Some Comparative Principles of Educational Stratification." *Harvard Educational Review* 47 (February): 1–27.

———. 1979. *The Credential Society.* New York: Academic Press.

———. 1980. "On the Microfoundations of Mascrosociology." *American Journal of Sociology* 85: 984–1014.

"Community Colleges Make Big Impact on Economy." 1978–1979. *Community and Junior College Journal* 49 (December–January): 51.

Commonwealth of Massachusetts. 1977. *Access to Action: A Guide for Employers in Employment and Training Resources in Massachusetts.* Boston: Commonwealth of Massachusetts.

Commonwealth of Massachusetts, Division of Employment Security. 1979. "High Technology Employment in Massachusetts and Selected States." Boston: Commonwealth of Massachusetts.

Commonwealth of Massachusetts, Office of the Governor. 1960–1979. *Governor's Budget Requests Series.* Boston: Commonwealth of Massachusetts.

———. 1979. *Executive Budget Recommendations.* Boston: Commonwealth of Massachusetts.

Compton, Wilson. 1956. "Responsibility and Opportunity in the Two-Year Colleges." *Junior College Journal* 27 (September): 3–9.

Conant, James Bryant. 1938. "The Future of Our Higher Education." *Harper's Magazine* 176 (May): 561–570.

———. 1940. "Education for a Classless Society." *Atlantic Monthly* 165 (May): 593–602.

———. 1948. *Education in a Divided World*. Cambridge, Mass.: Harvard University Press.

———. 1953. *Education and Liberty*. Cambridge, Mass.: Harvard University Press.

———. 1956. *Citadel of Learning*. New Haven, Conn.: Yale University Press.

———. 1959. *The Child, the Parent, and the State*. New York: McGraw-Hill.

———. 1961. *Slums and Suburbs*. New York: McGraw-Hill.

———. 1964. *Shaping Educational Policy*. New York: McGraw-Hill.

Condren, Clive P. 1960. "A Case Study of the Master Plan and the Legislature." Unpublished paper, University of California, Systemwide Administration.

Conger, George R. 1968. "Leonard V. Koos: His Contribution to American Education During Half a Century," Ph.D. diss., Graduate School of Education, Florida State University.

Cookson, Peter W., and Caroline H. Persell. 1985. *Preparing for Power*. New York: Basic Books.

Coons, Arthur G. 1968. *Crises in California Higher Education*. Los Angeles: Ward Ritchie.

Coordinating Council for Higher Education. 1969. *The Undergraduate Student and His Higher Education: Policies of California Colleges and Universities in the Next Decade*. Sacramento: Coordinating Council for Higher Education.

Connell, Robert W., et al. 1982. *Making the Difference*. Sydney: Allen & Unwin.

Council for Financial Aid to Education (C7AE). 1973. *Two Year Colleges—The Current Phenomenon in Higher Education*. New York: Council for Financial Aid to Education.

Counts, George, S. 1922. *The Selective Character of American Secondary Education*. Chicago: University of Chicago Press.

———. 1928. *School and Society in Chicago*. New York: Harcourt, Brace.

Cremin, Lawrence. 1961. *The Transformation of the School*. New York: Vintage.

Cross, K. Patricia. 1968. *The Junior College Student: A Research Description*. Princeton, N.J.: Educational Testing Service.

———. 1970. "The Role of the Junior College in Providing Postsecondary Education for All," in *Trends in Postsecondary Education*. Washington, D.C.: U.S. Government Printing Office.

———. 1971. *Beyond the Open Door*. San Francisco: Jossey-Bass.

———. 1974. "What Do You Know About the Goals of Community College?" *Community and Junior College Journal* 44 (April): 34–35.

———. 1985. "Determining Missions and Policies for the Fifth Generation," pp. 34–50 in William L. Deegan, Dale Tillery, and Associates, *Renewing the American Community College*. San Francisco: Jossey-Bass Publishers.

Cross, K. Patricia, and Anne-Marie McCartan. 1984. *Revitalizing the Economy Through Education*. Los Angeles: ASHE-ERIC Higher Education Research Report no. 1.

Darknell, Frank. 1975. "The Carnegie Council for Policy Studies in Higher Education." *The Insurgent Sociologist* 3: 106–114.

———. 1980. "The Carnegie Philanthropy and Private Corporate Influence on Higher Education", pp. 385–411 in Robert Arnove, ed., *Philanthropy and Cultural Imperialism: The Foundations at Home and Abroad*. Bloomington: Indiana University Press.

Darley, John G. 1959. "Factors Associated with College Careers in Minnesota." Unpublished paper. Berkeley, Calif.: Center for the Study of Higher Education.

Davis, Ben. 1980. "Business and Higher Education, 1945–1980." Unpublished paper. Cambridge, Mass.: Huron Institute.

Davis, James A. 1966. "The Campus As a Frog Pond: An Application of the Theory of Relative Deprivation to Career Decisions of College Men." *American Journal of Sociology* 72: 17–31.

Davis, Mike. 1986. *Prisoners of the American Dream: Politics and Economy and the History of the U.S. Working Class.* London: Verso Editions.

Dearman, Nancy B., and Plisko, Valena White. 1980. *The Condition of Education.* National Center for Education Statistics. Washington, D.C.: U.S. Government Printing Office.

Deegan, William L., and R. Drisko. 1985. "Contract Training: Progress and Policy Issues." *Community and Junior College Journal* 55: 14–17.

Deegan, William L., Dale Tillery, and Associates. 1985. *Renewing the American Community College.* San Francisco: Jossey-Bass.

———. 1951. "Comparative Scholastic Achievement of Native and Transfer Students." *Junior College Journal* 22 (October): 83–85.

Dewey, John. 1966. *Democracy and Education.* New York: Free Press. First published in 1916.

Deyo, Donald E. 1967. *Access to Quality Community College Opportunities: A Master Plan for Massachusetts Community Colleges Through 1975.* Boston: Massachusetts Board of Regional Community Colleges.

DiMaggio, Paul. 1982a. "Cultural Capital and School Success: The Impact of Status Culture Participation on the Grades of United States High School Students." *American Sociological Review* 47(2): 189–201.

———. 1982b. "Cultural Entrepreneurship in 19th Century Boston—The Classification and Framing of American Art, pt. 2." *Media, Culture, and Society* 4(4): 303–322.

———. 1982c. "Cultural Entrepreneurship in 19th Century Boston—The Creation of an Organizational Base for High Culture in America, pt. 1." *Media, Culture and Society* 4(1): 33–50.

DiMaggio, Paul, and Walter W. Powell. 1983. "The Iron Cage Revisted: Institutional Isomorphism and Collective Rationality in Organizational Fields." *American Sociological Review* 48: 147–160.

Dober and Associates. 1975. *Matrix for Planning.* Belmont, Mass.: Dober and Associates.

Donovan, Richard A., et al. 1987. *Transfer: Making It Work.* Washington, D.C.: American Association of Community and Junior Colleges.

Dore, Ronald. 1976. *The Diploma Disease.* Berkeley and Los Angeles: University of California Press.

Dougherty, Kevin. 1980. "The Politics of Federal Higher Education Policy Making, 1945–1980." Unpublished paper. Cambridge, Mass.: Huron Institute.

———. 1983. "The Politics of Community College Expansion: The Cases of Illinois and Washington State." Ph.D. diss., Harvard University.

———. 1987. "The Effects of Community Colleges: Aid or Hindrance to Socioeconomic Attainment?" *Sociology of Education* 60 (April): 86–103.

———. 1988a. "Education Policy Making and the Relative Autonomy of the State: The Case of Occupational Education in the Community College." *Sociological Forum* 3(Summer): 400–432.

———. 1988b. "The Politics of Community College Expansion: Beyond the Functionalist and Class Reproduction Explanations.'' *American Journal of Education* 96 (May): 351–393.

Dow, Ernest A. 1973. "A Minority View on Career Education.'' *Community and Junior College Journal* 43 (May): 13.

Dudley, Charles W. 1974. "AACJC Approach. AACJC's Panel on Association Vitality.'' *Community and Junior College Journal* 44(9):4.

Duffus, R. L. 1936. *Democracy Enters College*. New York: Scribner.

Dukakis, Michael. 1975. "Governor's Inaugural Address to the Legislature.'' Boston: Commonwealth of Massachusetts.

Durkheim, Emile. 1938. *L'évolution pédagogique en France*. Paris: Presses Universitaires de France.

———. 1956. *Education and Sociology*. Glencoe, Ill.: Free Press.

———. 1964. *The Division of Labor in Society*. Glencoe, Ill.: Free Press. First published in 1893.

Dwyer, William G. 1964. "What's Behind the Open Door of the Two-Year College?'' *Technical Education News*, July, pp. 1–2.

Eckland, Bruce K., and L. B. Henderson. 1981. *College Attainment Four Years After High School*. Washington, D.C.: National Center for Educational Statistics.

Educational Commission of the States. 1971. "Comprehensive Planning for Postsecondary Education,'' pp. 37–41 in *Higher Education in the States*. Denver: Educational Commission of the States.

Eells, Walter Crosby. 1925. *The Junior-College Movement*. Boston: Ginn.

———. 1931a. *The Junior College*. Boston: Houghton Mifflin.

———. 1931b. "The Junior College—What Manner of Child Shall This Be?'' *Junior College Journal* 1(February): 309–328.

———. 1932. "A Suggested Basis for a New Standard.'' *Junior College Journal* 3(1): 1–2.

———. 1933. "The Junior College: Its Character and Prospects.'' *Journal of the National Education Association* 22 (May): 157–158.

———. 1935. "The Junior College and the Youth Problem.'' *Kadelpian Review* 15 (November): 9–13.

———. 1940a. *American Junior Colleges*. Washington, D.C.: American Council on Education.

———. 1940b. "Junior College Terminal Education.'' *Junior College Journal* 10 (January): 244–250.

———. 1941a. *The Present Status of Junior College Terminal Education*. Washington, D.C.: American Association of Junior Colleges, Terminal Education Monograph no. 2.

———. 1941b. *Why Junior College Terminal Education?* Washington, D.C.: American Association of Junior Colleges, Terminal Education Monograph no. 3.

———. 1943. "Success of Transferring Graduates of Junior College Terminal Curricula.'' *American Association of Collegiate Registrars Journal*, pp. 372–398.

Eells, Walter C., and R. R. Brand. 1930. "Student Opinion in Junior Colleges in California.'' *School Review* 38: 176–190.

Esping-Andersen, Gosta. 1984. *Politics Against Markets*. Princeton, N.J.: Princeton University Press.

Evans, Peter, et al., eds., 1985. *Bringing the State Back In*. Cambridge, England: Cambridge University Press.

Faltermeyer, Edmund K. 1970. "Let's Break the Go-to-College Lockstep.'' *Fortune* 82 (November): 98–103.

Featherman, David, and Robert M. Hauser. 1978. *Opportunity and Change*. New York: Academic Press.

Feinberg, Walter, et al. 1980. *Revisionists Respond to Ravitch*. Washington, D.C.: National Academy of Education.

Ferrin, Richard I. 1971. *A Decade of Change in Free-Access Higher Education*. New York: College Entrance Examination Board.

Fields, Ralph R. 1962. *The Community College Movement*. New York: McGraw-Hill.

Finley, Grace J. 1973. *Business and Education: A Fragile Partnership*. Conference Board Report no. 586. New York: Conference Board.

Finn, Chester E., Jr. 1976. *Education and the Presidency*. Lexington, Mass.: Heath.

Fitzpatrick, Sheila. 1970. *The Commissariat of Enlightenment: Soviet Organization of Education and the Arts Under Lunacharsky, October 1917–1921*. Cambridge, England: Cambridge University Press.

———. 1979. *Education and Social Mobility in the Soviet Union, 1921–1934*. Cambridge, England: Cambridge University Press.

Flexner, Abraham. 1930. *Universities: American, English, German*. New York: Oxford University Press.

Folger, John K., Helen S. Astin, and Alan E. Bayer. 1970. *Human Resources and Higher Education*. New York: Russell Sage Foundation.

Frankel, Martin, and Debra Gerald. 1982. *Projections of Education Statistics to 1990–91, Volume I*. National Center for Education Statistics. Washington, D.C.: U.S. Government Printing Office.

Freeman, Richard. 1971. *The Market for College-Trained Manpower*. Cambridge, Mass.: Harvard University Press.

———. 1975. "Overinvestment in College Training." *Journal of Human Resources* 10(3): 287–310.

———. 1976. *The Overeducated American*. New York: Academic Press.

Fretwell, Elbert K. 1954. *Founding Public Junior Colleges*. New York: Teachers College Press, Columbia University.

Friedlander, Jack. 1980. "An ERIC Review: Why Is Transfer Education Declining?" *Community College Review* 8: 59–66.

Furniss, W. Todd, and Marie Martin. 1974. "Toward Solving Transfer Problems: Five Issues." *Community and Junior College Journal* 44(5): 10–15.

Furth, Dorotea. 1982. "New Hierarchies in Higher Education." *European Journal of Education* 17(2): 145–151.

Garbin, A. P., and Derrald Vaughn. 1973. "The Democratization of Higher Education." *Community and Junior College Journal* 43 (May): 23–25.

Gardner, John. 1961. *Excellence*. New York: Harper & Row.

Gaventa, John. 1980. *Power and Powerlessness*. Urbana: University of Illinois Press.

Gleazer, Edmund, Jr. 1957. "Coats Off by the Two Year Colleges." *Junior College Journal* 27: 515–520.

———. 1959. Untitled. *Junior College Newsletter* 15 (September 23): 1.

———. 1960. "Junior College World." *Junior College Journal* 30: 112–113.

———. 1961. "A National Approach to Junior College Leadership." *Journal of Secondary Education* 36 (January): 58–64.

———. 1965a. "AAJC Approach: New Kellogg Commitment." *Junior College Journal* 36 (December): 4.

———. 1965b. "AAJC Approach: A Partnership in Occupational Education." *Junior College Journal* 35 (February): 4.

———. 1968. *This Is the Community College*. Boston: Houghton Mifflin.

———. 1969a. "AAJC Approach: International Assembly." *Junior College Journal* 40 (October): 7.

———. 1969b. "AAJC Approach: The Prestige Factor." *Junior College Journal* 40 (September): 5.

———. 1971a. "AAJC Approach: International Education Grant." *Junior College Journal* 41 (March): 7.

———. 1971b. "Project Focus: Some Impressions to Date." *Junior College Journal* 42 (August–September): 5.

———. 1972. "AACJC Approach: Annual Report." *Community and Junior College Journal* 49 (February): 2.

———. 1973. "AACJC Approach: Negativism or Consumerism." *Community and Junior College Journal* 43 (June–July): 3.

———. 1974a. "After the Boom: What Now for the Community Colleges?" *Community and Junior College Journal* 44 (December–January): 6–11.

———. 1974b. "Beyond the Open Door: The Open College." *Community and Junior College Journal* 45(1): 6–12.

———. 1977. "AACJC Approach: Education and Work." *Community and Junior College Journal* 47 (February): 3.

———. 1978. "AACJC Approach: Policy Questions." *Community and Junior College Journal*.

———. 1980. *The Community College: Values, Vision and Vitality.* Washington, D.C.: American Association of Community and Junior Colleges.

Gleazer, Edmund J., ed. 1960. *Junior College Directory.* Washington, D.C.: AAJC.

Goffman, Erving. 1959. *The Presentation of Self in Everyday Life.* Garden City, N.Y.: Doubleday.

Goodman, Robert. 1979. *The Last Entrepreneurs.* New York: Simon & Schuster.

———. 1980. " 'Free Training': Special For-Industry State-Subsidized Job Training Programs in Two States." Report Prepared for the National Institute of Education's Rural Vocational Education Study. Washington, D.C.

Goodwin, Gregory. 1971. "The Historical Development of the Community–Junior College Ideology." Ph.D. diss., University of Illinois at Urbana.

Gordon, Margaret S. 1974. *Higher Education and the Labor Market.* New York: McGraw-Hill.

Gorelick, Sherry. 1981. *City College and the Jewish Poor.* New Brunswick, N.J.: Rutgers University Press.

Gould, Stephen Jay. 1981. *The Mismeasure of Man.* New York: Norton.

Gouldner, Alvin W. 1954a. *Patterns of Industrial Bureaucracy.* New York: Free Press.

———. 1954b. *Wildcat Strike.* Yellow Springs, Ohio: Antioch College Press.

———. 1979. *The Future of Intellectuals and the Rise of the New Class.* New York: Oxford University Press.

Green, Mark, and Norman Waitzman. 1980. "Cost, Benefit and Class." *Working Papers for a New Society* 7 (May–June): 39–51.

Group Attitudes Corporation. 1982. *American Attitudes Toward Higher Education.* New York: Group Attitudes Corporation.

Grubb, W. Norton. 1984. "The Bandwagon Once More: Vocational Preparation for High-Tech Occupations." *Harvard Educational Review* 54 (November): 429–451.

Grubb, W. Norton, and Marvin Lazerson. 1975. "Rally Round the Workplace: Continuities and Fallacies in Career Education." *Harvard Educational Review* 45 (November): 452–474.

Grusky, David B., and Robert M. Hauser. 1984. "Comparative Social Mobility Revisted:

Models of Convergence and Divergence in 16 Countries.'' *American Sociological Review* 49(1): 19–33.

Haber, William. 1976. ''College and the Changing Job Market.'' *AFL-CIO Federationist* 83 (June): 23–25.

Habermas, Jürgen. 1975. *Legitimation Crisis*. Boston: Beacon Press.

Hale, W. W. 1930. ''Comparative Holding Power of Junior Colleges and Regular Four-Year Colleges.'' *Phi Delta Kappan* 13: 69–74.

Hall, Lawrence, and Associates. 1974. *New Colleges of New Students*. San Francisco: Jossey-Bass.

Hansen, W. Lee, and Burton A. Weisbrod. 1969. *Benefits, Costs, and Finance of Public Higher Education*. Chicago: Markham.

Harbeson, John W. 1926. ''Education for Initiative.'' *NEA Journal* 15: 260.

Harper, William Rainey. 1900. ''The Associate Degree.'' *Educational Review*. 18: 412–415.

Harris, Arthur. 1977. ''Socioeconomic Data on the Student Body.'' Unpublished paper. Bedford, Mass.: Middlesex Community College.

Harris, Norman C. 1962. ''Administrative Leadership in Vocational-Technical Education.'' *Junior College Journal* 32 (March): 350–387.

———. 1964. *Technical Education in the Junior College: New Programs for New Jobs*. Washington, D.C.: American Association of Junior Colleges.

Harris, Norman C., and John F. Grede. 1977. *Career Education in Colleges*. San Francisco: Jossey-Bass.

Harris, Seymour E. 1972. *A Statistical Portrait of Higher Education*. New York: McGraw-Hill.

Havighurst, Robert J., and Bernice L. Neugarten. 1957. *Society and Education*. Englewood Cliffs, N.J.: Allyn and Bauer.

Heath, Anthony. 1981. *Social Mobility*. London: Fontana.

Heidenheimer, Arnold J. 1973. ''The Politics of Public Education, Health and Welfare in the USA and Western Europe: How Growth and Reform Potentials Have Differed.'' *British Journal of Political Science* 3: 315–340.

———. 1981. ''Education and Social Security Entitlements in Europe and America,'' pp. 269–304 in Peter Flora and Arnold J. Heidenheimer, eds., *The Development of Welfare States in Europe and America*. New Brunswick, N.J.: Transaction Books.

Heineman, Harry, and Edward Sussna. 1977. ''The Economic Benefits of a Community College Education.'' *Industrial Relations* 16: 345–354.

Heller, B. R., et al. 1978. *1973 Career Graduates: A Profile of CUNY Community College Students*. New York: City University of New York.

Henry, David D. 1975. *Challenges Past, Challenges Present*. San Francisco: Jossey-Bass.

Hibbs, Douglas A. 1976. ''Industrial Conflict in Advanced Industrial Societies.'' *American Political Science Review* 70(4): 1033–1058.

———. 1977. ''Political Parties and Macroeconomics Policy.'' *American Political Science Review* 71(4): 1467–1487.

Higher Education Act of 1972. 1972. Public Law 92–318. 92nd Congress, 659, June 23.

Hillway, Tyrus. 1958. *The American Two-Year College*. New York: Harper Bros.

Hogan, David. 1985. *Class and Reform: School and Society in Chicago, 1880–1930*. Philadelphia: University of Pennsylvania Press.

Hoge, Dean P., et al. 1981. ''Trends in College Students' Values Between 1952 and 1979: A Return to the Fifties?'' *Sociology of Education* 49: 263–274.

Hollingshead, August B. 1949. *Elmtown's Youth*. New York: Wiley.

Hollinshead, Byron S. 1941. ''Personal Observation in Terminal Education in Selected

Junior Colleges," pp. 158–179 in W. C. Eells, ed., *Present Status of Junior College Terminal Education*. Washington, D.C.: American Association of Junior Colleges.

Hopper, Earl. 1971. "Educational Systems and Selected Consequences of Patterns of Mobility and Non-Mobility in Industrial Societies: A Theoretical Discussion," pp. 292–336 in Earl Hopper, ed., *Readings in the Theory of Educational Systems*. London: Hutchinson.

Howe, Irving. 1985. *Socialism and America*. San Diego: Harcourt Brace Jovanovich.

Huber, Joan, and William Form. 1973. *Income and Ideology*. New York: Free Press.

Hurlburt, Allan S. 1969. *State Master Plans for Community Colleges*. Washington, D.C.: American Association of Junior Colleges.

Husen, Torsten. 1972. *Social Background and Educational Career*. Paris: OECD.

———. 1979. *The School in Question*. New York: Oxford University Press.

"Impressions of the Berkeley Convention." 1931. *Junior College Journal 1*: 191–195.

Ingalls, Roscoe C. 1937. "Evaluation of Semi-Professional Courses." *Junior College Journal* 7 (May): 483–484.

Innes, J. T., P. B. Jacobsen, and R. J. Pellegrin. 1965. *The Economic Returns to Education: A Survey of the Findings*. Eugene: University of Oregon Press.

Jaffe, A. J., and Walter Adams. 1972. "Two Models of Open Enrollment," pp. 223–251 in Logan Wilson and Olive Mills, eds., *Universal Higher Education*. Washington, D.C.: American Council on Education.

Jaschik, Scott. 1985. "States Are Urging Community Colleges to Review Programs, Justify Expenses." *Chronicle of Higher Education*, October 16, pp. 1, 18.

Jencks, Christopher, and David Riesman. 1968. *The Academic Revolution*. Garden City, N.Y.: Doubleday.

Jencks, Christopher, et al. 1972. *Inequality*. New York: Basic Books.

———. 1979. *Who Gets Ahead?* New York: Basic Books.

"The Job Gap for College Graduates in the '70s." 1972. *Business Week*, September 23, pp. 48–58.

Johnson, B. Lamar. 1944. "Junior College Trends." *Junior College Journal* 14: 606–610.

———. 1965. "Guidelines and Trends in Post-Secondary Vocational-Technical Training." *Phi Delta Kappan* 46 (April): 376–380.

Johnson, Dennis L. 1977–1978. "Marketing the Un-Cola College." *Community and Junior College Journal* 48 (December–January): 14–17.

Joint Committee on Higher Education of the California Legislature. 1969. *The Challenge of Achievement*. Sacramento: Joint Committee on Higher Education of the California Legislature.

Jordan, David Starr. 1910. *The Blood of the Nation: A Study of the Decay of Races Through the Survival of the Unfit*. Boston: American Unitarian Association.

Kaestle, Carl E., and Maris A. Vinovskis. 1980. *Education and Social Change in Nineteenth Century Massachusetts*. Cambridge, England: Cambridge University Press.

Kanouse, David, et al. 1980. "Effects of Postsecondary Experiences on Aspirations, Attitudes, and Self-Conceptions." Report prepared for the U.S. Department of Health, Education and Welfare. Santa Monica, Calif.: Rand Corporation.

Kantor, Harvey, and David Tyack, eds. 1982. *Work, Youth, and Schooling: Historical Perspectives in American Education*. Stanford, Calif.: Stanford University Press.

Karabel, Jerome. 1972. "Community Colleges and Social Stratification." *Harvard Educational Review* 42: 521–562.

———. 1974. "Protecting the Portals: Class and the Community College." *Social Policy* 5: 12–18.

———. 1979. "The Reasons Why" (Review of Werner Sombart, *Why Is There No Socialism in the United States?*). *New York Review of Books,* February 8, 1979, pp. 22–37.

———. 1983. "The Politics of Structural Change in American Higher Education: The Case of Open Admissions at the City University of New York," pp. 21–58 in Harry Hermanns et al., eds., *The Compleat University: Break from Tradition in Three Countries.* Cambridge, Mass.: Schenkman.

———. 1984. "Status-Group Struggle, Organizational Interests, and the Limits of Institutional Autonomy: The Transformation of Harvard, Yale, and Princeton, 1918–1940." *Theory and Society* 13: 1–40.

———. 1986. "Community Colleges and Social Stratification in the 1980s." *New Directions for Community Colleges,* June, pp. 13–30.

Karabel, Jerome, and Alexander W. Astin. 1975. "Social Class, Academic Ability and College 'Quality.' " *Social Forces* 53: 381–398.

Karabel, Jerome, and A. H. Halsey, eds., 1977. *Power and Ideology in Education.* New York: Oxford University Press.

Karen, David. 1980. "Trends in Racial, Sexual, and Class Inequality in Access to American Higher Education: 1940–1980." Unpublished paper. Cambridge, Mass.: Huron Institute.

Katz, Michael B. 1968. *The Irony of Early School Reform: Educational Innovation in Mid-Nineteenth Century Massachusetts.* Cambridge, Mass.: Harvard University Press.

Katz, Michael S. 1982. "Critical Literacy: A Conception of Education As a Moral Right and a Social Ideal," pp. 193–223 in Robert Everhart, ed., *The Public School Monopoly.* Cambridge, Mass.: Ballinger.

Katznelson, Ira. 1978. "Considerations on Social Democracy in the United States." *Comparative Politics* 11(1): 77–99.

———. 1981. *City Trenches: Urban Politics and the Patterning of Class in the United States.* New York: Pantheon.

Katznelson, Ira, and Margret Weir. 1985. *Schooling for All.* New York: Basic Books.

Kelly, Robert L. 1940. *American Colleges and the Social Order.* New York: Macmillan.

Kemp, W. W. 1934. "Training in Social Intelligence: A Challenge." *Junior College Journal* 4: 333–334.

Kennedy, Gail, ed. 1952. *Problems in American Civilization.* Boston: Heath.

Kerckhoff, Alan. 1974. *Ambition and Attainment.* Washington, D.C.: American Sociological Association.

Kerr, Clark. 1963. *The Uses of the University.* Cambridge, Mass.: Harvard University Press.

———. 1978. "Higher Education: Paradise Lost?" *Higher Education* 7 (August): 261–278.

———. 1985. "Foreword," pp. vii–xii in William L. Deegan, Dale Tillery and Associates, *Renewing the American Community College.* San Francisco: Jossey-Bass.

Kerr, Clark, et al. 1960. *Industrialism and Industrial Man.* Cambridge, Mass.: Harvard University Press.

Kett, Joseph E. 1982. "The Adolescence of Vocational Education," pp. 79–109 in H. Kantor and D. Tyack, eds., *Work, Youth, and Schooling.* Stanford, Calif.: Stanford University Press.

Kluegel, James R., and Eliot R. Smith. 1986. *Beliefs About Inequality.* New York: Aldine De Gruyter.

Knoell, Dorothy, and Leland Medsker. 1964. *Articulation Between Two-Year and Four-Year Colleges.* Berkeley, Calif.: Center for the Study of Higher Education.

————. 1966. *From Junior to Senior College*. Washington, D.C.: American Council on Education.

Konrad, George, and Ivan Szelenyi. 1979. *The Intellectuals on the Road to Class Power*. New York: Harcourt Brace Jovanovich.

Koos, Leonard V. 1924. *The Junior College*. Minneapolis: University of Minnesota Press.

————. 1925. *The Junior College Movement*. Boston: Ginn.

————. 1927. *The American Secondary School*. Boston: Ginn.

————. 1930. "The Junior College," pp. 3–33 in Raymond A. Kent, ed., *Higher Education in America*. Boston: Ginn.

————. 1932. "Program of Guidance in the Junior College." *Junior College Journal* 2: 443.

————. 1944. "How to Democratize the Junior College Level." *School Review* 52 (May): 271–284.

————. 1947. "Rise of the People's College." *School Review* 55 (March): 139–149.

Korpi, Walter. 1978. *The Working Class in Welfare Captialism: Work, Unions, and Politics in Sweden*. London: Routledge & Kegan Paul.

————. 1983. *The Democratic Class Struggle*. London: Routledge & Kegan Paul.

Kotschnig, Walter. 1937. *Unemployment in the Learned Professions: An International Study of Occupational and Educational Planning*. London: Oxford University Press.

Krug, Edward A. 1964. *The Shaping of the American High School, 1880–1920*. Madison: University of Wisconsin Press.

Lagemann, Ellen C. 1983. *Private Power for the Public Good*. Middletown, Conn.: Wesleyan University Press.

Lane, David. 1982. *The End of Social Inequality?* London: Allen & Unwin.

Lane, David, and Felicity O'Dell. 1978. *The Soviet Industrial Worker*. London: Martin Robertson.

Lange, Alexis F. 1911. *Some Phases of University Efficiency*. Berkeley and Los Angeles: University of California Press.

————. 1915. "The Junior College with Special Reference to California," pp. 119–124 in *Proceedings of the National Education Association*. Oakland: National Education Association.

————. 1918. "The Junior College—What Manner of Child Shall This Be?" *School and Society* 7: 211–216.

————. 1920. "The Junior College." *Sierra Educational News* 16(October): 483–486.

Lapidus, Gail. 1976. "Socialism and Modernity: Education, Industrialization, and Social Change, 1917–1936." In Paul Cocks et al., eds., *The Dynamics of Soviet Politics*. Cambridge, Mass.: Harvard University Press.

————. 1978. "Educational Strategies and Cultural Revolution: The Politics of Soviet Development." In Sheila Fitzpatrick, ed., *Cultural Revolution in the USSR, 1928–1931*. Bloomington: Indiana University Press.

Larson, Magali Sarfatti. 1977. *The Rise of Professionalism: A Sociological Analysis*. Berkeley and Los Angeles: University of California Press.

Lavin, David E., et al. 1981. *Right Versus Privilege: The Open Admissions Experiment at the City University of New York*. New York: Free Press.

Lawson, John. 1977–1978. "Vocational Preparedness for a Technical Age." *American Vocational Journal* 48 (December–January): 20–27.

Lazerson, Marvin. 1973. "Revisionism and American Educational History." *Harvard Educational Review* 43 (May): 282–283.

Lazerson, Marvin, and W. Norton Grubb, eds. 1974. *American Education and Vocation-*

alism: A Documentary History, 1870–1970. New York: Teachers College Press, Columbia University.

Levin, Henry M. 1978. "Dilemmas of Comprehensive Secondary School Reforms in Western Europe." *Comparative Education Review* 22(3): 434–451.

Levin, Henry M., and Russell W. Rumberger. 1983. "Low-Skill Future of High Tech." *Technology Review* 86(6): 18–21.

Levine, David O. 1981. "The Functions of Higher Education in American Society Between World War I and World War II." Ph.D. diss., Harvard University.

———. 1986. *The American College and the Culture of Aspiration, 1915–1940*. Ithaca, N.Y.: Cornell University Press.

Levine, Steven B. 1980. "The Rise of the American Boarding Schools and the Development of a National Upper Class." *Social Problems* 28 (October): 64–94.

Levitt, Theodore. 1960. "Marketing Myopia." *Harvard Business Review*, July–August, pp. 45–56.

Liaison Committee of the Regents of the University of California and the State Department of Education. 1948. *The Needs of California in Higher Education*. Berkeley and Los Angeles: University of California Press.

———. 1955. *A Restudy of the Needs of California in Higher Education* (by T. C. Holy and H. H. Semans). Sacramento: California State Department of Education.

———. 1960. *A Master Plan for Higer Education in California 1960–1975*. Sacramento: California State Department of Education.

Lincoln, Abraham. 1861. "Message to Congress in Special Session, July 4, 1861," pp. 124–142 in T. Harry Williams, ed., *Selected Writings and Speeches of Abraham Lincoln*. 1943. Chicago: Packard.

Lindblom, Charles E. 1977. *Politics and Markets*. New York: Basic Books.

Lindsey, Fred D. 1956. "Crisis Building Up in College Classrooms." *Nation's Business*, June, pp. 56–63.

———. 1939. "Enrollments in Various Curriculums of California Public Junior Colleges." *California Schools* 10: 303–308.

Lipset, Seymour Martin. 1950. *Agrarian Socialism: The Cooperative Commonwealth Federation in Saskatchewan*. Berkeley and Los Angeles: University of California Press.

———. 1963. *The First New Nation*. New York: Basic Books.

———. 1977. "Why No Socialism in the United States?" In S. Bialer and S. Sluzar, eds., *Sources of Contemporary Radicalism*. Boulder, Colo.: Westview.

———. 1983. "Radicalism or Reformism: The Sources of Working-Class Politics." *American Political Science Review* 77(1): 1–18.

Lipset, Seymour Martin, and Reinhard Bendix. 1959. *Social Mobility in Industrial Society*. Berkeley and Los Angeles: University of California Press.

Lipset, Martin Seymour, et al. 1956. *Union Democracy*. Glencoe, Ill.: Free Press.

Lombardi, John. 1978. "Resurgence of Occupational Education." Los Angeles: ERIC Clearinghouse for Junior Colleges, Topical Paper no. 65.

———. 1979. "The Decline of Transfer Education." Los Angeles: ERIC Clearinghouse for Junior Colleges, Topical Paper no. 70.

———. 1982. "Foreword," pp. ix–xiii in Arthur Cohen and Florence Brawer, *The American Community College*. San Francisco: Jossey-Bass.

London, Howard B. 1978. *The Culture of a Community College*. New York: Praeger.

"A Look Ahead in Education." 1967. *Nation's Business*, April, pp. 27–28.

Love, Andrea. 1973. "As Soon As We Learn to Dance, You Change the Steps." *Community and Junior College Journal* 43 (May): 13–15.

Lowell, Abbott Lawrence. 1928. "The Outlook for the American College," pp. 281–288 in R. L. Kelly, ed., *The Effective College*. New York: Association of American Colleges.

Lukes, Steven. 1968. "Methodological Individualism Reconsidered." *British Journal of Sociology* 19(2): 119–129.

———. 1974. *Power*. London: Macmillan.

Lustberg, Lawrence S. 1979. "The Founding of Community Colleges in Massachusetts: A Study of Issues in Political Sociology." Undergraduate thesis, Department of Sociology, Harvard University.

Lynd, Robert S., and Helen Merrell Lynd. 1937. *Middletown in Transition*. New York: Harcourt Brace Jovanovich.

Lynn, Kenneth S. 1955. *The Dream of Success*. Boston: Little, Brown.

MacLeod, Jay. 1987. *Ain't No Makin' It*. Boulder, Colo.: Westview.

Maeroff, Gene. 1982. "Community Colleges Defy Recession." *New York Times*, August 22, Section 12, p. 1.

———. 1983. "Better Ideas Are Sought for Two-Year Colleges." *New York Times*, August 23, pp. C1, C10.

Malitz, Gerald S. 1978. *Associate's Degrees and Other Formal Awards Below the Baccalaureate: Analysis of Six-Year Trends*. Washington, D.C.: National Center for Educational Statistics.

March, James G., and Johann P. Olsen. 1984. "The New Institutionalism: Organizational Factors in Political Life." *American Political Science Review* 78(3): 734–749.

Marland, Sidney. 1972a. "Career Education and Community Colleges." *American Education* 8 (March): 11–12.

———. 1972b. "A Strengthening Alliance," pp. 210–219 in Logan Wilson and Olive Mills, eds., *Universal Higher Education*. Washington, D.C.: American Council on Education.

———. 1974. *Career Education: A Proposal for Reform*. New York: McGraw-Hill.

Marx, Karl. 1969. *The Eighteenth Brumaire of Louis Bonaparte*. New York: International Publishers. First published in 1852.

Mason, Edward R. 1941. "New Arms for Junior Colleges." *Educational Record* 22: 15–26.

Massachusetts Board of Commerce. 1982. *Massachusetts Leader in the Biotechnical Revolution*. Boston: Commonwealth of Massachusetts.

Massachusetts Board of Higher Education. 1978. "Report to the Special Commission for Reorganizing Higher Education." Boston: Massachusetts Board of Higher Education.

Massachusetts Board of Regents. 1980. "Working Paper on Public Higher Education Planning." Summary Report 1980. Boston: Office of the Secretary for Educational Affairs Commonwealth of Massachusetts, August 17, 1977.

Massachusetts Board of Regents of Higher Education. 1981. "December Visitations." Boston: Massachusetts Board of Regents of Higher Education.

———. 1982. "Enrollment Statistics, 1980–81." Boston: Massachusetts Board of Regents of Higher Education.

———. 1983. *Program Inventory. Form D*. Boston: Massachusetts Board of Regents of Higher Education.

———. 1984. "Budget Guidlines." Boston: Massachusetts Board of Regents of Higher Education.

Massachusetts Board of Regional Community Colleges. 1958–1980. "Minutes of Board Meetings." Boston: MBRCC.

———. 1960–1980. "Enrollment Statistics." Boston: MBRCC.

———. 1965. "Vocational-Technical Education in Massachusetts Community Colleges." Boston: MBRCC.

———. 1969–1979. "Summary of Federal Aid Awarded . . . 1969–1979." Boston: MBRCC.

———. 1971. "Outline for New Occupational Program Proposals." Boston: MBRCC.

———. 1977. "Career Programs in Massachusetts Community Colleges." Boston: MBRCC.

Massachusetts Committee on High Technology. 1979. "Proceedings of Conference on Engineering Education." Boston: Massachusetts Council on High Technology.

Massachusetts House of Representatives. 1958. *Massachusetts General Law Chapter 15, Sections 27 and 28*. Boston: Commonwealth of Massachusetts.

McCabe, Robert H., and Suzanne B. Skidmore. 1983. "New Concepts for Community Colleges," pp. 232–248 in George B. Vaughan and Associates, *Issues for Community-College Leaders in a New Era*. San Francisco: Jossey-Bass.

McCartan, Ann-Marie. 1983a. "The Community College Vision: Present Challenges and Future Visions." *Journal of Higher Education* 54(6): 676–692.

———. 1983b. "Reorganizing Higher Education in Massachusetts." Cambridge, Mass.: Institute of Educational Management, Harvard University.

McConnell, T. R. 1962. *A General Pattern for American Public Higher Education*. New York: McGraw-Hill.

McDermott, John. 1969. "Campus Missionaries: The Laying On of Culture." *The Nation*, March 10, 2–7.

McDill, Edward L., and Lee C. Rigsby. 1973. *Structure and Process of Secondary Schools: The Academic Impact of Educational Climates*. Baltimore: Johns Hopkins University Press.

McDowell, Floyd M. 1919. *The Junior College*. U.S. Bureau of Education, Bulletin no. 35. Washington, D.C.: U.S. Government Printing Office.

Medsker, Leland. 1943. "The Wartime Role of Our Junior Colleges." *School Executive* 62: 19–40.

———. 1952. "Junior Colleges in This Period of Crisis." *Junior College Journal* 23 (January): 249–256.

———. 1960. *The Junior College: Progress and Prospect*. New York: McGraw-Hill.

Medsker, Leland, and Dale Tillery. 1971. *Breaking the Access Barrier*. New York: McGraw-Hill.

Medsker, Leland L., and James W. Trent. 1965. "The Influence of Different Types of Public Higher Institutions on College Attendance from Varying Socioeconomic and Ability Levels." Unpublished paper for the Center for the Study of Higher Education, University of California, Berkeley.

Mertins, P. E., and N. J. Brandt. 1979. *Financial Statistics of Institutions of Higher Education: Current Funds Revenues and Expenditures*. Washington, D.C.: National Center for Educational Statistics.

Merton, Robert K. 1968. *Social Theory and Social Structure*. New York: Free Press.

Meyer, John W. 1977. "The Effects of Education as an Institution." *American Journal of Sociology* 83: 55–77.

Meyer, John W., and Michael Hannan, eds. 1979. *National Development and the World System*. Chicago: University of Chicago Press.

Meyer, John W., and Brian Rowan. 1977. "Institutionalized Organizations: Formal Structure As Myth and Ceremony." *American Journal of Sociology* 83: 340–363.

———. 1978. "The Structure of Educational Organizations," pp. 78–109 in M. Meyer et al., eds., *Studies on Environments and Organizations*. San Francisco: Jossey-Bass.

Meyer, John W., and Richard W. Scott. 1983. *Organizational Environments: Ritual and Rationality.* Beverly Hills, Calif.: Sage Publications.

Meyer, John W., et al. 1979. "Public Education As Nation-Building in America." *American Journal of Sociology* 85: 978–986.

Meyer, Thomas J. 1984. "Two-Year Colleges Facing Serious Enrollment Decline." *Chronicle of Higher Education,* November 7, p. 3.

Michels, Robert. 1962. *Political Parties.* New York: Free Press. First published in 1911.

Middleton, Lorenzo. 1978. "NAACP Concerned over Racial Isolation in Cleveland's Community College." *Chronicle of Higher Education,* June 19, p. 9.

———. 1982. "Two-Year Colleges Beneficiaries of Hard Times." *Chronicle of Higher Education,* April 14, p. 2.

Miliband, Ralph. 1969. *The State in Capitalist Society.* New York: Basic Books.

Mills, C. Wright. 1956. *The Power Elite.* New York: Oxford University Press.

Mink, Gwendolyn. 1986. *Old Labor and New Immigrants in American Political Development: Union, Party, and State, 1875–1920.* Ithaca, N.Y.: Cornell University Press.

Monk-Turner, Elizabeth. 1982. "Education, Occupation, and Income: The Effect of Attending a Community College on the Labor Market Outcomes of Young Men and Women." Ph.D diss., Brandeis University.

———. 1983. "Sex, Educational Differentiation and Occupational Status: Analyzing Occupational Differences for Community and Four-Year College Entrants." *Sociological Quarterly* 24: 393–404.

———. 1985. "Sex Differences in Type of First College Entered and Occupational Status: Changes over Time." *Social Science Journal* 22 (January): 89–97.

Monroe, Charles R. 1972. *Profile of the Community College.* San Francisco: Jossey-Bass.

Murphy, Janet G. 1974. "Reorganization of Public Higher Education in the Commonwealth of Massachusetts." Ph.D. diss., University of Massachusetts.

Myrdal, Gunnar. 1944. *An American Dilemma: The Negro Problem and Modern Democracy.* New York: Harper Bros.

Nasaw, David. 1979. *Schooled to Order.* New York: Oxford University Press.

National Center for Educational Statistics. 1966–1985. *The Condition of Education.* Washington, D.C.: Department of Health, Education and Welfare. Published annually.

———. 1970. *Digest of Educational Statistics.* Washington, D.C.: U.S. Government Printing Office.

———. 1981. *Digest of Educational Statistics.* Washington, D.C.: U.S. Government Printing Office.

———. 1983. *Digest of Educational Statistics.* Washington, D.C.: U.S. Government Printing Office.

National Center for Educational Statistics. 1969–1977. *Financial Statistics of Higher Education: Current Funds, Revenues, and Expenditures.* Washington, D.C.: U.S. Government Printing Office.

———. 1984. *Projections of Educational Statistics to 1993–94.* Washington, D.C.: U.S. Government Printing Office.

National Education Association. 1957. *Higher Education in a Decade of Decision.* Educational Policies Commission. Washington, D.C.: National Education Association.

Neumann, William, and David Riesman. 1980. "The Community College Elite." *New Directions for Community Colleges* 8(4): 53–72.

Newman, Frank, et al. 1971. *Report on Higher Education.* Washington, D.C.: U.S. Government Printing Office.

Nixon, Richard. 1970. "March 19 Message to Congress on Higher Education," pp. 37a in *Congressional Quarterly Almanac.* Washington, D.C.: Congressional Quarterly.

Noeth, Richard J., and Gary Hanson. 1976. "Research Report: Occupational Programs Do the Job." *Community and Junior College Journal* 47 (November): 28–30.

O'Connell, Thomas. 1968. *Community Colleges: A President's View.* Urbana, Ill.: University of Illinois Press.

O'Connor, James. 1973. *The Fiscal Crisis of the State.* New York: St. Martin's Press.

Offe, Claus. 1973. "The Theory of the Capitalist State and the Problem of Policy Formation," pp. 125–144 in Leon Lindberg et al., eds., *Stress and Contradiction in Modern Capitalism.* Lexington, Mass.: Heath.

———. 1974. "Structural Problems of the Capitalist State," pp. 31–57 in Klaus von Beyme, ed., *German Political Studies.* London: Sage.

———. 1984. *Contradictions of the Welfare State.* Cambridge, Mass.: MIT Press.

———. 1985. *Disorganized Capitalism.* Cambridge, Mass.: MIT Press.

Ogbu, John U. 1978. *Minority Education and Caste.* New York: Academic Press.

———. 1983. "Minority Status and Schooling in Plural Societies." *Comparative Education Review* 27(2): 168–190.

Olivas, Michael A. 1979. *The Dilemma of Access: Minorities in Two-Year Colleges.* Washington, D.C.: Howard University Press.

Olson, Keith W. 1974. *The G.I. Bill, the Veterans, and the Colleges.* Lexington: University Press of Kentucky, 1974.

O'Neill, David M., and Peter Sepielli. 1985. *Education in the United States: 1940–1983.* U.S. Bureau of the Census, Special Demographic Analysis, Washington, D.C.: U.S. Government Printing Office.

O'Neill, June A. 1973. *Sources of Funds to Colleges and Universities.* New York: McGraw-Hill.

"Open the Doors." 1970. *Newsweek,* July 6, p. 77.

Organization for Economic Cooperation and Development. 1973. *Short-Cycle Higher Education.* Paris: OECD.

———. 1983. *Policies for Higher Education in the 1980s.* Paris: OECD.

Organization for Social and Technical Innovation (OSTI). 1973. *A Master Planning Process for Higher Education in Massachusetts: A Report to the Board of Higher Education.* Boston: Organization for Social and Technical Innovation.

Oromaner, Mark. 1984. "Insiders, Outsiders, and the Community College: A Sociology of Knowledge Perspective." *Research in Higher Education* 21(2): 226–235.

Ossowski, Stanislaw. 1963. *Class Structure in the Social Consciousness.* London: Routledge & Kegan Paul.

O'Toole, James. 1975a. "The Reserve Army of the Underemployed: I—The World of Work." *Change* 7(May): 26–33, 63.

———. 1975b. "The Reserve Army of the Underemployed: II—The Role of Education." *Change* 7(June): 26–33, 60–63.

———. 1977. *Work, Learning, and the American Future.* San Francisco: Jossey-Bass.

Padgett, John F. 1981. "Hierarchy and Ecological Control in Federal Budgetary Decision-Making." *American Journal of Sociology* 87: 75–129.

Palmer, George Herbert. 1927. "The Junior College." *Atlantic Monthly,* April, pp. 497–499.

Parker, Garland G. 1974. *Career Education and Transfer Program Enrollments in Two-Year Colleges, 1973–1974.* ACT Special Report no. 11. Iowa City, Ia.: American College Testing Program.

———. 1975. *Collegiate Enrollees in American Two-Year Institutions: 1974–1975 Statistics, Interpretations and Trends.* ACT Special Report no. 14. Iowa City, Ia.: American Testing Program.

Parkin, Frank. 1979. *Marxism and Class Theory: A Bourgeois Critique*. New York: Columbia University Press.

Parnell, Dale. 1982. "President's Column: Putting America Back to Work." *Community and Junior College Journal* 53: 12–15.

Pasqua, Tom. 1974. "It Can Aid Transfer." *Community and Junior College Journal* 44(5): 30–31.

Passow, A. Harry, et al. 1976. *The National Case Study: An Empirical Comparative Study of Twenty-One Educational Systems*. New York: Wiley.

Peng, Samuel. 1977. *Transfer Students in Institutions of Higher Education*. Washington, D.C.: National Center for Educational Statistics.

Peng, Samuel, Elizabeth Ashburn, and George Duncan. 1977. "Withdrawals from Institutions of Higher Education: An Appraisal with Longitudinal Data Involving Diverse Institutions." NLS–Sponsored Report Series. Washington, D.C.: National Center on Educational Statistics.

Pepper, Suzanne. 1980. "Chinese Education After Mao: Two Steps Forward, Two Steps Back, and Begin Again?" *China Quarterly* 81 (March): 1–65.

Perkinson, Henry J. 1977. *The Imperfect Panacea*, 2nd ed. New York: Random House.

Perrow, Charles. 1984. *Normal Accidents: Living with High-Risk Technologies*. New York: Basic Books.

———. 1986. *Complex Organizations*, 3rd ed. New York: Random House.

Pessen, Edward. 1971. "The Egalitarian Myth and the American Social Reality: Wealth, Mobility, and Equality in the Era of the Common Man." *American Historical Review*, October, pp. 989–1034.

Pfeffer, Jeffrey, and Gerald Salancik. 1978. *The External Control of Organizations: A Resource Dependence Perspective*. New York: Harper & Row.

Pifer, Alan. 1973. "The Nature and Origin of the Carnegie Commission on Higher Education," pp. 207–216 in *Priorities for Action: The Final Report of the Carnegie Commission on Higher Education*. New York: McGraw-Hill.

Pincus, Fred. 1974. "Tracking in Community Colleges." *Insurgent Sociologist* 4: 17–35.

———. 1980. "The False Promises of Community Colleges." *Harvard Educational Review* 50: 332–361.

———. 1986. "Vocational Education: More False Promises." *New Directions for Community Colleges*, June, pp. 41–52.

Pincus, Fred, and John Houston. 1978. "The Politics of 'Careers.' " *Politics and Education* 1(4): 11–14.

Piven, Frances Fox, and Richard A. Cloward. 1980. "Social Policy and the Formation of Political Consciousness," pp. 117–152 in Maurice Zeitlin, ed., *Political Power and Social Theory*. Greenwich, Conn.: JAI Press.

Plisko, Valena W., and Joyce D. Stern. 1985. *The Condition of Education*. National Center for Education Statistics. Washington, D.C.: U.S. Government Printing Office.

Poignant, Raymond. 1969. *Education and Development in Western Europe, the United States, and the U.S.S.R.*. New York: Teachers College Press, Columbia University.

Pollack, Andrew. 1983. "The Birth of Silicon Statemanship." *New York Times*, February 27, sec. III, pp. 1, 30.

Poulantzas, Nicos. 1973. *Political Power and Social Theory*. London: New Left Books.

———. 1975. *Classes in Contemporary Capitalism*. London: New Left Books.

Priest, Bill. 1956. "What Industrial Public Relations Can Teach Us." *Junior College Journal* 27 (September): 3–38.

Putnam, Roger. 1970. "Address to Advisory Council Members." Boston: Massachusetts Board of Regional Community Colleges.

Randour, Mary Lou, et al. 1982. "Women in Higher Education: Trends in Enrollments and Degrees Earned." *Harvard Educational Review* 52(2): 189–202.

Ravitch, Diane. 1978. *The Revisionists Revised.* New York: Basic Books.

———. 1983. *The Troubled Crusade.* New York: Basic Books.

Reich, Robert B. 1983. *The Next American Frontier.* New York: Times Books.

Reynolds, James W. 1965. *The Junior College.* New York: Center for Applied Research in Education.

Reynolds, Lloyd G., and Joseph Shister. 1949. *Job Horizons.* New York.

Reynolds, O. E. 1927. *The Social and Economic Status of College Students.* New York: Teachers College Press, Columbia University.

Rhine, Shirley H. 1972. "Technicial Education: Who Chooses It?" New York: Conference Board.

Rhoades, Gary. 1987. "Higher Education in a Consumer Society." *Journal of Higher Education* 58(1): 2–24.

Richardson, Richard C., et al. 1983. *Literacy in the Open-Access College.* San Francisco: Jossey-Bass.

Rickover, Hyman. 1959. *Education and Freedom.* New York: Dutton.

Ridgeway, James. 1968. *The Closed Corporation.* New York: Random House.

Riesman, David. 1956. *Constraint and Variety in American Education.* Lincoln: University of Nebraska Press.

———. 1980. *On Higher Education.* San Francisco: Jossey-Bass.

Riesman, David, and Reuel Denney. 1951. "Football in America: A Study in Culture Diffusion." *American Quarterly* 3: 309–325.

Ringer, Fritz, K. 1979. *Education and Society in Modern Europe.* Bloomington: Indiana University Press.

Rodriguez, Orlando. 1978. "Occupational Shifts and Educational Upgrading in the American Labor Force Between 1950 and 1970." *Sociology of Education* 51(1): 55–67.

Roper Organization. 1987. *The American Dream: A National Survey Conducted for the* Wall Street Journal *by the Roper Organization.* Princeton, N.J.: Dow Jones.

Rowe, Benjamin. 1957. "Public Relations and the Junior College." *Junior College Journal* 27(6): 339–342.

Rubinson, Richard. 1986. "Class Formation, Political Organization, and Institutional Structure: The Case of Schooling in the United States." *American Journal of Sociology* 92: 519–548.

Rudolph, Frederick. 1962. *The American College and University.* New York: Vintage.

———. 1977. *Curriculum: A History of the American Undergraduate Course of Study Since 1636.* San Francisco: Jossey-Bass.

Rumberger, Russell W. 1981. *Overeducation in the U.S. Labor Market.* New York: Praeger.

———. 1984. "The Job Market for College Graduates, 1960–1990." *Journal of Higher Education* 55(July–August): 433–454.

Saiter, Susan. 1982. "No Bell Towers or Fraternities, Little Football, Lots of Serious Study." *New York Times,* August 22, Section 12, pp. 32-33.

"Sally Gerhardt Finds B.A. Is of Little Help in Trying to Land Job." 1975. *Wall Street Journal,* January 30, p. 1.

Sawyer, Malcolm. C. 1976. *Income Distribution in OECD Countries.* Paris: OECD.

Schaefer, Carl, and Jacob Kaufman. 1968. *Occupational Education for Massachusetts: A Report Prepared for the Massachusetts Advisory Council on Education.* Boston: Advisory Council on Education.

Schmitter, Phillipe. 1974. "Still the Century of Corporatism?" *Review of Politics* 36: 85–131.

———. 1977. "Modes of Interest Intermediation and Models of Societal Change in Western Europe." *Comparative Political Studies* 10: 7–38.

Scott, Barbara Ann. 1983. *Crisis Management in American Higher Education.* New York: Praeger.

Scully, Malcolm G. 1980. "Volatile Decade Predicted for Community Colleges." *Chronicle of Higher Education,* March 31, p. 6.

Scully, Maureen. 1982. "Coping with Meritocracy: Education, Self-Esteem, and the Legitimation of Inequality." Senior Honors Thesis, Department of Social Studies, Harvard University.

Seashore, Carl E. 1940. *The Junior College Movement.* New York: Henry Holt.

Selby, David. 1980. "Short-Term Postsecondary Education and Work Four Years After High School." Washington, D.C.: Joseph Froomkin Inc. Report for the National Institute of Education.

Selznick, Philip. 1949. *TVA and the Grass Roots.* Berkeley, and Los Angeles: University of California Press.

Shannon, William G. 1971a. "AAJC Approach: The Convention and the Future." *Junior College Journal* 41 (May): 5.

———. 1971b. "AAJC Approach: Two Kellogg Projects End." *Junior College Journal* 41 (April): 7.

Shapiro, Harvey S. 1978. "Education and Ideology: A Sociological Study of Educational Thought in the American Radical Movement, 1900–1925." Ph.D. diss., Boston University.

———. 1982. "Education in Capitalist Society: Toward a Reconsideration of the State of Educational Policy." *Teachers' College Record* 83(4): 515–527.

———. 1983. "Habermas, O'Connor, and Wolfe, and the Crisis of the Welfare-Capitalist State: Conservative Politics and the Roots of Educational Policy in the 1980s." *Educational Theory* 33(3–4): 135–147.

Shirk, Susan L. 1982. *Competitive Comrades: Career Incentives and Student Strategies in China.* Berkeley and Los Angeles: University of California Press.

Shor, Ira. 1986. *Culture Wars: School and Society in the Conservative Restoration, 1969–1984.* Boston: Routledge & Kegan Paul.

Simon, Herbert. 1976. *Administrative Behavior.* 3rd ed. New York: Free Press.

Sinclair, Upton. 1922. *The Goose Step.* New York: Cornwall Press.

Singleton, Margaret. 1967. "Innovation at Oakland Community College." Unpublished paper. Albuquerque, N.M.: Westinghouse Research Laboratories.

Skaggs, Kenneth G. 1973. "Occupational Education: The Program Crisis." *Community and Junior College Journal* 43 (May): 11–12.

Skaggs, Kenneth G., Douglas W. Burris, and Lewis R. Fibel. 1967. "Report and Forecast: AAJC's Occupational Education Project." *Junior College Journal* 37 (March): 23–24.

Skocpol, Theda. 1979. *States and Social Revolutions.* Cambridge, England: Cambridge University Press.

Slosson, Edwin E. 1910. *Great American Universities.* New York: Macmillan.

Smith, David N. 1974. *Who Rules the Universities?* New York: Monthly Review Press.

Smith, Herbert L. 1986. "Overeducation and Underemployment: An Agnostic Review." *Sociology of Education* 59 (April): 85–99.

Smith, L. W. 1928. "Junior College Objectives." *Proceedings of the Ninth Annual AAJC Meeting.* Fort Worth, Tex.: American Association of Junior Colleges.

Snyder, William H. 1931. "The Real Function of Junior College." *Junior College Journal* 2: 74–80.

———. 1941. "Philosophy of Semi-professional Education," pp. 256–266 in Walter C. Eells, ed., *Why Junior College Education?* Washington, D.C.: American Association of Junior Colleges.

Spenner, Kenneth L., and David Featherman. 1978. "Achievement Ambitions," pp. 373–420 in Ralph Turner, James Coleman, and Renee Fox, eds., *Annual Review of Sociology,* vol. 4. Palo Alto, Calif.: Annual Reviews.

Spilerman, Seymour. 1983. "Careers, Labor Market Structure, and Socioeconomic Achievement." *American Journal of Sociology.* 83: 551–593.

Sproul, Robert Gordon. 1931. "Certain Aspects of the Junior College." *Junior College Journal* 1(5): 274–280.

———. 1938. *Before and After the Junior College.* Los Angeles: College Press.

———. 1958. "Many Millions More." *Educational Record* 39(2): 97–103.

Squires, Gregory. 1979. *Education and Jobs: The Imbalancing of the Social Machinery.* New Brunswick, N.J.: Transaction Books.

Stafford, Richard. 1980. "Massachusetts Higher Education and the Politics of Reorganization." Ph.D. diss., Harvard University.

Stafford, Richard, and Lawrence S. Lustberg. 1978. "Higher Education in Massachusetts: Issues in their Context." Unpublished paper. Cambridge, Mass.: Sloan Commission on Government and Higher Education.

Starr, Kevin. 1986. *Americans and the California Dream, 1850–1915.* New York: Oxford University Press.

Starr, Paul. 1982. *The Social Transformation of American Medicine.* New York: Basic Books.

State of New York. 1950. *The Master Plan: Two-Year and Four-Year Colleges.* Albany: State University of New York.

State University of New York. 1976. *Application and Enrollment Patterns of Transfer Students, Fall 1974.* Report no. 6–76. Albany, N.Y.: Central Staff Office of Institutional Research, SUNY.

Steinberg, Stephen. 1981. *The Ethnic Myth.* New York: Atheneum.

Stinchcombe, Arthur L. 1965. "Social Structure and Organizations," pp. 142–193 in James G. March, ed., *Handbook of Organizations.* Chicago: Rand McNally.

Strong, Michael. 1980. "The Media's Perspective on the Problems of Underemployment, 1968–1979." Unpublished paper. Cambridge, Mass.: Huron Institute.

Stuart, Mary Clark. 1980. "Clark Kerr: Biography of an Action Intellectual." Ph.D. diss., University of Michigan.

Talbot, Richard. 1978. "SES, Program Enrollment and Outcome." M.A. thesis, University of New Hampshire, Department of Sociology and Anthropology.

Taylor, Bernard. 1957. "Alumni Fund for the Junior College." *Junior College Journal* 27: 10–14.

Thomas, Charles W. 1961. "Financing the Public Community College." *Junior College Journal* 31 (March): 365–369.

Thomas, Frank Waters. 1926. "A Study of the Functions of the Public Junior College." Ph.D. diss., Stanford University.

Thomas, Russell. 1962. *The Search for a Common Learning: General Education, 1800–1960.* New York: McGraw-Hill.

Thornton, James W. 1972. *The Community Junior College.* New York: Wiley.

Thurow, Lester. 1975. *Generating Inequality: Mechanisms of Distribution in the U.S. Economy.* New York: Basic Books.

Tillery, Dale. 1973. *Distribution and Differentiation of Youth*. Cambridge, Mass.: Ballinger.

Tinto, Vincent. 1971. "Accessibility of Colleges As a Factor in the Rates and Selectivity of College Attendance." Ph.D diss., University of Chicago.

———. 1973. "College Proximity and Rates of College Attendance." *American Educational Research Journal* 10(4): 277–293.

———. 1975. "The Distributive Effects of Public Junior College Availabilty." *Research in Higher Education* 3(3): 261–274.

Tobin, Daniel. 1977. "Research Report no. 77: Student Profile." Worcester, Mass.: Quinsigamond Community College.

Touraine, Alain. 1974. *The Academic System in American Society*. New York: McGraw-Hill.

Trent, James, and Leland Medsker. 1968. *Beyond High School*. San Francisco: Jossey-Bass.

Trow, Martin. 1961. "The Second Transformation of American Secondary Education." *International Journal of Comparative Sociology* 2 (September): 144–166.

———. 1970. "Reflections on the Transition from Mass to Universal Higher Education." *Daedelus* (Winter): 1–42.

Turner, Ralph H. 1966. "Modes of Social Ascent Through Education," pp. 449–458 in Reinhard Bendix and Seymour Martin Lipset, eds., *Class, Status and Power,* 2nd ed. New York: Free Press.

Tyack, David. 1974. *The One Best System*. Cambridge, Mass.: Harvard University Press.

———. 1976. "Ways of Seeing: An Essay on the History of Compulsory Schooling." *Harvard Educational Review* 46(3): 355–389.

Tyack, David, and Elizabeth Hansot. 1982. *Managers of Virtue*. New York: Basic Books.

Tyack, David B., Robert Lowe, and Elizabeth Hansot. 1984. *Public Schools in Hard Times: The Great Depression and Recent Years*. Cambridge, Mass.: Harvard University Press.

Unger, Jonathan. 1982. *Education Under Mao: Class and Competition in Canton Schools, 1960–1980*. New York: Columbia University Press.

United States Bureau of the Census. 1975. *Historical Statistics of the United States: Colonial Times to 1970*. Washington, D.C.: U.S. Government Printing Office. Bicentennial ed., pts. 1 and 2.

———. 1987. *Statistical Abstract of the United States 1987*. Washington, D.C.: U.S. Government Printing Office.

United States Bureau of Education, Bulletin no. 19, pt. II. 1922. *National Conference of Junior Colleges, 1920, and First Annual Meeting of AAJC, 1921*. Washington, D.C.: U.S. Government Printing Office.

United States Department of Education, Center for Statistics. 1986. *Digest of Education Statistics, 1985–1986*. Washington, D.C.: U.S. Government Printing Office.

United States Department of Health, Education and Welfare. 1973. *Career Education: Implications for Minorities*. Washington, D.C.: Department of Health, Education and Welfare.

United States Department of Labor, Bureau of Labor Statistics. 1977. *Occupational Training Information in New England: An Evaluation, Volume II*. Boston: New England Regional Commission.

United States House of Representatives, Committee on Education and Labor. 1971a. *Higher Education Amendments of 1971, Hearings Before the Special Subcommitte on Education*. 92nd Cong., 1st sess. Washington, D.C.: U.S. Government Printing Office.

————. 1971b. *Report to Accompany H.R. 7248* (House Report 92–554). Washington, D.C.: U.S. Government Printing Office.

————. 1975a. *Hearings on Occupational and Vocational Education Amendments, H.R. 3036*. Washington, D.C.: U.S. Government Printing Office.

————. 1975b. *Vocational and Occupational Education, Hearings Before the General Subcommittee on Education*. 94th Cong., 1st sess. Washington, D.C.: U.S. Government Printing Office.

United States Office of Education. 1930–1958. *Biennial Survey of Education*. Washington, D.C.: Department of Health, Education and Welfare. Series published every two years.

————. 1944. *Statistics of Higher Education 1939–1940 and 1941–1942,* vol. 2. Washington, D.C.: Department of Health, Education and Welfare.

United States President's Commission on Higher Education. 1948. *Higher Education for American Democracy*. New York: Harper Bros. Orignially released on December 11, 1947.

United States President's Committee on Education Beyond the High School. 1956. *First Interim Report to the President*. Washington, D.C.: U.S. Government Printing Office.

United States Senate. 1975. *Hearings on Vocational Education Amendments*. Washington, D.C.: U.S. Government Printing Office.

University of California Systemwide Administration. 1978. *Beyond High School Graduation: Who Goes to College?* Berkeley.

University of Massachusetts. 1977. *Cooperative Institutional Research Program—Summary of Data on Entering Freshman 1977*. Washington, D.C.: American Council on Education.

Unruh, Adolph. 1949. "What's in a Name?" *Junior College Journal* 20 (October): 73–74.

Useem, Elizabeth. 1982. "Education in a High Technology World: The Case of Route 128." Unpublished paper. Boston: New England Institute for Interdisciplinary Study of Education.

————. 1986. *Low-Tech Education in a High-Tech World*. New York: Free Press.

Vaughan, George B., ed. 1980. *Questioning the Community College Role*. San Francisco: Jossey-Bass.

Vaughan, George B., and Associates. 1983. *Issues for Community College Leaders in a New Era*. San Francisco: Jossey-Bass.

Veblen, Thorstein. 1918. *The Higher Learning in America*. New York: B. W. Huebsch.

Velez, William. 1985. "Finishing College: The Effects of College Type." *Sociology of Education*. 58(3): 191–200.

Venn, Grant. 1964. *Man, Education and Work*. Washington, D.C.: American Council on Education.

Veysey, Lawrence R. 1965. *The Emergence of the American University*. Chicago: University of Chicago Press.

Wagenaar, Theodore C. 1984. *Occupational Aspirations and Intended Field of Study in College*. Washington, D.C.: National Center for Education Statistics.

Walsh, John. 1964. "Manpower Development." *Junior College Journal* 34(May): 8.

Warner, W. Lloyd. 1962. *American Life*. Chicago: University of Chicago Press.

Warner, W. Lloyd, and Paul S. Lunt, 1941. *The Social Life of a Modern Community*. New Haven, Conn.: Yale University Press.

Warner, W. Lloyd, et al. 1944. *Who Shall Be Educated?* New York: Harper & Brothers.

Watkins, Beverly T. 1982. "Community Colleges and Industry Ally to Provide 'Customized' Job Training." *Chronicle of Higher Education,* October 27, p. 4.

298   Bibliography

Weber, Max. 1978. *Economy and Society*. 2 vols. Berkeley and Los Angeles: University of California Press. First published in 1922.
Wechsler, Harold S. 1977. *The Qualified Student*. New York: Wiley.
Weersing, Frederick J. 1931. "Misconceptions Regarding the Junior College." *Junior College Journal* 2: 363–369.
Weinberg, Meyer. 1977. *A Chance to Learn: A History of Race and Education in the United States*. Cambridge, England: Cambridge University Press.
Wellinger, J. F. 1926. "The Junior College As Viewed by Its Students." *School Review* 34: 760–767.
Welter, Rush. 1962. *Popular Education and Democratic Thought in America*. New York: Columbia University Press.
Whitney, Frederick. 1928. *The Junior College in America*. Greeley: Colorado State Teachers College.
"Who Needs College?" 1976. *Newsweek*, April 26, pp. 60–69.
Wiebe, Robert H. 1967. *The Search for Order, 1877–1920*. New York: Hill & Wang.
Wilber, F. Parker. 1968. "Meeting the Job Demand." *Nation's Business*, April, p. 127.
Wildavsky, Aaron. 1974. *The Politics of Budgetary Process*, 2nd ed. Boston: Little, Brown.
Wilensky, Harold L. 1975. *The Welfare State and Equality*. Berkeley and Los Angeles: University of California Press.
Willey, Malcolm M. 1937. *Depression, Recovery and Higher Education*. New York: McGraw-Hill.
Williams, Robin. 1970. *American Society*, 3rd ed. New York: Knopf.
Williams, T. Harry, ed. 1943. *Selected Writings and Speeches of Abraham Lincoln*. Chicago: Packard.
Willis, Paul. 1978. *Learning to Labour*. London: Routledge and Kegan Paul.
Wilms, Welford W. 1974. *Public and Proprietary Vocational Training: A Study of Effectiveness*. Berkeley, Calif.: Center for Research and Development in Higher Education.
———. 1980. "Vocational Education and Social Mobility." Unpublished paper. Los Angeles: University of California, Graduate School of Education.
———. 1987. "Proprietary Schools." *Change*, January–February, pp. 10–22.
Wilms, Wellford, and Stephen Hansell. 1982. "The Dubious Promise of Post-Secondary Vocational Education: Its Payoff to Dropouts and Graduates in the USA." *International Journal of Educational Development* 2: 43–59.
Wilson, William Julius. 1978. *The Declining Significance of Race*. Chicago: University of Chicago Press.
———. 1987. *The Truly Disadvantaged*. Chicago: University of Chicago Press.
Winslow, Guy M. 1933. "Junior Colleges in New England: A Contrast." *Junior College Journal* 3: 342–346.
Wirth, Arthur G. 1972. *Education in the Technological Society: The Vocational-Liberal Studies Controversy in the Early Twentieth Century*. Scranton, Pa.: Intext.
Wohl, R. Richard. 1966. "The 'Rags to Riches Story': An Episode of Secular Idealism," pp. 501–506 in Reinhard Bendix and Seymour Martin Lipset, eds., *Class, Status, and Power*, 2nd ed. New York: Free Press.
Wolfe, Alan. 1971. "Reform Without Reform: The Carnegie Commission on Higher Education." *Social Policy* 2(May–June): 18–27.
———. 1974. "Carnegie Again." *Social Policy*, November–December, pp. 60–63.
———. 1977. *The Limits of Legitimacy*. New York: Free Press.
Wolfe, Lisa. 1985. "Enrollment at 2-Year Colleges Starting to Slip." *New York Times*, February 24, pp. 1, 34.

Wolfle, Dael. 1954. *America's Resources of Specialized Talent.* New York: Harper & Row.

Wood, William R. 1950. ''Professional Personnel for Community Colleges.'' *Junior College Journal* 20: 516–519.

Wrigley, Julia. 1982. *Class Politics and Public Schools: Chicago, 1900–1950.* New Brunswick, N.J.: Rutgers University Press.

Wyllie, Irwin G. 1954. *The Self-Made Man in America.* New Brunswick: Rutgers University Press.

Young, Michael. 1958. *The Rise of the Meritocracy.* London: Thames and Hudson.

Zook, George F. 1922. ''The Junior College.'' *The School Review* 30: 575–583.

———. 1929. ''Is the Junior College a Menace or a Boon?'' *The School Review* 37: 415–425.

———. 1932. ''Implications of the Junior College Movement.'' *Junior College Journal* 2 (February): 249–250.

———. 1940. ''The Past Twenty Years—The Next Twenty Years.'' *Junior College Journal* 10: 617–623.

———. 1945. *The Role of the Federal Government in Education.* Cambridge, Mass.: Harvard University Press.

———. 1946. ''Changing Patterns of Junior College Education.'' *Junior College Journal* 16 (May): 411–417.

Zwerling, L. Steven. 1976. *Second Best.* New York: McGraw-Hill.

———, ed. 1986. *The Community College and Its Critics.* San Francisco: Jossey-Bass.

List of Interviews

Asquino, Daniel (Dean of Administration, Cape Cod Community College). August 19, 1984.

Bartlett, Irving (Former President, Cape Cod Community College). April 12, 1979.

Buckley, Paul (Development Officer, Bunker Hill Community College). October 5, 1978.

Capeci, Pat (Dean of Admissions, Berkshire Community College). June 22, 1984.

Carifio, Jim (Chief, Management Information Systems, Massachusetts Board of Regents). July 27, 1984.

Case, Ethel (Dean of Students, Greenfield Community College). May 20, 1983.

Casik, Robert (Psychology Faculty Member, Massasoit Community College). May 7, 1984.

Chase, Theodore (Former Chairman, Massachusetts Board of Regional Community Colleges). March 12, 1979.

Chisholm, Patricia (Dean of Students, Bunker Hill Community College). October 5, 1978.

Cleaments, Evelyn (Counselor, Middlesex Community College). February 13, 1979.

Cody, Gail (Counselor, Roxbury Community College). March 19, 1979.

Collins, James (Representative to the Massachusetts State Legislature. Member, Joint Committee on Education). September 7, 1978.

Costello, John (Executive Director, Massachusetts Board of Regional Community Colleges, Central Office). October 17, 1978.

———. March 15, 1983.

Cotoia, Anthony (Dean of Continuing Education, Massasoit Community College). June 25, 1984.

Crossa, James (Placement Counselor, Bristol Community College). July 3, 1983.

Day, Frank (Chemistry Faculty Member, North Shore Community College). March 4, 1983.

Denhard, George (Program Specialist, Bay State Skills Corporation). July 27, 1984.

Derderian, Lucille (Dean of Students, North Shore Community College). March 20, 1983.

———. June 25, 1984.

DiCarlo, Robert (Director, Program Planning, Greenfield Community College). August 31, 1978.

Doherty, Frank (Counselor, Cape Cod Community College). March 18, 1983.

Doscher, Jeff (Director of Counseling, Berkshire Community College). March 18, 1983.

Dunn, John (Dean of Academic Affairs, Springfield Community College). June 22, 1984.

Dwyer, William (Former President, Massachusetts Board of Regional Community Colleges). February 9, 1979.

———. March 11, 1983.

Farrell, Robert (Manager, Digital Electronics Corporation). March 6, 1979.

Frugoli, Pam (Program Specialist, Commonwealth of Massachusetts, Division of Employment Services). May 14, 1979.

Furcolo, Foster (Former Massachusetts Governor. Member, Massachusetts Board of Regents of Higher Education). August 2, 1984.

Gerlach, Richard (Admissions Director, Berkshire Community College). March 18, 1983.

Gernhart, Jack (Former National Secretary, American Association of Community and Junior Colleges). January 14, 1983.

———. February 1, 1983.

Grande, James (Labor Representative and Chairman, Commission for Occupational/Vocational Education). July 26, 1978.

Haley, Arthur (President, Mount Wachusett Community College). March 4, 1983.

Hall, James (President, Cape Cod Community College). June 22, 1984.

Hamilton, Charles (Chairman, Massachusetts Board of Regional Community Colleges). February 6, 1979.

Hammerling, Henry (Mathematics Faculty Member, North Shore Community College). March 4, 1983.

Harrington, Kevin (Former President, Massachusetts Senate). August 3, 1984.

Harris, Arthur (Registrar, Middlesex Community College). February 13, 1979.

Hartley, Susan (Member, Commonwealth of Massachusetts, Department of Employment and Security, Manpower Services Council). April 30, 1979.

Haskins, Kenneth (Former President, Roxbury Community College). July 25, 1984.

Hicks, Everett (Budget Officer, Massachusetts Board of Regional Community Colleges). March 13, 1979.

Hudnall, Jack (Former President, Bristol Community College). July 24, 1984.

Jacobsen, Erroll (Member, Massachusetts Board of Regional Community Colleges). August 23, 1978.

Kamar, Richard (Assistant Dean of Students, Holyoke Community College). March 19, 1983.

Kataoka, Sara (Former Speech Instructor, Berkshire Community College). April 19, 1979.

King, Mel (Representative to the Massachusetts State Legislature. Member, Joint Committee on Education). September 26, 1978.

Krim, Bob (Economics Faculty Member, Roxbury Community College). July 26, 1978.

Landry, Barbara (Counselor, Mount Wachusett Community College). March 18, 1983.

Locey, Penny (Counselor, Massachusetts Bay Community College). March 19, 1979.

Mallan, John (Former Advisor to Governor Foster Furcolo. Former Chairman, Special Commission to Audit State Needs. Former Member, Massachusetts Board of Regional Community Colleges). March 18, 1983.

Massasoit Community College Students (Interviews with Twelve Students). May 8, 1984.

McDermott, Marie (Budget Officer, Massachusetts Board of Regional Community Colleges). March 19, 1979.

McGuire, Ed (Chancellor, Board of Higher Education). October 23, 1978.

McLaughlin, Paul (Staff Member, Joint Committee on Education, Massachusetts State Legislature). July 24, 1978.

Merriam, Robert (Development Officer, Greenfield Community College). August 31, 1978.

Moeser, Jeremy (Admissions Counselor, Massasoit Community College). March 19, 1979.

Morrissey, Kermit (Former Chairman, Massachusetts Board of Regional Community Colleges). March 12, 1979.

Murgo, John D. (Economics Faculty Member, Massasoit Community College). May 7, 1984.

Murphy, Richard (Placement Director, Massasoit Community College). May 7, 1984.

Musselman, John (Former President, Massasoit Community College). June 26, 1984.

Najarian, Michael (Staff Member, Massachusetts Board of Regional Community Colleges). September 14, 1978.

O'Connell, Thomas (Former President, Bristol Community College). February 15, 1978.

Offenberger, Richard (Staff Member, Massachusetts Board of Higher Education). October 23, 1978.

Olsen, Oscar (Former Executive Director, Beverly Chamber of Commerce). June 25, 1984.

O'Meara, Bill (Placement Counselor, Holyoke Community College). July 3, 1984.

Otis, John (Associate Dean of Student Affairs, Massasoit Community College). May 7, 1984.

Otis, John (Dean of Student Services, Massasoit Community College). March 18, 1983.

Pagano, Jules (President, Massachusetts Board of Regional Community Colleges). September 15, 1978.

Parks, Paul (Secretary of Educational Affairs, Commonwealth of Massachusetts). August 1, 1978.

Pyle, Gordon (Directory, Academic Planning, Massachusetts Board of Regional Community Colleges). July 10, 1978.

———. September 21, 1978.

———. October 16, 1978.

Rahaim, Charlotte (Professor of Education, University of Massachusetts). May 23, 1983.

Rininger, Don (Counselor, Massachusetts Bay Community College). May 2, 1979.

Rogers, George (Psychology Faculty Member, Massachusetts Bay Community College). March 4, 1983.

Roman, Frances P. (Former Admissions Director, Massasoit Community College). March 21, 1983.

Ross, Bob (Counselor, Bunker Hill Community College). October 5, 1978.

Rotundo, Bernie (Counselor, North Shore Community College). March 19, 1979.

Rowe, William (Business Faculty Member, North Shore Community College). March 4, 1983.

Saval, Allan (Dean of Administration, Bunker Hill Community College). March 4, 1983.

Scott, Patricia (Director of Academic Advisement, Bristol Community College). March 15, 1983.

Shively, Harold (President, Bunker Hill Community College. Former President, North Shore Community College). October 5, 1978.

———. June 25, 1984.

Simha, O. Robert (Member, Massachusetts Board of Regional Community Colleges). October 10, 1978.

Smith, Murray (Counselor, Middlesex Community College). February 13, 1979.

Spence, Robert (Manager, Digital Electronics Corporation). March 6, 1979.

Suhn, Andrew (Research Director, Commonwealth of Massachusetts, Department of Manpower Development). May 21, 1979.

Sullivan, James (Counselor, North Shore Community College). May 7, 1984

Trace, James (Admissions Director, Holyoke Community College). March 18, 1983.

Viaux, Frederick B. (Dean, Middlesex Community College). February 13, 1979.

Walsh, Betty (Assistant Admissions Director, Berkshire Community College). March 18, 1983.

Weston, John (Academic Programs Officer, Massachusetts Board of Regents). November 2, 1987.

Yacubian, Rob (Placement Officer, Bristol Community College). July 3, 1984.

Yess, James P. (Dean of Academic Affairs, Massasoit Community College). May 7, 1984.

Zekan, Donald (Dean of Administrative Services, Massasoit Community College). May 8, 1984.

Index